Dogs in the North

Dogs in the North offers an interdisciplinary, in-depth consideration of the multiple roles that dogs have played in the North. Spanning the deep history of humans and dogs in the North, the volume examines a variety of contexts in North America and Eurasia. The case studies build on archaeological, ethnohistorical, ethnographic, and anthropological research to illuminate the diversity and similarities in canine–human relationships across this vast region. The book sheds additional light on how dogs figure in the story of domestication, and how they have participated in partnerships with people across time. With contributions from a wide selection of authors, *Dogs in the North* is aimed at students and scholars of anthropology, archaeology, and history, as well as all those with interests in human–animal studies and northern societies.

Robert J. Losey is Associate Professor in the Department of Anthropology at the University of Alberta, Canada. His current research involves the study of humans' relationships with dogs as evidenced in the archaeology of Eastern Russia.

Robert P. Wishart is Lecturer in the Department of Anthropology at the University of Aberdeen, UK. His current research involves ethnographic, ethnohistorical, and history of science research focused on colonialism and human–animal relations in the Canadian North.

Jan Peter Laurens Loovers is Research Fellow in the Department of Anthropology at the University of Aberdeen, UK. As part of the ERC Arctic Domus Project, his research concerns the relationships between humans, dogs, fish, and caribou in the Canadian circumpolar North and the history of domestication in the Arctic.

Arctic Worlds
Communities, Political Ecology and Ways of Knowing
Series Editors: David Anderson and Robert J. Losey

This series aims to integrate research from across the circumpolar Arctic from across the humanities, social sciences, and history of science. This region – once exotised as a remote and unknown "blank spot" – is now acknowledged to be the homeland of a variety of indigenous nations, many of whom have won or are seeking home rule.

The Arctic was the central axis of frozen confrontation during the Cold War. At the start of the twenty-first century it is a resource hinterland offering supplies of petroleum and minerals for aggressively new markets with great cost and risk to the environment. The indigenous nations of the region are unique for their "ways of knowing" which approach animals and landscape as alive, sentient entities. Many share cultural commonalities across the Arctic Ocean, sketching out a human community that unites disparate continents.

This series takes history seriously by bringing together archaeological work on ancient Arctic societies with ethnohistorical studies of the alternate idioms by which time and meaning are understood by circumpolar peoples, as well as science and technology studies of how the region is perceived by various scientific communities.

Titles in series

Negotiating Personal Autonomy
Communication and Personhood in East Greenland
By Sophie Elixhauser

Dogs in the North
Stories of Cooperation and Co-Domestication
Edited by Robert J. Losey, Robert P. Wishart, and Jan Peter Laurens Loovers

www.routledge.com/Arctic-Worlds/book-series/ARCTICW

Dogs in the North
Stories of Cooperation and
Co-Domestication

Edited by
**Robert J. Losey, Robert P. Wishart,
and Jan Peter Laurens Loovers**

LONDON AND NEW YORK

First published 2018
by Routledge
2 Park Square, Milton Park, Abingdon, Oxon OX14 4RN

and by Routledge
711 Third Avenue, New York, NY 10017

Routledge is an imprint of the Taylor & Francis Group, an informa business

© 2018 selection and editorial matter, Robert J. Losey, Robert P. Wishart and Jan Peter Laurens Loovers; individual chapters, the contributors

The right of Robert J. Losey, Robert P. Wishart and Jan Peter Laurens Loovers to be identified as the authors of the editorial material, and of the authors for their individual chapters, has been asserted in accordance with sections 77 and 78 of the Copyright, Designs and Patents Act 1988.

All rights reserved. No part of this book may be reprinted or reproduced or utilised in any form or by any electronic, mechanical, or other means, now known or hereafter invented, including photocopying and recording, or in any information storage or retrieval system, without permission in writing from the publishers.

Trademark notice: Product or corporate names may be trademarks or registered trademarks, and are used only for identification and explanation without intent to infringe.

British Library Cataloguing-in-Publication Data
A catalogue record for this book is available from the British Library

Library of Congress Cataloging-in-Publication Data
A catalog record has been requested for this book

ISBN: 978-1-138-21840-6 (hbk)
ISBN: 978-1-315-43773-6 (ebk)

Typeset in Times New Roman
by Out of House Publishing

Contents

List of figures vii
List of contributors viii

1 Telling stories of co-domestication and cooperation: An introduction 1
ROBERT P. WISHART

2 Domestication and the embodied human–dog relationship: Archaeological perspectives from Siberia 8
ROBERT J. LOSEY, TATIANA NOMOKONOVA, LACEY FLEMING, KATHERINE LATHAM, AND LESLEY HARRINGTON

3 Hunters in their own right: Perspectival sharing in Soiot hunters and their dogs 28
ALEXANDER C. OEHLER

4 Dogs, reindeer and humans in Siberia: Threefold synergetic in the northern landscape 45
VLADIMIR DAVYDOV AND KONSTANTIN KLOKOV

5 Northern relations: People, sled dogs and salmon in Kamchatka (Russian Far East) 61
LISA STRECKER

6 The archaeology of human–dog relations in Northwest Alaska 87
ERICA HILL

7 An ethnohistory of dogs in the Mackenzie Basin (western Subarctic) 105
PATRICIA A. McCORMACK

8 The police and dogs during the early patrol years in the Western Canadian Subarctic: An inter-species colonial cooperation? 152
ROBERT P. WISHART

9 Threatening the fantasy of an Arctic welfare state: Canada, Quebec and Inuit dogs in Qikiqtaaluk and Nunavik between 1957 and 1968 172
FRANCIS LÉVESQUE

10 'Hard times are coming': Indeterminacy, prophecies, apocalypse, and dogs 191
JAN PETER LAURENS LOOVERS

11 Dogs among others: Inughuit companions in Northwest Greenland 212
KIRSTEN HASTRUP

12 Prehistory of dogs in Fennoscandia: A review 233
SUVI VIRANTA AND KRISTIINA MANNERMAA

13 "A dog will come and knock at the door, but remember to treat him as a human": The legend of the dog in Sámi tradition 251
NUCCIO MAZZULLO

14 Dogs in Saapmi: From competition to collaboration to cooperation to now 267
MYRDENE ANDERSON

15 Conclusion: Dogs in the North 278
JAN PETER LAURENS LOOVERS, ROBERT J. LOSEY, AND ROBERT P. WISHART

Index 293

Figures

0.1	Map of study locations examined in the volume	xi
2.1	Skeleton of a dog buried at the Pad' Kalashnikova site on the Angara River near Lake Baikal in Siberia	12
2.2	Cross-section of dog femur (L) and tibia (R) with planes of maximum and minimum bending strength indicated in lower row	14
2.3	Examples of some of the different types of harnesses used in Siberia during the ethnographic period	15
3.1	Aslan, Tsydyp's hunting-watchdog	38
3.2	A typical sable boulder patch, shown in summer	39
5.1	Sergey Lastochkin driving his dogs	63
5.2	Several sled dog teams resting in a village in Central Kamchatka	70
5.3	Fish camp outside of Karaga, Northern Kamchatka	75
6.1	Illustration of Ipiutak Burial 132 showing remains of a dog interred with an adult human and infant	88
6.2	Map showing sites discussed in the chapter	90
7.1	Hare Indian Dog. Sketch from Richardson (1829)	114
7.2	Hare Indian Dog. Illustration by J.W. Audubon, 1845–48	117
9.1	Map of Qikiqtaaluk and Nunavik, Canada	173
10.1	Breeding dogs: Abe Stewart Junior with Oscar	203
10.2	Training dogs: Abe Stewart Junior with his dog team	206
12.1	Map of the sites mentioned in the chapter	234
12.2	Dog mandible from the grave at Luistari in Eura, Finland	239
12.3	The Finnish Spitz	243
13.1	Herding dogs in their daily activities in the seventeenth century	255
13.2	Turi's drawing of herders and their dogs	256
14.1	Runne-Beana's descendant, Muste-Beana (born 2004 in Finland, photographed in 2012), living with cats in a temperate zone, Indiana, USA	273
14.2	Another descendant of Runne-Beana, Muste-Junior (Yuni) in Calgary, Alberta, Canada	274

Contributors

Myrdene Anderson, Associate Professor of Anthropology, Linguistics, and Semiotics at Purdue University in Indiana, USA, is an ethnographer with more than eight years spent amongst Saami in north Norway since 1971, focusing on reindeer husbandry, herding dogs, lichens, and folk natural history.

Vladimir Davydov is Head of the Siberian Ethnography department at Peter the Great Museum of Anthropology and Ethnography (Kunstkamera), Russian Academy of Sciences, Russian Federation. He received his PhD at the University of Aberdeen (2012). He is an ethnologist with a focus on human-nature relations in Baikal Siberia and Taimyr.

Lacey Fleming, a PhD candidate at the University of Alberta, Canada, is an archaeologist specializing in human–animal relationships and stable isotope analyses. She has worked with collections in North America and Siberia.

Lesley Harrington is Assistant Professor in the Department of Anthropology at the University of Alberta, Canada. She is a bioarchaeologist with a focus on bone functional adaptation and dental anthropology.

Kirsten Hastrup is Professor of Anthropology at University of Copenhagen, Denmark. She has worked extensively in the North, first in Iceland and more recently in Northwest Greenland. Her main thematic interest is the intertwinement of natural and social histories.

Erica Hill is Associate Professor of Anthropology at the University of Alaska Southeast, USA. She was a Fulbright–NSF Arctic Research Scholar in 2016–2017; her current work focuses on human–animal relations in the Western Arctic.

Konstantin Klokov is Professor and the Chair of Regional Politics and Political Geography, Saint-Petersburg State University, Russian Federation. Issues of reindeer herding and traditional hunting of indigenous peoples of Siberia are the main focus of his research.

Katherine Latham is a PhD student in the Department of Anthropology at the University of Alberta, Canada. Her research focus is on human–dog working relationships and the archaeological evidence of these interactions in past societies.

Jan Peter Laurens Loovers is Research Fellow at the University of Aberdeen, UK. He is an anthropologist with a focus on ecology, pedagogy and Indigenous people, and has primarily conducted research in northern Canada.

Francis Lévesque is Associate Professor at the School of Indigenous Studies, Université du Québec en Abitibi-Témiscamingue, Canada. He is an anthropologist with a focus on human–animal relations and has been conducting research in Nunavut and Nunavik.

Robert J. Losey is Associate Professor at the University of Alberta, Canada. He is an archaeologist with a focus on human–animal relations, particularly those between humans and dogs, and has primarily conducted research in Siberia.

Patricia A. McCormack is Professor Emerita, Faculty of Native Studies, University of Alberta, Canada, and currently operates Native Bridges Consulting. Her research focuses on the histories and cultures of Aboriginal people of the western Subarctic and northwestern Plains.

Kristiina Mannermaa works as researcher at the University of Helsinki, Finland. She is an archaeologist with a main focus on environmental archaeology, hunter-gatherers and human–animal relations in the North.

Nuccio Mazzullo is a Senior Researcher at the Arctic Centre, University of Lapland, Finland. He is an anthropologist and his research focuses mainly on the perception of the environment, place, and identity and human–animal relations among Sámi reindeer herders in Finnish Sámiland.

Tatiana Nomokonova is a Lecturer at the University of British Columbia (Okanagan), Canada. Her scholarly interests include human–animal relationships, ethnoarchaeology, and the zooarchaeology of Siberia.

Alexander C. Oehler is Assistant Professor at the University of Northern British Columbia, Canada. He is a social anthropologist studying human–animal and landscape relations in Siberia and Arctic Canada.

Lisa Strecker is a PhD student in Anthropology at the University of Alaska Fairbanks and faculty for the Alaska Ethnobotany program. Her interdisciplinary research on human–environment interactions (ethnobotany, invasive plants, sled dogs) is based in Kamchatka in the Russian Far East.

Suvi Viranta is Senior Lecturer in anatomy and paleobiology in the University of Helsinki, Finland. She works on functional anatomy and evolution of carnivores.

Robert P. Wishart is Lecturer at the University of Aberdeen, Scotland, United Kingdom. He is a social anthropologist with a focus on political ecology and human–environment relations, and has primarily conducted research in the Canadian Subarctic.

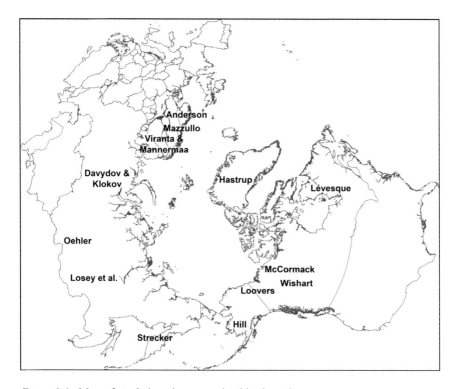

Figure 0.1 Map of study locations examined in the volume
Map by Robert Gustas.

1 Telling stories of co-domestication and cooperation
An introduction

Robert P. Wishart

No one is really sure when it happened but sometime in the distant past, and perhaps somewhere in what is now Siberia or Europe, some select wolves entered into a new relationship with another species for the first time. This meeting probably happened many times across the North, either through a process of copying or independent realisation of positive inter-species reciprocity, but it must have happened somewhere for the first time and it changed everything. Wolves and people came together; the wolves' ancestors probably had a history of their own in interacting with this other species, realising what the human hunters afforded in their own life-worlds. Hunters, no matter how efficient and careful, always leave scraps and sometimes maim their prey, making for easy wolf pickings. Working with this human affordance in their wolf lives meant that the wolves could prosper, and have more young, which would also be taught to work with people. However, it also would have come with a heavy price because the wolves were preyed upon for their meat and fur, and might have been killed to remove hunting competition. It is speculated that these wolves were already accustomed to humans but may have had lower levels of stress hormones than their contemporaries, allowing them to act on their own curiosity and come closer to people during opportune times (Coppinger and Coppinger 2001). The lower degree of stress might have meant that they displayed behaviours less frightening and more pleasing to people. The people, out of their own curiosity about the behaviour of these wolves, may have allowed their presence, and became accustomed to them. The wolves would have been rewarded with first pickings of the scraps and it is possible that just like today there was an urge among people to share their food with other animals. Wherever and whenever the first realisation of this special relationship occurred, the two species of wolves and humans came closer together through the generations to follow, with each species finding benefit in this new relationship. Wolves, in their transformation to dogs, benefited from human provisions and protection, but so too did the people benefit from their new hunting and protective companions. The capacity of dogs to transport people or goods came later but it is also a crucial part of our northern mutual story.

Who the wolves were and who the people were may never be known. Archaeology provides us with some tantalising clues about the early days of this unfolding relationship and some of the chapters assembled here allow us a glimpse through time at the lives of some of the characters involved in its unfolding. Whoever the originals were, we are all indebted to them; for human history would be very different without the wolves who became our dog partners. It is not too much of a stretch to say that without dogs there would be no humanity as we know it (Haraway 2007) and perhaps this is most true in the North. If we were to imagine the North as being inscribed with the footprints of the generations of humans who have made it their home, we must realise that there are also footprints of the dogs who walked beside, in front or followed our own, and who made our own lives in the North possible.

Our inter-species histories are so entangled that we continue to find fascination and comfort in imagining how we first came together and try to see that relationship in our own dogs today. It would be wrong to ignore this allure but it can also lead to unsupported conclusions. Dogs have such strong appeal that when pitching the original idea for this book we half joked about its marketability by asking the acquisition representative if they had ever seen sled dog puppies. Despite being present in the North to do serious work, researchers often fall in love with northern dogs because of this appeal—myself and the authors assembled here included—and stories of time spent in the North often include a lament for the dogs and their haunting howling. However, while the chapters provide a sense of this attachment and the charm of living alongside of dogs, we have tried to go much further than that of a sled dog calendar or coffee table book by asking a variety of questions about the way this unique set of relationships unfolded and how they have changed.

One of the drivers for this book is a realisation that the master narrative for domestication has ignored the North, and this collection of papers is indebted to the European Research Council Advanced Grant ERC-2011-ADG_20110406, Arctic Domestication: Emplacing Human–Animal Relationships in the Circumpolar North (Arctic Domus for short). Idioms of domestication written by people in the South for southern consumption often forget this original northern inter-species experiment of mutuality where animals including people came closer together for what each afforded the other (Anderson et al. 2017), preferring instead stories of grain and tamed food-animals. Those stories often rely on models that champion human inventiveness and the domination of the natural world without thought for the other beings who have shared this journey, although that too is changing with a shift in multiple disciplines away from human exceptionalism. However, we must also realise that the emerging relationships between dogs and people represent various histories in the circumpolar North, and some are troubling. The desire to find the primordial in modern northern relationships has led to many anthropological mistakes in the past and often fuels a continuation of simplistic popular imaginaries. These misrepresentations must be guarded against because both have a difficult relationship with the colonisation of the North to further southern interests. The chapters to follow provide many examples of how complex the story really is. These are stories of emerging dog types, varieties of northern human sensibilities about dogs, the many ways dogs were used by various human actors sometimes in ways that are profoundly dominating, the partnerships which were formed between dogs and people and the often tragic dissolving of those partnerships, the way that dogs became part of the expansion of empires and the establishment of colonial authority in the North, and finally how dogs are imagined to be future partners in northern people's lives.

The chapters in this book are arranged in a loose geographical manner across the circumpolar North. It was our intention to provide chapters with archaeological, ethnographic and historical appeal for each of the regions in the circumpolar North but this was not always possible due to lacunae in research in these areas and other reasons of suitable authors having other commitments. One of the dangers in a geographical ordering is that readers will focus on the region which matches their own interests and research, but I would ask the reader to indulge their canine and northern interests to read beyond their region because this collection taken as a whole provides ethnological evidence which has great use across the entire circumpolar North.

Given the current Anglo-centric world of academic publishing, it is common within a geographical ordering to start in the West and finish in the East, but we break that trend; because the story of dogs may begin in Siberia it seems apropos to follow that lead. The organisation makes no claims about the diffusionary direction of dogs because that is not the task we have set ourselves. The ability to work with dogs and transform them can be seen in many northern practices of interbreeding where the art of domestication is continually in practice. However with these caveats in place, we will start in Siberia and move generally eastward from there. Within each region the papers are arranged to provide alternating visions of archaeological, ethnographic and historical focus which tend to jump around in the region itself so it is not a strict east–west organisation in this sense.

Robert Losey, Tatiana Nomokonova, Lacey Fleming, Katherine Latham and Lesley Harrington open the book by asking some fundamental questions about dogs in both Siberia and archaeology. Going beyond the meta-narrative of dog origins, these authors describe what we can know about human and dog entanglements in the deep history of this region. By starting from the position that dogs are inherently social beings they are able to describe archaeological data in ways that move profoundly beyond utility. Proceeding from the perspective that elements of humans' relationships with dogs, and dogs' interactions with other things within their environment, are literally embodied, a careful attention to the physical remains of dogs can enlighten us about multiple relationships emerging in the region. It is a particularly appropriate opening chapter because it brings to attention the aspects of the human–dog world which other chapters describe in historical times and the present day such as human–dog emotional bonds, ritual practice involving dogs, working lives with dogs, and dog diets and provisioning practices. These studies help bridge archaeology with human–animal studies in the humanities and social sciences to show how archaeology can describe a rich human–dog life-world.

Alexander Oehler continues the conversation about human–dog life-worlds in Siberia with his chapter on Soiot-dog perspectival sharing. Using a carefully tuned theoretical ontological framework borrowed from human–animal studies, the chapter describes how dogs and humans inhabit a hunting world where each can rely on the senses of the other to bring about valuable shared perspectives that provide mutual benefit through collaboration. Historically locating the study with a group that have undergone tremendous change due to shifting political landscapes in post-revolutionary Russia, demonstrates how enduring the human–dog relationship is, and moreover it places a hunting way of life with dogs as partners in the present as opposed to a set of long-ago practices. Emerging out of this work is a clear sense that dogs and people live in a world inhabited by multiple other beings which are always at play in a field of relations.

Vladimir Davydov and Konstantin Klokov continue the discussion on assemblages of beings in Siberia by taking a comparative approach that demonstrates two important observations. The first is that Siberian ethnography has been fixated on one type of human–animal relationship: that between people and reindeer. The second is that dogs in Siberia co-exist with and are a part of the reindeer-herding life. The chapter illuminates how national ethnographic traditions have led to differing imaginaries about dogs in the North. Bringing together the literatures on dog breeding with that of reindeer breeding enriches our perspective on the intricate web of human–animal relations in Siberia.

Moving to the far east of Siberia, Lisa Strecker brings another assemblage of species to our attention. In Kamchatka there is a long history of keeping sled dogs which is made possible by the provisioning of dogs with salmon. Here, unlike that in the previous chapter, we have a human–dog–salmon world which has undergone significant changes in recent history but still exists in a modified form. Insights and information about the current situation of sled dog keeping are the result of the author's work in the region that illustrates the durabilities and weaknesses of the sled dog world. Here, like other areas of the North where dogs were relied on for transport, the arrival of the snowmobile has meant a lessened role for dogs but not an extinguishment of the relationships between the species.

Jumping across the Bering Strait we arrive in North America and Erica Hill presents us with a fascinating glimpse into the human–dog world of the Thule inhabitants about 1500 years ago. A single grave contains a tantalising and moving tableau of a family buried together with a dog. The scene tells of an entangled world of dogs and humans moving through and settling in what is now coastal Alaska, and it demonstrates potential continuity with ritual practices on the borders of Siberia and western North America. This grave points to a type of relationship between people and dogs which pre-dates the use of dogs for transportation. The treatment of the dog as a family member speaks through the ages of the mutual importance of all the parties, human and dog alike, in moving and hunting during this time. The paper hypothesises that once dogs became crucial for transportation their position in society changed. In North America the role of dogs in the North is tied to the sled in living history, but there was a time when that was not the case and certainly much changed once dogs became beasts of burden.

Patricia McCormack provides an ethnohistorical approach to what happened to dogs during the fur trade in the western Subarctic. Here, the arrival of fur traders stimulated a change in human–dog relations from one where dogs were hunting companions to being hitched to a sled for the transportation of goods and the efficient opening of trap-lines. McCormack demonstrates how these changes affected human sociality as well as that with other animals. Moving between Athapaskan ontology regarding shared life-worlds and the archival evidence for the impacts of the fur trade, the chapter brings the spiritual world and the economic world into a conversation where dogs take the centre stage in their contribution to the fur trade. Because dogs became the main mode of overland transportation in this region prior to the invention of motorised snow transport, they could be claimed to have become the tools of Indigenous people, traders and everyone else staking a claim to the Canadian North, but this mechanised understanding glosses over many intricacies in keeping and using sled dogs.

Robert Wishart continues the discussion of how dogs were used in the Western Canadian Subarctic but shifts the focus to a study of settler society and northern colonialism. Canada exerted its sovereignty in the North-West through the institution of police patrols, and in the nineteenth and early twentieth centuries patrolling the northern regions of Canada required sled dogs. The relationship between police and dogs in this case is not the same as the public imagination of canine units in today's police forces. Using the reports of the police posts and other evidence available from archives, the chapter documents how dogs were positioned in police technical inventories and how provisioning the dogs lead to multiple financial problems and solutions. The chapter asks how much we can know about the non-human actors in the unfolding of even the most scrutinised historical events when the animals were regarded at the time as tools rather than partners. The police in the North also gave up their dogs with the coming of snow-mobiles, and dog teams around this time became problematic to Canadian control of northern resources.

Francis Lévesque picks up the story of Canadian colonisation and settlement of the North with an investigation into the complexities of how dogs became a threat to the Canadian welfare state in the Eastern Arctic. In the mid-twentieth century, Canadian agents including the police force reportedly slaughtered Inuit dogs during a time when the state was relocating people into permanent settlements. The chapter takes a balanced approach in investigating why this occurred and how the story is more complex than originally reported with some colonial agents trying to feed and vaccinate dogs rather than killing them. However, in the end the goal was the same: to create a sedentary Inuit population beholden on the welfare state for their subsistence. Sled dogs became an obstruction to this overarching goal and it is a chapter that demonstrates how colonialism worked and continues to work in northern contexts where animal partners must be converted or destroyed.

The chapter by Peter Loovers completes the papers on North America with a return to the Western Canadian Subarctic where Gwich'in are including dogs in their visions of the future. In Gwich'in communities a syncretic Christian prophesy of the future holds that hard times are coming when people will have to abandon modern conveniences like snow-mobiles and trucks and return to using the transportation technologies of their elders. The reasonable realisation that the world of petroleum-fuelled lifeways is a short interlude in their history means that the people are preparing by maintaining human–dog relationships and keeping sled dog skills alive for the benefit of the future generations. This preparation includes a myriad of practices but also a sense of the plasticity of breeds and an ability to re-make good sled dogs out of a current stock more attuned to being house pets and racing dogs.

Greenland is a part of the Danish Kingdom but has an Indigenous population linked closely with Canada and physiographically it is part of North America; as such it is a circumpolar bridge between Canada and Fennoscandia. Kirsten Hastrup provides a chapter that examines the role of dogs as a companion species in Northwest Greenland where they are part of an assemblage making up the living landscape of Inughuit hunters who continue to use dogs to assist in their mobile world. Using historical and ethnographic evidence, the chapter examines the depth of the relationship between people and dogs, which is familiar to that of Northern Canada, but also how the companionship bends and stretches under various historical and Danish colonial pressures. The chapter portrays the relationship as an important continuity but while dogs always were and still are essential for transport and survival in the region, they are also part of a comprehensive assemblage of living and material forces that make up the fragile landscape of the hunters.

The final geographical area is Fennoscandia, and Suvi Viranta and Kristiina Mannermaa provide an overview of how dogs were a part of this region's prehistory. Using evidence from occupations, cult-sites, human graves and separate dog burials, the authors trace the development of dog types and their position within society. They argue that dogs are an inseparable part of Fennoscandian prehistory but went through multiple changes. Mesolithic dogs were large in size which was probably related to their position as hunters. During the Neolithic dogs became diverse in size and morphology, probably indicating various tasks for dogs. Robust dogs appeared with agriculture. It is also apparent in the archaeological evidence that there were multiple regional variations in dog preference, again probably related to the cultural expectations of dog partnerships, and these prehistoric trends may permeate to the present with differing Fennoscandian preferences.

Moving from a Fennoscandian overview to a specific story of human–dog relatedness, Nuccio Mazzullo offers us an intricate analysis of a part of Sámi oral tradition. Sámi maintained a central role for dogs as co-workers and family members despite changing economic roles. Today Sámi are most closely associated with reindeer husbandry but dogs have always had a place in how this economic adventure came to be. Codified in their stories we can find contracts between people and dogs which provided rules for how each party should treat the other. As a set of defined rules, we can also find a deeper sense of the importance of this enduring relationship which also includes reindeer and other animals in its ordering of sensibilities.

Finally we have a chapter written by Myrdene Anderson that both reflects on her long history of studying Saami human–dog relationships and also on the speculative question of the original dog–human experiment in inter-species cooperation and mutual domestication. Moving between conjectural but archaeologically evidenced deep history and a profound understanding of how dogs have been part of Saami history and life, the chapter metonymically reflects on how dogs became our partners and how we may have largely abandoned them at our convenience in order to pursue economic adventures where our partners were no longer required, only to discover the disenchantment of a world divorced from our canine friends and a longing once more for social co-development as reflected in current theorising on a post-human world view.

What the future may hold for the special northern relationship between people and dogs is difficult to predict but what we do know is that over the long, entangled history of this special inter-species relationship we can find guidance and many colonial 'mistakes' (Tester and Kulchyski 1994) from which we can learn. Authors such as Jack London found their muse in reflecting on the complexities of these northern lives, and in a scholarly sense so have the authors collected here, who tell multiple stories of cooperation, co-domestication and the challenges inherent in maintaining and cultivating these relationships.

Bibliography

Anderson, D.G., J.P.L. Loovers, S.A. Schroer, S.A. and R.P. Wishart. 2017. Architectures of Domestication: On Emplacing Human–Animal Relations in the North. *Journal of the Royal Anthropological Institute*, 23(2): 398–416.
Coppinger, R. and L. Coppinger. 2001. *Dogs: A Startling New Understanding of Canine Origin, Behavior, and Evolution*. New York: Scribner.
Haraway, D. 2007. *When Species Meet*. Minneapolis: University of Minnesota Press.
Tester, F. and P. Kulchyski. 1994. *Tammarniit (Mistakes): Inuit Relocation in the Eastern Arctic, 1939–63*. Vancouver: UBC Press.

2 Domestication and the embodied human–dog relationship

Archaeological perspectives from Siberia

Robert J. Losey, Tatiana Nomokonova, Lacey Fleming, Katherine Latham, and Lesley Harrington

Introduction

Archaeologists have tended to address a distinct set of questions in regard to the domestication of the dog. Typically these include where and when dogs first emerged, how and why this process occurred, and how dogs dispersed across various regions. These are metanarrative accounts of origins, causation, and biological colonization. Domestication itself is variously and contentiously defined (Russell 2012), but nonetheless is widely regarded as a major evolutionary transition in human history (Larson and Fuller 2014; Zeder 2015). As such, domestication is a fundamental area of research in archaeology (Kintigh et al. 2014), one that attracts significant funding and public attention, and helps to build major academic careers. The challenge faced by archaeologists when confronting this dominant perspective is that many aspects of past human–dog relations—such as how dogs were managed and provisioned, how we collaborated on daily tasks, how we affected each other's health and wellbeing—are glossed over and relegated to the periphery. They are not about domestication, but rather post-domestication husbandry practices that are considered to be of lesser historical, evolutionary, and academic significance. As a result, most high profile articles written by archaeologists on dog domestication are largely taxonomic efforts to classify early skeletal specimens as being from earliest dogs. How such animals went about being with people on a daily basis in the past is far more rarely explored.

The persistence of such implicit understandings of domestication among many archaeologists is striking because scholars in many disciplines, including archaeology itself, have clearly argued that domestication is a continuing and multidirectional process that is very much social. For example, Larson and Burger (2013:198), writing in *Trends in Genetics*, state that, '(b)ecause the evolution of domestic animals is ongoing, the process of domestication has a beginning but not an end'. From this perspective, dog domestication cannot be relegated to its Late Pleistocene origins but rather must be seen as an enduring project. Drawing on biological literature on species associations such as commensalism and symbiosis, O'Connor (1997) pointed to the mutualistic aspects of domestication. He argued that such relationships are better conceived of as a form of coevolution that involved adaptations among both humans and animals. In other words, domestication affects multiple species at once and is not a unidirectional process. Anthropologists have also scrutinized these traditional notions of domestication, highlighting the agencies of non-humans in these processes and demonstrating that our entanglements with other creatures are fundamentally social (Cassidy 2007; Haraway 2003; DeMello 2012; Fijn 2011; Lien 2015). Rather than biocommodities produced and used by society, domesticates and other animals are instead shown to also be part of what constitutes society. Humans and animals are significant others for one-another, neither being passive or wholly in control of the lives and experiences of the other.

Perhaps a useful way forward is not to redefine domestication to encompass these critical points (it is already defined this way by the authors just cited), but rather to demonstrate that they can be rigorously addressed using archaeological materials, and that what results are far more thorough and interesting accounts of our long-term meaningful relationships with animals. Archaeologists are in some ways in similar positions to anthropologists who study 'other than human socialities' (Tsing 2013). We cannot converse with our subjects and thus are forced to find other ways to study the social relationships we are interested in, including those of domestication. In archaeological settings this involves studying skeletal remains and their associations with other material traces of the past. Such studies begin from the proposition that various aspects of domestication are literally embodied—they help to form the body itself, including its bony core. For example, they can include osteological traces of a dog's habitual activities, such as their regular participation with people in carrying or pulling loads. Further, chemical traces in the bone can be examined to assess the long-term structure of their diets, including how they were provisioned by their human companions, and how they were sometimes also feeding themselves. Even traumatic episodes in life histories can sometimes be evidenced, including experiences of severe punishment at the hands of humans. Embodied in the skeletons of domestic animals then are not just the morphological and genetic changes that are said to mark specimens as 'domesticated' or 'wild', but also details of life histories that emerged in concert with other species, things, and places. They help to show the social facets of domestication, how it was enacted.

This chapter describes some of the opportunities and challenges involved with studying dog domestication in archaeology as social practice. To do this, we use examples drawn from our current archaeological research in Siberia. This vast region has a material record of human–dog engagements that spans thousands of years. The social and ecological variation in Siberia over this long period of time offers a wealth of settings within which to explore various ways of being with dogs in the past. Using this diversity, we examine a set of inter-related issues. First, we show how archaeological context can be used to explore emotional bonds between dogs and humans and how some dogs appear to have achieved 'other than human' forms of personhood. Second, we describe how human–dog labour practices can be assessed, including sled pulling and burden carrying. Third, the process of studying dog diets and provisioning is outlined. We conclude the paper by offering some ideas on further expanding the study of dog domestication in archaeology.

Dogs in Siberia

Siberia here is defined as the region of the Russian Federation east of the Ural Mountains, including the lands along the country's east coast. This region is larger than the whole of Europe, and given its size, it is impractical here to thoroughly review its archaeological record of dogs. Here we highlight only a few key patterns to provide a temporal setting for the following discussions.

The latest genetic research argues that the domestication of dogs from Eurasian wolves was initiated at least twice and in two separate regions: East Asia and Europe (Frantz et al. 2016). These relationships began at least 15,000 years ago, with the East Asian dogs apparently spreading to the west and largely replacing those originating in Europe by the Middle Holocene. However, far earlier domestications have been proposed, including in Siberia, where a single specimen dating to just over 33,000 years ago from the Altai was identified as an early dog (Ovodov et al. 2011)[1]. Other possible early dogs in Siberia include one ~17,000-year-old cranium from Yakutia (Germonpré et al. 2017), several Late Pleistocene canid specimens from just west of Lake Baikal (Birula 1929; Germonpré et al. 2014; Losey et al. 2013b), a single specimen from the Krasnoiarsk region in southwestern Siberia (Ovodov 1999), and a whole skeleton from the Ushki site on the Kamchatka Peninsula, also from this same period (Dikov 1977; Goebel et al. 2008). It is well established that by 7000–8000 years ago dogs were present in the northern Siberian Arctic at what is now Zhokhov Island (Lee et al. 2015; Pitulko and Kasparov 2016), and widespread in the Baikal region (Losey et al. 2011, 2013b, 2014). Dog remains of similar age also have been identified in Trans-Baikal by roughly the same period (Losey et al. 2014), and by 5000 or so years ago on the Pacific Coast of Siberia near Vladivostok (Losey, unpublished data). In Western Siberia, dogs appear to have been fairly numerous by about 5000 years ago (Kuznetsov 1998; Kosintsev and Nekrasov 1999), and were present just west of the Urals and in Kazakhstan somewhat earlier than this (Matyushin 1986; Olsen 2000).

This evidence indicates dogs were living with humans in Siberia for much of the Holocene and were inhabiting a range of habitats by at least 5000 years ago, ranging from steppe and forest steppe, to marine coastlines, to boreal forest, and even the far northern Arctic tundra. Such relationships began long prior to the presence of other domesticated animals in Siberia. For example, horse domestication was initiated about 5000–6000 years ago in Kazakhstan (Anthony 2007; Outram et al. 2009), and these and other west Asian herd animals probably arrived in Southwest Siberia no more than a millennium later (Koryakova and Epimakhov 2007). East of this region around Lake Baikal and along the Amur River to the Pacific Coast, domesticated herd animals appear even later, around 3500 years ago at the earliest (Kuzmin 1997; Losey et al. 2017; Nomokonova et al. 2010, 2015). Most scholars also argue that reindeer domestication was first set in motion in Siberia around 3500 years ago or so (Laufer 1917; Pomishin 1990; Vasilevich and Levin 1951; Vainshtein 1980). In sum, dogs appear to have held a unique place in Siberian communities for millennia, being the only animal conspicuously living with people, but by the Middle to Late Holocene were becoming parts of broadening multispecies entanglements.

Emotional bonds

While all living things have the ability to be social with beings outside of their species, dogs do this in ways that are overtly obvious to many people, perhaps resulting in them regularly being the subjects of extensive study (Hare and Tomasello 2005; Miklósi 2015). These unique ways of being undoubtedly contributed to dogs' longstanding history of co-habitation with people and other animals, and at the same time were a key part of the reasons that emotional relationships emerged between dogs and others. This raises the question of how might such social relationships be manifest in the archaeological record.

Using a wide array of archaeological data, Darcy Morey (2006) showed that dogs are the most commonly buried animals in the world, a practice that began early in their history of cohabiting with humans. For example, the Bonn-Oberkassel canid skeleton from Germany, widely considered to be from one of the very earliest dogs anywhere, was buried alongside two humans (Benecke 1987). In Siberia, canid burials also appear very early, with the oldest being at the Ushki site in Kamchatka, mentioned above. Here, a poorly preserved skeleton was found in a pit in the floor of a house, and alongside it were ochre (a reddish pigment) and several stone tools (Dikov 1979). While the Ushki canid has yet to be thoroughly studied, its context is clear—it is an intentional burial of a whole animal. Just as importantly, two human children were interred at Ushki in the same manner, namely buried in simple pits in the floors of other houses. In other words, this canid appears to have been treated much like a human upon its death, and no other animals at Ushki received such post-mortem care. In death it was literally domesticated—made part of the home.

Siberian dog burials are best documented in the Lake Baikal area, where studies have revealed that a few dogs were afforded mortuary rites similar to those given to humans (Losey et al. 2011, 2013b). Foraging communities living along the shore of the lake and its nearby rivers began regularly burying their human dead in cemeteries about 7500 years ago (Weber et al. 2016). Dogs buried in these cemeteries show no indication of being intentionally

Figure 2.1 Skeleton of a dog buried at the Pad' Kalashnikova site on the Angara River near Lake Baikal in Siberia. The dog was buried just over 6000 years ago with several implements, some of which are visible near the cranium. A round stone was also placed in its mouth at the time of burial

Photograph by Archive of the Institute of Archaeology, Russian Academy of Science.

killed by humans, as might be expected with sacrificed animals (Figure 2.1). Further, the dogs' graves are not set apart from those of humans, but rather intermixed among them. The dogs themselves were most often adults at the time of death and were regularly interred with implements and ornaments, including one dog that was buried wearing a necklace of red deer teeth (Losey et al. 2013b). At another cemetery, previously interred human remains were moved within the grave to make way for a later dog burial (Losey et al. 2011), while at yet other locations, dogs were buried to the left and right sides of a human in a relatively elaborate grave (Konopatskii 1982; Losey et al. 2013b).

We have argued that these Baikal dog burials were created because of several inter-related factors (Losey et al. 2011, 2013b). First, close personal and emotional relationships emerged between some people and dogs, and this meant that their deaths would have been mourned. In other words, these dogs were not merely living technologies exploited by people in accomplishing tasks (dogs are sometimes portrayed in this manner in archaeology), but rather were significant social actors for the humans with whom they lived. Second, 'human communities' of this region and time period enacted a way of being in which some animals could achieve human-like status. Such ways of being are common among many historic indigenous groups of Siberia (e.g., Iokhel'son 2005; Golovnev 1995; Khangalov 2004; Lukina and Ryndina 1987; Perevalova 2004; Taksami 2007), who know some animals as being particularly sentient, interactive, and ensoul much like humans—they can achieve a form of other-than-human personhood. Dogs are among the most common such animals to have such characteristics in the North (Ingold 1986; Paulson 1968). These animals' uniquely powerful characteristics meant that their deaths required certain actions be taken, which were meant to both placate their spirits and ensure their regeneration. They were not just mourned, but also required being sent to the afterlife. Third, what those specific actions were was heavily influenced by the mortuary practices for the human dead, which were also mourned and sent to the afterlife. Dogs were buried in cemeteries because cemetery burial was the most common practice for treating the dead in this region starting around 7500 years ago. In fact, ritualized interment of bears and one wolf also is evidenced in some of these same cemeteries (Losey et al. 2011, 2013a). If cremation or platform burial were the dominant human mortuary practices of the time, for example, then one might expect dogs not to have been buried but rather treated in these manners.

Working lives

Historically, dogs and humans in Siberia have collaborated in many daily and seasonal tasks, including hunting, herding, migrating, transporting loads, and protection of the community (e.g., Alekseev et al. 2012; Bat'ianova and Turaev, 2010; Bogoraz 1904 and 1907; Iokhel'son 1997, 2005; Gemuev et al. 2005; Khomich 1966; Levin and Potapov 1961; Samar 2010; Turov 2010). All of these activities require enskillment—the selective breeding involved in domestication alone does not produce dogs that effectively pull sleds, herd reindeer, or hunt. Rather, dogs and people learn to do these tasks by repeatedly engaging in them together, and in concert with other things such as landscapes, other human and non-human animals (including other dogs), and the crafts of domestication such as sleds, packs, and harnesses (Loovers 2015). This matters in archaeology because these practices are repetitive and involve bodies and other material things, thus potentially leaving behind physical traces that can be analysed, including parts of the body itself.

Archaeological study of habitual activity in animals is in its infancy (see Niinimäki and Salmi 2014; Shackelford et al. 2013), but is a well-developed area of study in human osteology, which offers some useful pathways forward in understanding past dogs' working lives. Conceptually such research can be divided into two areas, namely how skeletons become more robust in response to repetitive activities, and how they break down because of them. The first approach is referred to as the study of bone functional adaptation (Ruff 2007). This research relies upon the fact that bone responds to repeated strains and stresses by becoming more robust—it grows to accommodate the forces placed upon it, up to a point. These changes in robusticity are often studied by examining the cross-sectional structural parameters (strength) of

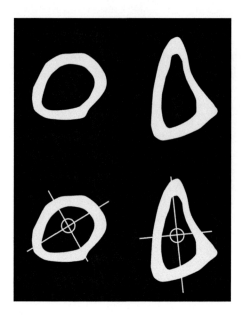

Figure 2.2 Cross-section of dog femur (L) and tibia (R) with planes of maximum and minimum bending strength indicated in lower row. Images were obtained through CT scanning

Image by Robert Losey.

individual bones using X-rays or CT scans (Figure 2.2). This is often comparative research examining individuals with known or assumed activity patterns as baselines against which others can be compared.

Perhaps the best examples of bone functional adaptation involve work with living humans. For example, a study of tennis players demonstrated that the bones of their dominant arms were far more robust than those of their non-dominant sides (Jones et al. 1977). Other studies have shown that the lower leg bones of field hockey players and runners can be distinguished by the multidirectional versus unidirectional nature of the movements performed. Runners' leg bones are predominantly strained in one direction during exercise and correspondingly strengthen mostly in this plane (Shaw and Stock 2009b). Conversely, field hockey players, who perform more complex and variable movements in their sport, have limb elements that are strengthened in all directions, not just in one plane. Further, swimmers have been shown to have more symmetrical arm bones than those of cricket players, as the former consistently use their left and right arms while moving, while the latter regularly favour the use of one arm over the other (Shaw and Stock 2009a). These studies illustrate that specific activities may produce a pattern of loading that leaves a unique signature in the structural properties of limb bones.

Archaeological perspectives from Siberia 15

Figure 2.3 Examples of some of the different types of harnesses used in Siberia during the ethnographic period. Styles are based on those in Levin and Potapov (1961)
Illustration by Emily Hull.

Several challenges face the application of the bone functional adaptation approach to understanding dogs' working lives. First is the need to have skeletons from modern dogs that performed repetitive tasks similar to those undertaken in the past. In our experience, such specimens are rare, particularly from dogs regularly involved in herding, pack hauling, and sledding. Second is disentangling the non-activity factors that also influence bone robusticity, including age, sex, body size, and even breed type. This is particularly challenging when dealing with partial skeletons and isolated bones, which are far more common than burials of whole skeletons in archaeological sites throughout the North. Third is that some activities undertaken by past dogs may have had little measurable effect on the skeleton due to their infrequency and short duration. For example, we know little about harness variation across the long-term history of Siberia, as these items seemingly were constructed out of perishable materials. Harness types vary historically in the region (Levin and Potapov 1961; Figure 2.3), and different forms of harnesses could load and strain dogs in quite different ways. Historic sledding practices, particularly their intensity and duration, might also not provide adequate analogies for past practices. Most existing sled dog skeletons in museums are from racing teams, Arctic expeditions, or Inuit communities of the North American Arctic. Such specimens may be extreme cases that compare poorly to other regions and time periods where sledding was practised over much shorter seasons and distances.

Archaeologists have already suggested a series of skeletal lesions are linked to dogs' working lives, particularly their roles in sled pulling and burden carrying. A key issue, however, has been the lack of baseline data on such lesions in dogs with known life histories—we poorly understand what sorts of problems typically develop in the dog skeleton in relation to specific habitual activities, and how these might be differentiated from the effects of other processes and factors such as ageing and breed type. Given that comparative skeletal lesion data is now usefully employed to investigate the working lives of other fauna (Bartosiewicz et al. 1997; Cupere et al. 2000; Pluskowski et al. 2010; Rossel et al. 2008; Salmi and Niinimäki 2016; Taylor et al. 2015; Telldahl 2012; Thomas 2008), creation of such basic osteological datasets for dogs is clearly warranted.

Spinal lesions in particular have been linked in multiple archaeological studies to working lives in dogs. One of the most common conditions is spondylosis deformans, a degenerative disease in which bony growths called osteophytes develop at the margins of vertebral endplates following damage to the intervertebral disc (Burt et al. 2013; Morgan 1967:8). It has been claimed that spondylosis deformans in archaeological dog remains was caused by repeatedly carrying burdens on the back or the excessive strain experienced during sled pulling (Arnold 1979; Losey et al. 2011; Millar 1978; Snyder 1995; Warren 2004). However, the occurrence of spondylosis deformans is correlated with age and breed type in dogs (Bellars and Godsall 1969:28, 34; Morgan et al. 1967:57; Morgan et al. 1989:458), and there is currently no published data indicating it is more common in sled or pack dogs than in other individuals. Many of the same archaeological studies have linked deformations of spinous processes to these same habitual activities. Spinous processes are the projections of bone along the upper (dorsal) side of the vertebrae, which in some archaeological specimens are noticeably bent or twisted. Some variability in these spinal parts is normal, but bent or twisted spinous processes also could form due to compression caused by wearing packs or harnesses. Notably, fractures of the spinous processes might also produce such deformations by the processes subsequently healing out of proper alignment—in bent or twisted shapes. If such trauma-related deformations can be ruled out, perhaps through the use of X-rays of the affected portions, then these irregular vertebrae may be better linked to habitual activities.

Some of the studies of spinal deformations also link osteoarthritic changes in the limbs and fracture patterns in various elements to dogs' working lives (Losey et al. 2011; Millar 1978; Snyder 1995; Warren 2004). Again, these studies' findings remain tenuous because the observed patterns cannot presently be linked to specific habitual activities. For example, one might reasonably expect that dogs involved in hunting larger ungulates such as elk (*Alces alces*) and red deer (*Cervus elaphus*) might be prone to certain types of fractures, particularly from being crushed underfoot by these animals defending themselves. However, it is unclear how such injuries might be differentiated from those resulting from being corporally punished by humans, or even from trampling experienced during herding larger animals such as cattle or horses. Survey of veterinary literature on injuries among hunting and herding dogs could help reveal useful patterns (c.f., Dennis et al. 2008; Houlton 2008), as would ethnographic fieldwork focused on the lived experiences of such working animals.

Diets and provisioning

Dogs' diets and the provisioning practices involved with them also are critical to many aspects of domestication. First, while domestication is thought of as a process that enables humans in many ways, it is also clearly constraining in that such relationships involve multiple obligations and entanglements with other species, things, and places. One of those obligations is providing food when animals cannot effectively self-provision—humans have to fish, hunt, harvest, store food, and move for reasons beyond just 'their own' needs. Dogs can feed themselves by hunting and scavenging, but their ability to do so is context dependent—some environments, seasons, working lives, pack sizes, prey types, and so on are more suitable for this than others (c.f., Hughes and Macdonald 2013; Young et al. 2011). In Siberia dogs probably are and were better able to survive by scavenging in sedentary human agriculture-based communities producing extensive edible waste, and by hunting in areas with abundant small game, particularly in summer. During winter, hunting, fishing, and herding communities in taiga and tundra regions might be poor hunting and scavenging environments for dogs. Further, activities like sled pulling and burden carrying are both time consuming and energy-intensive. Both settings likely require at least some provisioning by humans. Historically, dog provisioning in Siberia is quite variable, ranging from providing dogs with fish (Alekseenko 1967; Bat'ianova and Turaev 2010; Chikachev 2004; Iokhel'son 1997; Khomich 1966; Orlova 1999; Samar 2010), to hunting terrestrial and marine mammals and birds to feed dogs (Bat'ianova and Turaev 2010; Iokhel'son 2005; Savin 2005; Turaev 2010), to dogs being almost totally self-reliant (Bogoraz 1904, 1907; Iokhel'son 1997; Khomich 1966). These approaches vary between and among communities, and over the life course of individual dogs, including seasonally, with dogs being regularly provisioned when required to pull sleds in winter, for example, and left to scavenge and hunt in summer when such tasks are far less common (c.f., Bogoraz 1904, 1907).

Second, some scholars argue that dog domestication was initiated by permanently changing feeding habits in a subset of wolves, namely those that began to specialize in scavenging food remains around human residences (Coppinger and Coppinger 2001). This 'self-domestication' hypothesis also has been tied to the reduction of body size in dogs relative to wolves and during their initial period of domestication. Size reduction is thought to have occurred because this scavenging environment offered relatively low energy foods in comparison to other niches, and inhabiting it would have favoured smaller body sizes, and different body proportions, including smaller heads and teeth. We argue here that dogs' food environments have continued to change since these animals started living with people and persist in shaping their evolution and life histories, not just their initial domestication. Finally, genome analysis has revealed that many modern dogs possess several genes that are distinct from those in wolves that have roles in the digestion of starches (Axelsson et al. 2013). These genetic differences presumably emerged early in the history of their domestication, allowing some dogs to more effectively digest foods such as grain. Most human diets in Siberia were probably relatively starch poor, with the exceptions being communities inhabiting the south of this region, where cultivation of some grains, particularly millet, has occurred for at least 3500 years or so in Western Siberia, and at least 4000 years in southern Primor'e (Kuzmin et al. 1998; Svyatko et al. 2013).

Stable isotope analysis is a commonly used archaeological technique for investigating past diets (DeNiro and Epstein 1981; Schoeninger and DeNiro 1984). In this technique, ratios of the stable isotopes of carbon and nitrogen are measured in organic tissues, most typically bone collagen. An individual's collagen isotope ratios differ in a predictable manner from those of the foods that made up the bulk of its diet. To be best interpreted, the isotopic values of the consumer are compared to the isotopic ratios of these potential foods. However, stable carbon and nitrogen isotope analysis often cannot identify the specific foods that were eaten because many foods have identical or overlapping isotope ratios. Instead, the approach is best able to provide an estimate of the relative contributions of groups of food to the diet, such as relative importance of freshwater fish, terrestrial plants or animals, or marine fauna to the diet. In Siberia, consumption of some plants also is readily evidenced by stable isotope data due to their regionally unique photosynthetic pathways, with foxtail and common millet, both introduced cultivated plants, being the best examples. The isotopic ratios of bone collagen reflect the structure of the diet over relatively long periods. For adult human bones, this is often the last ten years or so of life, while for dog bones anywhere from a few months to three years is represented (Martin et al. 1998).

Stable carbon and nitrogen isotope values have been determined for numerous archaeological dog remains (e.g., Murphy et al. 2013; Pechenkina et al. 2005), but assessing dogs' diets has only rarely been the goal of such studies (but see Losey et al. 2011, 2013b; McManus-Fry et al. 2016; White et al. 2001). Rather, the dogs' values are used as proxies for those of local humans, with the assumption being that dog and human diets will have very similar structures. This is known as the canine surrogacy approach (Guiry 2012, 2013), and is utilized in situations where human remains are absent or unavailable. We currently have several stable isotope studies of Siberian dog remains underway, and preliminary data indicate human–dog dietary similarity in some areas and time periods, and dissimilarity in others. Further, the studies show significant variation in ancient dog diets, ranging from diets largely of freshwater fish near Lake Baikal and in the Arctic along the lower Ob' River, terrestrial mammal diets in some parts of Buriatia and eastern Trans-Baikal, and marine diets in southern Primor'e. The freshwater fish diets in particular are indicative of human provisioning, as dogs were probably very inefficient at procuring these foods on their own. Marine and terrestrial mammal diets are less clear indicators of dogs being fed, as they perhaps could have more effectively hunted or scavenged in such environments. Further, at Lake Baikal, some dogs from hunter-gatherer communities had diets that are distinctly non-local, suggesting they moved to the regions where they were buried shortly prior to death (Losey et al. 2013b).

An additional way of examining dog provisioning and diet is through study of dental health, particularly the loss or fracture of teeth prior to death. High rates of tooth breakage and loss are expected when dogs recurrently chew dense materials such as bone, which would occur when scavenging is common and competition over food is high—they spend more time trying to extract nutrients from poor-quality foods resulting in more damage to their teeth. If dogs were well provisioned by humans who gave them soft foods such as fish and sea mammal meat or blubber, lower rates of tooth loss and fracture should occur. In a study of modern dog and wolf skulls from across the circumpolar North, Losey et al. (2014) found that dogs overall suffered more tooth loss and fracture than wolves, suggesting dogs were regularly resorting to scavenging upon hard foods, perhaps as a result of food stress resulting from being poorly fed by humans. However, the rates among dogs were highly variable, indicating very localized diets and provisioning practices, only some of which involved food stress. Similar studies of large numbers of prehistoric canid remains has yet to occur, but could prove useful in examining food stress in the past, including when wolves first supposedly began feeding on human food waste.

Ways forward with past dogs

The above examples of how domestication practices can be literally embodied could be further expanded, including additional studies of the body, but also work on other material things that are enmeshed in these relationships. In regard to the former, some potential ways forward would be to study dog mobility and migration patterns through analyses of strontium and oxygen isotopes in tooth enamel. These isotopes potentially provide an indicator of where on the landscape a dog or other animal was living when their teeth were developing—the chemistry of the region's bedrock is in a sense 'written' in them while they form. Repeatedly sampling a single tooth, and sampling teeth that formed over different periods of the individual's growth, then provides a way of tracking residency (c.f., Britton et al. 2009 for such work on caribou). Such analyses could be carried out on the remains of dogs, people, and reindeer from a single site, providing a glimpse of multi-species mobilities and how they compare and contrast within a given community. Another approach would be to study the sharing of parasites and diseases among human and non-human animals, traces of which can sometimes be found in or around body remains, but also in site sediments (Roberts and Manchester 2007; Waters-Rist et al. 2014). These studies could help to highlight the multi-species aspects of domestication, and how they can sometimes involve unanticipated and problematic relationships that have profound effects for those involved.

Dog domestication will be best understood when such studies are integrated with analyses of other forms of evidence, including the more common genetic and morphological studies that typify archaeological domestication research. Beyond this work with dog bodies, we might also involve archaeological data on the architecture involved in domestication, which ranges from remnants of houses to pens and corrals, all of which were parts of the social worlds of humans, dogs, and other creatures. Crafts used in habitual activities such as sleds, harnesses, packs, leashes, and whips also could be studied to better understand how dogs physically engaged in their tasks, but also how people communicated their intentions and needs to these animals through these material things. Finally, even the soil itself should bear chemical and physical traces of cohabiting with canids, which might be particularly useful when their skeletal remains are not present. Many of these suggested ways forward already have well-established methodologies. What remains largely absent in archaeology is a thorough consideration of domestication as a social process and practice, not merely an evolutionary state.

Acknowledgements

Funding for this research was provided by the Social Science and Humanities Research Council of Canada (SSHRC IG 435-2014-0075) and the European Research Council (Arctic Domus, no. 295458). Emily Hull is acknowledged for producing the illustration used in Figure 2.3. Losey also acknowledges the Centre for Advanced Study, Norwegian Academy of Science and Letters for providing writing time to complete this chapter.

Note

1 The identification of all possible dog remains older than ~15,000 years ago is contentious and subject to extensive debate.

Bibliography

Alekseenko, E.A. 1967. *Kety. Istoriko-Etnograficheskie Ocherki*. Leningrad: Nauka.
Alekseev, N.A., E.N. Romanova and Z.P. Sokolova (eds.). 2012. *Iakuty (Sakha)*. Moscow: Nauka.

Anthony, D.W. 2007. *The Horse, the Wheel, and Language: How Bronze Age Riders from the Eurasian Steppes Shaped the Modern World*. Princeton, NJ: Princeton University Press.

Arnold, C.D. 1979. "Possible Evidence of Domestic Dog in a Paleoeskimo Context." *Arctic*, 32, 3: 263–265.

Axelsson, E., A. Ratnakumar, M.-L. Arendt, K. Maqbool, M.T. Webster, M. Perloski, O. Liberg, J.M. Arnemo, A. Hedhammar, and K. Lindblad-Toh. 2013. "The genomic signature of dog domestication reveals adaptation to a starch-rich diet." *Nature*, 495, 7441: 360–364.

Bartosiewicz, L., W. van Neer, and A. Lentacker. 1997. *Draught Cattle: Their Osteological Identification and History*. Tervuren: Royal Museum of Central Africa.

Bat'ianova, E.P. and V.A. Turaev (eds.). 2010. *Narody Severo-Vostoka Sibiri*. Moscow: Nauka.

Bellars, A.R.M. and M.F. Godsall. 1969. "Veterinary studies of the British Antarctic Survey's sledge dogs: II. Occupational osteoarthritis." *British Antarctic Survey Bulletin*, 22: 15–38.

Benecke, N. 1987. "Studies on early dog remains from Northern Europe." *Journal of Archaeological Science*, 14, 1: 31–49.

Birula, A.A. 1929. "Rapport préliminaire sur les mammifères "des débris de cuisine" d'une station de l'homme préhistorique de l'âge de pierre sur le mont Verholensk près Irkoutsk." *Doklady Akademii Nauk SSSR*: 91–93.

Bogoraz, W. 1904 and 1907. *The Chukchee*. Memoirs of the American Museum of Natural History, Vol. 11, Parts 1–2. New York: EJ Brill Ltd. and GE Stechert & Co.

Britton, K., V. Grimes, J. Dau, M.P. Richards. 2009. "Reconstructing faunal migrations using intra-tooth sampling and strontium and oxygen isotope analyses: a case study of modern caribou (Rangifer tarandus granti)." *Journal of Archaeological Science*, 36, 5: 1163–1172.

Burt, N.M., D. Semple, K. Waterhouse, N.C. Lovell. 2013. *Identification and Interpretation of Joint Disease in Paleopathology and Forensic Anthropology*. Springfield: Charles C. Thomas.

Cassidy, R. 2007. "Introduction: Domestication Reconsidered." In *Where the Wild Things are Now: Domestication Reconsidered*, edited by Rebecca Cassidy and Molly Mullin, 1–27. Oxford: Berg.

Chikachev, A.G. 2004. *Ezdovoe Sobakovodstvo Iakutii*. Iakutsk: SO RAN.

Coppinger, R. and L. Coppinger. 2001. *Dogs: A Startling New Understanding of Canine Origin, Behavior & Evolution*. New York: Scribner.

Cupere, B. de, A, Lentacker, W. van Neer, M. Waelkens, and L. Verslype. 2000. "Osteological evidence for the draught exploitation of cattle: first application of a new methodology." *International Journal of Osteoarchaeology*, 10: 254–267.

DeMello, M. 2012. *Animals and Society: An Introduction to Human–Animal Studies*. New York: Columbia University Press.

DeNiro, M.J. and S. Epstein. 1981. "Influence of diet on the distribution of nitrogen isotopes in animals." *Geochimica et Cosmochimica Acta*, 45: 341–351.

Dennis, M.M., S.N. Nelson, G.H. Cantor, D.A. Mosier, J.E. Blake, and R.J. Basaraba. 2008. "Assessment of necropsy findings in sled dogs that died during Iditarod Trail sled dog races: 23 cases (1994–2006)." *Journal of the American Veterinary Medical Association*, 232(4): 564–573.

Di Cosmo, N. 1994. "Ancient Inner Asian nomads: their economic basis and its significance in Chinese history." *The Journal of Asian Studies*, 53: 1092–1126.

Dikov, N.N. 1977. *Arkheologicheskie Pamiatniki Kamchatki, Chukotki i Verkhnei Kolymy*. Moscow: Nauka.

Dikov, N.N. 1979. *Drevnie Kul'tury Severo-Vostochnoi Azii: Aziia na Styke s Amerikoi v Drevnosti*. Moscow: Nauka.

Fijn, N. 2011. *Living with Herds: Human–Animal Coexistence in Mongolia*. Cambridge: Cambridge University Press.

Frantz, L.A.F., V.E. Mullin, M. Pionnier-Capitan, O. Lebrasseur, M. Ollivier, A. Perri, A. Linderholm, V. Mattiangeli, M.D. Teasdale, E.A. Dimopoulos, A. Tresset, M. Duffraisse, F. McCormick, L. Bartosiewicz, E. Gál, E.A. Nyerges, M.V. Sablin, S. Bréhard, M. Mashkour, A. Bălășescu, B. Gillet, S. Hughes, O. Chassaing, C. Hitte, J.-D. Vigne, K. Dobney, C. Hänni, D.G. Bradley, and G. Larson. 2016. "Genomic and archaeological evidence suggest a dual origin of domestic dogs." *Science*, 352: 1228–1231.

Gemuev, I.N., I.V. Molodin, and Z.P. Sokolova, (eds.). 2005. *Narody Zapadnoi Sibiri. Khanty, Mansi, Sel'kupy, Nentsy, Entsy, Nganasany, Kety*. Moscow: Nauka.

Germonpré, M., M. Lázničková-Galetová, R.J. Losey, J. Räikkönen, and M.V. Sablin. 2014. "Late canids at the Gravettian Predmosti site, the Czech Republic: the mandible." *Quaternary International*, 359(36): 261–279.

Germonpré, M., S. Fedorov, P. Danilov, P. Galeta, E.-L. Jimenez, M. Sablin, and R.J. Losey. 2017. "Palaeolithic and Prehistoric Dogs and Pleistocene Wolves from Yakutia: Identification of Isolated Skulls." *Journal of Archaeological Science*, 78: 1–19.

Goebel, T., M.R. Waters, and D.H. O'Rourke. 2008. "The late Pleistocene dispersal of modern humans in the Americas." *Science*, 319: 1497–1502.

Golovnev, A.V. 1995. *Govoriashchie Kul'tury: Traditsii Samodiitsev i Ugrov*. Ekaterinburg: UrO RAN.

Guiry, Eric J. 2012. "Dogs as analogs in stable isotope-based human paleodietary reconstructions: a review and considerations for future use." *Journal of Archaeological Method and Theory*, 19: 351–376.

Guiry, Eric J. 2013. "A canine surrogacy approach to human paleodietary bone chemistry: past development and future directions." *Archaeological and Anthropological Sciences*, 5: 275–286.

Haraway, D. 2003. *A Companion Species Manifesto: Dogs, People, and Significant Otherness*. Chicago: Prickly Paradigm.

Hare, B. and M. Tomasello. 2005. "Human-like social skills in dogs?" *Trends in cognitive sciences*, 9(9): 439–444.

Houlton, J.E.F. 2008. "A survey of gundog lameness and injuries in Great Britain in the shooting seasons 2005/2006 and 2006/2007." *Veterinary and Comparative Orthopaedics and Traumatology*, 21(3): 231–237.

Hughes, J. and D.W. Macdonald. 2013. "A review of interactions between free-roaming domestic dogs and wildlife." *Biological Conservation*, 157: 341–351.

Ingold, T. 1986. *The Appropriation of Nature*. Manchester: Manchester University Press.

Iokhel'son, V. 1997. *Koriaki. Material'naia Kul'tura i Sotsial'naia Organizatsiia*. St. Petersburg: Nauka.

Iokhel'son, V. 2005. *Iukagiry i Iukagirizirovannye Tungusy*. Novosibirsk: Nauka.

Jones, H.H., J.D. Priest, W.C. Hayes, C.C. Tichenor, and D.A. Nagel. 1977. "Human hypertrophy in response to exercise." *Journal of Bone and Joint Surgery*, 59(2): 204–208.

Khangalov, M.N. 2004. *Sobraniie Sochinenii*. Vol. III. Ulan-Ude: Respublikanskaia Tipografiia.
Khomich, L.V. 1966. *Nentsy: Istoriko-Etnograficheskie Ocherki*. Moscow: Nauka.
Kintigh, K.W., J.H. Altschul, M.C. Beaudry, R.D. Drennan, A.P. Kinzig, T.A. Kohler, W.F. Limp, H.D.G. Maschner, W.K. Michener, T.R. Pauketat, P. Peregrine, J.A. Sabloff, T.J. Wilkinson, H.T. Wright, and M.A. Zeder. 2014. "Grand Challenges for Archaeology." *American Antiquity*, 79(1): 5–24.
Konopatskii, A.K. 1982. *Drevnie Kul'tury Baikala*. Novosibirsk: Nauka.
Koryakova, L.N., A.V. Epimakhov. 2007. *The Urals and Western Siberia in the Bronze and Iron Ages*. Cambridge: Cambridge University Press.
Kosintsev, P.A. and E.A. Nekrasov. 1999. "Promyslovaia deiatel'nost' liudei is poselenii, raspolozhennykh na beregy ozera Mergen' (Mergen' 5 i 6) v neolite i eneolite." In *Ekologiia Drevnikh i Sovremennykh Obshchestv*, edited by N.P. Matveeva, 100–105. Tiumen: Izd-vo Instituta Problem Osvoeniia Severa SO RAN.
Kuzmin, Y.V. 1997. "Vertebrate Animal Remains from Prehistoric and Medieval Settlemetns in Primorye (Russian Far East)." *International Journal of Osteoarchaeology*, 7: 172–180.
Kuzmin, Y.V., A.J.T. Tull, and G.A. Jones.1998. "Early agriculture in Primorye, Russian Far East: new radiocarbon and pollen data from Late Neolithic sites." *Journal of Archaeological Science*, 25: 813–816.
Kuznetsov, N.A. 1998. Pogrebeniia Sobak na Srednem Yenisee kak Arkheologicheskii Istochnik. PhD dissertation, Novosibirsk State University.
Larson, G. and J. Burger, 2013. "A population genetics view of animal domestication." *Trends in Genetics*, 29(4): 197–205.
Larson, G. and D.Q. Fuller. 2014. "The evolution of animal domestication." *Annual Review of Ecology, Evolution, and Systematics*, 66: 115–136.
Laufer, B. 1917. "The reindeer and its domestication." *Memoirs of the American Anthropological Association*, 4(2): 91–147.
Lee, E.J., D.A Merriwether, A.K. Kasparov, P.A. Nikolskiy, M.V. Sotnikova, E. Yu., V. Pavlova, and V.V. Pitulko. 2015. "Ancient DNA Analysis of the Oldest Canid Species from the Siberian Arctic and Genetic Contribution to the Domestic Dog." *PLoS One*, 10, 5: e0125759.
Levin M.G., and L.P. Potapov (eds.). 1961. *Istoriko-Etnograficheskii Atlas Sibiri*. Moscow: Izdatel'stvo Akademii Nauk SSSR.
Lien, M.E. 2015. *Becoming Salmon: Aquaculture and the Domestication of a Fish*. Oakland: University of California Press.
Loovers, J.P.L. 2015 "Dog-craft: A history of Gwich'in and dogs in the Canadian North." *Hunter-gatherer Research*, 1(4): 387–419.
Losey, R.J., V.I. Bazaliiskii, S. Garvie-Lok, M. Germonpré, J.A. Leonard, A.L. Allen, M.A. Katzenberg, and M.V. Sablin. 2011. "Canids as persons: Early Neolithic dog and wolf burials, Cis-Baikal, Siberia." *Journal of Anthropological Archaeology*, 30: 174–189.
Losey, R.J, V.I. Bazaliiskii, A. Lieverse, A. Waters-Rist, K. Faccia, A. Weber. 2013a. "The Bear-able Likeness of Being: Ursine Remains at the Shamanka II Cemetery, Lake Baikal, Siberia." In *Relational Archaeologies*, edited by C. Watts, 65–96. London: Routledge Press.
Losey, R.J., S. Garvie-Lok, J.A. Leonard, M.A Katzenberg, M. Germonpré, T. Nomokonova, M.V. Sablin, O.I. Goriunova, N.E. Berdnikova, and N.A. Savel'ev.

2013b. "Burying Dogs in Ancient Cis-Baikal, Siberia: Temporal Trends and Relationships with Human Diet and Subsistence Practices." *PLoS One,* 8(5): e63740.

Losey, R.J., E. Jessup, T. Nomokonova, and M. Sablin. 2014. "Craniomandibular Trauma and Tooth Loss in Northern Dogs and Wolves: Implications for the Archaeological Study of Dog Husbandry and Domestication." *PLoS One,* 9(6): e99746.

Losey, R.J., A. Waters-Rist, T. Nomokonova, and A.A. Kharinskii. 2017. "A second mortuary hiatus on Lake Baikal in Siberia and the arrival of small-scale pastoralism." *Scientific Reports,* 7: 2319.

Lukina, N.V. and O.M. Ryndina (eds.). 1987. *Istochniki po Etnografii Zapadnoi Sibiri.* Tomsk: Izd-vo TGU.

McManus-Fry, E., R. Knecht, K. Dobney, M.P. Richards, and K. Britton. 2016. "Dog–human dietary relationships in Yup'ik western Alaska: the stable isotope and zooarchaeological evidence from pre-contact Nunalleq." *Journal of Archaeological Science Reports,* 15: 1–9.

Martin, R.B., D.B. Burr, N.A. Sharkey, and D.P. Fyhrie. 1998. *Skeletal Tissue Mechanics,* New York: Springer.

Matyushin, G. 1986. "The Mesolithic and Neolithic in the southern Urals and Central Asia." In *Hunters in Transition: Mesolithic Societies of Temperate Eurasia and their Transition to Farming,* edited by M. Zvelebil, 133–150. Cambridge: Cambridge University Press.

Miklósi, A. 2015. *Dog Behaviour, Evolution, and Cognition.* Oxford: Oxford University Press.

Millar, J.F. 1978. *The Gray Site: An Early Plains Burial Ground, Vol. I and II.* Parks Canada Manuscript, No. 304. Winnipeg: Parks Canada.

Morey, D.F. 2006. "Burying Key Evidence: the social bond between dogs and people." *Journal of Archaeological Science,* 33(2): 158–175.

Morgan, J.P. 1967. "Spondylosis Deformans in the Dog: A Morphologic Study with Some Clinical and Experimental Observations." *Acta Orthopaedica,* 38(1): 1–88.

Morgan, J.P., K. Hansson, and T. Miyabayashi. 1989. "Spondylosis deformans in the female beagle dog: A radiographic study." *Journal of Small Animal Practice,* 30 : 457–460.

Morgan, J.P., G. Ljunggren, and R. Read. 1967. "Spondylosis Deformans (Vertebral Osteophytosis) in the Dog a Radiographic Study from England, Sweden and USA." *Journal of Small Animal Practice,* 8: 57–66.

Murphy, E.M., R. Schulting, N. Beer, Y. Chistov, A. Kasparov, and M. Pshenitsyna. 2013. "Iron Age pastoral nomadism and agriculture in the eastern Eurasian steppe: implications from dental paleopathology and stable carbon and nitrogen isotopes." *Journal of Archaeological Science,* 40: 2547–2560.

Niinimäki, Sirpa and A-K. Salmi. 2014. "Entheseal Changes in Free-Ranging Versus Zoo Reindeer—Observing Activity Status of Reindeer." *International Journal of Osteoarchaeology,* 26(2): 314–323.

Nomokonova, T., R.J. Losey, O.I. Goriunova, A.G. Novikov, and A.W. Weber. 2015. "A 9,000 Year History of Seal Hunting on Lake Baikal, Siberia: The Zooarchaeology of Sagan-Zaba II." *PLoS One,* 10(5): e0128314.

Nomokonova, T., R.J. Losey, A.W. Weber, O.I. Goriunova. 2010. "Late Holocene subsistence practices among Cis-Baikal pastoralists, Siberia: zooarchaeological insights from Sagan-Zaba II." *Asian Perspectives,* 49(1): 157–179.

O'Connor, T.P. 1997. "Working at relationships: another look at animal domestication." *Antiquity*, 71: 149–156.
Olsen, S.L. 2000. "The secular and sacred roles of dogs at Botai, North Kazakhstan." In *Dogs Through Time: An Archaeological Perspective*, edited by S.J. Crockford, 71–92. Oxford: Archaeopress.
Orlova, E.P. 1999. *Itel'meny. Istoriko-Etnograficheskii Ocherk*. St. Petersburg: Nauka.
Outram, A.K., N.A. Stear, R. Bendrey, S. Olsen, A. Kasparov, V. Zaibert, N. Thorpe, R.P. Evershed. 2009. "The earliest horse harnessing and milking." *Science*, 323(5919): 1332–1335.
Ovodov N.D. 1999. *Pleistotsenovye sobaki Sibiri*. Chetvertyi s"ezd teriologicheskogo obshchestva, 179. Moscow: Teriologicheckoe obshchestvo RAN.
Ovodov, N.D., S.J. Crockford, Y.V. Kuzmin, T.F.G. Higham, G.W.L. Hodgins, and J. van der Plicht. 2011. "A 33,000 year old incipient dog from the Altai mountains of Siberia: evidence of the earliest domestication disrupted by the Last Glacial Maximum." *PLoS One*, 6: e22821.
Paulson, I. 1968. "The Preservation of Animal Bones in the Hunting Rites of Some North-Eurasian Peoples." In *Popular Beliefs and Folklore Traditions in Siberia*, edited by Vilmos Diószegi, 451–457. The Hague: Mouton and Co.
Pechenkina, E.A., S.H. Ambrose, M. Xiolin, and A.B. Robert Jr. 2005. "Reconstructing northern Chinese Neolithic subsistence practices by isotopic analysis." *Journal of Archaeological Science*, 32: 1176–1189.
Perevalova, E.V. 2004. *Severnye Khanty: Etnicheskaia Istoriia*. Ekaterinburg: UrO RAN.
Pitulko, V.V. and A.K. Kasparov. 2016. "Early Holocene dog bones from the Zhokhov Site (Eastern Siberian Arctic) and the question of the reliability of identification of early *Canis familiaris* from archaeological excavations." *Stratum Plus*, 1: 171–207.
Pluskowski, A., K. Seetah, and M. Maltby. 2010. "Potential osteoarchaeological evidence for riding and the military use of horses at Malbork Castle: Poland." *International Journal of Osteoarchaeology,* 20: 335–343.
Pomishin, S.B. 1990. *Proiskhozhdenie olenevodstva i domestikatsiya severnogo olenya*. Moscow: Nauka.
Roberts, C. and K. Manchester. 2007. *Archaeology of Disease*. Ithaca: Cornell University Press.
Rossel, S., F. Marshall, J. Peters, T. Pilgram, M.D. Adams, and D. O'Connor. 2008. "Domestication of the donkey: Timing, processes, and indicators." *Proceedings of the National Academy of Sciences of the United States of America*, 105(10): 3715–3720.
Ruff, C.B. 2007. "Biomechanical analyses of archaeological human skeletons." In *Biological Anthropology of the Human Skeleton*, edited by M.A. Katzenberg and S.R. Saunders, 183–206. Hoboken: Wiley-Liss Inc.
Russell, N. 2012. *Social Zooarchaeology*. Cambridge: Cambridge University Press.
Salmi, A.-K. and S. Niinimäki. 2016. "Entheseal changes and pathological lesions in draught reindeer skeletons—four case studies from present-day Siberia." *International Journal of Osteoarchaeology*, 14: 91–99.
Samar, A.P. 2010. *Traditsionnoe Sobakovodstvo Nanaitsev*. Vladivostok: Dal'nauka.
Savin, A.A. 2005. *Pishcha Iakutov do Razvitiia Zemledeliia*. Iakutsk: AN RS (IA).
Schoeninger, M.J. and M.J. DeNiro. 1984. "Nitrogen and carbon isotopic composition of bone collagen from marine and terrestrial mammals." *Geochimica and Cosmochimica Acta,* 48(4): 625–639.

Shackelford, L., F. Marshall, and J. Peters. 2013. "Identifying Donkey Domestication Through Changes in Cross-Sectional Geometry of Long Bones." *Journal of Archaeological Science*, 40(12): 4170–4179.

Shaw, C.N. and J.T. Stock. 2009a. "Habitual throwing and swimming correspond with upper limb diaphyseal strength and shape in modern human athletes." *American Journal of Physical Anthropology*, 140(1): 160–172.

Shaw, C.N. and J.T. Stock. 2009b. "Intensity, repetitiveness, and directionality of habitual adolescent mobility patterns influence the tibial diaphysis morphology of athletes." *American Journal of Physical Anthropology*, 140(1): 149–159.

Snyder, L.M. 1995. Assessing the Role of the Domestic Dog as a Native American Food Resource in the Middle Missouri Subarea AD 1000–1840. PhD dissertation, University of Tennessee.

Svyatko, S.V., R.J. Schulting, J. Mallory, E.M. Murphy, P.J. Reimer, V.I. Khartanovich, Y.K. Chistov, and M.V. Sablin. 2013. "Stable isotope dietary analysis of prehistoric populations from the Minusinsk Basin, Southern Siberia, Russia: a new chronological framework for the introduction of millet to the eastern Eurasian steppe." *Journal of Archaeological Science*, 40(11): 3936–3945.

Taksami, Ch.M. 2007. *Nivkhi. Etnicheskaia Kul'tura Nivkhov – Aborigenov Tikhookeanskogo Severa i Dal'nego Vostoka*. Novosibirsk: Nauka.

Taylor, W.T.T., J. Bayarsaikhan, and T. Tuvshinjargal. 2015. "Equine cranial morphology and the identification of riding and chariotry in late Bronze Age Mongolia." *Antiquity*, 89(346): 854–871.

Telldahl, Y. 2012. "Skeletal changes in lower limb bones in domestic cattle from Eketorp ringfort on the Öland Island in Sweden." *International Journal of Paleopathology*, 2: 208–216.

Thomas, R. 2008. "Diachronic trends in lower limb pathologies in later medieval and post-medieval cattle from Britain." In *Limping Together Through the Ages: Joint Afflictions and Bone Infections,* edited by G. Grupe, G. McGlynn, and J. Peters, 187–201. Rahden/Westf: Verlag Marie Leidorf GmbH.

Tsing, A. 2013. "More-than-Human Sociality, A Call for Critical Description." In *Anthropology and Nature*, edited by Kirsten Hastrup, 27–42. New York: Routledge.

Turaev, V.A. (ed.). 2010. *Istoriia i Kul'tura Dal'nevostocnykh Evenkov: Istoriko-Etnograficheskie Ocherki*. St. Petersburg: Nauka.

Turov, M.G. 2010. *Evenki Economy in the Central Siberia Taiga at the end of the 20th century. Principles of Land Use*. Edmonton: Canadian Circumpolar Institute Press.

Vainshtein, S.I. 1980. *Nomads of South Siberia: the Pastoral Economies of Tuva*. Cambridge: Cambridge University Press.

Vasilevich, G.M. and M.G. Levin. 1951. "Tipy olenevodstva i ikh prioiskhozhdeniya." *Sovetskaya Ethnografiya*, 1: 63–87.

Warren, D.M. 2004. Skeletal Biology and Paleopathology of Domestic Dogs from Prehistoric Alabama, Illinoi, Kentucky and Tennessee, Volume I. PhD dissertation, Indiana University.

Waters-Rist, A.L., K. Faccia, A. Lieverse, V.I. Bazaliiskii, M.A. Katzenberg, and R.J. Losey. 2014. "Multicomponent analysis of a hydatid cyst from an Early Neolithic hunter-fisher-gatherer from Lake Baikal, Siberia." *Journal of Archaeological Science*, 50: 51–62.

Weber, A.W., R.J. Schulting, C.B. Ramsey, V.I. Bazaliiskii, O.I. Goriunova, and N.E. Berdnikova. 2016. "Chronology of middle Holocene hunter-gatherers in the Cis-Baikal region of Siberia: Corrections based on examination of the freshwater reservoir effect." *Quaternary International*, 419: 74–98.

White, C.D, M.E.D. Pohl, H.P. Schwarcz, and F.J. Longstaffe. 2001. "Preclassic Maya patterns of deer and dog exploitation: The isotopic evidence from Colha, Belize." *Journal of Archaeological Science*, 27: 89–107.

Young, J.K., K.A. Olson, R.P. Reading, S. Amgalanbaatar, and J. Berger. 2011. "Is wildlife going to the dogs? Impacts of feral and free-roaming dogs on wildlife populations." *Bioscience*, 61: 125–132.

Zeder, M.A. 2015. "Core questions in domestication research." *Proceedings of the National Academy of Sciences of the United States of America*, 112(11): 3191–3198.

3 Hunters in their own right

Perspectival sharing in Soiot hunters and their dogs

Alexander C. Oehler

Introduction

This chapter is concerned with the ways in which Oka-Soiot herder-hunters of South Central Siberia collaborate with their dogs in the hunt for sable and other fur-bearing animals. Thus the chapter contributes to the anthropological literature of dog–human relations in collaborative hunting contexts within and beyond the North (e.g. Corkran 2015; Laugrand and Oosten 2015; McGranaghan 2015; Koster 2009; Kohn 2007; Ikeya 1994; Anderson 1986). The material presented here comes from participant observations made during my doctoral fieldwork in the Oka district of the Republic of Buriatia, Russian Federation, between 2013–2014. My analysis of dog–human relations is part of a larger multi-species ethnography, which involves dynamic Soiot practices and beliefs relating to reindeer, horses, yak, and wolves. Formerly known as "hunters who have reindeer" (Andreeva and Leksin 1999:92), rather than herders who occasionally hunt, indigenous Soiots and their Tofa, Tozhu, and Dukha neighbors had in common what has been called the 'Saian-style' of reindeer herding (Vasilevich and Levin 1951:76–77). However, Soiot households began shifting their focus to other species, particularly yak, possibly as early as the mid-1800s (e.g. Petri 1927). This shift in species focus is generally attributed to the arrival of Buriat settlers in the Eastern Saian Mountains, which was accompanied by extensive intermarriage between both social groups (Pavlinskaia 2002:49–50, 56). Although we lack a date for the arrival of dogs to Soiot households, pre-revolutionary accounts from neighboring regions describe the presence of dogs in Tozhu (e.g. Olsen 1915) and Tofa (e.g. Vasil'ev 1910) nomadic hunting and reindeer-herding households.

The fieldwork observations provided in this chapter seek to illuminate how dogs and humans in Oka were seen not only to live side by side, but how they actively engaged in each other's embodied perspectives of the landscape. As part of the so-called 'ontological' and 'animal turns' in anthropology (e.g. Weil 2010; Ingold 2013), a concern has arisen not only with defining what is (and for whom), but also an interest in how communication is facilitated between beings of distinct life-worlds. One theoretical approach to the intersection of the perceptive worlds of humans and other beings has been Eduardo Viveiros de Castro's (1996, 1998) Amerindian perspectivism. Drawing on the ethnography of Amerindian peoples, Viveiros de Castro postulates a radical relationalism between human and other beings. Hidden behind the external corporeality of all beings (i.e. their diverse bodies) lies a common (human) nature. Viveiros de Castro summarizes this ontological shift by contrasting multinaturalism with multiculturalism. Yet much of this perspectivist approach seems to imply that the perceptive capacity of a given being remains, for the most part, trapped inside its specific body. While Soiots do not share the belief in an underlying common humanity, in my observations with dogs and hunters Viveiros de Castro's ontological imprisonment is broken. This is evidenced in how canines and humans collectively construct meaning, each actively drawing on the perceptive advantages they recognize in the other's perspective. This inter-perspective is not unique to the dog–human interface. Rather, it can be observed in multiple other collaborative animal-human relations in Oka, including in horse-human and reindeer-human encounters. However, the dog–human interface lends itself particularly well to an analysis of this inter-perspective because of the proximate and primarily non-touch-based nature of co-joint pursuit in hunting tasks relating to small fur-bearing animals.

In the context of dogs and humans, I will refer to this phenomenon as perspectival sharing. Sharing speaks to the interaction of assemblages of perspectives which, like sentences in a book, "space themselves out and disperse, or else jostle together and coexist…" (Deleuze and Guattari 2013[1987]:25). Although assemblages remain a reality, they do not in themselves address the kind of conversational responsiveness that seems to be characteristic of life, as Tim Ingold points out (2015). In this study of dog–human relations I attempt to qualify this responsiveness by showing how Soiot hunters and their dogs not only exhibit a string or assembly of interchangeable perspectives in the taiga, but a deliberate sharing in body-specific perspectives. All participants in the hunt engage in this perspectival sharing as they invoke a degree of multi-sensorial interdependence. Divergent perspectives of the landscape are engaged here on the basis of a mutual attribution of autonomy. Human hunters recognize dogs as hunters in their own right, relying on, and encouraging their body-specific skills. Reversely, dogs are seen to rely on the body-specific abilities of their human collaborators. Together they share in joint tasks, while maintaining the ability to lend their perspectives to other assemblages.

Feeding patterns

Unlike many Western contexts, in which dogs are objects of affection, Soiot dogs were not considered pets in this sense. None of the dogs I came to know at Uro were accustomed to affectionate physical contact, although they were highly communicative. Once a dog had proven itself a useful watchdog, or a skillful hunter, it had an established position within the household. Positioned close to the human abode, people relied on their dogs as intruder alarms. Several watchdogs had been killed by wolves in the past, but in most cases a dog's barking would allow householders to scan the horizon, check on their sheep, and load a rifle if need be. Both men and women fed dogs, and children freely played with pups. But a dog's primary relation with the household was established by the master of the household (Rus. *khoziain*) during the seasonal practice of hunting. Hunting, watching, and feeding were closely interrelated, as a sense of hunger was thought to keep a dog alert and ready to take initiative at all times. Going back and forth between periods of tight leashing and loose rambling, a dog's relations with household and master were characterized not so much by seasonal fluctuation in proximity, as by variation in communicative and collaborative intensity. The annual high point of their interactions undoubtedly lay in autumn and early winter hunting. Although a hunter's recognition of his dog's intentions never called into question his authority as master, there was a deep understanding of interdependency between dogs and humans, in which dogs were understood as hunters in their own right.

Historically, in Oka the composition of a dog's diet fluctuated seasonally, depending on the availability of food scraps and the importance of the dog to the household. Although there is little information on how Soiot dogs were fed in the past, some historical information exists for Tofa dogs who lived under similar circumstances to those of Oka. L.V. Mel'nikova (1994:46) writes:

> In summer they barely fed them, only once a day they would provide some batter (Tof. talkhan-bulkhar; Rus. boltushka). One to two handfuls of flour were dissolved in hot water. [The liquid] was poured into separate bowls for each dog. [Dogs] scavenged[1] [Rus. dobivali] for the remainder of their subsistence. But prior to the hunt, and during the hunt, dogs were fed well. The dogs lived in chums together with people, sleeping near the hearth. Every hunter had two to three dogs on average. Pups were carefully nursed (hunting dogs gave birth in chums where a warm corner was specially set aside for them).[2]

The feeding pattern in this account of historic Tofa dogs is largely consistent with contemporary Soiot dog keeping.

One afternoon in late September, when I was visiting Soiot elder Tseren-Dorzho[3] at his cabin in Uro, his three dogs were furiously barking at a chipmunk outside his cabin. The dogs had not caught the chipmunk yet—primarily because they were chained to three wooden boxes which served as their huts. Whenever I came to visit, the dogs would stand atop their boxes, barking relentlessly. Panda (who looked like a black and white bear) was the eldest at 14 years.[4] He had lost his hearing and looked genuinely tired of life. Sharik (Rus. for 'Little Ball') was five years old, and Druzhok (Rus. for 'Little Friend') was the youngest at three years of age. The chipmunk had reminded

Tseren-Dorzho of his hungry dogs, allowing me to see how dogs were fed: "Flour, water, milk. They don't eat much," Tseren-Dorzho explained. He poured two large ladles of flour into a basin with cold water: "This way it doesn't lump." Transferring the flour water into a metal bucket, he added some leftover milk and set the mix on his hearth. Over the glowing ambers the feed slowly thickened. Reminded of Tofa tradition, I asked whether dogs were ever let into the house. "No!" he replied. But, then he recalled how in winter, when his dogs were puppies, he had allowed them into the cabin. At first he had wanted to kill them, but feeling sorry for them, he had let them into the house. And, it turned out, "they liked candy!"

According to Igor V. Rassadin (2000:40–41), Tofa dogs were used in obtaining all kinds of game, but they received special training to go fur hunting (cf. Petri 1928). Larger meat-bearing fauna (e.g. Manchurian wapiti, bears, red deer, musk deer) were obtained serendipitously during the fur hunt. Squirrel and sable had been mainstays for trade until the preputial glands of Siberian musk deer (*Moschus moschiferus*) took their place in recent years.[5] Dogs were trained to specialize in tracking either squirrel or sable,[6] and it was rare to find one truly skilled in tracking both. During training, as well as later in a dog's life, Tofa hunters would use squirrel carcasses and intestines of other prey as lure for their dogs. More choice meat was rarely part of the feed provided by a hunter to his dogs. Instead, scraps served as reward and communicative means in forging and sustaining behavioral associations, especially in young dogs. When a novice hunting dog had located a squirrel on a tree, the squirrel was shot and skinned, and its carcass was fed to the dog immediately. This sequence of events cemented a link between the taste of squirrel meat and the task of tracking and cornering the animal. Meat was therefore a relatively rare supplementation to a dog's diet, and it signified a time of year when humans and dogs collaborated intimately in the taiga.

A combination of significantly reduced hunting responsibilities, and low grain stashes, meant that Tofa dogs were fed minimal rations and expected to fend for themselves during the summer (Rassadin 2000; Mel'nikova 1994; Petri 1928). Having to scavenge for part of their own diet, they would hunt for rodents and other small game, activities that were thought to intensify their hunting instincts (Rassadin 2000:41).[7] Little information exists on historical dog–human interaction for these times of year. Conversely, autumn and winter months were so labor intensive in a dog's life that independent scavenging for small game became impossible. To keep their hard-working dogs alive during these intense times, Tofa hunters "fed a rye flour mash, the stock of which was transported to hunting taigas specifically on their behalf" (Rassadin 2000:41). Thus, the ways in which hunting dogs obtained and consumed food throughout the year stood in direct relation to their seasonal importance within a hunter's household.

With a rise in the importance of cattle and other livestock for Soiot households, it is reasonable to assume that the role of dogs had to shift as well. During my fieldwork at least three scenarios were most common: Firstly, there were dogs who were raised specifically for hunting purposes. The relationship between hunters and such dogs still much resembled the pattern described for traditional Tofa dogs, even if larger game had replaced the focus on sable and squirrel in recent years. Several of these dogs were well known for their skill, and people were keen on borrowing them, which I will describe below. Secondly, there were dogs who served primarily as chained watchdogs, but who were occasionally taken out to hunt, especially in autumn. This was perhaps the most common scenario. Less training effort went into such dogs, but a number of them were quite prolific hunters nonetheless. Finally, there were dogs who never went hunting, and whose sole purpose was to watch over the comings and goings of the household in both summer and winter residences. In no case were dogs used to herd cattle, yak, or even sheep.

Sharing bodies, building skill

Sometime in autumn, my neighbor Borzhon (b. 1966) invited me to join him and his sons on one of their hunting trips to the upper Sorok River. On our second day in the bush I noticed that one of our three dogs was limping from a trauma he had received in his right rear leg. I could not recall any of Borzhon's dogs limping. His thick legs, strong chest, and whitish coat, made the animal stand out from Borzhon's dogs, and I soon realized that it did not, in fact, belong to Borzhon's household. To whom did this experienced tracker belong? After studying the dog more closely, it occurred to me that he had visited my cabin in the past, feeding on leftovers. Later, one of Borzhon's sons told me how several years earlier the 'limping dog' had plummeted from a steep cliff, along with a musk deer. The hunters had been surprised the dog survived, and since it had not lost its skill, they continued to take him along in spite of the limp. Shortly after our return, I visited former reindeer herder Iumzhap. Aware of our hunting trip, he asked me if his dog had joined us. The one with the limp, also known as White Sheik (Rus. *belyi sheikh*), had been missing for a few days. I confirmed his dog's collaboration, and Iumzhap did not seem in the least annoyed, nor did he seem to anticipate a share of game for his dog's services.[8]

Neither Borzhon nor Iumzhap had arranged for White Sheikh to join our hunt. Having previously slipped off his chain, the dog had been roaming among the winter residences of the other side of the valley on the morning of our departure. As our group were leaving the valley, White Sheik adjoined himself to the trot of Borzhon's dogs. On the following day, with White Sheik still among us, Borzhon set him on track for musk deer, alongside his own dogs. Familiar with Borzhon, with his sons and their dogs, White Sheik obeyed Borzhon's orders. Not only was the dog familiar with the members of the party he had chosen to join, he was also deeply familiar with the landscape, its trails, creeks, slopes, and rocky outcrops, the latter onto which he was to chase musk deer. Clearly, White Sheik had been here many times. And, quite likely, a good number of these outings had not been initiated by his master, Iumzhap. Although we had not deliberately taken him along on this trip, White Sheik had lent us his skill as a fellow hunter in a place deeply familiar to him.

I soon learned this kind of dog sharing was not unusual. One morning, late in autumn, Afanasiev called my host Baianbata from the village of Sorok. Afanasiev was a respected elder and former director of the now defunct collective farm in the village of Sorok. He said he was planning to hunt for sable, and he was asking for our neighbor Alesha's dogs to be sent to Sorok. I asked Baianbata whether Afanasiev would pay Alesha for the use of his dogs. Baianbata shook his head. When I saw Alesha's friend Regdel later that day, I asked again whether Alesha would get anything in return for lending his prized dogs to Afanasiev. "Of course he will not get anything in return!" Instead, Regdel estimated that Alesha would deliver the dogs to Sorok at his own cost, to ensure Afanasiev would take them hunting. It was in Alesha's interest to have his dogs taken out by another hunter. 'Better for the dogs to be out hunting than to be sitting in the yard on their chains.' Each hunt would increase their skill—no matter who took them to the forest. Each outing made them more versatile hunters, adding to their value for Alesha's household.

Alesha and Iumzhap's dogs provide examples of several related dynamics: the boundaries of belonging to specific masters was suspended as the dogs moved back and forth between social engagements with other households, lending their dog perspectives to diverse assemblages. In addition, in the case of White Sheik, there emerged a degree of dog autonomy in which the dog opportunistically decided which household to join in the hunt. Although no one would sell[9] or otherwise exchange a prized hunting dog, even the best of dogs could circulate among hunters. Increased sharing meant increasing skill in one's dogs, even if this came at the price of risking the loss of one's dog during another hunter's outing. As sharing could occur without the owner's knowing, and as the result of a dog's own volition to join another hunting party, there seemed to occur an interplay of human and dog interests above and beyond common claims of ownership. Dogs were navigating between households, and humans were responding to this navigation. But aside from recognizing that one's dogs sometimes chose with whom to hunt, they were also understood to co-determine when to hunt.

Dogs as hunters in their own right

Although hunters collaborated with their dogs during the hunt, it could also be said that dogs were understood to hunt on behalf of their human masters. Ilia, a seasoned hunter who in winter resided on Tustuk River, illustrated this point in describing how he would let his dogs run off into the forest. He told me one day: "My dogs hunt for me." After releasing his dogs, he would ride his horse to the base of the nearest cliff, an outcrop well known to his dogs. At the base of the cliff he would wait with his firearm in position, his horse tied off to the side. It could take Ilia's dogs two or three hours before their barking would announce their approach from the forest. At this point their prey would appear at the edge of the cliff. Once his excited dogs had cornered their prey, Ilia would aim at it and shoot. This account is consistent, if generalized, with my own observations and the accounts of many other hunters in Oka. Ilia was a confident subsistence hunter, regularly bringing home meat for his immediate family, but sharing also with his aging mother and with his brothers. Taking pride in his WWII era German-made rifle, Ilia understood himself as an experienced hunter—but a hunter, nonetheless, primarily by way of his dogs.

Not all hunters I encountered took pride in the work of hunting dogs. Two avid hunters from Sorok (b. ca. 1980), for instance, did not hunt with dogs at all: "It's not interesting!" 'The dogs do all the work while the hunter merely shoots the animal at the end.' These young men preferred tracking prey on their own, from the saddle of their horses. For them, too, dogs were hunters in their own right. The two had felt that their skill as hunters was brought into question by the work and skill of dogs. Both men were also employed as water truck drivers in Sorok, and drawing on a monthly paycheck they were less likely to rely on hunted meat quite to the same extent as did my friends in the valley of Uro. In either case, Ilia's account, and the water truck drivers' preferences, are among multiple other examples which testify to the ways in which dogs were recognized as skilled hunters, and not merely as assistants in the hunting process. Understanding dogs as autonomous hunters would undoubtedly also have been foundational to Tofas, who historically released their dogs to fend for themselves during the summer months.

Talking about the hunt, its right timing and balance between hunter, landscape, and local spirit master, Iumzhap once explained: "You get up in the morning and look at your [lead] dog to see what mood he is in. You then decide whether to go hunting or not." If the dog is running in circles, pulling on his chain, and barking—it means that he is in a good mood (or in the right mood). If he is lying lazily by his hut, then he is in a bad mood (or in the wrong mood). It followed that only after one's dogs had been assessed one made decisions regarding the hunt. While many factors played into the right timing, it made little sense for Iumzhap to head into the forest with dogs that were found to be in the wrong mood. A dog's disposition was so important for a hunter to assess, precisely because his relations with the dog were not defined merely by his authority as master. Iumzhap knew he could coerce his dogs into tracking game, but he also knew that by forcing his dogs to work for him, he was ultimately working against himself. Unable to establish a space for productive collaboration, the balance in their relationship would be endangered. Waiting for the right disposition in his dogs allowed Iumzhap to tap into his dogs' intentions, which afforded him far better collaboration.[10]

Selecting for self-initiative and fearlessness

In early June, two days before our household was to migrate to summer pastures, Tsydyp's female hunting dog Strelka gave birth to five pups. Two of her litter were females, three were males. When I arrived at her wooden dog hut on the day of our departure, several men were gathered around it, attempting to pull her out from it. Resisting with all her might, Strelka desperately defended her litter. When the men had succeeded in separating her from her offspring, they held her tightly to the ground, while Tsydyp reached into the hut, bringing forward her pups. One by one he lay them in a box of corrugated board. It was my assumption that he was going to drown the pups, but instead he put the box in his jeep. As we departed Uro to travel to summer camp on upper Tustuk River, Strelka was left to run behind the jeep. Weakened by her pregnancy, and having been tied up since the previous winter, we soon lost sight of her. Tsydyp stopped the jeep and climbed on the roof to call for her. After some time she appeared on the horizon, driving a herd of sheep that did not belong to Tsydyp, and which were not supposed to come with us. Shouting and throwing sticks, Tsydyp was able to convince the sheep to return to the side valley from whence they had come. When Strelka reached us, she was allowed to join her pups in the jeep, where she settled into feeding them.

According to Tsydyp, the average lifespan of a dog in Oka was eight to nine years. Iumzhap, Tsydyp's elder brother and owner of White Sheik, had owned a bitch who had produced for him a last litter before falling to her death from a cliff. From this litter Iumzhap had chosen several good-looking pups who had grown into his current hunting dogs. The remainder of the litter he had culled. According to Iumzhap it was common practice to cull all female offspring on the spot, unless one were looking for a bitch. To be able to tell which members of a litter had promising features, one had to wait for several weeks. The runt had to be identified, and the fastest growing and stoutest looking pups were then selected. At summer camp Tsydyp periodically checked on the growth of Strelka's litter. It was unclear who had fathered the litter. All were growing slowly compared to other litters that season. Two or three weeks after our arrival at summer pasture, the first runt had died, and four slow-growing pups now remained. Tsydyp decided to let the litter live, at least until their first hunt.

The first hunt in a dog's life was a pivotal point in the selection of dogs. Ilia, whom I described earlier, was known as an expert horse breeder as well as a skillful dog enthusiast. He described his dogs as descending from "first-class" animals. One of their grandmothers had been an East Siberian Laika [probably a Siberian Husky or Iakut Laika], which had come to him from Iakutia. Another ancestor had been a very talented hunter, the origin or breed of which Ilia could not recall. What made a great hunting dog, according to Ilia, was the skill to quickly identify a track and to follow it until the prey animal was located. In this regard, Ilia had seen many "lazy"

(Rus. *lenivyie*) dogs. While some dogs were lazy, other dogs were "fearful."[11] Neither trait made for a good hunting dog. Such dogs were 'done away with' immediately. According to Iumzhap, 'Once a dog is a year old, it is taken on a hunting trip during which it is trained to identify tracks, following them over long distances, and to drive the prey in direction of the hunter.' For this purpose Iumzhap brought along an experienced dog, like White Sheik. The yearling would pick up tracking skills from the senior dog, and with every subsequent hunt it would build on its skill. A yearling who only followed the human hunter, was shot on the spot. What counted was a dog's fearlessness and self-initiative. White Sheik always led the way—whether we went to fetch sand or sable. In the words of Iumzhap, "This is how you select a hunting dog."

Castration and burial

Docking and castration were rarely practiced in Oka. One exception were Uncle Ivan and Aunty Irina's dogs. Living a distance away from Uro proper, Ivan kept three dogs, two of which he had castrated. Ivan did not fear unwanted offspring—both were good dogs. Instead, he sought to prevent them from running after bitches belonging to households in Uro proper. Ivan was concerned that his 'well mannered' dogs would be in contact with 'badly mannered' dogs from Uro. He described bad manners as nipping yak, chasing cows, and other unruly behavior that would potentially disturb or harm his herds. Were such habits to rub off on his dogs, they would become useless to him. Good demeanor around livestock he saw not as a genetic trait, so much as learned behavior that was exceedingly difficult to instill in Oka dogs. Although there had been no record of herding dogs in Oka, sensitivity to stock in dogs had become increasingly important to Ivan, especially since the decline in fur prices over the past few years, which meant that his dogs spent more time around domestic stock than out on hunting trails.

Ivan's topographic isolation from the rest of Uro's households had more than grazing reasons, and his dog castrations may well be framed in this context. There existed observable tensions between members of his household and several individuals at Uro proper. In Oka overall disposition, mood, or character of an animal or even of a herd were understood to reflect the mood or character of their owners, and particularly of the owning household's male head. In Ivan's case, castrating his dogs seemed to have been a way to demarcate the good demeanor of his own household from that of certain male heads and their households in Uro. This link between people and their animals was illustrated in Ivan's eldest dog who had lost his hearing. Although Ivan described him as 'mean' (Rus. *zloi*), he had no intention of putting him down. Quite to the contrary: Ivan valued the dog's irritation with certain people. 'The dog "senses" (Rus. *chustvuet*) people with a temper and will attack them.' Ivan went on to list the names of men from Uro whom the dog could not stand, adding: 'the dog will not bother any women or people of 'gentle' [Rus. *smirnyi*] character.' Dog castration in this chase not only prevented the corruption of dog behavior, but it also symbolized and accentuated inter-household distinctions.

After years of service, a good dog's life was celebrated with a special last rite, which elder Tseren-Dorzho explained as follows:

> When a dog gets too old, or when it is hurt, it is killed—its tail is chopped off [docked] and put under its head, and a piece of fat (Rus. salo) or butter, or something else that is delicious, is put in its mouth. That's how we bury our dogs. That's how I do it too. […] A dog is usually hanged. Or it can be shot. But usually it is hanged.

When I visited Tseren-Dorzho in the spring, he had already laid his eldest dog, Panda, to rest. Although I had not been there for the procedure, I imagined his body resting in the ground, somewhere near Tseren-Dorzho's cabin, with his lower jaw perched on his scruffy black tail, and with a piece of cured pork on his old tongue. Anthropologist Bernard Charlier (2015:38) explains the meaning of this ritual in Mongolia as "a process supposed to guarantee its human reincarnation." Tseren-Dorzho never offered such explanations, but the Soiot variant of this last rite seemed to blend Tofa and Mongolian traditions in which a dog was thanked for its many years of faithful service. According to B.E. Petri's (1928:33) account, a Tofa hunter would walk his aging but revered dog to "a good place"—usually atop a hill—where he "fed it for the road." He would say: "Mende, good-bye; do not be angered; you served me well; always helped me out on the hunt and in life; step now into your place; mende!" Then he would shoot the dog and cover it with boughs and moss.

Hunting sable with Tsydyp, Strelka, and Aslan

First snow had fallen in the night, and I could tell from the south-facing window in my cabin that my neighbor Borzhon had already caught his riding horse. Shaking his black mane, the stallion was eagerly awaiting his master to emerge from his cabin. By the time my breakfast water had boiled, Borzhon had long disappeared into the hills, with his rifle across his back. I walked across the valley to see Tsydyp, with whom I had arranged to go hunting at first snow. I could tell from the snow around his cabin that no one had left yet. Dagzama, his wife, poured me a cup of tea, while Tsydyp readied his rifle in the lean-to. Minutes later we were on our way—on foot—into the hills east of Uro. Both of Tsydyp's dogs had come with us; Aslan, his less experienced two-year-old male (Figure 3.1), and Strelka, his more experienced bitch.

Scrambling up a steep hillside, Tsydyp recalled seeing a sable in the area. Today there was no sign of it. Strelka and Aslan had run well ahead of us, and we were following in their tracks, scanning the snow cover for signs of life. Tsydyp was confident that if the sable was not here, we would find it further uphill. It was difficult to move at Tsydyp's pace, while at the

Figure 3.1 Aslan, Tsydyp's hunting-watchdog
Photograph by Alexander Oehler.

same time remaining attentive to the forest. So I decided to follow Tsydyp between the trees, mimicking his movements. Perhaps I would see what he saw, if I aligned my gate and gaze to his, much in the way in which Aslan was to learn from Strelka. We had climbed for a good while when we heard barking in the distance. I asked Tsydyp which of his dogs had barked and why. He said it was Aslan who had probably picked up the track of a deer. We pushed on through the snow, until both dogs stopped beneath two trees which were leaning on each other. Both dogs were intently looking up the trunk, barking. When we reached the trees, the dogs were sniffing the ground. Soon Tsydyp found sable tracks, so elusive that I could not see them. The uneven ground, strewn with rock boulders the size of large cushions, was covered under a white blanket. Walking here was a slippery and treacherous task. For small animals like sable, the countless holes and cracks between the boulders provided innumerable possibilities to disappear (Figure 3.2).

I was standing on a raised boulder, dizzied by the endless number of possible directions in which the sable might have run, when I noticed Aslan and Strelka closing in on several distinct boulders. Tsydyp and I quickly circled the area in a 10-meter radius, checking for tracks that might break our circle. Our foot and paw prints were now covering the site. Neither Tsydyp nor I could see the sable. Although I felt like we were chasing a ghost, my companions'

Figure 3.2 A typical sable boulder patch, shown in summer
Photograph by Alexander Oehler.

confidence that a sable was near made me yearn to see the forest as they did. Keeping the boulders in sight, Tsydyp and I swiftly collected dry brush and needles from beneath nearby larches. With the aid of some newspaper, we set four fires, placing them strategically throughout the boulder patch. The flames we fed with moss, lichen, and dry grass to intensify their smoke. With a thin board, Tsydyp directed the smoke into several cracks near the dogs. Strelka and Aslan were now intently moving between two or three openings, while Strelka suddenly sat back on one side of the boulder patch, while Aslan frantically wiggled a rock slab, attempting to gain access to what lay beneath. Pointing to Strelka, Tsydyp joked: "There, that's what old age does." Seconds later, Tsydyp identified a fresh set of tracks leading away from the boulders. The sable had escaped. Strelka had not sat back from fatigue, she had registered the loss of scent, while Aslan's lack of experience led him to dig harder. Not seeing it leave, she had sat back to observe the scene. Upset that we had missed the escape, Tsydyp pursued its tracks, immediately followed by his dogs.

Further downhill Tsydyp picked up on the tracks again, keeping a close eye on his dogs. Several minutes had passed when Aslan and Strelka began circling another boulder patch, similar to the previous one. Strelka was now focused on a slab, sniffing intently, and scratching with her paws in one direction. Tsydyp was certain the sable was here. I still could see nothing; no tracks, no sable. Again we set fires—three this time—fanning smoke into adjacent cracks. With increased certainty of success, the dogs reversed roles. Aslan was now watching from a slight distance, while Strelka was intently waiting at the opening under a rock slab. We spent a good while feeding and fanning our fires, and Tsydyp was as certain as Strelka that the sable was still under one of the slabs. Then Strelka changed position, and gazing at an adjacent opening, both dogs froze in perfect silence. Out of the stillness, Tsydyp suddenly cried out as something black and furry shot past me from under the cracks. The dogs took after it, chasing it uphill.

Tsydyp grabbed his rifle, following the dogs. A stone's throw up the hill, one of the dogs had got hold of the sable, then lost it again. By the time we had reached the dogs, Aslan was in control of the fighting sable, refusing to release it. Showering curses on his dog, and beating him vigorously with a thick branch, Tsydyp eventually convinced Aslan to release the sable. The sable leaped uphill, but catching up with it, Tsydyp held down its neck with the arch of his boot. He grabbed a stick and knocked it over the head three times. Its fur was crusted with frozen canine saliva, but it had remained unharmed from the dogs' fangs. Tsydyp's blows to the head had killed it, and its warm body now hung lax from his grip. Its shiny eyes were wide open and its mouth slightly ajar, exposing glistening gums and sharp little teeth. It was a smaller sable with little claws, about one-third smaller than the regional 'ideal'. I held it for a while, inspecting its shape and distinct facial expression, as its body was stiffening in my hands. Still excited, Aslan and Strelka attempted to take the body off my hands. We put the sable in Tsydyp's backpack, left our fires smoking, and departed.

On our return home, Tsydyp and I talked about the sable's escape at the first boulder patch. He said he had noticed the sable's escape before his dogs had. Yet, when Tsydyp saw Strelka sitting down, he had initially misread her behavior. She had not 'tired', and as soon as Tsydyp had discovered the new tracks, Strelka's actions gained new meaning. Having lost the sable's scent, she had no longer focused on the hole alone. Instead, she had sat back to visually consult the movements of Aslan, Tsydyp, and myself. When she noticed Tsydyp's excitement further downhill, she interpreted it as the missing link that had grounded her for several moments. She swiftly picked up on the fresh tracks and proceeded to direct us to the second boulder patch, once again relying on her olfactory abilities. This back-and-forth between the senses of three hunters had fueled the hunt: Tsydyp had relied on his dogs' capacity to track scent, while they in turn had relied on his eyes. When one system had broken down, each would look to the other to recalibrate their own search. Thus Tsydyp's eyes helped Strelka bridge the gap she had encountered in the sable's scent trail. At the same time, both Strelka and Tsydyp had been guessing the meaning of each other's responses to changes in the situation. In so doing, both were collaborating by sharing in each other's perspectives of the landscape.

Conclusion

The purpose of this chapter was to illustrate Soiot human–dog relations in terms of communication and collaboration. For my Soiot friends, it was paramount to ascribe their dogs a degree of autonomy, even if this resulted in some unpredictability, which was evident in their need to consult a dog's demeanor prior to departing for the taiga. Successful collaboration had to take into account another's disposition. Yet the level of attention paid to dogs by households and masters fluctuated seasonally, and in dependence on the relative economic importance of dogs as hunters at a given time of year. Hunting dogs enjoyed greater attention during the autumn months when collaborative activities peaked, which was also reflected in the mode and quality of feeding. Rather than asserting perfect control over their canine partners, Soiot householders allowed their more mature dogs periodic free roaming. Yet, even where dogs spent the majority of time on a chain, intermittent releases enabled some to join the hunting activities of other households on their own accord, further affirming their status as hunters in their own right. Meanwhile, there also existed a sharing practice of dogs among hunters. This sharing of dog skill and perspective maximized the animal's time spent in actual pursuit of prey, and thereby increased its value to the household, even if no payment was received for lending it.

In selecting dogs as hunters, self-initiative and fearlessness were the two most prized qualities, followed by the animal's ability to collaborate as part of a team. The success of a hunting team, consisting of humans and dogs, and sometimes also of horses or reindeer, relied on effective communication between the perspectives of each member. A good team was able not only to align their diverse intentions under a human master, but also to jointly profit from the bouquet of sensorial skills that emerged in their coming together. By drawing on each other's body-specific perceptual capacities, such as heightened sense of smell, superior eyesight, body size, or stature, dogs and humans intentionally bridged the gaps each encountered in their own perception of sequences in the landscape. By drawing on another's embodied sensory advantages, an assemblage of inter-species perspectives became interactive. Perspectival sharing between dogs and humans, then, serves as an ethnographic example of the conversational responsiveness that Ingold sees to occur within assemblages, and which is foundational to all of life.

Acknowledgements

The author would like to thank Professor Dr. David Anderson for his insightful comments on earlier drafts of this chapter. The fieldwork underlying this text was made possible by ERC Advanced Grant 'Arctic Domus', as well as 'The North Theme' and its Northern Colonialism program at the University of Aberdeen, Scotland.

Notes

1 This "searching," in Tofa dogs, according to B.E. Petri (1928:31), was a matter of being "intrusive," and "trying to carry off or lick up [anything they could find]." For most of the day, however, the dogs would sleep, "running nowhere, catching [not even] mice" (Petri 1928:31).
2 Charlier (2015: 38) explains that Mongolian herders from Uvs district attempted to keep their dogs at a distance from the yurt due to associations of uncleanliness. This does not seem to have applied, historically, to Tofas. Contemporary Soiots, however, rarely seemed to allow dogs into their homes.
3 Names of people have been anonymized, except where individuals chose to be named by their real names. Verbatim quotations (word-for-word recordings) are indicated by double quotation marks ("…"), interpretative quotations (based on field jottings) are indicated by single quotation marks ('…').
4 It was uncommon for a hunting dog to live to the age of 14. A dog would normally die earlier of natural or accidental (often hunting-related) circumstances, or its master would kill it around retirement age.
5 The decline in pelt prices has led to changes in hunting emphases all over the Saian Mountain region. It is to be expected that the training of hunting dogs reflects these changes. In Tofalariia, where hunting still constitutes the majority of a household's annual income, the illegal sale of musk deer glands has taken the place of sable and to a lesser degree of squirrel. But musk deer were an important prey long before the drop in fur prices (e.g. Mel'nikova 1994:45).
6 Rassadin (2000:42) explains further, "When a sable track was found, the young dog would be incited to follow it. If the dog was by nature to be a sable hunter (Rus. *soboliatnitsa*), then it would immediately follow its trail, sometimes even completely ignoring squirrel tracks. Such a dog would remain a *soboliatnitsa* for life."
7 This observation contradicts B.E. Petri's (1928:31) findings described above.
8 Iumzhap's family lived across the river from Borzhon's. He belonged to one of two main extended families that had taken abode in the valley, each of their respective households being located on opposite sides of the river. The fact that a dog from a non-kin household joined our hunt further confirms extended sharing of dogs. Although Iumzhap's younger brother had joined us on the hunt, he had not taken command over his elder brother's dog, leaving me under the impression that the dog had belonged to Borzhon.
9 B.E. Petri (1928:32) reported that although Tofa hunters would generally not sell their dogs, a good hunting dog was worth two horses.
10 In Tofalariia, hunters I spent time with had similar experiences. For them, too, dogs were hunters in their own right, and their services were shared by people. But in recent years, as they had observed, hunting dogs were increasingly following their own agendas. Particularly in certain locations, such as a rocky outcrop (Rus. *tstoi*) we passed during one outing, it was exceedingly difficult to corner Siberian musk deer because the dogs would not drive them all the way to the cliff. Most hunters seemed dissatisfied with contemporary dogs because often they would hunt for one species when the hunter had intended to obtain another. Whether this reported increase in the failure to reconcile intentional discrepancies resulted from a decrease in proper training, breeding, or field communication was unclear.

11 Although all Iumzhap's dogs feared wolves, they were not considered fearful dogs. According to Iumzhap, White Sheik was a fearless dog, yet he rightfully feared wolves. He said, wolves could easily eat White Sheik, given they were bigger than him: "All they would leave of him is his tail." But Iumzhap had already docked the tail.

Bibliography

Anderson, M. 1986. "From Predator to Pet: Social Relationships of the Saami Reindeer-Herding dog." *Central Issues in Anthropology*, 6(2): 3–11.
Andreeva, E. and V. Leksin. 1999. "Traditional land use: from state planning to a self-sufficient model." In A. Pika (ed.), *Neotraditionalism in the Russian North*, 89–108. Edmonton: Canadian Circumpolar Institute.
Charlier, B. 2015. *Faces of the Wolf: Managing the Human, Non-human Boundary in Mongolia*. Leiden: Brill.
Corkran, C. 2015. "'An Extension of Me': Handlers Describe Their Experiences with Bird Dogs." *Society & Animals*, 23: 231–249.
Deleuze, G. and F. Guattari. 2013[1987]. *A Thousand Plateaus: Capitalism and Schizophrenia*. London: Bloomsbury.
Ikeya, K. 1994. "Hunting with Dogs Among the San in the Central Kalahari." *African Study Monographs*, 15(3): 119–134.
Ingold, T. 2013. "Anthropology Beyond Humanity." *Suomen Anthropologi: Journal of the Finish Anthropological Society*, 38(3): 5–23.
Ingold, T. 2015. "One World Anthropology." Visiting speakers series at the Department of Anthropology at McGill University, Montreal. Oct. 9.
Kohn, E. 2007. "How Dogs Dream: Amazonian Natures and the Politics of Transspecies Engagement." *American Ethnologist*, 34(1): 3–24.
Koster, J. 2009. "Hunting Dogs in Lowland Neotropics." *Journal of Anthropological Research*, 65(4): 575–610.
Laugrand, F. and J. Oosten. 2015. *Hunters, Predators and Prey: Inuit Perceptions of Animals*. New York: Berghahn.
McGranaghan, M. 2015. "Hunters-with-Sheep': The |Xam Bushmen of South Africa Between Pastoralism and Foraging." *Africa*, 85(3): 521–545.
Mel'nikova, L.V. 1994. *Tofy: Istoriko-Etnograficheskii Ocherk (Tofas: an ethnohistorical sketch)*. Irkutsk: Vostochno- Sibirskoe Knizhnoe Izd-vo.
Olsen, Ø. 1915. *Et Primitivt Folk: de Mongolske Rennomader (A Primitive People: the Mongolian Reindeer Nomads)*. Oslo: Cappeln.
Pavlinskaia, L.R. 2002. *Kochevniki Golubykh Gor (Nomads of the Blue Mountains)*. St. Petersburg: Evropeiskii Dom.
Petri, B.E. 1927. *Etnograficheskie Issledovania Sredi Malykh Narodov v Vostochnykh Saianakh: Predvoritel'nye Dannye (Ethnographic Researches Among the Small Numbered Peoples of the Eastern Saians)*. Irkutsk: Izdanie Irkutskovo Universiteta.
Petri, B.E. 1928. *Promysli Karagas (Subsistence strategies of the Karagas)*. Irkutsk: Izdanie Irkutskovo Universiteta.
Rassadin, I.V. 2000. *Khoziaistvo, Byt i Kultura Tofalarov (Subsistence Practices and Culture of Tofas)*. Ulan-Ude: Institut Mongolovedenia, Buddologii i Tibetologii CO RAN.

Vasil'ev, V.N. 1910. "Kratkii Ocherk Byta Karagasov (A Brief Description of Karagas Livelihood)." *Etnograficheskoe Obozrenie*, 1–2: 46–76.

Vasilevich, G.M. and G.M. Levin. 1951. "Tipy Olenevodstva i Ikh Proiskhozhdenie. (Reindeer Herding Types and Their Origins)." *Sovietskaia Etnografia*, 1: 63–87.

Viveiros de Castro, E. 1996. "Images of Nature and Society in Amazonian Ethnology." *Annual Review of Anthropology*, 25: 179–200.

Viveiros de Castro, E. 1998. "Cosmological Deixis and Amerindian Perspectivism." *The Journal of the Royal Anthropological Institute*, 4(3): 469–488.

Weil, K. 2010. "A Report on the Animal Turn." *Differences*, 21(2): 1–23.

4 Dogs, reindeer and humans in Siberia

Threefold synergetic in the northern landscape

Vladimir Davydov and Konstantin Klokov

Introduction: Socio-biological mechanisms of landscape appropriation in human–dog–reindeer communities

Dogs and reindeer are animals which can be met in many northern communities, but the question of their co-existence has been rarely discussed in anthropological literature. In many cases they have been represented in separate texts devoted either to 'reindeer breeding' or to 'dog breeding'. These two activities were represented in the ethnographic literature as two separate spheres and two different domains of knowledge. The purpose of this chapter is bring these spheres and domains together and to discuss the effect of their mutual involvement in the process of northern landscapes appropriation. In this context we approach human–animal–landscape interaction as a type of social relation. We try to avoid the dualistic representation of northern communities by approaching them as human–dog–reindeer communities (HDR-communities) and put the stress on dog, reindeer and human interaction and co-existence, rather than analyzing dog breeders and reindeer breeders as separate and independent groups. In this sense, ethnographic narratives can sometimes go beyond the research strategy of stressing symmetry and equality to represent many agents that can collaborate and together create the conditions for routine everyday life (Anderson et al. 2016: 21; 2017). Therefore we are trying to stress that the landscape appropriation in the North is not just an outcome of the intensive involvement of tools and equipment, but it can be seen as a result of the action of particular socio-biological mechanisms.

Contemporary exploitation of northern and Arctic territories, e.g. in the oil and gas industry, as well as in the process of mineral extraction, has a mechanical character. In this context the landscape is appropriated by the use of heavy equipment. This extensive exploitation has certain negative ecological effects that are exemplified in local environmental discourses (Sirina and Fondahl 2006). In contrast to this industrial model, many local people appropriate northern landscapes not only with tools and vehicles, but also with the help of other beings. Active participation and collaboration of humans, dogs and reindeer is very important here. This way of landscape appropriation is less harmful for the environment and is based on a combination of social and biological factors. The purpose of this chapter is to discuss the mutual involvement of humans, dogs and reindeer in the process of landscape appropriation using extensive examples from our own fieldwork in different regions in Siberia. This ethnographic data shows that appropriation is not a mechanical process but involves active engagement of human and non-human persons.

'Invisible' co-existence

In many respects, 'reindeer herding' and 'dog breeding' have been understood as distinctive activities. In classical ethnographic works, for example, they are discussed in separate chapters or articles (Bogoraz 1991; Vasilevich 1969). This separation can also be traced in museum collections, which were classified by the collectors and registrars according to region, ethnicity and thematic attribution. This created sets of objects used to portray either 'reindeer herding' of 'dog breeding'. The same logic was implemented for the collection of visual materials. If we investigate Siberian ethnographic photo collections of the Museum of Anthropology and Ethnography (Kunstkamera), Russian Academy of Sciences (MAE RAS), we can see that most pictures represent the use of either reindeer or dogs. For instance, there are more than 500 photo prints of reindeer in this collection while the number of photos picturing dogs is almost ten times smaller. Most dogs are represented in the context of hunting. There are a few photos of sled dogs, and the pictures of reindeer-herding dogs are especially rare. Finally, there are just a few pictures showing dogs and reindeer together (see e.g. MAE RAS coll. И426–7, И426–71 and И1811–67).

At the same time it is obvious that humans, dogs and reindeer inhabit the landscape together. What are the reasons and implications for such misrepresentation of dogs? After analyzing our own field experience we realized that we did almost the same during our expeditions. The number of pictures with reindeer was always much bigger. For some reason the co-existence of humans, dogs and reindeer remained invisible both in ethnographic collections and in our own observations. There was a lack of multispecies ethnography reflecting on humans, dogs, and reindeer co-presence.

These anthropological practices are partly due to the fact that reindeer were more exotic animals for the observers than dogs, which were far more familiar animals. Both of these animals help facilitate people's movements and other daily activities in the North and Siberia. However, their co-presence in particular communities was not reflected in collections and archival documents, and most historical sources showed or described the use of reindeer and dogs as separate activities. In this sense, the invisibility of dog and reindeer co-existence was connected with a strong focus on reindeer herding and hunting as two main occupations of northern peoples. Therefore, reindeer became the main heroes of ethnographic texts devoted to reindeer herding, while dogs were mostly described in the context of hunting. Some works, however, concentrated on the use of dogs as transport animals (Vasil'ev 1936; Levin and Potapov 1961).

Cultural differences in human–animal interaction

There are certain cultural differences which affect human–animal relations. This idea was reflected in Russian classical ethnographic works, which distinguished four types of reindeer herding (Vasilevich and Levin 1951) and five types of sled dog breeding (Levin 1946). The way in which people interact and train animals depends on cultural context. This idea was reflected in the accounts of Russian travelers and ethnographers of the eighteenth and nineteenth centuries. Thus, G. A. Sarychev (1802) was one of the first to mention that behavior of Siberian dogs varied from place to place and depended on the way that people treated them. This idea was further developed by V. G. Bogoraz (Bogoraz-Tan 1934), who described the differences between reindeer trained by Tungus (Evens) and Chukchis. He wrote that Tungus' reindeer behaved in a different manner and they were 'more expensive and much better than Chukchis' reindeer' (Bogoraz-Tan 1934: 144). Some contemporary researchers mentioned different skills and behavioral manners of dogs, which were raised in different cultural environments. For instance, T. Safonova and I. Sántha (2012, 2013) stressed the differences between Buriat and Evenki dogs which arise from different models of these animals' socialization. An interesting observation made by these authors was that children play an important role in the socialization of dogs, and dogs in the socialization of children. Both children and puppies are in contact from the very early stages of their socialization and become accustomed to one another (see also McCormack, this volume). In this sense, people become emotionally connected with other living beings from the early age. The same kind of early socialization with reindeer takes place in the families of reindeer herders.

With some exceptions, ethnographic accounts generally lack descriptions of experimental activities and small-scale everyday tasks done with animals, as well as small-scale domestication architecture. For instance, people in Yakutia tried to use reindeer to plow the land instead of horses or bulls in the 1920s (see e.g. MAE RAS coll. И1475–29). Northern Baikal Evenkis used some exercises for reindeer and riders: young men tried to keep their balance standing on reindeer back similarly to horse riders in a circus (MAE RAS coll. И1811–26). Evenkis from the northern Zabaikal region confirmed that they tried this way of training.

Some ethnographic accounts described a special type of a dog, one that is used in tundra reindeer herding (Rus. *olenegonnaia sobaka*) (see e.g. Kvashnin 2007; Adaev 2013, 2014). In many places it was introduced during the Soviet period, in the 1940s–1950s, in order to provide better control of animals' movements in large herds (Sirina 2016). These dogs were used as a kind of mediator between people and reindeer, which helped people to keep herds in certain places and were able to follow herders' commands. In this sense, we can speak about different patterns of use of space which depend on the division of tasks between reindeer and dogs. Traditionally it was not used by Chukchis, but they spread widely in Chukotka in the Soviet period (Golovnev et al. 2015: 79). This type of a Siberian Laika is considered by Taimyr reindeer herders as especially intelligent compared to other dogs. When such dogs are trying to bring back the runaway groups of reindeer, they lead the process themselves and may follow these reindeer for several kilometers.

In many places in Siberia dogs became employed for cargo transportation. In Taimyr, northern Baikal, and the Yenisei River regions dogs helped people to bring water or ice. People employed dogs for short-term trips on the river. Siberian hunters used dogs to pull special small sledges with cargo. All these tasks, even though they were never in the center of researchers' attention, played an important role in the process of human–animal interaction. Domestication is not a quality of an animal; rather it is a continuous process involving everyday tasks. These tasks vary from place to place and in part determine the quality of human–animal relations.

Monopolization of transport function

Dogs and reindeer work in close cooperation together with humans in herding and hunting, but in some areas both are also a means of conveyance. Typically, participation in transportation is 'monopolized' in communities either by dogs or reindeer. This monopolization was later reflected in ethnographic texts which described dog breeding and reindeer herding as separate and not intersecting spheres (Antropova and Levin 1961). V. G. Bogoraz even wrote, that 'reindeer herding is incompatible with dog breeding' (Bogoraz-Tan 1934: 4).

In Siberia, it is a well-established ethnographic fact that reindeer transport is generally not used together with dog transport in individual communities. For example, according to the data from the Polar Census concerning the households of indigenous peoples of the northern Russia, 89% of the sled dogs belonged to settled households, while 91% of the transport reindeer (Rus. *ezdovovye oleni*) were from nomadic households (calculated on data from *Pokhoziaistvennaia perepis'*, TsSU 1929: 13–14).

The use of dog sledges for transport correlated with the resources available for feeding dogs. These practices occurred in the regions rich in fish and sea mammals such as shores of big spawning rivers and shores of the Pacific and Arctic Oceans (Bogoslovskaia 2005; Samar 2010: 21). Chikachev (2004) reports that in winter a sled dog would eat an average of 1.5–2 kg of fish or meat per day, and in summer would consume far less. In order to feed one team of sled dogs consisting of ten animals, one would need about 3–4 tons of fish per year (Chikachev 2004: 18). Dogs are also considered hardier than reindeer: a dog pulls a sledge until it is no longer able to stand, but a tired reindeer often just lies down. During blizzards when visibility is extremely poor, dogs can usually manage to direct sledges back to dwellings.

During such bad weather reindeer are often guided by the wind and can easily become disoriented. According to Dolgan informants, reindeer are able to bring sledges back to a camp as well; however, they need much better weather conditions than dogs (Fieldnotes Davydov, Taimyr Peninsula). Dogs are much lighter than reindeer, who often fall through the snow, while dogs are able to stay suspended on the snow crust (Tugolukov 1979: 80; Chikachev 2004: 41). Dog sledges are faster than reindeer sledges in case people travel short distances. For instance, in the past, fishermen on dog sledges and reindeer herders on reindeer sledges participated in the competitions and at short distances dogs would outrun reindeer (Fieldnotes Klokov, Yamal Peninsula).

At the same time people may combine these two modes of transportation for completing different tasks. For instance, Dolgan reindeer herders use reindeer transport, while fishermen and people residing in the villages employ dog sledges. Reindeer herders from the Taimyr Peninsula explain this by the fact that reindeer can be scared by a large number of dogs. Currently, small numbers of sled dogs remain in the Siberian North, while reindeer sledges are used more often. However, in some regions such as Chukotka and the Taimyr Peninsula dog sledge races have become a part of 'reindeer herders' day' celebration (see Strecker, this volume). For instance, sled dog races have taken place in Chukotka since 1991, and they usually consist of 15–20 dog sledges that cover a distance of several hundred kilometers along the Pacific Coast (Bogoslovskaia 2011: 38–65).

Domestic animals and religious beliefs

V. G. Bogoraz wrote that dogs were more important than reindeer in the context of religious beliefs (Bogoraz-Tan 1934: 4). Thus, Bogoraz mentioned that a dog can protect a person from evil inclinations, but a reindeer does not have this protection power (Ibid.).

In many Siberian cultures a dog was considered as a mediator between people and spiritual beings (Samar 2010: 89), and it always played a significant role in cult practices, shamanic rituals (Ibid.: 101, 103; Novikov 2001), and mythology (Miller 1875). Rites of reindeer sacrifice are now widespread in the north of Siberia (Khariuchi 2012: 98–101; Vaté 2005: 54–55), while sacrifice of dogs is mostly a thing of the past and only rarely now takes place. However a special attitude toward dogs is still preserved. Thus, Nenets reindeer herders from the Tazovskaia tundra do not kill old reindeer-herding dogs. These animals are often given to fishermen camps, where they perform a useful ecological function by clearing the area of fish waste by eating it. If a reindeer herder still needs to get rid of an old dog, he makes a loop and ties it to its neck, and then binds the animal to a sledge and moves so fast on it that the dog cannot keep up. Arriving at a new location, the owner 'accidentally' discovers that the dog has died (Kvashnin 2009: 153).

In other regions customs are different. According to the stories told by Yamal Nenets, a prohibition to kill a dog exists only in some kin groups. The others can kill an old dog in case of need, but they carry out a special ritual in this case. For instance, they cover a killed dog with deer skin and lay a piece of bread or fish nearby (Fieldnotes Klokov, Yamal Peninsula). Several years ago, in Chukotka, a case where a dog was sacrificed during a funeral took place. A dog was killed after a woman, who was its owner, had died. This tradition has long ceased to be regularly followed (Fieldnotes Klokov, Chukotka).

Relative autonomy and animal agency

Co-existence with dogs and reindeer helps people in certain periods of time to rely just on local resources. Dogs and reindeer provide people with transport, food and skins, the latter of which are used as both building materials and for clothing. Therefore, dogs and reindeer provide local people with relative autonomy from state resources and neighboring groups. It is obvious that reindeer herders, through intensive exchange with others, acquire certain resources, and full autonomy will never be possible. However, the use of reindeer and dogs helps them to live for certain periods of time autonomously. They are part of what enables people to appropriate landscapes while relying on their own resources, and generally make people less dependent on state infrastructure.

In comparison to some other species, dogs and reindeer can provide people with more autonomy, because they can be relatively autonomous themselves. We can speak only about a high degree of autonomy, because absolute autonomy is not possible in this context. Evenkis had a practice of self-provision of dogs that is similar to that of reindeer. This is often not the case with other domestic animals such as cattle and horses. At the same time, in this case the idea of relative autonomy may create an illusion of animals less dependent on humans and a smaller degree of animal domestication (Anderson et al. 2016: 6). The idea of autonomy correlates with the idea of personhood. People in Siberia at times perceive dogs and reindeer as persons who themselves know how to act in certain situations. Reindeer and dogs are active agents of social interaction and people give them significant freedom of movement. Animals themselves can decide where to move. Reindeer herders and hunters are skillful in seeing and predicting the intentions of animals.

The relationships between dogs and reindeer are especially interesting for research but are often quite ambiguous. The dogs from settlements (Rus. *poselkovye*) as well as hunters' dogs can potentially traumatize reindeer. Cases when reindeer, which had arrived in the village and were left unattended by the herders, were bitten, mutilated, or killed by dogs are not rare. Dogs which live together with reindeer herders pass through a strong selection process where people take into account their loyalty to the reindeer. Reindeer herders punish dogs strictly, and if this does not work – kill those dogs which continue biting reindeer. However, for the safety of calves, which are the most vulnerable, reindeer herders do not keep large dogs. The classic reindeer herders' dog is a Siberian Laika, which is of a rather small size. Further, as Nenets reindeer herders say, a small dog is very convenient because it can be easily carried with people on sledges.

It might be assumed that the training of reindeer-herding dogs requires a significant number of special techniques. However, reindeer herders usually do not agree with this statement. Both Nenets and Dolgan reindeer herders particularly emphasized the innate capacities of local Siberian Laikas and their ability to learn from interacting with more experienced dogs. People do not specially teach dogs. As people say, a dog either receives the qualities of good reindeer-herding from nature, or learns from an older dog (Fieldnotes Klokov, Yamal Peninsula; Fieldnotes Davydov, Taimyr Peninsula). As a Nenets reindeer herder said, 'Nenets dogs have a skill to herd reindeer from God. But Russian dogs as well as Russian people are not able to do this. An old dog teaches a younger one' (Fieldnotes Klokov, Yamal Peninsula). Another informant emphasized: 'Even a bad dog is better than nothing, since reindeer see a dog and gather themselves in a group' (Fieldnotes Klokov, Yamal Peninsula). The opinions of the reindeer herders can be confirmed by observations of ethnologists. L. M. Baskin (2009: 152–153), who researched reindeer herding and animals' behavior for many years, argues that there is no need to teach a reindeer-herding dog to run after reindeer – this is an inherent instinct. Rather, a herder's task is to not allow a puppy to do this aimlessly. The main method of working with such a dog is to send it to the side of a group of reindeer and have it direct them to join the main herd. This task can be performed by a dog on its own. It is simplified by the fact that due to the herd's instincts, in most cases frightened reindeer will cluster together, regardless of the direction in which the dog first chases them. As soon as a herder makes sure that the reindeer have turned and are moving to the herd, he recalls the dog to him. An experienced dog does it itself, and does not wait for a herder's call. In addition, following its instinct, a dog, like a wolf, does not usually break into a herd, but rather rushes along its edges, making animals walk close to each other. This is exactly what reindeer herders need. Conversely, dogs from settlements have this instinct broken; they can disperse a herd instead of collecting it. That is why reindeer herders always use only their own dogs.

Co-domestication of dogs and reindeer in HDR-communities?

Food sharing with dogs and reindeer is a widely spread practice in Siberia. Domesticated reindeer eat bread from people's hand. We have observed this practice among Evenki and Dolgan reindeer herders. For instance, Dolgans call a reindeer that is accustomed to eating bread from people's hands *aku*. They say that *aku* is an especially tamed reindeer, which is not afraid of people. This type of reindeer develops when a calf loses his mother and people have to feed him from a bottle. As informants say, in these cases a reindeer can be as domesticated 'as a dog and usually walks behind people like a dog'. Some informants say that *aku* recognizes his name when people call for him (Fieldnotes Davydov, Taimyr Peninsula). Feeding dogs from the hands is widely spread among different groups of Siberian reindeer herders. Evenki reindeer herders from Tiania in Olekminskii district of Yakutiia sometimes fed meat to a reindeer. Afterwards this particular animal received the name Cannibal or Gannibal. People said that this animal 'used to eat almost everything from people's hands'. In some cases people may use the same food both for reindeer and dogs. For instance, on Sakhalin Island people feed both dogs and reindeer with fish. Reindeer are fond of fish because it is salted (Fieldnotes Davydov, Yakutia). As Uilta informants from Val village said, in these cases reindeer can walk behind fishermen 'like dogs and are waiting for the catch' (Fieldnotes Davydov, Sakhalin).

The process of human–animal interaction involves the use of different sorts of constructions. Some of these structures are built especially for animals. Architecture plays an important role in the process of domestication. It can restrict animals' movements as well as create more comfortable environments for them. People may construct special structures of comfort (Anderson et al. 2016) for animals, for instance dog shelters and sheds for reindeer. People may use the same strategies both for dogs and reindeer to limit their movements. One of these strategies is tethering animals to poles, trees, thick roots or structures. As we have observed in the field they may start doing this when the animals are rather young. For instance, Evenki herders bind reindeer calves to poles in order to make them calmer. They do the same with puppies in order to teach them to wear collars. Training of both dogs and reindeer may involve using a leash when people move animals together with them. During this training animals learn how to walk at the same speed as a person.

Another technique is the use of small logs, called both by Evenkis and Dolgans *chengai*. These are tied to the neck of the animal, and their main purpose is to slow down the amplitude of its movements. People use these items as a way to 'release' transport reindeer overnight, which prevents them from moving far away from the camp. A *chengai* usually beats animals' legs when it moves too fast, making rapid movement uncomfortable. The idea behind using a *chengai* is similar to tethering, but it gives some freedom to an animal to be able to find food. With dogs, people do this in order to train sled dogs and to make dogs with a bad character calmer. This technique is widely spread throughout the Siberian taiga, and people may employ the same techniques and tools for both dogs and reindeer.

The wealth that walks on the land

The nomadic economy of a typical Nenets reindeer herder's family ideally consists of an unbroken chain, including a host husband, housewife and children-heirs, several hundred reindeer, and about a dozen dogs, where each plays its role. The loss of one of the elements in the chain weakens or completely destroys the economy (Kvashnin 2009: 16–17). Reindeer serve as a measure of success in this economy. For example, Nenets say 'Everyone who wants can earn money, but one is rich if he has many reindeer' (Martynova 2014: 164). However, a reindeer-herding dog is valued no less than a sledge reindeer, because 'one cannot gather a herd without a dog'. In our conversations with Yamal herders, it was said that a good young dog can be exchanged for a leading (Rus. *peredovoi*) reindeer (Fieldnotes Klokov, Yamal Peninsula). In the past, in the areas where sedentary indigenous inhabitants were engaged primarily in hunting and fishing, people valued sled dogs more than reindeer. Thus, in the Indigirka and Kolyma River Basins, an offer to sell a lead dog in a sledge team often was followed by the answer: 'Yes, I will better give a wife than a leading dog!' (Chikachev 2004: 38).

A variety of animal types rather than one type

Cooperation in the HDR-communities was achieved through the natural and acquired abilities of each of the three participants. Some of these abilities are probably genetic, while others were acquired in the course of their joint activities (Stépanoff 2012). The development of relevant capacities allowed everyone to contribute to the overall synergistic activity of the community, and the performance of a specific set of functions was integrated in various combinations in each particular type of community. On the one hand, these combinations depended on local conditions such as the relations of local communities with the landscape. On the other hand, they were connected with the historical traditions of a cultural group, and with the process of transmission of skills from one community to another. As a result, even within the same type of natural environment the structure of HDR-communities and the role of each of the three participants are often significantly different.

This argument is supported by the numerous local categories of dogs and reindeer used by Siberian indigenous groups. In many respects, the official statistical documents often misrepresent the ways in which people and animals appropriate landscapes. They represented the quantitative data, but they did not show particular relations which existed between people and animals. This created the image of 'reindeer herding' and 'dog breeding' as something uninfected, stable and based on a single type of an animal which can be classified according to gender and age. However, the particularities and ethnographic descriptions of these relations were often missing. The qualitative characteristics of human–dog–reindeer relations varied from place to place.

We can observe diverse 'types' of dogs and reindeer in the North depending on their training, diets, and relations to people and other animals: sledge reindeer, riding reindeer, interbred wild/domestic reindeer, sledge dogs, guard dogs, and hunting dogs. These animals participate in multiple activities and many of the types are based not just on the pedigree and physical form, but rather depend on the socialization process and training. Thus, the tundra and taiga reindeer vary by size, leg length and other ecological adaptations. In total there are four pedigrees of domestic reindeer in Siberia, each of which has several variations (Klokov 2013). Dogs for reindeer herding, hunting and sledges are variable not only in size and appearance, but also in their skills and behavior. A Siberian hunting dog is known as a Laika, which means a 'bark-dog'. The hunting Laika are represented by a number of different pedigrees, and reindeer-herding dogs by only one pedigree, which is known as the 'Nenets reindeer herding Laika'. In the past more than ten groups characterized by different coat and body forms were distinguished among the native Siberian sled dogs. However, only one of them, which is officially named the Chukchi sled dog, still survives (Shereshevskii et al. 1946: 20–51; Bogoslovskaia 2011: 99–106).

However, all native dog 'types' encompass a range of individual variability. For instance, there are quiet and 'delicate' dogs among the Nenets reindeer-herding dogs which are used for pasturing female deer with calves, but more aggressive dogs, which can scare and even bite disobedient reindeer, are also present. Nenets from the Taz River have special words to describe dogs of various 'specialties', such as dogs for collecting a herd, bringing a herd home, and even search dogs, which look for and bring back deer that have strayed from the herd (Adaev 2014: 27–28). Many Nenets reindeer herders have four to six dogs of different temperaments, but they usually take just one or two with them to drive reindeer.

People and dogs appropriate new spaces together. Many nomadic groups became involved in the sedentarization policy. In the 1920s–1930s many tenure settlements were created and both people and dogs became the inhabitants of these new settlements. Sedentarization of Arctic indigenous groups led to division between tundra and settlement (Rus. *tundrovye i poselkovye*) dogs. Local people in eastern Taimyr mentioned many differences in behavior of dogs that inhabit the settlements or the tundra. For instance, they mentioned that tundra dogs are much more intelligent compared to dogs in settlements. They added that tundra dogs never eat garbage when they are in the village. In contrast, settlement dogs 'Eat garbage and can steal food' (Fieldnotes Davydov, Taimyr Peninsula). For such people a dog is not just a dog, but rather a certain type of an animal whose behavior depends on the environment where it grew up.

Reflection on movement

The spatial aspect of human–animal relations plays a very important role in the process of domestication. People employ different structures and techniques to limit and direct the movements of dogs and reindeer and, at the same time, constantly move themselves through different locations. Building, the use of different techniques, and movements usually take into consideration the needs of animals. In many respects local people correlate their seasonal rhythms with the interests of reindeer. At the same time, the needs of dogs can put serious limitations on the economic activity of people. For example, when people plan a trip on dog sledges they need to consider the possibility that food (fish or meat) will need to be provided for them.

Reindeer herders and hunters are involved in intensive movements and are surrounded by movements of multiple agents. They constantly reflect upon these movements in order to plan their next actions. The plans of reindeer herders and hunters strongly depend on the current situation. Interaction of dogs and reindeer takes place in the context of intensive movements of people and animals themselves. On the one hand, reindeer herders move from place to place to save pastures. On the other hand, people and animals periodically return to the same places (Davydov 2014). Some places, such as locations where one can escape from biting insects, find salt, food or water, may themselves attract animals in certain periods of the year. The everyday tasks of people in HDR-communities involve constant reflection upon movements of different types. Reindeer herders are very skillful in understanding and anticipating domestic animals' and predators' actions. They constantly try to keep in mind the direction in which they can find reindeer and recall the places which might be visited by predators. This way of reflecting upon the numerous moves of multiple agents can be compared with playing chess (Davydov 2015). In fact, it is not surprising that chess and other strategic games have become a significant part of reindeer herders' leisure activities in between different tasks. Reindeer herders often use self-made chess pieces that they carve from wood.

The metaphor of chess is rather old in ethnography. For instance, A. F. Middendorf (1869: 705), a researcher who worked in Siberia in the nineteenth century, employed the metaphor of chess for his analysis of Tungus patterns, which were compared to those Samoyedic groups. He writes that in contrast to Samoyeds, the movements of Reindeer Tungus 'cannot be reduced to a single chess move' (Ibid.). Chess is also a local metaphor for reindeer herders' movements. For instance, Evenkis and Orochens of China even play a special variant of chess – a reindeer chess where the main figures are reindeer and dogs (Davydov, Inner Mongolia).

Reindeer herders and hunters are inspired by the strategy of a game. It is play which takes place in a certain space and is not limited by only one potential move. While playing chess one needs to think about the moves of his various figures, which have different spectrums of action, and try to predict the actions of his opponent. Chess requires predicting a multiplicity of variants for future action. Thus, the strategy of the game itself has many similarities with everyday practices of reindeer herders. Reindeer herding involves reflection on small changes in the environment such as change of wind speed and direction, in order to anticipate the direction in which reindeer moved and to define potentially dangerous places, which can attract predators.

Tracking predators' movements is a very important task in reindeer herding. This practice helps to prevent a herd from the predators' attacks. Siberian reindeer herders are very skillful in their ability to 'read the tracks'

(Brandišauskas 2009: 133–134) and to reconstruct movements of multiple agents (Spasskii 1822: 45–46; Tugolukov 1969: 34). Many authors describing these practices employed the metaphor of 'reading' (Dokolev 1957: 3). Similarly to chess play, reindeer herding and hunting are strategic and reflexive activities which involve a kind of 'battle' or competition with the 'opponents', which are represented by predators, prey and other actors. In this sense, dogs help people to be more reflexive and more sensitive to changes around the HDR-community; they can extend human senses. In this sense the use of dogs has some similarities with chess, since they help humans to expand their operative knowledge concerning the activities of different agents on surrounding territory. It helps people to analyze the current situation and to make strategic decisions. Dogs help people to monitor movements of different kinds. They have a very fast reaction and can warn people in case of danger. Visual and sound cognition play an important role here. Moreover, dogs have a fine sense of smell, and are particularly sensitive to predators' scent. In the Zabaikal region reindeer herders' camps are surrounded by dogs in order to track all directions of potential predators' movements. Dog barking can signal potential danger and alert others to the movements of people and animals approaching a camp (Fieldnotes Davydov, Zabaikal region).

The internal cooperation of these HDR-communities would not be possible without the participation of other non-domesticated species living in the same shared habitat. For example, dogs play an intermediate role in the relations of humans with other species in hunting and reindeer herding. We can say that dogs and reindeer are stakeholders in the relations between human and other species, revealing other animals' locations and directing their moves, as well as transporting humans towards the places where wild fauna are plentiful. In the tundra dogs help people to coordinate a herd's movements. Dogs in a sense decrease the spectrum of actions of wild and domestic animals. They provide an extension of reindeer herders' and hunters' bodies. As a reindeer herder from Taimyr emphasized: 'Dog is my right hand!' The practice of scaring a reindeer is very important here (Golovnev et al. 2015: 79; Davydov 2016: 199). Reindeer are scared of dogs and can change the direction of their movement depending on the location of a dog. In the taiga people sometimes use fences to keep reindeer in particular places. In the Arctic tundra dogs are used instead of fences (they perform the same function within their movements). They help people to collect reindeer in particular places. They can run much faster than a person and are able to run rather long distances to bring reindeer to a camp.

Conclusion: Changes and innovations in human–dog–reindeer communities

During the last few decades several types of northern human–dog–reindeer-communities have disappeared and others have undergone significant changes. These are connected to the transformation of movement regimes framed by particular forms of human–dog–reindeer co-existence and cooperation, and started the process of gradual replacement of sled dogs and transport reindeer by vehicles such as snowmobiles and all-terrain-vehicles (ATVs).

A well-known 'snowmobile revolution' (Pelto 1973) took place in the North and changed the structure of people's movements. Snowmobiles were actively employed in reindeer herding and in many places replaced reindeer transport, being used in many cases instead of dogs for collecting the herds (Ibid.; see also Loovers, this volume). Similar processes took place in Siberia. As a result, fewer animals are trained for use in transport from year to year. Thus, in 2014–2016 the number of trained reindeer and transport dogs significantly decreased in the Taimyr Peninsula. Some brigades were completely lacking riding reindeer. In some places people started to use ATVs instead. This process rapidly changes the structure of local people's movements. In order to move, people have to transport fuel in barrels and search for new sources of income to purchase or exchange for them (Fieldnotes Davydov, Taimyr Peninsula).

In some northern regions fuel is extremely expensive. For instance, in Taimyr dogs are still used for completion of small-scale transport tasks. Dogs are used for bringing water and small-scale trips in fishery. This helps people to economize on fuel that is used for longer-distance transport activities. For this reason, some families now specially train sled dogs.

Both reindeer and dogs became an important part of reindeer herders' day celebrations in spring. This celebration was established during the Soviet era and became very popular among reindeer herders (Dudeck 2013). People usually receive valuable prizes at the competitions during these occasions, which are sponsored by the state. In many cases the celebration is supplemented by racing on reindeer sledges and sled dog races which are often motivated by the opportunity to win a valuable prize. For instance, in 2014 in Taimyr the first prize was a 'Buran'-brand snowmobile produced in Russia; a second prize was a motor for a boat (Davydov, Taimyr Peninsula). Even though some people especially train animals to take part in these competitions, every year the number of trained sled dogs and reindeer decreases.

In any case, we see that in some places people do not refuse to use reindeer and dogs for transportation. People continue to explore the landscapes both through the use of equipment and by continuing to move together with their animals. This shows the ability of local people to sustain their own way of life with the pragmatic incorporation of new elements.

In this chapter we discussed the synergetic effect of mutual human–dog–reindeer agency. Co-existence of humans with these two species helped people effectively extract local resources, facilitate movements, and to reflect them better. This synergetic effect helped Siberian indigenous people to appropriate huge territories in the tundra and taiga. This way of landscape appropriation is based on local knowledge and helped to provide local people with a strong sense of autonomy. In this sense HDR-communities are based on certain ways of cooperation with animals that helps people to rationalize their mobility and enables them to use certain territories, facilitates cargo transportation, and intensifies economic exchange.

Original sources

Fieldnotes Davydov – Taimyr Peninsula, 2014, 2015, 2016; Yakutia, 2013; Zabaikal region, 2013; Sakhalin Island, 2013; Inner Mongolia, China, 2015.

Fieldnotes Klokov – Yamal Peninsula, 2013; Chukotka, 2016.

Muzei Antropologii i Etnografii im. Petra Velikogo (Kuntskamera) Rossiiskoi Akademii Nauk (Museum of Anthropology and Ethnography (Kunstkamera), Russian Academy of Sciences).

Muzei Istorii Buriatii Imeni M. N. Khangalova (Museum of the History of Buryatia), No. 8735-1.

Bibliography

Adaev, V.N. 2013. "Nenetskie Olenegonnye Laiki Tazovskoi Tundry." *AB ORIGINE*, 5: 120–142. Tumen: Vektor Buk.

Adaev, V.N. 2014. "Olenegonnye laiki tundrovykh Nentsev: osobennosti ekster'era i vypolniaemye funktsyi." *Nauchnyi Vestnik Iamalo-Nenetskogo Avtonomnogo Okruga*, 1(82): 25–33.

Anderson, D.G., J.P.L. Loovers, S.A. Schroer, and R.P. Wishart. 2016. "Prostranstvennye Arhitektury v Otnosheniiakh Mezhdu Liud'mi, Zhivotnym Mirom i Landshaftom na Severe." In *Arkheologiia Arktiki: Sbornik*. Edited by D.S. Tupakhin and N.V. Fedorova. Kaliiningrad: ID ROS-DOAFK.

Anderson, D.G., J.P. L. Loovers, S.A. Schroer, and R.P. Wishart. 2017. "Architectures of Domestication: On Emplacing Human–Animal Relations in the North." *Journal of the Royal Anthropological Institute*, 23(2): 398–416.

Antropova, V.V., and M.G. Levin. 1961. "Upriazhnoe sobakovodstvo." In *Istoriko-Etnografisheskii Atlas Narodov Sibiri*. Moscow: Nauka, 55–77.

Baskin, L.M. 2009. *Severnyi olen'. Upravlenie povedeniem i populiatsyiami. Olenevodstvo. Okhota*. Moscow: Tovarishchestvo nauchnykh izdanii KMK.

Bogoraz V.G. 1991. *Material'naia Kul'tura Chukchei*. Moscow: Nauka.

Bogoraz-Tan, V. G. 1934. *Chukchi. Part 1*. Leningrad: Izdatel'stvo instituta narodov Severa Tsyk SSSR.

Bogoslovskaia, L. 2005. "Dog Sledge in Northern Eurasia". In *Encyclopedia of the Arctic*, Vol. 1. Edited by M. Nuttall, 501–502. London: Routledge.

Bogoslovskaia, L.S. (Ed.) 2011. *Nadezhda – Gonka po Kraiu Zemli*. Moscow: Institut Naslediia.

Brandišauskas, D. 2009. Leaving Footprints in the Taiga: Enacted and Emplaced Power and Luck among Orochen-Evenki of the Zabaikal Region in East Siberia. PhD Dissertation. Aberdeen: University of Aberdeen.

Chikachev, A.G. 2004. *Ezdovoe Sobakovodstvo Iakutii*. Iakutsk: IaF GU 'Izdatel'stvo SO RAN'.

Davydov, V.N. 2014. "Coming Back to the Same Places: The Ethnography of Human-Reindeer Relations in the Northern Baikal Region." *Journal of Ethnology and Folkloristics*, 8(2): 7–32.

Davydov, V.N. 2015. "Khod konem: shakhmaty u evenkov-olenevodov Severnogo Baikala i Pribaikal'ia." In *Radlovskii Sbornik: Nauchnye Issledovaniia i Muzeinye proekty MAE RAN v 2014 g.* Edited by I.K. Chistov, 241–246. St. Petersburg: MAE RAN.

Davydov, V.N. 2016. "Veter v evenkiiskikh landshaftakh Severnogo Baikala i Zabaikal'ia." In *Radlovskii Sbornik: Nauchnye Issledovaniia i Muzeinye Proekty MAE RAN v 2015 g.* Edited by I.K. Chistov, 198–202. St. Petersburg: MAE RAN.

Dokolev, V.E. 1957. Evenkiiskii kolkhoz imeni Vtoroi Piatiletki. Unpublished typescript.

Dudeck S. 2013. *Der Tag des Rentierzüchters: Repräsentation indigener Lebensstile zwischen Taigawohnplatz und Erdölstadt in Westsibirien.* Norderstedt: SEC Publications.

Golovnev, A.V., E.V. Perevalova, I.V. Abramov, D.A. Kukanov, A.S. Rogova and S.G. Useniuk. 2015. *Kochevniki Arktiki: Tekstovo-visual'nye Miniatiury.* Ekaterinburg: "Alfa print".

Khariuchi, G. P. 2012. *Priroda v Traditsyonnom Mirovozzrenii Nentsev.* St. Petersburg: Istoricheskaia illustratsyia.

Klokov, K.B. 2013. "Geograficheskie vzaimosviazi mezhdu tipami olenevodstva, porodami domashnego i podvidami dikogo severnogo olenia." In *Integratsyia Archeologicheskikh i Etnograficheskikh Issledovanii, Sbornik Nauchnykh Trudov.* Vol. 1, 295–298. Irkutsk: Idatel'stvo IRGTU.

Kvashnin, Iu. N. 2007. "Olenegonnaia sobaka v khoziaistve sibirskikh tundrovykh nentsev." In *Materialy mezhdunarodnoi konferentsii "Vtorye istoricheskie chteniia Tomskogo gosudarstvennogo pedagogicheskogo universiteta", posviashchennoi 105-letiiu TGPU, 75-letiiu obrazovaniia istoricheskogo fakul'teta TGPU* (20–21 noiabria 2007 goda). Part 2, 236–239. Tomsk: Izd-vo TGU.

Kvashnin, Iu. N. 2009. *Nenetskoe Olenevodstvo v XX – nachale XXI veka.* Salekhard; Tiumen': Reklamno-izdatel'skaia firma 'Koleso'.

Levin, M.G. 1946. "O proiskhozhdenii i tipakh upriazhnogo sobakovodstva." *Sovetskai Etnografiia,* 4: 76–108.

Levin, M.G. and Potapov, L. P. (Eds.) 1961. *Istoriko-etnograficheskii Atlas Sibiri.* Moscow: Izdatel'stvo akademii nauk SSSR.

Martynova, E.P. 2014. "Predstavleniia o bogatstve u nentsev Iamala." *Sibirskii Sbornik – 4. Grani Sotsial'nogo: Antropologicheskie Perspektivy Issledovaniia Sotsial'nykh Otnoshenii i Kul'tury.* Edited by V.N. Davydov and D.V. Arziutov, 161–170. St. Petersburg: Kunstkamera.

Middendorf, A.F. 1869. *Puteshestvie na Sever i Vostok Sibiri. Chast' II. Sever i Vostok Sibiri v Estestvenno-istoricheskom Otnoshenii.* St. Petersburg: Tipografiia Imperatorskoi Akademii Nauk.

Miller, V.F. 1875. "Znachenie sobaki v mifologicheskikh verovaniiakh." *Drevnosti: Trudy Moskovskogo Arkheologicheskogo Obshchestva,* 6: 193–210.

Novikov, A.V. 2001. "Sobaki v mirovozzrenii i ritual'noi praktike drevnego naseleniia lesostepnoi i iuzhnotaezhnoi zon Zapadnoi Sibiri." *Arkheologiia, Etnografiia i Antropologiia Evrazii,* 5(1): 72–83.

Pelto, P.J. 1973. *The Snowmobile Revolution: Technology and Social Change in the Arctic.* Menlo Park, Calif.: Cummings Publishing Co.

Safonova, T. and I. Sántha. 2012. "Stories about Evenki People and their Dogs: Communication through Sharing Contexts." In *Animism in Rainforest and Tundra: Personhood, Animals, Plants and Things in Contemporary Amazonia and Siberia.* Edited by M. Brightman, V.E. Grotti and O. Ulturgasheva, 82–95. New York; Oxford: Berghahn Books.

Safonova, T. and I. Sántha. 2013. *Culture Contact in Evenki Land: a Cybernetic Anthropology of the Baikal Region.* Leiden; Boston: Global Oriental.

Samar, A.P. 2010. *Traditional Dog Breeding of the Nanai.* Vladivostok: Dal'nauka.
Sarychev, G.A. 1802. *Puteshestvie Flota Kapitana Sarycheva po Severovostochnoi Chasti Sibiri, Ledovitomu Moriu i Vostochnomu Okeanu, v Prodolzhenie Os'mi let, pri Geograficheskoi I Astronomicheskoi Morskoi Ekspeditsyy, Byvshei pod Nachal'stvom Flota Kapitana Billingsa, s 1875 po 1793 g.* Part 1. St. Petersburg: Tipografiia Shnora.
Shereshevskii, E.I., P.A. Petriaev and V.G. Golubev. 1946. *Ezdovoe Sobakovodstvo.* Moscow; St. Petersburg: Izdatel'stvo Glavsevmorputi.
Sirina, A.A. 2016. *Zametki ob olenegonnykh sobakakh u evenov* (draft paper in print).
Sirina, A.A. and G. Fondahl. 2006. *Evenki Severnogo Pribaikal'ia i Proekt Stroitel'stva Nefteprovoda 'Vostochnaia Sibir' – Tikhii Okean'.* Issledovaniia po prikladnoi i neotlozhnoi etnologii, 186. Moscow: Institut Etnologii i Antropologii.
Spasskii, G. 1822. "Zabaikal'skie Tungusy." *Sibirskii Vestnik*, 17:1–66.
Stépanoff, C. 2012. "Human–Animal 'Joint Commitment' in a Reindeer Herding System." *HAU: Journal of Ethnographic Theory*, 2(2): 287–312.
TsSU (Tsentral'noe Statisticheskoe Upravlenie). 1929. *Pokhoziaistvennaia Perepis' Pripoliarnogo Severa SSSR 1926/27 goda. Territorial'nye i Gruppovye Itogi Pokhoziaistvennoi Perepisi.* Moscow: Statizdat TsSU SSSR.
Tugolukov, V.A. 1969. *Sledopyty Verhom na Oleniakh.* Moscow: Nauka.
Tugolukov, V.A. 1979. *Kto vy, Iukagiry?* Moscow: Nauka.
Vasil'ev, Iu. A. 1936. "Transportnoe sobakovodstvo Severa." *Sovetskaia Arktika*, 4: 78–88.
Vasilevich, G.M. 1969. *Evenki. Istoriko-etnograficheskie Ocherki (XVIII – nachalo XX v.).* Leningrad: Nauka.
Vasilevich, G.M. and G.M. Levin. 1951. "Tipy olenevodstva i ikh proiskhozhdenie." *Sovetskaia Etnografiia*, 1: 63–87.
Vaté, V. 2005. "Maintaining Cohesion through Rituals: Chukchi Herders and Hunters; A People of the Siberian Arctic." In *Pastoralists and their Neighbors in Asia and Africa.* Edited by K. Ikeya. Senri Ethnological Studies, 69: 45–68.

5 Northern relations

People, sled dogs and salmon in Kamchatka (Russian Far East)

Lisa Strecker

Introduction

In the past, the Kamchatka region in the Russian Far East was famous for its sled dogs, the breed of the Kamchatka sled dog, the type of sled used and for the fact that people travelled on sleds hauled by dogs. From the outside, sled dog keeping in Kamchatka was regarded as a curiosity and local characteristic feature; similar to reports about the use of fly agaric, sled dogs were an almost obligatory component of every travel account of Kamchatka and were relatively abundant. In this chapter, I reconstruct the history of sled dog husbandry in Kamchatka based on data retrieved from ethnographic and historical sources as well as from personal observations and anthropological fieldwork.

Beginning with the earliest written accounts available from the early eighteenth century, I will demonstrate how the people[1]–sled dog relationship has always played a central role in the local people's household economies, social and spiritual lives, and later in the regional economy, in the private or government sectors. Before the sparse road network that exists on the peninsula today was developed in the second half of the last century, travelling over land during summer months was arduous and time consuming. In the long and snowy Kamchatkan winters, however, one could travel much faster and more easily on a sled pulled by a team of dogs or reindeer.

In recent years, sled dog keeping and driving has been experiencing some sort of revival in Kamchatka. The current interest in sled dogs is mainly related to the Kamchatkan long-distance sled dog race, the Beringia. The start day of the race recently became a regional holiday and sled dog rides became a popular tourist activity for locals and visitors alike. The Beringia race labels itself a 'traditional sled dog race'. As will be shown in this chapter, the definition of 'traditional' remains largely vague; a situation that creates room for interpretations and conflict at the same time. Since most dog teams in Kamchatka are now kept as a result of or for the sole purpose of participating in this race, I will dedicate the final part of this chapter to the Beringia and how it has shaped contemporary sled dog keeping in Kamchatka.

Insights and information about the current situation of sled dog keeping are preliminary results of my ongoing fieldwork for the thesis project 'Fishing for sled dogs or fishing for snowmobiles in Kamchatka, RF'.[2] At the same time, I have spent significant time in Kamchatka learning about sled dog keeping, training a dog team and finally participating with a team of local sled dogs in the Beringia race. Both approaches to learning about sled dog keeping in Kamchatka have equally contributed to this chapter. Sled dog keeping in Kamchatka is largely based on the local abundance of salmon. Salmon served and still serves as the staple food for dogs (and humans) and thus fuelled this efficient form of transportation; therefore, salmon always needs to be considered when talking about sled dogs in Kamchatka.[3]

Sled dogs in Northern Kamchatka

Sled dogs and other animals employed for mobility

In the past, most dogs in Kamchatka probably were sled dogs (Figure 5.1). Herding dogs were introduced by the Russians only after the Soviet collectivization of reindeer herding in the first half of the twentieth century. Even today, reindeer herders in Kamchatka rarely use herding dogs (Levin and Potapov 1956). The other main type of working dog, the hunting dog, was usually not employed as a sled dog (Sil'nitskiy 2011:15; Sergeev 1936:616). Sled dogs were generally considered completely useless as watchdogs; they hardly ever bark and are either afraid of people or overly friendly to everyone (Jochelson 2005: 62; Shereshevskiy et al. 1946:22–23). In addition to employing dogs for pulling sleds, hunting, and for personal and spiritual reasons, some dogs were also kept for their fur, which was used to trim clothes. In general, dog fur was used to decorate and make warm winter clothes and sleeping bags, which were highly valued. Unlike reindeer fur, dog fur does not shed (Kasten and Dürr 2013:83; Langsdorff 2011:275; Gülden 1992:187; Dürr 2011:526).

Besides dogs, reindeer were involved in winter transportation, primarily for pulling sleds and hauling loads. Reindeer can run fast for short distances, but they fatigue more quickly than dogs (Kocheshkov and Turaev 1993:51). Unlike the fish eaten by dogs, the food of the reindeer, lichen, does not have to be transported and stored. As lichen has fewer calories than dog food, the reindeer need to eat more often and for longer durations, which requires that the travellers make regular stops (about every 10 km) (Langsdorff 2011:278). Problems arise when there is no lichen or if the slowly recovering feeding places have been depleted in the past (Shereshevskiy et al. 1946:9). For these and other reasons, many travellers preferred dogs for travelling (Panyukhina 2001).

In Kamchatka, sled dogs and reindeer were generally regarded as a very bad match. If sled dogs were not restrained from attacking reindeer, they would most likely kill and eat them. Sled dogs were considered a bigger risk for reindeer than wolves (Kennan 2004: chapt. XVII; Svanberg 1986:162;

Figure 5.1 Sergey Lastochkin driving his dogs. Sled dogs in Kamchatka are hitched in pairs with relatively short tug lines (connection between harness and central line) and no necklines. The dogs pull rather from the side but can switch sides whenever they want to. Karaga, Northern Kamchatka, Feb 2011
Photograph by Lisa Strecker.

Gapanovich 1932:29). In order to not attack reindeer, sleds dogs had to be trained or grow up with them. This is also the reason why drivers of reindeer sleds would never travel to a village, which would typically contain many dogs that had not been socialized with reindeer (Bergman 1926:137, 154). Reindeer herders would use dogs for trips to the settlements and to get wood or provisions, or while checking traps. For moving the reindeer herders' camp from one location to the next and for visiting other herders, reindeer were used (Vdovin 1973).

The preferred time for travelling on dog sleds was spring when the interplay of thawing during the day and freezing at night builds up a snow crust. Unlike horses that would break through this surface, dogs can easily run on the crust, and ideally the ice crust carries the sled well.[4]

The Kamchatkan sled dog breed: **Kamchatskaya ezdovaya**

In the past, Kamchatkan sled dogs were considered to be the largest of all Siberian sled dogs (Jochelson 2005:64) but could not always be clearly distinguished from the sled dog breeds of neighbouring regions. The cynologist Boris Shereshevskiy described the Kamchatka sled dog together with those from the lower reaches of the Yenisei, Yakutia (Kolyma), Chukotka, Anadyr, Sakhalin and the Amur as the 'North Eastern sled dog of the Soviet Union' (Shereshevskiy et al. 1946:21). The *Kamchatskaya ezdovaya* (Kamchatkan sled dog) became a registered breed only in 1991. When talking to elders about the dogs that they used to have in the past, they would usually describe to me the following type of dog that was adapted to travel in deep snow. Sled dogs had to be tall (long legged) and strongly built; at the same time, they should not be too heavy, so they would not sink through the snow crust in spring. The dogs had thick coats so they could cope with the winter temperatures but their fur should not be too fluffy so that snow clumps would get stuck in it or that they would overheat during warm days in spring. People would always mention the great strength and endurance of the dogs in the past that, in relatively small teams, hauled large loads over long distances.

One of the aims of the Kamchatkan Beringia sled dog race was to revitalize this formerly famous sled dog breed. However, 12 of the 76 dogs that appeared for the first start of the race showed signs of poodle, shepherd and other Western breed ancestry (Panyukhina 2001). This diverse ancestry was seen as a likely impediment to the required properties of sled dogs such as the ability to withstand Arctic climatic conditions and a heavy workload, good performance under low temperatures and high winds, steady pulling whilst being fed only once per day, the ability to digest frozen food, and a fast recovery after fasting periods. A disadvantageous property of the *Kamchatskaya ezdovaya* and other old sled dog breeds is the tendency to fight with one another, especially in times when the dogs do not work or have to wait (Shereshevskiy et al. 1946:25).

The decay of the breed has been explained by several authors. The introduction of agriculture in Kamchatka along with livestock animals required that dogs be tied up during summer instead of being set free to feed themselves (Kittlitz 2011:311; Jochelson 2005:58; Starkova 1976:73; Slyunin 1900:629). Sled dogs were often described as the main inhibiting factor for the development of livestock husbandry (Barrett-Hamilton and Jones 1898:290; Cook 1785:344). The fact that the tied-up sled dogs could not feed themselves but rather depended on the poor feed that they were given during summer is considered one of the reasons for the degeneration of the breed (Jochelson 2005:64; Starkova 1976:73). Prior to the introduction of agriculture in Kamchatka, dogs were set free during summer and able to roam around freely eating whatever they would find. Some owners kept supplementing the diet of their off-chain dogs. After spawning, the salmon die and their carcasses accumulate on the river banks; this way, there is always plenty of food for the dogs. Usually, the dogs would gain weight from eating during this period and recovered well from their hard winter labour.[5] Being tied up also prevented the dogs from digging holes in the earth to protect themselves from mosquitoes, which led to a general deterioration of the health of the dogs (Kittlitz

2011:283, 286). Others have explained that the deterioration of the breed is linked to the practice of castrating the good sled dogs to make them more useful working dogs, which subsequently left reproduction to less ideal individuals (Sil'nitskiy 2011:16; Jochelson 2005:64). The introduction of pet dogs and other working dogs (e.g. herding dogs) to Kamchatka further contributed to the degeneration of the sled dog breed (Panyukhina 2001).

Another factor that reduced the number of aboriginal dogs were diseases introduced by Russian colonization starting at the end of the seventeenth century (Slyunin 1900:629). In 1889 alone, a disease outbreak killed well over half of the sled dogs in the Petropavlovskiy Okrug, reducing their numbers from 11,000 to 6,500 (Sil'nitskiy 2011:16). After the Beringia sled dog race in 2012, I personally witnessed a similarly severe outbreak of an unknown (and, according to the state veterinarians, unstudied) epidemic that killed and crippled many sled dogs throughout Kamchatka. From conversations with mostly indigenous dog owners, I learned that this was not an exceptional event, but that severe dog diseases tend to occur regularly (Jochelson 2005:59; Sergeev 1936:617).

To date, no known cynological work has been conducted on Kamchatkan sled dogs. When targeted sled dog breeding happens, dog mushers select from the dogs that are locally available and for the properties required for sled dogs today. With the general shift in using sled dogs for competitive sport mushing instead of hauling freight, the physiognomy of the dogs has changed. The image of a typical sled dog commonly displayed in popular entertainment media, a blue-eyed Siberian husky, has certainly influenced how sled dogs look in Kamchatka today. All the factors mentioned make it difficult to tell what remained of the *Kamchatskaya ezdovaya* breed (Molchanov 2015).

Dog food

One of the key factors tying humans and their sled dogs together is the fact that salmon was the main staple food for both. Even today, some natives still state that 'fish is our bread'. Fish being the main food source had the advantage that the process of food procurement for humans and dogs – fishing – is the same (Jochelson 2005:53).

Salmon for the dogs is preserved by fermenting the entire fish or drying it sliced into halves that are connected at the tail (dry fish known as *yukola*). When processing the freshly caught salmon for human consumption, the sides (fillets) are separated from the bones and the head in such a way that the two sides were still connected by the fish's tail (Nagayama 2011:44). The bones and the head were dried to be fed to the dogs during winter trips (Sil'nitskiy 2011:12). When not travelling, dog owners cooked a soup for the dogs called *opana* in a large kettle. The ingredients of an *opana* can be fresh, fermented or dry whole salmon, salmon bones and heads, other fish and human food scraps, any meat or seal blubber, or even store-bought dog food. *Opana* is still considered the ideal food for sled dogs, even those involved in racing. Many summer and winter settlements usually had and still have a special straw hut or other form of shelter for cooking the dog soup. Today, fish for the dogs is also preserved by freezing in large walk-in freezing units (Kasten and Dürr 2013:8; Jochelson 2005:53).

Other fish species were also harvested for the dogs, such as capelin, flounders, sticklebacks, saffron cod and stint (Kasten and Dürr 2013:99). During Soviet times, dogs were partly fed with *kombikorm*, an industrially produced animal feed (Plattet 2005:126). Besides fish, dogs have to be fed fat, and ideally also meat. During cold periods in the winter and when they work hard, seal meat and blubber is added to the dogs' diets. In rare cases, the dog feed stock ran out in spring. During these times, dogs could starve (Jochelson 2005:53; Cochrane 1825; Lesseps 1790).

Today, store-bought dog food is accessible only to a small group of urban sled dog keepers. The work-intensive and sometimes expensive procurement of fish for dog feed, as well as the legal access restrictions and challenges of catching salmon, are central topics in conversations with dog owners.

Social and spiritual roles of dogs

Anthropologist Alex King's observation that 'dogs are also part of the domestic socio-spiritual world of the Koryaks (but in a way much different than deer)' applies to other groups as well. This special role of dogs extends to their importance as sacrifice animals. Sacrifices of dogs were described in the earliest accounts, and in a few places are still practised today (Kasten and Dürr 2013:100; Dürr 2011:526; King 2011:246; Plattet 2005:267; Irimoto 2004:96; Kennan 2004: chapt. XXII; Jochelson 1908:519).

The way sled dogs are generally treated by their owners differed between those classified by anthropologist Waldemar Jochelson as 'real dog-breeders', as opposed to other groups living in the North, such as the Yakuts, who arrived in this region far more recently and who are known for their cattle and horse husbandry. The author explained that the difference in these attitudes towards sled dogs was partly caused by the belief among the Yukaghirs, Koryaks, Chukchis and Itelmens [longer-term inhabitants of the region] that the door to the country of the shadows was guarded by dogs. These mythological guarding dogs had to be bribed in order to get them to let in the souls of the newly deceased. These same dogs gave 'a very ugly reception to the dead who, while alive, tortured dogs' (Jochelson 2005:54). Today, the treatment of dogs varies strongly between individual dog keepers.

In the past, sled dog keeping was generally regarded as men's business and continues to be seen that way. This does not mean that women were excluded from interacting with sled dogs. In addition, there long have been and still are women who drive dog sleds. I have met several families where the dog owner's wife raises the puppies and makes sure that the young dogs, as well as their mother, get the care and feed that they need, making sled dog care part of family life (Kasten and Dürr 2013:317; Jochelson 2005:57).

Diachronic analysis of the role of sled dogs in Kamchatka

I fully acknowledge that, where possible, it is important to embed facts in a historical context in order to be able to interpret them. Most researchers and travellers producing historical reports of Kamchatka were keen on recording the assumed genuine and 'authentic' culture that they might have missed because of ongoing cultural change caused by contact with the colonizers and their culture. Even one of the first ethnographers, Georg Steller, recorded descriptions about the 'earlier times' in order to capture what he might have missed. Considering the devastating impact of early colonization in Kamchatka, even Steller and Stepan Krasheninnikov who travelled in Kamchatka in the 1740s encountered a situation that was characterized by the disastrous consequences of Russian rule in Kamchatka (Murashko et al. 1994:27).

It also has to be considered that certain developments, e.g. mechanization, are not unilinear. In what is known as the Russian North today, different forms of mechanized mobility (e.g. snowmobiles) historically have been adopted, abandoned and re-adopted. Traditional forms of natural resource use once assigned to the past were revived in the context of economic crisis and general cultural revival during the *perestroika* years (Pika 1999). This situation makes it sometimes difficult to decide whether to write about practices or facts in the past or present tense.

Eighteenth–nineteenth centuries

When the first authors of historical sources arrived in the early eighteenth century, the only domestic animal in Kamchatka, besides reindeer, were dogs (Kasten and Dürr 2013:138; Cook 1785:353). The dog sled as a means of transportation was immediately adopted by all newcomers for its convenience and efficiency. By the beginning of the eighteenth century, Krasheninnikov reports that both natives and Cossacks[6] travelled on dog sleds (Krasheninnikov 1949:395).

In the eighteenth and nineteenth centuries, the numbers of sled dogs were still relatively low (Vdovin 1973:29). In general, people would have three to four dogs per team and, especially if the sled was loaded, would walk beside or along it (Kasten and Dürr 2013:138; Vdovin 1973:29, 126, 191, citing Lindenau; Krasheninnikov 1949:395–401; Lesseps 1790:116).

The low number of dogs available to the Itelmens reflects their relatively limited travel and transportation needs. It is assumed that the number of dogs was always outweighed by the labour input necessary to procure the feed for them. According to Steller, Itelmens were generally not fond of travelling; they travelled in order to obtain food or for fur hunting. Other than that, they left their home only for visiting friends or in the case of warfare (Kasten and Dürr 2013:368). However, Steller mentioned the newly imposed necessity to travel in order to hunt fur-bearing animals, which were used almost exclusively as tribute (*yasak*) payments or as commodities for trade. The extraction of pelts was one of the driving forces behind the colonization of Siberia and later Kamchatka. Among other obligations, the colonized peoples were forced to pay the aforementioned *yasak* in the form of animal pelts. Steller documented the changes in mobility he observed first-hand: due to the Russian occupation and imposed labour service, the Itelmens were often busy doing errands for others, including often transporting heavy loads for several hundred kilometres (Kasten and Dürr 2013:268; Starkova 1976:72).

In the Itelmen culture, the shift in the importance and purpose of mobility is also reflected in the transition from an artfully decorated lightweight sled that certainly served as a status symbol to a relatively simple type freight sled that was used all over Siberia for hauling loads with dogs. Today, the latter type of sled is regarded as the generic dog sled, or the so-called traditional dog sled – a labelling that became relevant in the contemporary sled dog racing scene in Kamchatka. The old-style Itelmen sled disappeared in the middle of the eighteenth century. Its elaborate decorations and sole use as a one-person travel sled positions it in a time and culture, where people must have enjoyed a general economic surplus and plenty of leisure time (Koester 2002). With the catastrophic impact of colonization, not only the leisure time was gone, but also the majority of the potential sled builders and users were dead (Zuev 2007:131; Murashko et al. 1994).

Twentieth century

In Kamchatka and other regions of the Russian Far East, sled dogs have always been a central part of their owner's economy (Sil'nitskiy 2011:15). With the growing role of cash economy and globalization, the importance of dogs correspondingly increased. The economic well-being of the inhabitants of Kamchatka was completely dependent on the successful hunt for fur and sea mammals (Sil'nitskiy 2011:22). Both activities required dogs as a means of transportation. Economic well-being was also linked to the accessibility of goods which in turn required mobility. Thus, there was a direct link between modern economic well-being and the presence and number of sled dogs (Shereshevskiy et al. 1946:12; Sergeev 1936:615; Bilibin 1934:13; Jochelson 1908).

The numbers of sled dogs fluctuated throughout the nineteenth century and varied extensively from place to place. The general trend was an increase in sled dogs, in particular towards the turn of the twentieth century. Dogs were the primary means of transportation for natives and non-natives alike. Merchants, *yasak* collectors, clergymen and local people all travelled on dog sleds (Sil'nitskiy 2011:34; Jochelson 2005:18; Vdovin 1973:127).

The abundance of salmon in Kamchatka has been repeatedly described. A popular form of illustrating this bounty of fish was to mention that the Itelmens could catch their main staple food and the feed for their dogs within a few weeks of intense labour (Shnirelman 1994:172; Jochelson 1908:524).

This implied that the fishermen were actually at home during the time of the salmon run. While travelling through Kamchatka, the researcher Kegel observed how everyone capable of work often had to run nonsensical errands for the colonial administration and therefore missed the salmon run with devastating consequences (Gülden 1992:153). The rising numbers of dogs also directly related to the travel and transportation needs of the colonial administration. For transportation services that were part of the tax obligations, the natives had to keep 10–20 dogs, which in turn required huge amounts of fish. Additionally, they had to feed the dog teams that travelled through. Another reason for keeping a relatively larger team was the involvement in trade (Krusenstern 2011:33, 35; Sergeev 1936:615; Slyunin 1900:490; Cochrane 1825:173, 195).

The combination of high variability in salmon runs from year to year and the exploitative socio-economic situation led to severe famines and misery for the native population (Gülden 1992:130, 153). An unusually low salmon run was a rare and random event with dire consequences for the people who depended on these fish. The lack of salmon could be more easily compensated for by food from other sources (e.g. gathering, hunting, and exchange with reindeer herders (Bilibin 1934)) if they did not have to feed artificially high numbers of dogs, and if they were not overly occupied with fulfilling their tribute and labour obligations.

In the early 1900s, half of the Koryak households in Kamchatka's northern Penzhina area had only two to eight sled dogs. According to Jochelson, they used their dogs for household chores like hauling wood and bringing dried fish from the summer to the winter camps. Those who had more dogs (20 dogs or two teams) were engaged in trade themselves or served the Russians, Cossacks or merchants (Vdovin 1973:158). In 1911 each Itelmen household kept 8 to 15 dogs (Jochelson 2005:65), which roughly corresponds to two teams of dogs or two transportation units.

The ethnographer Innokentiy Vdovin related the increasing numbers of sled dogs to the growing need of sled dog-related mobility, but also to the capability of feeding the dogs through improved means of catching fish (Vdovin 1973:126). The nets made from nettle fibre (Kasten and Dürr 2013:83; Kittlitz 2011:99; Gülden 1992:143) and sometimes reindeer sinew thread (Jochelson 1908:527–528) were replaced by hemp fibre or other imported twine if available. The new material increased the longevity of the nets significantly (Gülden 1992:142; Erman 1848:160, 308). Hemp was one of the first cultivated plants introduced to Kamchatka and became one of its main crops (Sil'nitskiy 2011:167; Gülden 1992; Erman 1848:160, 308).

The rise of the Soviet Union came along with ambitious developmental goals and major changes in the local economy. Summer transportation became increasingly mechanized, and winter transportation remained powered by reindeer and dogs (Levin and Potapov 1956:975).

In 1938, there were 50,000 sled dogs in Kamchatka (Kamchatskaya Oblast'). This number was, however, not seen as sufficient to satisfy the demands of

Figure 5.2 Several sled dog teams resting in a village in Central Kamchatka. One of the teams belongs to the Swedish travellers Sten and Dagny Berman and Rene Malaise. 1920s

Photograph by Sten Bergman expedition team, courtesy of Jens Sucksdorff.

the growing economy (Shereshevskiy et al. 1946:7). Around 1,200 dogs (100 teams) were employed just for postal service in Kamchatka (on Sakhalin – 1,000 dogs) (Shereshevskiy et al. 1946:11). It should be noted that dogs were not kept because of an economic surplus or as a status symbol for the well-off, but rather were a labour-intensive necessity for economic success. During this time, dog-sled transportation was a central pillar of the state economy. A document from 1936 enlists three '[dog sled] trails of regional importance' (*tropy oblastnogo znacheniya'*) with a total trail length of 950 km; many trails had shelter cabins for travellers and some sort of trail maintenance (Gavrilov 2006; Sergeev 1936:613; Slyunin 1900:491).

The rising numbers of dogs and dog feed requirements are also reflected in the travel accounts of Swedish scientist Sten Bergman (Figure 5.2). In the village Kamaki, he observed that every man 15 years of age or older had his own team of ten dogs (Bergman 1926:58). One night, the Bergmans stayed with their ten dogs at a local Kamchadal's[7] house together with a large group of other travellers. The host fed all the guests' dogs, which amounted to 110 fish (salmon) for one feeding episode (Bergman 1926:124). On some sections of their route, the Swedish group travelled in a caravan composed of 17 sleds which transported mostly international merchants. On one day, they met a caravan of 250 dogs. These traders carried imported goods such as tea, sugar, iron ware and cloth that they sold to the local population or more likely, exchanged for fur (Bergman 1926:134, 160). The high numbers of dogs eventually led to a severe socio-economic downside for the Itelmens. In the 1930s, dog keeping had become unprofitable and people often suffered from hunger in spring because all the fish were fed to the dogs. As the demand for dog food rose and the capacity to actually catch and process the fish shrank, times of hunger occurred even in winters that followed a good fishing year. The amount of salmon needed for one winter became hard to estimate and to satisfy (Sergeev (1936) cited by Starkova 1976).

The attitude of local governmental agencies toward sled dog transportation was very contradictory. The decision to develop this mode of transport contrasted with the limitation of fishing quotas for dog food. Nevertheless, the sled dog husbandry developed successfully during pre-war years, and sled dogs still played a central part in the Soviet economy in Kamchatka (Shereshevskiy et al. 1946). In 1940, official sources show that there were 20,000 dogs in Kamchatka. Dogs were kept also by companies, various organizations and institutions (Kocheshkov and Turaev 1993:53). In May 1941, the *okrispolkom* (district executive committee) adopted a plan to develop sled dog husbandry in Northern Kamchatka. The goal was to improve the sled dog breed and to raise their numbers by 30% by January 1, 1942. At the same time, a stable feed source based on fish with low mercantile value was to be established. This plan was never realized because of WWII. Even though sled dogs were employed by the Soviet army, their numbers sharply decreased during the war and kept decreasing in subsequent years in Kamchatka.

In 1950, 11,646 sled dogs were still being kept mainly for private use (Kocheshkov and Turaev 1993:54). This relatively large number of dogs reflects the fact that sled dogs were still the most important means of winter transportation (Krushanov 1990:72). In the second half of the 1950s, the collective farms (*kolkhozes*) grew bigger and became more mechanized. It was at this time that the importance of sled dog transportation diminished sharply. Another factor enforcing this trend was the closure of so-called 'unpromising settlements' by the Soviet administration (Gritsay 2003:78; Forsyth 1994:362; Grant 1995). As many small settlements and seasonal camps were abandoned, the distances between places inhabited by people became very large (King 2011:67; Kocheshkov and Turaev 1993:54) and travel between them almost always required mechanized transportation. People were forced to move to larger settlements where sled dog keeping was very difficult or impossible (Panyukhina 2001).

According to the literature, in the 1960s sled dogs were kept only by Koryak and Itelmen hunters who had teams of about 10 dogs (Kocheshkov and Turaev 1993:54; Starkova 1976:73). This is the time when 'dogs are usually kept in places far away from the settlements for sanitary and hygienic reasons'

(Starkova 1976:74). This coincides with a massive influx of workers from the Russian mainland to Kamchatka, which quickly made the Kamchatka natives a minority (Gritsay 2003:81). Keeping dogs further away from homes means having them out of sight and commuting to them. Both aspects are rather unfavourable for dog keepers and it can be assumed that they had been forced to do so through social or administrative pressure (Panyukhina 2001).

There are very few published sources documenting anti-sled dog policies by the government and the replacement of sled dogs by snowmobiles in Northern Kamchatka. Elena Panyukhina who, together with her husband Sergey, was essentially involved in a project to salvage the once famous breed of the Kamchatkan sled dog, drew a dramatic picture of the events starting in the late 1960s when, according to Panyukhina, 'warfare was declared on the sled dogs'. Sled dogs were seen as a remnant of the past that had to be overcome; the dogs ate too much salmon and were declared a risk to people through diseases and biting. They were also seen as a nuisance in villages for making noise and spreading filth. Sled dogs were systematically shot and within a few years, disappeared from the villages in the North. There are contradictory voices about the extent of the dog shootings, and it is well possible that such practices were more prevalent in some regions of Kamchatka than others (Panyukhina 2001).

1980s – 2000: *Perestroika*, neotraditionalism and native peoples' sled dogs

The radical political, economic and social changes that took place during the 80s and 90s were euphemistically summarized as *perestroika* (ru., rebuilding). The Soviet Union disintegrated and the economy crashed, which led to the necessity and short-term opportunity to actually rebuild and reorganize social, political and economic lives. In this context, a general cultural and national revitalization movement gained steam across the former Soviet Union (Pika 1999; Grant 1995:151; Slezkine 1994:371).

During the last two decades of the century, Soviet and Russian publications describing the transportation system in the Russian Far East no longer mention sled dogs (Radnaev 1996; Yazev 1987). Sled dog transportation had lost its economic importance and was generally regarded as belonging to the past. During this time, dog and reindeer sleds transformed into becoming important symbols of ethnic identity (Hancock 2001:117). Some researchers interpret the increase of dog teams among the Koryak in the 80s and the popularity of sled dogs races as a reflection of a raised ethnic awareness (Kocheshkov and Turaev 1993:55).

Regarding the harsh economic conditions during and after *perestroika*, it is indispensable to interpret this neotraditionalism (Pika 1999) mainly as an economic necessity for many, as sled dogs became again the only accessible means of winter transportation. This is still the case for some people living in remote settlements in Northern Kamchatka today (Patrick Plattet Jan 2014, personal communication; Kasten 2012:69; Plattet 2005:118). The economic breakdown during the *perestroika* years together with rising energy prices led to an ongoing energy, supply and transportation crisis in the North. People in Northern Kamchatka state that it was the sled dogs that saved them in the worst years of crisis when the means of mechanical transportation, their parts, and fossil fuels were very hard or impossible to come by (see Loovers, this volume for a Canadian perspective). The situation was aggravated by the fact that traditional native ways of mobility had been replaced by the Soviet mechanized system all over the North. The breakdown of this Soviet-style transportation network led to a high degree of isolation in rural areas. This explains how sled dogs became once again the only reliable means of winter transportation; however, not every household still owned sled dogs (Beyseuov and Dogorov 2015; Kasten 2012:69; Campbell 2003:118; Plattet 2005:118; Rethmann 1996:25).

Nevertheless, the observation that dog-sled driving can serve as a marker of ethnic identity is still valid today. Recall that before dog numbers were diminished by killings and the growing use of mechanized transportation, dog sleds were the common means of transportation for everyone, not just native people. The revived practice of keeping sled dogs, though, was considered a predominantly native occupation. In these years, the average team size was six to seven dogs, which was enough for average subsistence economy travel needs (Kocheshkov and Turaev 1993:55). Around the turn of millennium, sled dog competitions were showcased in public events as a typical trait of native identity: '[D]uring contemporary heritage festivals and celebrations of native holidays and traditions, ceremonial *balagans* [fish store houses on stilts] are constructed and dog teams and sleds race in competitions' (Hancock 2003:162). Much more than the sled dogs, salmon helped people to cope with the wide-reaching impact of the crisis after the collapse of the Soviet Union. Salmon not only provided sustenance, but also cash flow through the commodification of its roe as caviar.

Salmon poaching beyond all imagination had its advent during the *perestroika* years and thereafter. As most of the salmon for roe is harvested illegally, everything but the roe is usually thrown away to rot. Only in recent years has the stabilization of the national economy, and a more powerful and less corrupt law enforcement service, contributed to a decline of salmon poaching (Sergeev and Spiridonov 2006:14; Shevlyakov 2013). This salmon stock threatening problem has been extensively described in media and literature (Gerkey 2011:82; Maksimov and Leman 2008:5). Native people were and are engaged in various forms of illegal harvesting, as are non-native individuals. Some native people 'stretch' their quota up to tenfold to get enough food for themselves and their dogs as well as to procure roe for cash. Others run criminal poaching enterprises with devastating harvest practices. During the two decades around the turn of the millennium, a popular approach of organized crime groups was to form pseudo-indigenous communities under the name of a native person in order to receive the privileged resource access that is granted to such native communities (ru.: obshiny (pl.), obshina (s.)) in order to maintain a traditional lifestyle (Sobolevskaya and Divovich 2015).

Restrictive salmon-fishing regulations for individuals, even for native people, led to a situation where subsistence fishing automatically equalled poaching. Native small-scale poachers often express a feeling of entitlement to salmon as it always has been the basis of their existence. As the anthropologist Andrew Gerkey pointed out, the Russian verb '*brosat'* is used to describe the harvesting technique where only the roe is extracted but the rest is discarded. This verb means 'to throw away' but also 'to dump someone in a close relationship'. 'Abandoning fish (ru.: *brosat' rybu*)' is regarded as an 'egregious moral transgression' and people clearly distinguish the different forms of poaching (Gerkey 2011:82–83). The wasteful practice of harvesting roe for commercial purposes has certainly altered the human-salmon relationship (Koester 2012:62).

2000 – present: Urban sled dog keepers, subsistence and race dog teams in Northern Kamchatka

Some ethnic Russians[8] have started to keep smaller recreational sled dog teams in recent years. Non-native Russians, regardless of how many years or generations they reside in Northern Kamchatka, do not currently have subsistence access to salmon. This legal situation was established in 2007 (Vakhrin 2014) and explains why keeping sled dogs became a mere native occupation: in a subsistence environment with limited monetary resources, Russians simply could not feed their dogs. Whereas native sled dog keepers can illegally overexploit their subsistence fishing quota in a way so that they harvest enough fish for their dogs, non-native sled dog keepers have no legal document that would even explain their mere presence close to a fishing net (Gerkey 2011:81). In this context it becomes clear that for the new Russian mushers, keeping sled dogs requires significant monetary resources. This expensive hobby and status symbol of modern lifestyle could not be more different from the sled dog husbandry in a native subsistence setting in Northern Kamchatka.

Only a minority of native people keep dog teams as a tribute to their native identity. They have sled dogs for the mere reason that they themselves as well as their forefathers have always kept dogs. They enjoy living with and taking care of the dogs as well as travelling on a dog sled. Having a dog team in Northern Kamchatka means to engage in subsistence practices such as fishing and hunting and also to be watching out for other opportunistic dog food sources, such as donations from a fish plant, winter fishing or picking up leftover food from commercial kitchens (e.g. at hospitals). Besides sourcing the dog food itself, most dog owners cook for their dogs every day, or every second day. The activities, which involve getting firewood, building fires, hauling water, cooking the food, letting it cool off and finally feeding it to the dogs, take a considerable amount of time. Dog owners breed their own dogs, trade puppies and raise them. All of

Figure 5.3 Fish camp outside of Karaga, Northern Kamchatka. These store houses on stilts (*yukolniki*) keep dried fish protected from hungry bears and other animals. Fish is usually hung up to dry under a *yukolnik*. Since there are hardly any sled dogs left in Karaga, the *yukolniki* are empty as well. August 2015

Photograph by Lisa Strecker.

these activities involve daily interactions with the dogs that certainly shape a dog owner family's routine. Children play with the puppies, and a few free ranging dogs, maybe retired sled dogs, pregnant females or just trusted individuals, roam around freely and share the same living spaces as humans, for example in fish camp. Besides the dogs themselves, the dog owners have to build or acquire gear and sleds as well as warm winter travel clothing. Usually, several family members if not entire families are involved in the different aspects of sled dog keeping.

The Beringia sled dog race (1990 to present)

Most of the records about sled dog keeping in Kamchatka for the post-Soviet period are linked to the Beringia or a variety of newly installed sled dog sprint races in Petropavlovsk-Kamchatsky. Only a few people living in rural areas still use sled dogs as their primary means of transportation and for everyday chores (Kasten 2012; Plattet 2005). Currently, the importance of dogs diminishes as the accessibility of snowmobiles increases.

In 1990, the Kamchatkan Traditional Sled Dog race, the Beringia, was founded. The Beringia started out as a project by a group of enthusiastic volunteers that gathered around the charismatic founder of the race, Aleksandr Pechen. Pechen spent a year in Alaska before he returned to Kamchatka and invented the Beringia. It is well possible that was inspired by Alaskan sled dog races; however, the format of the early Beringia has no comparison in the Alaskan sled dog racing world where races are generally more individualistic and competitive. The core idea of the early Beringia was to support native people and their culture in Northern settlements. Thus, besides being a sports event, the early race had a clear cultural as well as a humanitarian mission. The physician of the race would treat mushers as well as people living in the settlements, and the race volunteers handed out books, clothes and toys to the children. The Beringia was designed as an expedition to Northern settlements that were, at that time, very isolated and marked by severe economic hardship and a plethora of concomitant social issues. The race would stop in every settlement on the way where the community welcomed and celebrated the mushers in cultural events that usually included native and modern dance performances. The fact that most of the winners of the early races were natives certainly added to the popularity of the Beringia in Northern communities. Particularly for off-road settlements, the Beringia was, and partly continues to be, one of the most important events of the year. Keeping sled dogs as a trait of native culture was generally considered outdated and incompatible with modern lifestyle. The message of a native person excelling in a competition that receives high regional, national and even international attention was very important during these times of hardship. For the most part, financial support came from mining companies, other businesses and private donors. The government also financially contributed to the race (Brekhlichuk 2016; Pechen' 2015).

Since its inception, the race has been held almost every year. The Beringia has certainly contributed to popularizing sled dogs again and to keeping the sled dog husbandry in Kamchatka alive. Even though the Beringia race does not claim to be a native people's race, its organizers insist on it being a 'traditional' race. As elaborated on further below, there is little agreement and heated ongoing dispute among participants on what 'traditional' exactly means.

After 20 years, the leadership and structure of the Beringia changed. In 2010, Pechen retired and 'his' race that was initiated and conducted as a strictly non-governmental event was taken over by the Government Department of Sports of the Kamchatskiy Kray. The acting governor of Kamchatka, Vladimir I. Ilyukhin, an enthusiast of the Beringia, labelled the race as 'the flagship of Kamchatka' (VechernyeVESTI Petropavloska 2016) and the day of the opening of the race became a public holiday. The race now receives substantial government funding and media attention. The opening ceremony of the Beringia turned into an impressive show event with enormous fireworks, TV stars flown in from Moscow, and exotic banquets.

With the onset in 2014 of very high prize money awards[9] for the Beringia race and the concurrent boom in sled dog tourism, large-sized kennels appeared in the vicinity of the capital Petropavlovsk (PK). The kennels around PK are predominantly owned by ethnic Russians. Currently the largest kennel, *Snezhnye psy*[10] rose from about 45 dogs in 2011 to almost 200 in 2015. The main income for large kennels is generated through sled dog-related activities year round. Urban sled dog owners have to purchase the bulk of their dog food, such as fish and processed dog food. A popular programme among winter tourists in Kamchatka is a sled dog tour in combination with an ethnic programme and dance performance by Kamchatka natives. Only recently have native sled dog keepers tried to tap into the market of sled dog-related ethnic tourism. When the large ethnic Russian kennels send teams to the start of the Beringia, they have a large number of dogs to choose from, and they also have access and means to acquire lightweight sleds and modern racing gear.

The predominantly native sled dog owners in Northern Kamchatka who participate in the Beringia now own more dogs than would be necessary for mere transportation. Dogs in Northern Kamchatka are generally fed fish, meat (mainly brown bear or seal), seal blubber, and kitchen scraps only. The high purchase and transportation costs of processed, dry dog food makes this dog food alternative a rare addition to the dogs' diets, if they get to eat it at all. Commercial dry dog food is purchased by a few sled dog keepers in Northern Kamchatka in small amounts and if they can afford it – the convenience of feeding out-processed food as opposed to having to cook for the dogs is certainly appreciated by many. Some sled dog keepers of Northern Kamchatka relate the success of capital-based mushers to their access to high quality commercial dog food. This view is, however, not shared by all native sled dog owners. In particular the successful native mushers still claim that there is no better dog food out there than fish, meat and fat.

Being in remote locations, the sled dog owners cannot tap into financing through tourism, which means that they cannot operate with large amounts of money. They still have to go fishing and hunting to be able to feed their dogs. If they use a snowmobile for getting dog food and fuel to cook for the dogs, then these snowmobiles and fuel are usually purchased and maintained with money originating from wage labour or salmon poaching.

The aforementioned conflict among Beringia participants about the vague definition of 'traditional' can be interpreted as a protest against highly unequal economic situations between the rural, mostly native North and the rich, predominantly Russian South.

The high purse of the Beringia has not only created a fierce competition among the racers, but has also led to outspoken protest by racers who still use wooden sleds. The generic dog sled used in Kamchatka is a wooden sled with usually three pairs of stanchions. Traditionally, the sled dog driver sits sideward on the sled and sets his or her feet on the runners. With one hand, the dog sled driver holds on to a bow that goes over the bed of the sled, with the other, he or she holds the *ostol*, a wooden steering and breaking pole with a sharp metal tip. The *ostol* is the only tool for speed control and anchoring sled and dog team on the snow; its use certainly requires some training and also strength. Every dog team owner builds his own sled from material locally available. The runners for the sleds are covered with plastic pipes that are cut in half and nailed to the broad wooden runners. Because of the weight of the wooden sled combined with the rarely ideal gliding properties of the pipe runners, the user of this type of sled is usually outcompeted by sled dog drivers using modern race sleds. The runner plastic of the lightweight racing sleds can easily be exchanged in response to the changing temperatures, trail and snow conditions. Modern, imported sleds come with a price tag of several thousand US Dollars or Euros, and parts and runner plastic have to be imported as well.

In 2016, the mushers from the northern Karaginsky Okrug announced they would boycott the race if they, on their wooden sleds, were to compete with mushers using professional race sleds. In order to pacify this group, an alternative purse for 'Fidelity to the Traditions of the North' was installed. The winners of this prize money, however, declared that they would use their money to purchase a modern sled (Kinas 2016; Kamchatka-Inform 2014a). Within the last two years, three competitive native sled dog owners and their dog teams have moved to Central and Southern Kamchatka where all three of them immediately set up tourist enterprises in a similar pattern to the other sled dog-oriented tourist businesses of the capital area. This recent development has certainly shifted the division line between North and South; however, it remains a fact that the economic situation of sled dog owners living in Northern Kamchatka is still very different from their colleagues in or near PK.

With the Beringia becoming more competitive, the type of dog used for racing has changed as well. There is currently no cynological work on sled dogs conducted in Kamchatka and thus, we lack a more exact description of the modern dog type (Molchanov 2015). There are at least two government-funded kennels that were created as part of this revitalization initiative to successfully breed and sustain sled dogs. Unfortunately for the Kamchatkan sled dog breed, the initiators do not apply any professional cynological expertise. In a press release, the programme proudly reported about a freshly imported breeding pair – two Siberian Huskies (Kamchatka-Inform 2014b). The so-called revitalization of Kamchatkan sled dog husbandry promoted by the Kamchatkan government is also partly a re-invention of local sled dog traditions. One of the core missions of the early Beringia race was to save the Kamchatkan sled dog breed from disappearing (Panyukhina 2001). Despite all well-intended effort, it is now even harder to find a dog with characteristic traits of the Kamchatkan sled dog breed than it was in the early days of the Beringia in the 1990s. The majority of the Beringia participants is, understandably, more interested in the race performance of their dogs than in their genetic make-up. Competitive sled dog keepers seek to import dogs for breeding from Alaska as well as from race kennels in western Russia (Molchanov 2015).

Another contradiction of the revitalization program is the fact that these government-initiated and supported kennels do not necessarily possess the required fishing and hunting allocations to legally sustain their dogs. Currently, about 200 kg of salmon are allocated to every native person in Northern Kamchatka per year.[11] Despite repeated calls of native Beringia participants for fishing allocations that allow them to feed their dogs without poaching, the legal situation has not changed.

Conclusion

Throughout the past 280 years, sled dogs have played important roles in Kamchatka. Their presence or absence was and is a relatively reliable indicator of the economic strategy and well-being of the dogs' owners and the broader political and economic arena. Before the onset of motorized winter travel, sled dogs were an integral part of the lifestyle, culture and economy of sedentary native people in Kamchatka. This lifestyle was based on salmon fishing. The dog-powered form of winter mobility was made possible by the abundance of salmon and other marine resources as food for the dogs. Upon their arrival in Kamchatka about 300 years ago, the Russian colonizers immediately appropriated the native way of winter travelling, at which point dog sled transportation became, in addition to the less prevalent reindeer sledding, the general form of winter mobility for everyone in the region.

The colonizers claimed *yasak* from the native population, as well as other forms of tribute. Many were directly or indirectly related to sled dogs and salmon fishing, including transportation services, maintenance of the trail system as well as providing dog food for teams travelling through. The colonial practices, in combination with local manifestations of the global market economy in the form of travelling traders, brought sled dogs into great demand, significantly increasing their numbers.

Sled dogs were also heavily employed to support the eager developmental goals of the Soviet administration, and consequently dog numbers kept rising before WWII. With the onset of mechanized winter travel, sled dogs were regarded as obsolete, and their high food requirements detrimental for the economy. Dog keeping was ostracized; in some areas, the official anti-sled dog policy even led to systematic dog shootings.

The years of *perestroika* and thereafter were characterized by severe economic hardship and a general transportation crisis, particularly in remote areas. Then, sled dogs were in use once again, since the mechanized means of transportation could not be fuelled or repaired. At the same time, sled dogs advanced to a marker of ethnic identity of native people. This coincided with the foundation of the annual long-distance stage race, the Beringia. The race contributed tremendously to the popularization of sled dog driving in Kamchatka, in both the native communities and in the predominantly

Russian south of the peninsula. As non-native inhabitants of Northern Kamchatka lost their right to subsistence salmon fishing in 2007, sled dog keeping became all the more a native occupation. Representatives of other groups could simply not afford to feed a dog team.

To date, sled dogs are highly popular in Kamchatka. In comparison to earlier times, though, there are relatively few people who actually own a team. The main forms of dog keeping are urban, sportive sled dog teams mainly owned by ethnic Russians; large-scale professional and touristic dog kennels; and teams owned by native people in rural areas. The current sled dog landscape in Kamchatka has been significantly shaped by the Beringia race. When the organization of the race was taken over by the government, highly lucrative purses offered sled dog keepers a new avenue of making a living with sled dogs. In urban areas, sled dog tourism contributes to turning dogs into an economic strategy again. Rural sled dog keepers feel left out of the financial opportunities from tourism or modern competitive racing. They stress their native traditional approach or try to catch up with their urban competitors.

Sled dog husbandry in Kamchatka, as well as the sled dogs themselves, are currently changing at a very fast rate. The government-sponsored revitalization of sled dog keeping is very show-effective; however, it lacks cynological expertise, as well as measures to make the effort sustainable. The current legal situation does not allow individual sled dog keepers to catch the fish that they need to feed their dogs. As a consequence, rural sled dog keepers are, to a lesser or greater degree, poachers. The ecological impact of this form of poaching is, however, minor compared to the large-scale poaching enterprises of organized criminal structures. Their reckless harvesting methods signify a serious threat to the salmon stock, and hence, to the different forms of salmon-based lifestyles in Kamchatka of which sled dogs have always been an integral part.

Acknowledgements

The material presented in this article is based upon fieldwork supported by the National Science Foundation under Grant No. 1417707. The research project would not have been possible without the friendship and support that I experienced during all my stays in Kamchatka. In particular, I would like to thank Aleksandr Pechen, Aleksandr Molchanov and the Beringia organization team and the participants of the 2010 and 2011 race for patiently sharing their knowledge with me. I owe them as well as many of the Kamchatkan dogs for teaching me about sled dog keeping and driving. The generous in-kind, moral and financial support from various sides allowed me to realize my dream to participate in the race in these two years. When I participated in the Beringia, I had no idea that this would become a future topic of research; still, most of my knowledge about the Kamchatkan way of sled dog keeping comes from my role as a genuinely observing and learning participant. The list of people that generously hosted me and shared their dog and fishing stories with me is very long and I am grateful to every single one of them. Friends who have most contributed to this work are Larisa and Vladimir Yakimenko and Lyubov' Sokolova – thank you!

Notes

1 In my research, I consider all sled dog keepers, past and present, in Kamchatka, non-native and native, such as a variety of local groups generally summarized as Itelmens, Nymylans, Koryaks (reindeer Koryaks and sedentary Koryaks), Evens and Chukchis. Most groups of sedentary native people as well as a few reindeer herders owned sled dogs. If no ethnic affiliation of a native person or group is given in this text, then it is because it was not available.
2 The project investigates how the human–sled dog–salmon relationship in Northern Kamchatka has changed under the different socio-economic and political regimes of the last hundred years.
3 As the subject of keeping and feeding sled dogs in Northern Kamchatka always touches on the legally sensitive aspect of salmon poaching, no names or other identity markers of sled dog keepers are revealed in this publication.
4 After being introduced by the Russians, horses were used during the snow-free seasons (Kittlitz 2011: 295–296).
5 The aforementioned practice of setting sled dogs free as soon as the snow thaws in spring so that they can feed themselves is still practised in remote regions of Northern Kamchatka. Some people keep a few dogs tied up in their summer fishing camps so that the dogs can warn them about visiting bears (Kasten and Dürr 2013: 90; Kittlitz 2011: 311; Jochelson 2005: 58; Erman 1848: 136).
6 Cossacks are a rather diverse Slavic ethnic group that defines itself by being warriors. In pre-Soviet times, the Cossacks formed a social rank with their own rights and privileges. In exchange they secured the thinly populated borderlands and several of their military units served in the army. As many ethnic groups, the Cossacks experienced a strong revival after the disintegration of the Soviet Union. In Kamchatka, one of the shorter sled dog races in Central Kamchatka is called *kazachiy put'* [The Trail of the Cossacks] (Enciklopediya Brokgauza i Efrona).
7 Before 1927, 'Kamchadal' was used to denominate a native person of Kamchatka (Murashko 1997: 181).
8 There are two translations for 'Russian': *Rossiyanin* – citizen of the Russian Federation and *russkiy* – ethnic Russian.
9 In 2014, the purse increased tenfold; now, the winner receives 3 Mio Roubles. In Oct. 2017, this amount equals 52,000 US Dollars, in 2014 it would have been worth 85,000 US Dollars. As a comparison: the winner of the prestigious Alaskan Iditarod sled dog race received 71,250 US Dollars in 2017 (Hanlon 2017; Kamchatka-Inform 2014a; www.oanda.com/currency/converter/, accessed October 11, 2017).
10 Based on the owner's, Andrey Semashkin's, native affiliation, this kennel is legally owned by a native community (*obshchina*). Until a few years ago, not many people were aware that Andrey was Aleut. He and his family are commonly perceived as Russians (SnowDogs Kamchatka n.d.).
11 Fishing allocations for *obshchiny* might be bigger. Not every native dog owner is a member of an *obshchina*. Fishing allocations for native individuals in Southern Kamchatka are significantly smaller.

References

Barrett-Hamilton, G.E.H. and H.O. Jones. 1898. "A Visit to Karaginski Island, Kamchatka". *The Geographical Journal*, 12(3):280–299.
Bergman, S. 1926. *Vulkane, Bären und Nomaden. Reisen und Erlebnisse im wilden Kamtschatka*. Stuttgart: Strecker & Schröder.
Beringiya. 2014. "Beringiya-2014" finishirovala: Andrey Semashkin – chempion! ['Beringia 2014' Finished, Andrey Semashkin is Champion!]. Electronic document, http://beringia41.ru/?p=1365, accessed September 1, 2016.
Beyseuov, S. and S. Dogorov. 2015. Russkie gonki [Russian Races]. 90 min.
Bilibin, N. 1934 *Obmen u Koryakov [Exchange of the Koryaks]*. Leningrad: Izdatel'stvo Instituta Narodov Severa.
Brekhlichuk, E. 2016. *Aleksandr Pechen'. Komandor svoey sud'by [Aleksandr Pechen'. Commander of his Destiny]*. Kamchatskiy Kray – Edinaya Kamchatka, August 31, 2016. http://kam-kray.ru/news/10801-aleksandrpechen-komandor-svoei-sudby.html, accessed October 24, 2016.
Campbell, C. 2003. "Contrails of Globalization and the View from the Ground: An Essay on Isolation in East-Central Siberia". *Polar Geography*, 27(2):97–120.
Cochrane, J.-D. 1825. *"Capitän J. Dundas Cochrane's" Fußreise durch Rußland und die sibirische Tatarey, und von der chinesischen Gränze nach dem Eismeer und Kamtschatka. Aus dem Englischen übersetzt*. Wien: Strauß.
Cook, J. 1785. *A Voyage to the Pacific Ocean. Undertaken, by the Command of His Majesty, for Making Discoveries in the Northern Hemisphere. Performed Under the Direction of Captains Cook, Clerke, and Gore, in His Majesty's Ships the Resolution and Discovery; In the Years 1776, 1777, 1778, 1779, and 1780*, 2. London: Printed by H. Hughs for G. Nicol and T. Cadell.
Dürr, M., ed. 2011. *Karl von Ditmar: Reisen und Aufenthalt in Kamtschatka in den Jahren 1851–1855. Erster Teil. Historischer Bericht nach den Tagebüchern (1890)*. Fürstenberg/Havel: Kulturstiftung Sibirien.
Enciklopediya Brokgauza i Efrona. Kazaki [The Cossacks]. In: 2009–2015 Enciklopedii & Slovari. Kollekciya enciklopediy i slovarey. http://enc-dic.com/brokgause/Kazaki-112280.html, accessed October 11, 2017.
Erman, A. 1848. *Die Ochozker Küste, das Ochozker Meer und die Reisen auf Kamtschatka im Jahre 1829. Reise um die Erde durch Nord-Asien und die beiden Oceane in den Jahren 1828, 1829 und 1830*. Berlin: Reimer.
Forsyth, J. 1994. *A History of the Peoples of Siberia. Russia's North Asian Colony, 1581–1990*. Cambridge, New York: Cambridge University Press.
Gapanovich, I.I. 1932. *Kamchatskie Koriaki. Sovremennoe polozhenie plemeni i znanie ego olennogo khoziaistva [The Kamchatkan Koryaks. The Current State of the Tribe and Knowledge About Their Reindeer Husbandry]*. Tientsin: Serebrennikoff & Co.
Gavrilov, S. V. 2006. *Kamchatskoe nasledie: istoricheskie ocherki [Kamchatkan Heritage: Historical Sketches]. Kak na Kamchatke khoteli stroit' zheleznuyu dorogu [How They Wanted to Build a Railway in Kamchatka]*. Kamchatskiy pechatnyy dvor Knizhnoe izdatel'vsto.
Gerkey, D. 2011. "Abandoning Fish: The Vulnerability of Salmon as a Cultural Resource in a Post-Soviet Commons". *Anthropology of Work Review*, 32(2):77–89.
Grant, B. 1995. *In the Soviet House of Culture. A Century of Perestroikas*. Princeton paperbacks. Anthropology. Princeton, NJ: Princeton University Press.

Gritsay, I.V. 2003. "Pereustroystvo obraza zhizni korennykh narodov Kamchatki za gody sovetskoy vlasti: popytka retrospektivnogo sravnitel'nogo analiza" [The Reorganization of the Lifestyle of the Indigenous Peoples of Kamchatka During Soviet Times: An Attempt of an Retrospective Analysis]. *Vestnik KRAUNTS – Humanities*, 2:77–85.

Gülden, W.F., ed. 1992. *Forschungsreise nach Kamtschatka. Reisen und Erlebnisse des Johann Karl Ehrenfried Kegel von 1841 bis 1847.* Köln: Böhlau.

Hancock, N. 2001. Ethnicity and State Measures: Social and Political Construction of Kamchadal Identity, 1700–2000. Doctoral dissertation, Columbia University.

Hancock, N. 2003. "Regimes of Classification and the Paradox of Kamchadal Heritage". *Polar Geography*, 27(2):159–173.

Hanlon, T. 2017. *Iditarod. Cash-strapped Iditarod cuts purse for 2018 race by about $250,000.* Alaska Dispatch News. September 22, 2017. www.adn.com/outdoors-adventure/iditarod/2017/09/22/cash-strapped-iditarod-reduces-minimum-payout-to-mushers-for-2018-race/, accessed October 11, 2017.

Irimoto, T. 2004. *The Eternal Cycle. Ecology, Worldview, and Ritual of Reindeer Herders of Northern Kamchatka.* Senri Ethnological Reports, 48. Osaka, Japan: National Museum of Ethnology.

Jochelson, W. 1908. *The Koryak. Jesup North Pacific.* Leyden: Brill.

Jochelson, W. 2005. *The Kamchadals.* Unpublished. Typescript prepared by I. Summers and D. Koester. Typed in spring 1993. The original typescript is held in the New York Public Library, Waldemar Jochelson Papers, Manuscripts and Archives Division. Electronic document 2005, www.facultysite.sinanewt.on-rev.com/JochelsonTheKamchadals.pdf.

Kamchatka-Inform. 2014a. *Na "Beringiyu" v etom godu potratyat 20 millionov rubley iz kraevogo byudzheta i 6 millionov sponsorskikh sredstv [This Year, the Beringia Will be Funded With 20 Billion From the Regional Budget and 6 Billion From Sponsorships].* January 15, 2014. https://kamchatinfo.com/mob/page/542/?ELEMENT_ID=3723, accessed October 24, 2016.

Kamchatka-Inform. 2014b. *Dva shchenka khaski dostavleny v Palanu dlya razvitiya ezdovogo sporta (Kamchatka) [Two Husky Puppies Were Delivered to Palana for the Development of the Sled Dog Sport (Kamchatka)].* June 3, 2014. http://kamchat.info/novosti/dva_wenka_haski_dostavleny_v_palanu_dlya_razvedeniya_kamchatskoj_ezdovoj_porody_kamchatka/, accessed November 6, 2016.

Kasten, E. 2012. "Koryak Salmon Fisheries: Remembrances of the Past, Perspectives for the Future". In *Keystone Nations. Indigenous Peoples and Salmon Across the North Pacific*. Benedict J. Colombi and James Brooks, eds, 65–88. School for Advanced Research Advanced Seminar Series. Santa Fe: School for Advanced Research Press.

Kasten, E. and M. Dürr 2013. *Georg Wilhelm Steller: Beschreibung von dem Lande Kamtschatka. Mit einem Essay von Erich Kasten.* Fürstenberg/Havel: Kulturstiftung Sibirien.

Kennan, G. 2004 [1910]. *Tent Life in Siberia, a New Account of an Old Undertaking.* New York. www.gutenberg.org: Project Gutenberg. E-Book, accessed August 24, 2016.

Kinas, E. 2016. *Beringiya 2016: Gonka menyaet imidzh [Beringia 2016: The Race Changes Its Image].* Kamchatka-Inform, February 22, 2016. https://kamchatinfo.com/epicentre/detail/13428/, accessed October 11, 2016.

King, A.D. 2011. *Living with Koryak Traditions. Playing with Culture in Siberia*. Lincoln: University of Nebraska Press.

Kittlitz, F.H. 2011. *Denkwürdigkeiten einer Reise nach dem russischen Amerika, nach Mikronesien und durch Kamtschatka. Auszüge aus den Werken von Friedrich Heinrich von Kittlitz*. Herausgegeben von Erich Kasten. Bibliotheca kamtschatica. Fürstenberg/Havel: Kulturstiftung Sibirien.

Kocheshkov, N.V., Turaev, V.A. 1993. "Material'naya kul'tura" [Material Culture]. In: *Krushanov, Andrei Ivanovich. Istoriia i kul'tura koryakov [History and Culture of the Koryaks]*. Leningrad: Nauka, pp. 25–55.

Koester, D. 2002. "When the Fat Raven sings: Mimesis and environmental alterity in Kamchatka's environmentalist age". In: *People and the Land: Pathways to reform in post-Soviet Siberia*. Seattle: University of Washington Press, 45–62.

Koester, D. 2012. "Fish, Fishing and Itelmen Cultural History". In *Keystone Nations. Indigenous Peoples and Salmon Across the North Pacific*. B.J. Colombi and J. Brooks, eds, 47–64. School for Advanced Research Advanced Seminar Series. Santa Fe: School for Advanced Research Press.

Krasheninnikov, S.P. 1949. *Opisanie zemli Kamchatki: s prilozheniem raportov, donesenii i drugikh neopublikovannykh materialov [Description of the Land of Kamchatka: with Reports, Communications and Other Unpublished Materials]*. Moskva: Izd-vo Glavsevmorputi.

Krusenstern, A.J. von. 2011. Über den jetzigen Zustand von Kamtschatka, aus: Reise um die Welt in den Jahren 1803, 1804, 1805 und 1806. Zweiter Teil. St. Petersburg 1811. (8. Kapitel). In *Forschungsreisen auf Kamtschatka; Auszüge aus den Werken*. Marie-Theres Federhofer, ed, 11–36. Fürstenberg: Kulturstiftung Sibirien.

Krushanov, A.I. 1990. *Istoriia i Kul'tura Itel'menov [History and Culture of the Itelmens]*. Leningrad: Nauka.

Langsdorff, G.H. von. 2011. "Georg Heinrich Freiherr von Langsdorff, Bemerkungen auf einer Reise um die Welt in den Jahren 1803–1807, 2 Bde, Frankfurt am Main 1812". [Bd. 2: 217–284]. In *Forschungsreisen auf Kamtschatka; Auszüge aus den Werken*. Marie-Theres Federhofer, ed, 38–94. Fürstenberg: Kulturstiftung Sibirien.

Lesseps, J.J. de. 1790. *Travels in Kamchatka*. London.

Levin, M.G., and L.P. Potapov, eds. 1956. *Narody Sibiri [The Peoples of Siberia]*. Moskva: Izdatel'stvo Akademii Nauk SSSR.

Maksimov, S.V., and V.N. Leman. 2008. *Regional'naya Koncepciya Sokrashcheniya Nezakonnoy Dobychi Lososevykh Ryb v Kamchatskom Krae [Regional Conceptional Framework to Reduce Illegal Salmon Harvest in Kamchatskiy Kray]*. Moskva.

Molchanov, A. 2015. Conversation with a Dog Breeder About Kamchatka Sled Dogs. Personal communication. Elizovo, Kamchatka, RF.

Murashko, Olga. 1997. "Itelmens and Kamchadals: Marriage Patterns and Ethnic History". *Arctic Anthropology*, 34(1):181–193.

Murashko, O., I.I. Krupnik, and E.W. Davis. 1994. "A Demographic History of the Kamchadal/Itelmen of Kamchatka Peninsula: Modeling the Precontact Numbers and Postcontact Depopulation". *Arctic Anthropology*, 31(2):16–30.

Nagayama, Y. 2011. "Tradicionnoe ispol'zovanie rybnykh i rastitel'nykh resursov korennymi narodami Kamchatki" [Traditional Use of Fish and Plant Resources by the Indigenous People of Kamchatka]. In *Sokhranenie Bioraznoobraziya Kamchatki i Prilegajushchikh Morey. Mater. XI Mezhdunar. Nauch. Konf.* A.M. Tokranov, V.F Bugaev, and O.A Chernyagina, eds, 42–51. Petropavlovsk-Kamchatskiy: Kamchatpress.

Panyukhina, E. 2001. Perezhitok proshlogo [A Relic from the Past]. *Severnaya Pacifika*, 2(12). www.npacific.ru/np/magazin/2_01_r/np12018print.htm, accessed August 3, 2016.
Pechen', A.M. 2015. Beringiya. Personal communication. *Petropavlovsk-Kamchatskiy*.
Pika, A., ed. 1999. *Neotraditionalism in the Russian North. Indigenous People and the Legacy of Perestrojka*. Circumpolar Research Series, 6. Alberta: Canadian Circumpolar Institute Press.
Plattet, P. 2005. Le double jeu de la chance: imitation et substitution dans les rituels chamaniques contemporains de deux populations rurales du Nord-Kamtchatka (Fédération de Russie, Extrême-Orient sibérien): les chasseurs maritimes de Lesnaia et les éleveurs de rennes d'Atchaïvaiam. PhD thesis, Université de Neuchâtel, Neuchâtel.
Radnaev, B.L. 1996. *Transport Vostoka Rossii v Novoy Social'no-ekonomicheskoy i Geopoliticheskoy Situacii [Transportation in Eastern Russia Under the New Social-Economic Situation]*. Novosibirsk: Izdatel'stvo SB RAS.
Rethmann, P. 1996. Intimate Relations: Reflections on History, Power, and Gender in Koriak Women's Lives in Northern Kamchatka. Ph.D Thesis, McGill University, Department of Anthropology, Montreal.
Sergeev, M.A. 1936. *Narodnoe Khozyaystvo Kamchatskogo Kraya [National Economy of the Kamchatka Region]*. Moskva: Izd. Akademii Nauk SSSR.
Sergeev, S.N. and V.A. Spiridonov. 2006. *Ugrozy Lososevym Rybam Kamchatki [Threats to the Kamchatka Salmon]*. Moskva.
Shereshevskiy, E.I., P.A. Petryaev and V.G. Golubev. 1946. *Ezdovoe Sobakovodstvo [Sled Dogs Husbandry]*. Moscow-Leningrad: Glavsevmorputi.
Shevlyakov, E.A. 2013. "Struktura i dinamika nelegal'nogo beregovogo promysla tikhookeanskikh lososey v Kamchatskom regione v sovremennyy period" [Structure and Dynamics of the Illegal Coastal Salmon in the Kamchatka Region to Date]. *Rybnoe Khozyaystvo*, 2:58–64.
Shnirelman, V. 1994. "Chercher le Chien: Perspectives on the Economy of the Traditional Fishing-Oriented People of Kamchatka". In *Key Issues in Hunter-Gatherer Research*. Ernest S. Burch and Linda J. Ellanna, eds, 169–188. Explorations in Anthropology. Oxford [u.a.]: Berg.
Sil'nitskiy, A.P. 2011. "Kratkiy ocherk sovremennago sostoyaniya Petropavlovskoy okrugi (Kamchatki)" [Brief Sketch of the Current State of the Petropavlovsk Okrug]. In *Voprosy istoriy Kamchatki* S.V. Gavrilov ed, 6–38. Petropavlovsk-Kamchatsky.
Slezkine, Y. 1994. *Arctic Mirrors. Russia and the Small Peoples of the North*. Ithaca: Cornell University Press.
Slyunin, N.V. 1900. *Okhotsko-Kamchatskiy Kray; Estestvenno-Istoricheskoe Opisanie [The Okhotsk-Kamchatka Region; a Descriptive Natural History]*. Sankt-Peterburg: Izd. Ministerstva finansov.
SnowDogs Kamchatka. n.d. *TSO Deti Severa [Territorial* obshchina *'Kids of the North']*. Electronic document, www.snowdogskamchatka.com/105810571054-1044107710901080-105710771074107710881072.html, accessed October 12, 2016.
Sobolevskaya, A. and Esther D. 2015. *The Wall Street of Fisheries: The Russian Far East, a Catch Reconstruction from 1950 to 2010. Working Paper Series. Working Paper no. 2015 – 45*. The University of British Columbia: Fisheries Center.
Starkova, N.K. 1976. *Itelmeny-Materialnaya Kultura XVIII v.-60-e gody XX v [Itelmen – the Material Culture from the 18th Century to the 1960s]*. Moskva: Nauka.

Svanberg, I. 1986. "Traditional Reindeer Husbandry among the Evens of Kamchatka in the Beginning of the 1920's. From the Ethnographical Field Notes of Sten Bergman". In *Contributions to Circumpolar Studies*. H. Beach, ed, 151–180. Uppsala Research Reports in Cultural Anthropology. Uppsala: University of Uppsala.

Vakhrin, S.I. 2014. *Vylavlivayut Losos' Dlya Lichnogo Potrebleniya vse, Krome Starozhilov. Pochemu tak Proiskhodit? [Everybody But the Long-Term Residents Catches Fish for Subsistense Use. Why?]*. Ekspress Kamchatka. Online, June 14, http://express-kamchatka1.ru/sobytiya/10450-vylavlivayut-losos-dlya-lichnogo-potrebleniya-vse-krome-starozhilov-pochemu-tak-proiskhodit.html, accessed November 3, 2016.

Vdovin, I.S. 1973. *Ocherki Etnicheskoy Istorii Koryakov [Sketches of the Ethnic History of the Koryaks]*. Leningrad: Nauka.

VechernyeVESTI Petropavlovska. 2016. *Na biatlonnom komplekse proshlo otkrytie "Beringii-2016", – v etom godu prazdnik sobral rekordnoe kolichestvo gostey i uchastnikov [The Beringia 2016 Opening Took Place in the Biathlon Stadium. This Year, the Celebration Had Record-High Numbers of Visitors and Participants]*. February 21, 2016. www.vestipk.ru/?id=31579, accessed August 25, 2016.

Yazev, E.N., ed. 1987. *Intensifikaciya Razvitiya Regional'nykh Transportnykh Sistem Severo-vostoka SSSR [Intensification of the Development of Regional Transportation Systems in the Northeast of the USSR]*. Yakutsk: Yakut Branch SB AS SSSR.

Zuev, A.S. 2007. "Kamchatskiy bunt 1731 g. iz istorii russko-itel'menskikh otnosheniy" [The Kamchatkan Uprising of 1731: From the History of the Russian-Itelmen Relations]. In *Voprosy Istorii Kamchatki*. S.V. Gavrilov, ed, 108–191. Petropavlovsk- Kamchatskiy: Novaya Kniga.

6 The archaeology of human–dog relations in Northwest Alaska

Erica Hill

Some 1500 years ago, on a gravel spit extending into the Chukchi Sea, people living at the site of Ipiutak buried several members of their community. They excavated a shallow pit in the gravel and laid out a human adult, likely a woman. She was positioned on her back with her legs extended. An infant was placed at her right shoulder and she was provided with a stone knife and two chisels. Next, a dog was lowered into the grave. The dog's body was positioned along the woman's right leg; its head rested on her thigh, while the hindquarters covered her feet.

Burial 132 at Ipiutak (Larsen and Rainey 1948: 250), described here, provides a glimpse of an unusual practice in Alaska prehistory—the burial of a human and a dog together (Figure 6.1). Such burials demonstrate that the lives of dogs and humans have been entangled for nearly two thousand years along the coast of Alaska, where they cohabited until around AD 1000, when their relationship intensified and became one of codependency. Together humans and dogs developed the technologies and practices of the Thule lifeway, which enabled them to hunt and travel quickly and efficiently as they colonized the North American Arctic.

Thule people and their dogs probably descended from occupants of western Beringia in the Late Pleistocene (Raghavan et al. 2014; Tackney et al. 2016; on the genetics of dogs, see Brown, Darwent, and Sacks 2013; Germonpré et al. 2017). By the Early Holocene, humans and dogs had explored Zhokhov Island in the East Siberian Sea (Pitul'ko and Kasparov 2016). They were also cohabiting along the coast in Kamchatka, at the Ushki 1 site. There the remains of dogs and children were interred in similar ways (Dikov 1996). As Losey et al. (this volume) observe, the interment of a dog in the floor of an Ushki dwelling suggests the animal was "literally domesticated." By 5000 years ago, dogs had established themselves in human societies across Siberia; their treatment in death at Ushki and in Cis-Baikal (e.g., Losey et al. 2011; Losey et al. 2013) demonstrates that their relations with humans had already become complex, diverse, and ritualized.

Across Bering Strait in Alaska, the evidence for dogs in the Late Pleistocene and Early Holocene is scarce. Dog bones appear in midden and burial contexts at sites in Kachemak Bay and the Kodiak Archipelago in southern Alaska (de

Figure 6.1 Illustration of Ipiutak Burial 132 (after Larsen and Rainey 1948: pl. 100.3) showing remains of a dog interred with an adult human and infant
Illustration by Mark Luttrell.

Laguna 1956; Lantis 1980). In Northwest Alaska, evidence of dogs is negligible in the first centuries AD; their presence is known from a small number of disarticulated skeletal elements (e.g., Darwent 2006) prior to AD 500, a pattern similar to that described for Paleoeskimo sites in the Eastern Arctic (Morey and Aaris-Sørensen 2002).

Around AD 500, dogs become more archaeologically visible, appearing in burials at the site of Ipiutak on the Chukchi Sea coast. From the Ipiutak period onwards, zooarchaeological and artifactual evidence for dogs in the region increases. Their remains occur in small numbers at sites along the coasts of Chukotka and Alaska in house and midden contexts. At cemetery sites, like Ipiutak, dog elements occur in human graves, suggesting they had some cosmological significance.

Sometime between AD 700 and 1000, relations between humans and dogs in Northwest Alaska began to intensify. Dogs took on new roles in travel and transportation by providing traction. This development, part of the Thule phenomenon, fundamentally altered the way humans and dogs lived together. Dog traction enabled humans to travel farther and faster, and to colonize the High Arctic. But the labor of dogs required constant provisioning, compelling human hunters to adjust their subsistence practices to meet the demands of both human and canine dependents.

Though dog traction was a critical component of Thule and early historic Eskimo lifeways in Northwest Alaska, it represents only one facet of a complex set of human–animal relations manifest in technology, subsistence, and cosmology. This chapter identifies multiple lines of evidence for human–dog relations at sites in Northwest Alaska, on the islands in the Bering Sea, and along the coast of Chukotka. Artifactual evidence of dog traction and harnessing complements the osteological evidence of dogs in middens and houses. Burial evidence hints that dogs and their body parts had ritual significance as early as the Ipiutak period, AD 500. They cohabited with humans for several hundred years until intensification during the Thule period (AD 1000–1450) fundamentally changed the ways humans and dogs related.

Dogs in Ipiutak and Old Bering Sea contexts

Dated to AD 500–900, roughly contemporaneous with the Old Bering Sea culture, Ipiutak occupations (Figure 6.2) are known from several sites along the northwest coast of Alaska and the Seward Peninsula (Hilton et al. 2014; Mason 1998, 2014, 2016a). Evidence for dogs has been identified at a handful of sites dating to this time period: the Ipiutak component at Cape Krusenstern yielded zooarchaeological evidence for two or three dogs, albeit not in burial contexts (Giddings and Anderson 1986: 154). At Deering, on the Seward Peninsula, the skulls of two adult dogs and a nearly complete skeleton of a pup were found within an Ipiutak structure identified as a *qargi*, or ceremonial house (Saleeby et al. 2009: 197). Dog feces were found in the anteroom (Bowers 2009: 92; Larsen 2001: 22). A small number of dog bones were also identified in the faunal component from another house at the same site (Saleeby et al. 2009: 196). In Old Bering Sea contexts (AD 400–800) at sites on St. Lawrence and the Punuk Islands, dog remains roughly contemporary to Ipiutak have been found (Collins 1937: 249; 1940: 551).

The exception to this pattern of few bones in multiple contexts is the Ipiutak type site at Point Hope, where several dogs occur articulated in burials and as disarticulated elements in house contexts (Larsen and Rainey 1948: 186). To date, Ipiutak has yielded the only conclusive evidence for the burial of dogs by Eskimo of Alaska and Chukotka.[1] The rare occurrence of dog burials in Arctic Alaska and Canada contrasts with the high frequency of these features elsewhere in North America (Morey 2006) and in other northern regions, such as Scandinavia (Gräslund 2004; Larsson 1989; Mannermaa, Ukkonen, and Viranta 2014; Viranta and Mannermaa, this volume) and Siberia, where the burial of canids appears to have been a diverse and widespread practice (e.g., Dikov 1996; Losey et al. 2011; Losey et al. 2013). The rarity of dog burial in Northwest Alaska and the adjacent coast of Chukotka makes the finds at mortuary sites such as Ipiutak, where dogs and dog elements were found in multiple contexts, particularly noteworthy.

Following the typology suggested by Perri (2017), the features involving dogs at Ipiutak include one true dog burial (Burial 109), three "associated" depositions in which one or two dogs accompanied human burials (Burial nos. 131, 132, 137), and one elemental deposition comprised of two dog skulls (Burial 90) (Larsen and Rainey 1948).

Burial 109 contained a complete dog skeleton interred in a "tomb-like log structure with the head toward the west, exactly as in the human burials"

90   Erica Hill

Figure 6.2 Map showing sites discussed in the chapter
Map created by Erica Hill.

(Larsen and Rainey 1948: 121). There was no human skeleton in the tomb, nor were any artifacts found (Larsen and Rainey 1948: 248). Elsewhere in the cemetery, humans were buried in similar tombs, both with and without grave goods. Several archaeologists (e.g., Hill 2013; Losey et al. 2011; Morey 2006; Perri 2017) have interpreted the parallel treatment of humans and non-human animals in death as evidence that the species held similar ontological positions. Without additional evidence from other Ipiutak sites, such an interpretation must remain conjectural. However the treatment of the dog in Burial 109 was clearly distinct from that of conspecifics, indicating the animal held some significance deserving of unusual expenditures of time, energy, and resources.

Three other burials at Ipiutak contained humans and a total of four associated dogs. Burial 131 contained an articulated dog lying along the left hip of the human decedent. An arrow point was found within the dog's skeleton, though it is unclear whether this was the product of an earlier injury, taphonomic processes, or the dispatch of the animal prior to burial. Burial 132, containing an adult, an infant, and a dog in immediate physical proximity, has already been mentioned. Burial 137 contained a single adult human flanked by two dogs—one on each side (Larsen and Rainey 1948: 250).

The third type of dog-related deposition at the Ipiutak cemetery was elemental—the inclusion of individual canid skeletal elements in the burial of a human. Elemental depositions are common worldwide, and most often include dog skulls, mandibles (jawbones), and teeth (Perri 2017). Several examples exist at coastal sites in Alaska and Chukotka: Burial 90 at Ipiutak contained a young woman in a log coffin accompanied by two dog skulls (Larsen and Rainey 1948: 60, 243). In Chukotka at the site of Ekven and dating to generally the same time period as Ipiutak, a 14- to 15-year-old individual was buried with a dog mandible (Arutiunov and Sergeev 2006b: 11). At nearby Uelen cemetery, a dog skull was recovered from a human burial in an Old Bering Sea context (Arutiunov and Sergeev 2006a: 53).

Depositions of dog skeletal elements may be part of a broader pattern linking coastal peoples on both sides of Bering Strait. Based on descriptive information from early twentieth-century excavations, skulls and mandibles of dogs appear to be overrepresented in the archaeological record. For example, at Miyowagh on St. Lawrence Island, Collins (1930) recovered at least 26 right mandibles that he classified as domestic dog. At Kukulik to the east and at a later date, "several dozen" dog skulls were recovered (Geist and Rainey 1936: 62). One possible explanation for this pattern is excavation bias; in the absence of screens, only large and easily identifiable bones were collected and reported. A second possibility is that dogs were consumed and that mandibles and skulls, which contained little marrow and bone grease, were discarded rather than processed. Third, skulls and mandibles may have been preferentially curated following the death of the animal.

Archaeological features involving the skulls of bears (Hallowell 1926; Larsen 1969–1970), seals (Giddings and Anderson 1986: 130–131), walrus (Harritt 2004; Hill 2011), and beluga (Hill 2012, 2013) have been documented along the coast of Alaska. Dog skulls, too, may have been curated for multiple purposes, one of which was deposition in human burials. The evidence for unusual treatment of dogs at Ipiutak and the apparent pattern of elemental deposition in burials and *qargi*, as at Deering, suggest that at least some dogs (or their parts) were highly valued and some dog bones held ritual significance. What dogs signified in the first millennium AD remains unclear—they do not appear prominently in the spectacular ivory art of Old Bering Sea or Ipiutak, which features bears (Larsen 1969–1970) and anthropomorphic masks. Nor is there clear evidence for the consumption of dogs during this time period. Without systematic collection and analysis of additional faunal assemblages, understanding of human–dog relations in Ipiutak and Old Bering Sea societies will remain incomplete. Late in the first millennium AD, however, major shifts in subsistence, transport, and technology radically altered the lives of humans and dogs in Alaska.

Traction, food, and raw materials

The Birnirk culture (AD 700–1000) is known from several sites along the coast of Northwest Alaska, the Seward Peninsula, and Chukotka (Alix et al. 2015; Mason 1998) and overlaps temporally with some Ipiutak occupations along the coast (Gerlach and Mason 1992). Birnirk sites have yielded evidence for innovation in sledge transport and watercraft (e.g., Ford 1959; Stanford 1976: 151–156), perhaps among the earliest indicators that dogs were undergoing a radical transformation from commensal species to cultural keystone.

During the Thule period (AD 1000–1450), humans and dogs developed and refined the skills, technologies, and cultural norms that enabled them to rapidly colonize the North American Arctic. Thule culture was first identified by Mathiassen (1927: 6) in Central Canada on the basis of a distinctive set of hunting and transport technologies ideally adapted for Arctic life. The dog sled was one component of a sophisticated material culture that included watercraft, specialized hunting and fishing implements, and tools specific to life amid ice and snow, such as goggles and snow knives. While many of these tools and technologies were in use during the first millennium AD, Thule people refined their forms and adapted them to local conditions (Jensen 2016).

Thule culture likely originated north of Bering Strait on the Chukchi Sea coasts of Alaska or Chukotka around AD 1000 (Mason 2016b). Expert sea mammal hunters, Thule people migrated rapidly across the North American Arctic between about AD 1200 and 1400 (Friesen and Arnold 2008), finally reaching Greenland where they settled along the coast. Their rapid transcontinental migration was made possible by dog traction. Typical Thule artifacts associated with traction include sled parts and gear, such as harness buckles, swivels, whip handles and ferrules, most of which have precedents in Old Bering Sea, Ipiutak, Punuk (e.g., Collins 1937: 242), and Birnirk (e.g., Stanford 1976: 44) material culture. Burials at the Ipiutak site, for example, yielded dozens of swivels that were interpreted as ceremonial (Larsen and Rainey 1948: 129–130), in the absence of other evidence for traction. Ivory swivels were also used for kayak and *umiak* (large skin boat) lines and attached to floats, harpoons, and seal drags. Like swivels, ivory buckles and ferrule-like objects of antler or ivory had alternative uses or could be modified and repurposed, making their presence in archaeological assemblages difficult to interpret.

Sled parts, too, present interpretive challenges, as a kind of low, ladder-like sled with bone or ivory runners (Murdoch 1892: 354–355) was apparently in use for over a millennium on St. Lawrence and the Punuk Islands (Collins 1937: 338–341; Rainey 1941: 546), well before dog traction became common.

Remains of such sleds have also been identified on the coast of Chukotka at Cape Baranov, Kivak, and Sireniki (Bychkov et al. 2002: 109–111; Okladnikov and Beregovaya [1971] 2008: 82). These sleds were probably pulled by hand and used to transport meat, blubber, and watercraft across sea ice.

In contrast, Thule-era dog traction is generally associated with the "built up" or "railed" sled, which—based on ethnohistoric examples—tended to be longer and higher off the ground than the smaller, unrailed sleds. The railed sled used in northern Alaska and documented in nineteenth-century accounts dates to at least the mid-1500s, based on Giddings' finds of shoes, runners, and pegs at Kotzebue. Many of the artifacts were found in the men's house (House 7), where they may have been under construction or repair (Giddings 1952: 20, 61). Earlier Thule sleds were presumably similar, based on Eastern Arctic finds. However, use of sleds in Alaska appears to have been less uniform than in the Canadian Arctic. For example, Collins (1940: 340) believed the built-up sled on St. Lawrence was a recent introduction, likely in the mid-1700s, while on Nunivak Island, dog traction may never have been particularly important (Lantis 1980: 11).

The disparate use pattern evident in Alaska is likely related to local geography, as well as to personal circumstances. Team size was influenced by factors such as season, hunting and fishing success, ice conditions, family size, load size, distance traveled, and wealth. Teams during the Thule and early historic periods appear to have been comprised of only three to five dogs (Giddings 1952: 59; Ostermann and Holtved 1952: 121). Nelson (1899: 206) observed teams of five to nine dogs in use with heavily loaded railed sleds, while Murdoch (1892: 358) in Northwest Alaska reported that ten dogs would be considered a large team, and few Inupiat had that many. The travel and transportation benefits provided by dogs—hauling sleds in the winter, pulling boats upriver after spring breakup, and serving as pack animals on inland treks (Rainey 1947: 266)—were always offset by the time and energy expended in their care and provisioning.

Working dogs required six to seven pounds (2.7–3.2 kg) of fish or walrus each day (Spencer 1959: 468); they also reportedly ate the crushed bone of caribou (Murdoch 1892: 96), but not whale meat, "this being hateful to the whale" (Spencer 1959: 467). While dogs were fed in the winter when their traction was most needed, they generally ran loose in the summer to fend for themselves. Late nineteenth- and twentieth-century Inupiat participation in trapping, which required greater mobility, made larger teams necessary (Anderson et al. 1998: 22), while firearms made acquiring dog food much easier. Therefore, relations between humans and dogs in Arctic Alaska changed once again with the growth of Euro-American trade in the second half of the nineteenth century.

Use of dog traction accompanied changes in sled technology, as well as new forms of material culture, such as whips. Nelson (1899: 209–210) described both long- and short-handled whips with ivory ferrules and reported their widespread use on both sides of Bering Strait and on St. Lawrence Island.

Handles and ferrules—both more likely to survive than the whip lashes, have been identified from sites dating to the Thule and protohistoric periods, including two ferrules and a wooden whip handle from Kukulik on St. Lawrence Island (Geist and Rainey 1936: 106, 110, 142), a ferrule at Ambler Island on the Kobuk River (Giddings 1952: 62–63), and a handle at Utqiaġvik (Barrow) (Ford 1959: 152).

The use of whips by Thule people has implications for understanding relations between humans and dogs. Morey (2010: 148) has expressed doubt that Thule people established social bonds with their dogs, citing the "frankly harsh discipline" many dogs endured. Dog whips were in regular use on St. Lawrence and several other islands in the Bering Sea at contact (Nelson 1899: 209), and archaeological evidence supports their use during the Thule period. Dog treatment, however, appears to have varied by region and by time period. In the 1880s, an American naturalist in northern Alaska commented that "[t]he dog whip so universally employed by the eastern Eskimo, is not used [here] … " (Murdoch 1892: 359). Instead, adults ran alongside dog teams "reproving," "coaxing and encouraging" each dog by name (Murdoch 1892: 357–358; see also Ray 1892: xcvii).

That the situation differed elsewhere in the Arctic is clear from work by Morey (2010: 127–128) and Losey et al. (2014), who observed lesions in the frontal bones that they attributed to trauma in nearly 30% of the dogs they studied from Arctic Canada and Siberia. Losey's study supports earlier findings by Park (1987) of facial trauma in dogs from the Canadian High Arctic. Similar studies have yet to be conducted in Alaska; however, dog remains from Miyowagh on St. Lawrence Island reportedly displayed healed rib fractures (Collins 1930), suggesting the animals were kicked. Blunt force trauma resulting in fractures and cranial lesions has been documented elsewhere among domestic dogs, suggesting that cohabiting with humans sometimes had dire implications (e.g., Bartelle et al. 2010; Binois et al. 2013), including use of dogs as food items.

Osteological evidence for the possible consumption of dogs has been identified at Thule sites in Greenland and Canada (Morey 2010: 136–142; Morey and Aaris-Sørensen 2002; Park 1987). Dogs were reportedly consumed as famine food on St. Lawrence Island in the late 1800s (Crowell and Oozevaseuk 2006; Mudar and Speaker 2003; Nelson 1899: 269), by inland Alaska Eskimo (Spencer 1959: 374), and by Canadian Inuit in Nunavut (Laugrand and Oosten 2007: 356; 2015: 154). While ethnohistoric evidence for the practice in the 1800s is relatively clear, osteological evidence for the consumption of dogs during the Thule period in Alaska is only now beginning to accrue, after decades of speculation. Based on damage to the skulls recovered at Walakpa, in northern Alaska, Stanford (1976: 86) suggested that dogs were consumed. Butchered dog bones have also been reported from a Thule house at Deering, on Seward Peninsula (Saleeby et al. 2009: 193). More recently, a site in Southwest Alaska has yielded osteological evidence for consumption of dogs (McManus-Fry et al. 2016) in the protohistoric period.

On St. Lawrence Island, biologist Olaus Murie observed parietal lesions in dog skulls from Kukulik, which he attributed to extraction of the brain. His conclusions were influenced by reports that dogs were still being consumed on St. Lawrence in the 1930s and that it had been "common practice in early times" (Murie 1936: 356–357). Collins, describing Bering Sea prehistory more generally, suggested that dogs comprised a major food source since at least the Old Bering Sea period, well before their use for traction (Collins 1937: 249; 1940: 551). By contrast, no evidence of parietal lesions was reported on the dogs from Ipiutak, which Murie also analyzed (Murie 1948).

While dog traction and consumption are perennial issues in North American Arctic archaeology, dogs also served as sources of raw materials. Throughout the 1800s, Inupiat in Northwest Alaska used dog fur for ruffs, hide for mittens, and canine teeth for pendants and amulets (Lantis 1980: 10). Dog tails were apparently worn to decorate clothing, though a late nineteenth-century observer reported that wolverine tails were much more "fashionable" (Murdoch 1892: 729).

The Birnirk and Thule predecessors of the Inupiat likely made similarly intensive use of dog hide and fur, though the archaeological evidence is limited (but see Morey 2010: 128–136). At Birnirk, Ford (1959: 220) excavated pieces of dog skin that he interpreted as the remnants of clothing. More common are modified dog bones and teeth, including pairs of mandibles made into tiny sleds (Morey 2010: 142–144). Pendants made of dog teeth have been used in the region since Old Bering Sea times; they have been recovered as personal ornaments in human burials at sites such as Ekven (Arutiunov and Sergeev 2006b: 64), and occur in Birnirk and Thule contexts in Alaska (e.g., Ford 1959: 67; Stanford 1976: 60). While walrus ivory and bird and caribou bone were the most common raw materials for implements in Northwest Alaska, dog bone was occasionally used instead. At Cape Krusenstern, a dog ulna was used to make an awl or pin (Giddings and Anderson 1986: 183, pl. 105b). Three dog humeri were used to make pot hooks at the site of Kukulik, St. Lawrence Island (Geist and Rainey 1936: 107, 266) in the early historic period.

In sum, the role of dogs changed radically in Alaska with the advent of Thule and the spread of dog traction. Dogs appear to be more numerous at sites after AD 1000, when they became integral to the life of many Alaskan Thule and their Inupiaq Eskimo descendants. Use of dog traction was uneven, however, likely due to local conditions. The zooarchaeological evidence indicates that dogs were sources of meat, fur, and bone implements during the Thule and early historic periods. At some sites they formed part of the regular diet, while elsewhere, they constituted famine food. The uses to which dogs were put and the types of treatment considered acceptable are related to the ontological status assigned to dogs by their human cohabitants. Indicators of their status may be found not just in the burial evidence, as at Ipiutak, but also in ethnohistoric accounts of their association with illness, healing, and death.

The ontological status of dogs

In northern and western Alaska, as in Arctic Canada, dogs appear to have occupied an ambiguous ontological position during the protohistoric and early historic periods. Dogs were certainly not considered persons like "real people," that is, Inupiat or Yupiit. Nor were they persons in the sense that many sea mammals were. Nineteenth- and twentieth-century accounts indicate that dogs were inherited and owned by their human handlers. Under certain circumstances, dogs could be killed with impunity (Spencer 1959: 467). On the other hand, dogs reportedly had personal names, were given amulets, like humans, and possessed *inuat* (Inupiaq, sing. *inua*, "its person"). Further, there is considerable ethnohistoric evidence that dogs served as ritual substitutes for humans in case of illness.

The apparent inconsistencies in human attitudes toward and treatment of dogs in Alaska reflect their ambivalent status, a phenomenon also observed in Arctic Canada (Laugrand and Oosten 2002, 2015). This ambivalence is most marked in the realms of illness and death, and in the use of dogs as scapegoats, a practice well-documented among Canadian Inuit (i.e., Laugrand and Oosten 2002, 2015; Taylor 1993). Anecdotal accounts are scattered throughout the Alaska literature, suggesting that an association among dogs, illness, healing, and death was widespread in the North American Arctic at contact. This association—and dogs' reputation as unclean, indiscriminate consumers—may derive in part from their consumption of offal and human waste, and their role as disposers of both human and canine corpses (e.g., Nelson 1899: 321).

Several contact-era accounts describe a scenario involving some act of "brushing" illness onto a dog and then either abandoning or killing the animal to secure recovery. This procedure, which appears to vary by region, was intended to transfer a human illness to the dog. The dog was then killed—or died from the transfer—and the illness was cured or some sort of misfortune averted. A 1930 account from St. Lawrence Island describes the ritual that followed the killing of a dog:

> [its] intestines were pulled out. The family then walks thru the loop formed by the intestines thereby forestalling sickness. Also if a person is very sick he may be laid across a dog. A few pieces of baby seal hair dyed red is then sewed in the dog's ear and when the person recovers the dog is killed, the red hair or tip of ear is cut off or burned in an open fire and the person walks thru the loop of the dog's intestines, followed by others. If the person dies the dog is also killed … If [the] person recovers from illness, the skin of the sacrificed dog is kept and used for parka trimmings, but not used if [the] person dies.
> Henry B. Collins Collections, National Anthropological Archives box 55, notebook A, pp. 20–21[2]

Some twenty years later, a similar practice was still in effect in Northwest Alaska: illness was "brushed" onto a dog and the dog was then killed (Hughes 1960: 264). Possibly related is the belief that if a person was bitten by a dog, the human's life became dependent upon that of the dog (Spencer 1959: 467). Similarly, if several children died one after another, the surviving child might be given a dog's name to break the cycle (Spencer 1959: 466). Finally, the use of dog parts as amulets conferred specific dog characteristics onto the wearer, especially their ability to eat anything without adverse effect (Rainey 1947: 273).

Among Yup'ik Eskimo on the southwest coast of Alaska, dog behavior was used to predict outbreaks of illness—of specific concern was when dogs appeared to "communicate with each other like people" (Himmelheber 2000: 158). A dog crying like a human child indicated death was imminent. But if the dog was killed, the disaster could be averted (Fienup-Riordan 1994: 240). The apparent ritual substitution of the life of a dog for that of a person is consistent with a nineteenth-century Yup'ik Eskimo belief that dogs represented the spirits of the dead. The recently deceased might visit a village of "dog shades" where the dogs tormented those who had mistreated them in life (Fienup-Riordan 1994: 276). According to one account, the purpose was to enable people to "see how the living dogs feel when beaten by people" (Nelson 1899: 488).

Like humans, dogs in Northwest Alaska had personal names (Murdoch 1892: 357–358; Spencer 1959: 465), wore amulets, and according to some sources, possessed *inuat*, soul-like interior persons (Lantis 1990: 183; Nelson 1899: 435). In some cases, when a family had no children, a dog might be given the name of a deceased relative, taken indoors, and fed better than other dogs (Spencer 1959: 466). Like children, puppies were sometimes carried by girls and women in parka hoods (Murdoch 1892: 357–358; Ray 1892: xcvii; Spencer 1959: 467) and were sometimes allowed within the house, usually a forbidden space to dogs.

While dogs were not persons in Inupiaq and Yup'ik societies in the same way that humans were, they possessed names and *inuat*, like humans. They cohabited with Inupiat and Yupiit in ways that prey animals did not. Unlike prey animals, dogs were not a preferred food source. In the liminal realm of illness, the lives of dogs took on a ritual equivalency to those of humans; dogs could serve as scapegoats and even as replacements for human lives.

Conclusions

Artifactual and osteological evidence from Alaska, Chukotka, and the islands of the Bering Sea, in tandem with ethnohistoric accounts, indicate that dogs played multiple roles in prehistoric Eskimo societies: as cohabitants, providers of traction, food items, and ritual substitutes. In contrast to a worldwide pattern of dog burial, the interments of dogs and the occasional dog element in a human grave appear to be the exception, rather than the rule in Alaska. Other than at Ipiutak, no complete and articulated non-human animal has been identified in a human burial context in northern Alaska. In general, dog remains appear to have received no special treatment in death. This lack of elaboration may be due in part to the perception—known from nineteenth-century ethnohistoric accounts—that dogs were unclean and therefore offensive to sea mammals (Nelson 1899: 438), key subsistence resources. At Barrow, for example, no dogs were permitted on the ice during the whaling season, lest they offend the whale (Spencer 1959: 336). Such behaviors may reflect earlier, Thule attitudes as well. However, for at least a short time in Alaska prehistory, around AD 500, some dogs at Ipiutak held an ontological status analogous to that of humans.

The Ipiutak example highlights the fact that the temporal and spatial specifics of human–animal relations matter (Jennbert 2014; Watson and Warkentin 2013). In other words, relations between humans and animals have a history. Certain humans and certain animals were valued in vastly different ways from their fellows. There was something extraordinary about the dogs at Ipiutak, but the relationship between one particular dog and one particular person in Burial 132 is unique in prehistory. An example like this, an exception to the "no dogs" rule in Eskimo burials, tells us about the potentials inherent in human–animal relations, even amidst apparently contrary social norms.

Between AD 700 and 1000, the onset of the Thule era in Alaska, human–dog relations intensified, shifting from cohabitation to codependency. Though these lifeways are often elided in the literature, the distinction between cohabitation and codependency is a useful one. Dogs have cohabited with humans for tens of thousands of years; only in a handful of societies, however, has that cohabitation intensified to the point of codependency, as in the Arctic. Cohabitation includes a variety of activities that bring humans and animals into physical proximity, often benefitting both. For example, dogs may provide advance notice of strangers and dispose of waste while supplementing their diets with scraps from human meals. They may live in human structures and participate in the daily lives of humans, or they may simply stay near human camps and settlements, without establishing closer bonds. Cohabitation therefore covers a range of practices with varying benefits for humans and dogs. Most, perhaps all, human societies from prehistory to the present have cohabited with dogs.

In contrast, codependency evolves in circumstances in which dog and human cooperation significantly enhances the likelihood of mutual survival, or makes possible the habitation of certain environments. Perri (2016), for example, has argued that Jōmon exploitation of forests was made possible by hunting dogs, without which humans could not have taken certain prey. Dogs were also arguably instrumental in the survival of the Yanomami, who depended upon them for hunting, as trade goods, and as sentries (Cummins

2013). In the North American Arctic, Thule people and their dogs appear to have developed a codependent relationship based upon provisioning in exchange for traction.

A hallmark of the Thule lifeway, dog traction facilitated the spread of Thule people eastward, along with a sophisticated toolkit and innovations in watercraft. While artifactual evidence for dog traction in Alaska is negligible prior to the Thule period, the practice likely developed during the preceding Birnirk period. Objects such as swivels, buckles, and ferrules had multiple uses, making their presence at archaeological sites inconclusive evidence of traction. Ethnohistoric accounts provide analogs for prehistoric Thule human–dog relations and indicate that there were both regional and individual differences in technologies and in the ways that dog teams were managed.

Dogs appear to have been a regular food source during the Thule period in Alaska, as they were in Canada and Greenland. On St. Lawrence Island, their consumption may go back to an earlier date. That dogs were eaten during famine is supported by multiple sources (Crowell and Oozevaseuk 2006; Nelson 1899: 325), though some of these same sources describe villages where both humans and dogs were dying for lack of food (Nelson 1899: 354–355). Whether dogs were considered non-famine food apparently varied by community, region, and even by individual. One possible explanation for this apparent inconsistency is differing attitudes toward the ontological status of dogs.

The Western Arctic record suggests that, during the contact era, relations with dogs were characterized by ambiguity, findings that broadly parallel data from the Eastern Arctic (e.g., Laugrand and Oosten 2015). Dogs were essential to trade, travel, and transportation; their provisioning required intensified subsistence practices, and they often suffered abuse and death at the hands of their human cohabitants. Yet dogs were also treated as surrogates for humans in cases of illness and disease, had names, wore amulets, and were believed by some to have interior selves, all of which are indicative of personhood. Together, archaeological and ethnohistoric evidence suggests that a dynamic tension existed in the Western Arctic between humans and dogs, reflecting both the symbolic potential inherent in dog behavior and the ambivalence and fluidity of dog–human relations through time.

Acknowledgements

I thank Blaine Maley and Chuck Hilton for providing me with sex determinations for several human skeletons from the Ipiutak cemetery excavated by Larsen and Rainey (1948). Several scholars, including Rob Losey and Angela Perri, kindly shared their work with me prior to publication. I thank the volume editors for their many suggestions, which have greatly improved this chapter.

Notes

1 A possible Ipiutak dog burial was encountered in a trench excavation at the site of Deering on the Seward Peninsula, but was not excavated (Bowers 2009: 115).
2 Paul Silook of St. Lawrence Island, writing around 1917, describes a very similar procedure (Paul Silook journal vol. XII, pp. 50–51, Daniel S. Neuman Papers MS 162, folder 11, Alaska State Library Historical Collections).

Bibliography

Alix, C., O.K. Mason, N.H. Bigelow, S.L. Anderson, and J. Rasic. 2015. "Archéologie du cap Espenberg ou la question du Birnirk et de l'origine du Thulé dans le nord-ouest de l'Alaska." *Les Nouvelles de l'Archéologie*, 141 (September):13–19.

Anderson, D.D., W. Anderson, R. Bane, R.K. Nelson, and N.S. Towarak. 1998. *Kuuvaŋmiut Subsistence: Traditional Eskimo Life in the Latter Twentieth Century*. Washington, DC: National Park Service.

Arutiunov, S.A. and D.A. Sergeev. 2006a. *Ancient Cultures of the Asiatic Eskimos: The Uelen Cemetery*. Translated by Richard L. Bland. Anchorage, AK: Shared Beringian Heritage Program, National Park Service.

Arutiunov, S.A. and D.A. Sergeev. 2006b. *Problems of Ethnic History in the Bering Sea: The Ekven Cemetery*. Translated by R.L. Bland. Anchorage: Shared Beringian Heritage Program, National Park Service.

Bartelle, B.G., R.L. Vellanoweth, E.S. Netherton, N.W. Poister, W.E. Kendig, et al. 2010. "Trauma and Pathology of a Buried Dog from San Nicolas Island, California, USA." *Journal of Archaeological Science*, 37 (11):2721–2734.

Binois, A., C. Wardius, P. Rio, A. Bridault, and C. Petit. 2013. "A Dog's Life: Multiple Trauma and Potential Abuse in a Medieval Dog from Guimps (Charente, France)." *International Journal of Paleopathology*, 3 (1):39–47.

Bowers, P.M. (ed.). 2009. *The Archaeology of Deering, Alaska: Final Report on the Deering Village Safe Water Archaeological Program*. Fairbanks: Northern Land Use Research.

Brown, S.K., C.M. Darwent, and B.N. Sacks. 2013. "Ancient DNA Evidence for Genetic Continuity in Arctic Dogs." *Journal of Archaeological Science*, 40 (2):1279–1288.

Bychkov, V.V., I.A. Zagrebin, T.M. Zagrebin, E.V. Tagrina, and V.V. Zhurakov. 2002. *Catalog of Objects of Material and Spiritual Culture of Chukchi and Eskimos of the Chukchi Peninsula in the Provideniya Museum Collections*. Translated by R.L. Bland. Anchorage: Shared Beringian Heritage Program, National Park Service.

Collins, H.B., Jr 1930. "Natural History Collection—Mammal Bones, Molluscs & Barnacles," box 55, Henry B. Collins Collection, National Anthropological Archives, Smithsonian Institution, Washington, DC.

Collins, H.B, Jr. 1937. *Archeology of St. Lawrence Island*. Washington, DC: Smithsonian Institution.

Collins, H.B., Jr. 1940. *Outline of Eskimo Prehistory*. Washington, DC: Smithsonian Institution.

Crowell, A.L. and E. Oozevaseuk. 2006. "The St. Lawrence Island Famine and Epidemic, 1878–80: A Yupik Narrative in Cultural and Historical Context." *Arctic Anthropology* 43 (1):1–19.

Cummins, B. 2013. *Our Debt to the Dog: How the Domestic Dog Helped Shape Human Societies*. Durham, NC: Carolina Academic Press.

Darwent, C. 2006. "Reassessing the Old Whaling Locality at Cape Krusenstern, Alaska." In *Dynamics of Northern Societies*, edited by J. Arneborg and B. Grønnow, 95–101. Copenhagen: National Museum of Denmark.

de Laguna, F. 1956. *Chugach Prehistory: The Archaeology of Prince William Sound, Alaska*. Seattle: University of Washington Press.

Dikov, N.N. 1996. "The Ushki Sites, Kamchatka Peninsula." In *American Beginnings: The Prehistory and Palaeoecology of Beringia*, edited by F.H. West, 244–250. Chicago: University of Chicago Press.

Fienup-Riordan, A. 1994. *Boundaries and Passages: Rule and Ritual in Yup'ik Eskimo Oral Tradition*. Norman, OK: University of Oklahoma Press.

Ford, J.A. 1959. *Eskimo Prehistory in the Vicinity of Point Barrow, Alaska*. Anthropological Papers of the American Museum of Natural History, 47 (1). New York: American Museum of Natural History.

Friesen, T.M. and C.D. Arnold. 2008. "The Timing of the Thule Migration: New Dates from the Western Canadian Arctic." *American Antiquity*, 73 (3):527–538.

Geist, O.W. and F.G. Rainey. 1936. *Archaeological Excavations at Kukulik St. Lawrence Island, Alaska*. Washington, DC: U.S. Government Printing Office.

Gerlach, S.C. and O.K. Mason. 1992. "Calibrated Radiocarbon Dates and Cultural Interaction in the Western Arctic." *Arctic Anthropology*, 29 (1):54–81.

Germonpré, M., S. Fedorov, P. Danilov, P. Galeta, E.-L. Jimenez, et al. 2017. "Palaeolithic and Prehistoric Dogs and Pleistocene Wolves from Yakutia: Identification of Isolated Skulls." *Journal of Archaeological Science*, 78:1–19.

Giddings, J.L. 1952. *The Arctic Woodland Culture of the Kobuk River*. Philadelphia: University Museum, University of Pennsylvania.

Giddings, J.L. and D.D. Anderson. 1986. *Beach Ridge Archeology of Cape Krusenstern: Eskimo and Pre-Eskimo Settlements around Kotzebue Sound, Alaska*. Washington, DC: National Park Service.

Gräslund, A.-S. 2004. "Dogs in Graves—A Question of Symbolism?" In *Pecus: Man and Animal in Antiquity*, edited by Barbro Santillo Frizell, 167–176. Rome: Swedish Institute.

Hallowell, A.I. 1926. "Bear Ceremonialism in the Northern Hemisphere." *American Anthropologist*, 28 (1):1–175.

Harritt, R.K. 2004. "A Preliminary Reevaluation of the Punuk–Thule Interface at Wales, Alaska." *Arctic Anthropology*, 41 (2):163–176.

Hill, E. 2011. "Animals as Agents: Hunting Ritual and Relational Ontologies in Prehistoric Alaska and Chukotka." *Cambridge Archaeological Journal*, 21 (3):407–426.

Hill, E. 2012. "The Nonempirical Past: Encultured Landscapes and Other-than-Human Persons in Southwest Alaska." *Arctic Anthropology*, 49 (2):41–57.

Hill, E. 2013. "Archaeology and Animal Persons: Towards a Prehistory of Human–Animal Relations." *Environment and Society: Advances in Research* 4:117–136.

Hilton, C., E. Benjamin, M. Auerbach, and L.W. Cowgill (eds.). 2014. *The Foragers of Point Hope: The Biology and Archaeology of Humans on the Edge of the Alaskan Arctic*. Cambridge: Cambridge University Press.

Himmelheber, H. 2000. *Where the Echo Began and Other Oral Traditions from Southwest Alaska*. Translated by K. Vitt and E. Vitt. Fairbanks: University of Alaska Press.

Hughes, C.C. 1960. *An Eskimo Village in the Modern World*. Ithaca, NY: Cornell University Press.

Jennbert, K. 2014. "Certain Humans, Certain Animals: Attitudes in the Long Term." In *Exploring the Animal Turn: Human–Animal Relations in Science, Society and Culture*, edited by E.A. Cederholm, A. Björck, K. Jennbert and A.-S. Lönngren, 183–192. Lund: Pufendorfinstitutet.

Jensen, A.M. 2016. "Archaeology of the Late Western Thule/Iñupiat in North Alaska (A.D. 1300–1750)." In *The Oxford Handbook of the Prehistoric Arctic*, edited by T.M. Friesen and O.K. Mason, 513–536. New York: Oxford University Press.

Lantis, M. 1980. "Changes in the Alaskan Eskimo Relation of Man to Dog and Their Effect on Two Human Diseases." *Arctic Anthropology*, 17 (1):1–25.

Lantis, M. 1990. "The Selection of Symbolic Meaning." *Études/Inuit/Studies*, 14 (1–2):169–189.

Larsen, H. 1969–1970. "Some Examples of Bear Cult among the Eskimo and Other Northern Peoples." *Folk: Dansk Etnografisk Tidsskrift*, 11–12:27–42.

Larsen, H. 2001. *Deering: A Men's House from Seward Peninsula, Alaska*. Edited by M. Appelt. Copenhagen: Department of Ethnography and SILA, National Museum of Denmark.

Larsen, H. and F.G. Rainey. 1948. *Ipiutak and the Arctic Whale Hunting Culture*. New York: American Museum of Natural History.

Larsson, L. 1989. "Big Dog and Poor Man: Mortuary Practices in Mesolithic Societies in Southern Sweden." In *Approaches to Swedish Prehistory: A Spectrum of Problems and Perspectives in Contemporary Research*, edited by T.B. Larsson and H. Lundmark, 211–223. Oxford: British Archaeological Reports.

Laugrand, F. and J. Oosten. 2002. "Canicide and Healing: The Position of the Dog in the Inuit Cultures of the Canadian Arctic." *Anthropos*, 97 (1):89–105.

Laugrand, F. and J. Oosten. 2007. "Bears and Dogs in Canadian Inuit Cosmology." In *La nature des esprits dans les cosmologies autochtones / Nature of Spirits in Aboriginal Cosmologies*, edited by F. Laugrand and J. Oosten, 353–385. Université Laval, QC: Les Presses de l'Université Laval.

Laugrand, F. and J. Oosten. 2015. *Hunters, Predators and Prey: Inuit Perceptions of Animals*. New York: Berghahn.

Losey, R.J., V.I. Bazaliiskii, S. Garvie-Lok, M. Germonpré, J.A. Leonard, et al. 2011. "Canids as Persons: Early Neolithic Dog and Wolf Burials, Cis-Baikal, Siberia." *Journal of Anthropological Archaeology*, 30 (2):174–189.

Losey, R.J., S. Garvie-Lok, J.A. Leonard, M.A. Katzenberg, M. Germonpré, et al. 2013. "Burying Dogs in Ancient Cis-Baikal, Siberia: Temporal Trends and Relationships with Human Diet and Subsistence Practices." *PLoS ONE*, 8 (5):e63740.

Losey, R.J., E. Jessup, T. Nomokonova, and M. Sablin. 2014. "Craniomandibular Trauma and Tooth Loss in Northern Dogs and Wolves: Implications for the Archaeological Study of Dog Husbandry and Domestication." *PLoS ONE*, 9 (6):e99746.

Mannermaa, K., P. Ukkonen, and S. Viranta. 2014. "Prehistory and Early History of Dogs in Finland." In *Fennoscandia Archaeologica*, XXXI:25–44. Helsinki: Archaeological Society of Finland.

Mason, O. K. 1998. "The Contest Between the Ipiutak, Old Bering Sea, and Birnirk Polities and the Origin of Whaling during the First Millennium A.D. along Bering Strait." *Journal of Anthropological Archaeology*, 17:240–325.

Mason, O.K. 2014. "The Ipiutak Cult of Shamans and Its Warrior Protectors: An Archaeological Context." In *The Foragers of Point Hope: The Biology and Archaeology of Humans on the Edge of the Alaskan Arctic*, edited by Charles E. Hilton,

Benjamin M. Auerbach and Libby W. Cowgill, 35–70. Cambridge: Cambridge University Press.
Mason, O.K. 2016a. "From the Norton Culture to the Ipiutak Cult in Northwest Alaska." In *The Oxford Handbook of the Prehistoric Arctic*, edited by T. Max Friesen and Owen K. Mason, 443–467. New York: Oxford University Press.
Mason, O.K. 2016b. "Thule Origins in the Old Bering Sea Culture: The Interrelationship of Punuk and Birnirk Cultures." In *The Oxford Handbook of the Prehistoric Arctic*, edited by T.M. Friesen and O.K. Mason, 489–512. New York: Oxford University Press.
Mathiassen, T. 1927. *Archaeology of the Central Eskimos: The Thule Culture and Its Place within the Eskimo Culture*. Copenhagen: Gyldendal.
McManus-Fry, E., R. Knecht, K. Dobney, M.P. Richards, and K. Britton. 2016. "Dog–Human Dietary Relationships in Yup'ik Western Alaska: The Stable Isotope and Zooarchaeological Evidence from Pre-Contact Nunalleq." *Journal of Archaeological Science Reports*, 15:1–9.
Morey, D.F. 2006. "Burying Key Evidence: The Social Bond between Dogs and People." *Journal of Archaeological Science*, 33:158–175.
Morey, D.F. 2010. *Dogs: Domestication and the Development of a Social Bond*. Cambridge: Cambridge University Press.
Morey, D.F. and A. Aaris-Sørensen. 2002. "Paleoeskimo Dogs of the Eastern Arctic." *Arctic*, 55 (1):44–56.
Mudar, K. and S. Speaker. 2003. "Natural Catastrophes in Arctic Populations: The 1878–1880 Famine on Saint Lawrence Island, Alaska." *Journal of Anthropological Archaeology* 22:75–104.
Murdoch, J. 1892. *Ethnological Results of the Point Barrow Expedition*. Washington, DC: Government Printing Office.
Murie, O.J. 1936. "Appendix IV: Dog Skulls from St. Lawrence Island, Alaska." In *Archaeological Excavations at Kukulik St. Lawrence Island, Alaska*, edited by O.W. Geist and F.G. Rainey, 347–357. Washington, DC: US Government Printing Office.
Murie, O.J. 1948. "Appendix 4: Dog Skulls from Ipiutak." In *Ipiutak and the Arctic Whale Hunting Culture*, 255–259. New York: American Museum of Natural History.
Nelson, E.W. 1899. *The Eskimo about Bering Strait*. Washington, DC: Government Printing Office.
Okladnikov, A.P. and N.A. Beregovaya. [1971] 2008. *The Early Sites of Cape Baranov*. Translated by R.L. Bland. Anchorage: Shared Beringian Heritage Program, National Park Service.
Ostermann, H. and E. Holtved. 1952. *The Alaskan Eskimos as Described in the Posthumous Notes of Dr. Knud Rasmussen*. Translated by W.E. Calvert. Copenhagen: Gyldendal.
Park, R.W. 1987. "Dog Remains from Devon Island, N.W.T.: Archaeological and Osteological Evidence for Domestic Dog Use in the Thule Culture." *Arctic*, 40 (3):184–190.
Perri, A.R. 2016. "Hunting Dogs as Environmental Adaptations in Jōmon Japan." *Antiquity*, 90 (353):1166–1180.
Perri, A.R. 2017. "A Typology of Dog Deposition in Archaeological Contexts." In *Economic Zooarchaeology: Studies in Hunting, Herding and Early Agriculture*, edited by P. Rowley-Conwy, P. Halstead and D. Serjeantson, 89–99. Oxford: Oxbow Books.
Pitul'ko, V.V. and A.K. Kasparov. 2016. "Early Holocene Dog Bones from the Zhokhov Site (East Siberian Arctic) and the Question of the Reliability of

Identification of Early Canis familiaris from Archaeological Excavations." *Stratum Plus*, 1:171–207.

Raghavan, M., M. DeGiorgio, A. Albrechtsen, I. Moltke, P. Skoglund, et al. 2014. "The Genetic Prehistory of the New World Arctic." *Science*, 345 (6200).

Rainey, F.G. 1941. *Eskimo Prehistory: The Okvik Site on the Punuk Islands*. New York: American Museum of Natural History.

Rainey, F.G. 1947. *The Whale Hunters of Tigara*. New York.

Ray, P.H. 1892. "Ethnographic Sketch of the Natives of Point Barrow." In *Ethnological Results of the Point Barrow Expedition*. Washington, DC: Smithsonian Institution Press.

Saleeby, B., M.L. Moss, J.M. Hays, C. Strathe, and D.L. Laybolt. 2009. "Mammalian Remains from the Ipiutak and Western Thule Houses." In *The Archaeology of Deering, Alaska: Final Report on the Village Safe Water Archaeological Program*, edited by P.M. Bowers, 189–200. Fairbanks: Northern Land Use Research.

Spencer, R.F. 1959. *The North Alaskan Eskimo: A Study in Ecology and Society*. Washington, DC: U.S. Government Printing Office.

Stanford, D.J. 1976. *The Walakpa Site, Alaska: Its Place in the Birnirk and Thule Cultures*. Washington, DC: Smithsonian Institution Press.

Tackney, J., J. Coltrain, J. Raff, and D.H. O'Rourke. 2016. "Ancient DNA and Stable Isotopes: Windows on Arctic Prehistory." In *The Oxford Handbook of the Prehistoric Arctic*, edited by T.M. Friesen and O.K. Mason, 51–80. Oxford: Oxford University Press.

Taylor, J.G. 1993. "Canicide in Labrador: Function and Meaning in an Inuit Killing Ritual." *Études/Inuit/Studies*, 17 (1):3–13.

Watson, G.P.L. and T. Warkentin. 2013. "Introduction: Animals, Place and Humans." *Animal Studies Journal*, 2 (1):1–7.

7 An ethnohistory of dogs in the Mackenzie Basin (western Subarctic)

Patricia A. McCormack

In 1977, I spent seven months at Fort Chipewyan, an historically important fur trade center on Lake Athabasca in northern Alberta, doing dissertation research. I brought my two dogs along. One was an Alaskan Malemute, and the other, a Siberian Husky-Alaskan Malemute cross. They were companion dogs – "pets" – but I also had them carry laundry for me in their blue Gerry packs when I walked from my cabin at the western edge into town, where I had access to a washer and dryer. During one of those trips, an older trapper, clearly taken by the sight, stopped me on the trail to tell me about how he used to pack beaver skins in the spring on his own dogs. My dogs came with me everywhere, on my daily visits to people in the community and on trips into the bush. They were loose when we walked in town, though I tied them outside people's houses while I was inside. They were much admired for their beauty and friendly nature, although local people probably considered *pet* sled dogs to be yet another outsider quirk. Fort Chipewyan was at that time transitioning from an era of dog sleds to snowmobile transport, and the fur trade itself had been facing significant challenges since the 1950s. There were, however, still many sled dogs in the community. Had I stayed for the entire winter, I would probably have put my dogs in harness too, but it was not till many years later that I hitched another Malemute to a sleigh.

In the fall, my neighbor asked me to look after his sled dogs while he and his family were going out of town for a few weeks. With the exception of his daughter's puppy, his dogs were staked out in the bush at some distance from his house. He gave me a half bag of commercial dog food for them. I finished that bag the next day, and after that I fed them fish obtained from a local fisherman. I also wormed and vaccinated them with supplies I had brought from the city. When he returned, my neighbor was surprised that I had used up the dog food, which in my mind had been scant to begin with. His dogs, as with many other dogs in Fort Chipewyan and other northern communities, lived and were treated in ways I found distressing, at odds with my own ethic about animal treatment. I helped local dogs when I was able to do so, and otherwise I compartmentalized the subject of dogs, not studying them in any formal way. While I lost a valuable opportunity to learn about dog traditions, those informal experiences, some inscribed in my field journals and some only in memory, along with my life-long experiences with dogs and other domestic animals, have helped shape this article, which involved considerable personal reflexivity in the realm of thinking about relationships among the different "persons" or "selves" that most Euro-Canadians – but not most northern Aboriginal people – typically divide into opposing categories of "humans" and "animals."

Four other threads are also joined in this article. First is a new approach in anthropology that Eduardo Kohn has called "an anthropology of life," one "that situates all-too-human worlds within a larger series of processes and relationships that exceed the human" (2007:4, 6). This "anthropology beyond the human" (Kohn 2013:7) is related to "multispecies ethnography," which Eben Kirksey and Stefan Helmreich call "a new genre of writing and mode of research" (2010:545). Second, I am mindful of the accounts I have read about and heard for decades from Aboriginal people about the non-human persons and spiritual entities that populate the world and are active agents in their lives. These narratives constitute much of the meat of Subarctic ethnography and are an older but still current approach to research and writing about northern peoples. As oral traditions, they lie at the heart of Aboriginal knowledge and traditional spiritual belief and practice, yet they have rarely been comprehended by most Euro-Canadians, who impose very different understandings of animals and land. The Aboriginal traditions are typically dismissed by non-Aboriginal people as so much cultural baggage – "superstition" at worst, religion at best – rather than a rational but alternate reality.[1] A new multi-species ethnography may be one way to bridge these two approaches. Third, there is a burgeoning literature about the domestication of dogs and their arrival in the Americas, some of which addresses the agency of wolves in the domestication process. Last, there is literature about dogs, wolves, and other animals of the western Subarctic to be found in the writings of European explorers and northern ethnographers, though this literature tends to be meagre, scattered, and uneven in content. This textual record is supplemented and enhanced by artifact collections in museums and archival photographs.

My broader goal is to draw on the northern literature and museum and archival collections for historic evidence about the evolution of the northern dogs commonly called "sled dogs" (less commonly, "working dogs") and dog teams in the Mackenzie Basin, the eastern portion of the western Subarctic, along with the complex of technologies, decorative elements, and behaviors that evolved in tandem with the dogs themselves since the arrival of Europeans. In short, it is an ethnohistory of northern dogs and the people in their lives, one which raises many questions and tries to answer others. This chapter is a starting point for the larger work. It focuses on the time in the lives of northern peoples and their dogs *before* they became heavily involved in the fur trade, which opened up a new and often unhappy chapter in the North for both dogs and people. Some of the impacts of the fur trade on dogs and sled technology have already been explored in two earlier papers (McCormack

2014a, 2014b), but the need to complete a much wider literature review and to pursue new lines of investigation, along with the potential length of such an expanded study, means that it is beyond the scope of this chapter to address the full topic here. Also, I do not explore the subject of Inuit/Eskimo dogs and komatiks (sleds) of the Arctic, which involve different historical questions (see Hill, this volume). Following Kohn, I want to contribute to the question of what it means to be a *person* in the cultural and historic contexts of the Subarctic and Parkland regions of the Canadian Northwest. As Kohn argues, "[a]ttending to our relations with these beings that exist in some way beyond the human forces us to question our tidy answers about the human" (2013:6).

I begin this discussion by pointing to modern understandings and popular notions of northern dogs, or "sled dogs," in order to contrast these to their little known histories. I then address a series of four questions. Who were the original dogs of the western Subarctic? What is known about indigenous dogs of the western Subarctic? What were the early Aboriginal traditions about wolves and dogs? How did the early fur trade affect Aboriginal people and their dogs? I return to the topic of multi-species ethnography and ethnohistory by way of conclusion, pointing to how we might think about northern dogs as integral elements of human societies.

How are sled dogs stereotyped and mythologized?

My own dogs were classic sled dogs originating in the eastern Siberia-Alaska region, now the remnant lands of Beringia.[2] Today, these are considered some of the "ancient breeds" (e.g., Parker et al. 2004:1161). They are a type of "spitz" dog, which were dogs evolved for cold regions. Specifically, these dogs have a thick double coat, small erect triangular ears, thick fur on their paws, a bushy "expressive" tail, and a ruff of fur around the neck (e.g., DogsReviewed n.d.). While the lineage of these northern dogs is ancient, there were probably few or no *sled* dogs before Europeans arrived in the western Subarctic. While there were always dogs to interact with and assist humans in various ways, they rarely if ever pulled sleds, which were pulled instead mainly by women. And, it seems likely that dogs were both few in number and small.[3] The development of sled dogs/dog sleds implicates the fur trade and an expanding European-dominated capitalist economy in the North.

Yet Canadians and an international audience possess strong stereotypes of beautiful northern dogs pulling a sled, "driven" by a trapper riding behind, along a trail in the famed Canadian "wilderness." This image is promoted as contributing to the authenticity of modern dog sled experiences. As an article in a popular northern magazine contended, in a reversal of historical fact, "Since time immemorial, the Inuit and First Nations used dogs for travel across the sea ice and through the boreal forest. It [dog hauling] was kept alive despite the arrival of Europeans…" (Edwards 2015). This image of dog and wilderness is sometimes conflated with that of the also-iconic Royal Canadian Mounted Police. Radio and television programs *Sergeant Preston* of the 1950s and *Due South* of the 1990s articulated the modern dog sled image: a team of handsome huskies pulling a sleigh and driven by a man dressed for extremely cold weather. A plethora of media exists to celebrate dog sledding, especially competitive racing, which is considered a spectator sport and attracts fans just as other sports do. Dog sledding has also become an important recreational winter sport for residents and tourists everywhere there is snow, including Scotland and other countries. Dog sledding operations catering to tourists tend to use Siberian Huskies or other beautiful northern dogs, while racers who have bred their dogs for speed have often lost the distinctive spitz look, producing a new breed of sled dog far removed from ancestral forms and often, frankly, homely (e.g., Huson et al. 2010).

Sled dogs have also been embraced by non-Aboriginal people as family pets, which erases the boundary between the opposing and transformative Aboriginal domains of "pet" and "sled dog." Sled dogs as family members rarely have to work in transport as their ancestors did, which means a life of ease and care. These dogs can live to be very old, unlike sled dogs, who often suffer physical disabilities and are worn out by middle age. These differences parallel those for humans who live by hard physical labor and those who do not.

Sled dog paraphernalia has proliferated along with racing, tourism, and sled dogs as pets. People can buy a wide array of merchandise, from clothing and coffee mugs emblazoned with sled dog imagery to sled dog puppies, retired sled dogs, and dog sleds. In short, the northern dogs themselves, the multiple roles they play for Aboriginal and non-Aboriginal people today, and the sentiments attached to them are complex and continuing to evolve. Yet these are far removed from the realities of the northern indigenous dogs of the past. It is that other story that is the focus of this article.

Who were the original dogs of the western Subarctic?

This question concerns the dogs themselves, whose ancestry dates back to the very origin of domestic dogs, a matter much disputed, but which probably occurred during the Late Pleistocene – the time of the Upper Paleolithic – at a time when humans co-existed with the gray wolf, *Canis lupus*, a widespread species across the Northern Hemisphere and also the ancestor of domestic dogs.[4] This question is also related to the question of how America was peopled, because it was they who brought the first dogs into the Americas. (There is no evidence for the independent domestication of dogs in the Americas). Some authors have been considering information about dogs in the Americas as a proxy for information about human newcomers (e.g., Witt el al. 2015:106); however, one can also look at information about human migration as a proxy for the expansion of dog populations into the western hemisphere. The question is complicated by the fact that while dogs evolved differences from ancestral wolves in genetics, morphology, and behavior, they can still interbreed and in some regions (including North America) continued to do so even after domestication, a face known from genetic and ethnographic evidence. Until recently, dogs were classified as a distinct species – *Canis familiaris* – but since 2003 scientists have considered them to be a subspecies of wolf, *Canis lupus familiaris*.[5] The brief discussion here is intended only to point to some of the highlights of the expanding literature in the field, which comprises investigations into both wolves and dogs globally, and to draw on some leading work relevant to dogs in the Americas. This section also offers a few suggestions for future research on this topic.

The time, location, and process of dog domestication are critical for determining when dogs may have been available to enter the Americas with human travelers. One difficulty is that dogs may have remained morphologically similar to ancestral wolves as domestication proceeded and their behaviors changed (e.g., Vilà et al. 1997:1689; Morey 2014:306); today's researchers rely on both genetic and morphological evidence to help sort out that problem, which remains unresolved.[6] Carles Vilà and his colleagues proposed "multiple founding events" from several lineages of wolves during the Late Pleistocene, with continued interbreeding with wolves (1997:1687). Peter Savolainen and his co-authors (2002) contended that at least five female wolf lines were involved and speculated on a possible date of 40,000 years BP, with a probable date of 15,000 years BP origin in East Asia for Clade A, which is found in the indigenous dogs of the Americas. Much later work has brought forward new evidence and new analyses with a wide range of dates within this time range. Darcy Morey's review (2014) of genetic and morphological evidence led him to propose "sustained canid domestication" at about 17,000–16,000 years BP, but these activities were likely different from those of proto- or early-domestication from much earlier times.

One implication of undoubted skeletal evidence of dogs is that the processes leading up to domestication and the consequent morphological changes must have begun earlier (e.g., see Larson et al. 2012; Morey 2014). Morey's review of dog morphology pointed to three key skeletal features: an overall reduction in size, facial shortening, and tooth crowding (1992b:182; see Larson et al. 2012). He did not propose that these features resulted from deliberate selection, but rather that "transition to a domestic way of life entailed changes in diet, social behaviour, and reproductive strategy that were associated with selection for both body size reduction and alterations in reproduction timing" (Morey 1992b:197). Unfortunately, the behavioral and communicative changes that are at the heart of the domestic dog do not reveal themselves in skeletal remains and remain elusive in genetic studies (e.g., Wayne and Ostrander 2007:557, 565). They involve "tameness" and "social competence," characterized in dogs by increased docility, reduced aggressiveness, the ability to "read" "human social and communicative behavior" (Hare and Tomasello 2006:497), and overall the ability to bond with humans socially and emotionally (Hare 2004; Hare and Tomasello 2006; Hare et al. 2002; Miklósi and Topál 2013; Morey and Jeger 2015; Freedman et al. 2014).[7] These aspects suggest that the dynamics leading to domestication involved biocultural elements at a highly localized level that may have included a predominance of "pleasurable" rather than "painful" interactions between humans and ancestral wolves/proto-dogs, the (related) development of trust between dogs and humans, and the initial persistence of a level of dog autonomy that was lacking in later domestic animals and was eventually eroded among dogs too, as it became possible for humans to exploit them more fully (Balcombe 2009; Ingold 1994; Argent 2013:179). Estrus in dogs is not seasonally restricted, as it is in wolves, which engage in courtship and mating only in the spring (e.g., Mech 1970:117). That points to a major shift in dog reproductive behavior, undoubtedly enabled by the fact that dogs were fed, even if irregularly. Peter Saetre et al. (2004) have proposed that the differences in dog psychology – and perhaps these other differences? – may be less genetic *per se* than in "patterns of gene expression" and have found significant differences in gene expression in the hypothalamus. That could push the date for dog domestication much farther back than is suggested by direct genetic evidence.

The spread of domestic dogs to the Americas is similarly an unresolved matter, and it relates to human migrations south from Beringia. Antonio Torroni and colleagues have argued in various papers that there were two human migrations into the Americas: one by Amerind peoples between 37,500–18,750 years BP and a second later migration by Na-Dene peoples (Torroni, Sukernik, et al. 1993; Torroni, Schurr, et al. 1993; see Pedersen et al. 2016 for some recent dates). Eskimo-Aleut peoples were the last to arrive (e.g., Torroni, Schurr, et al. 1993:563; Shields et al. 1993:559), and contact among these peoples – and their dogs – has persisted across the Arctic from eastern Siberia to Greenland to the present (except during the Cold War of the late twentieth century).[8]

More recently, Erika Tamm et al. (2007) developed the "Beringian Incubation Model"; Hoffecker et al. (2016) have elaborated on this model and its implications. Also known as the "Beringian Standstill Hypothesis/Model," it proposes that modern humans arrived in northern Asia after c. 50,000 BP and after c. 30,000 BP became isolated in Beringia, a refugium during the Last Glacial Maximum, until glaciation began to recede in North America, c. 17,000–16,000 BP, allowing humans to enter the Americas between c. 16,000 and 13,000 BP.[9] Witt et al. have presumed that dogs were present in Beringia (2015:107). Given the cold climate of Beringia, the founding dogs were probably all spitz types, with the diverse phenotypes described in the literature on indigenous American dogs developing after dogs spread throughout the hemisphere.

The earliest dates proposed for the peopling of the Americas do not align with the dates for the domestication of dogs, and no one has yet published a study seeking to reconcile the various dates for humans and dogs. There is little evidence for human occupation in Beringia, let alone for dogs, given that most Beringian lands are now under water. If Amerind ancestors entered the Americas at a very early date, they may not have had dogs and would have had to obtain them from later arrivals (see van Asch et al. 2013:2). Ancestors entering at a later date – the Na-Dene and Eskimoan peoples – certainly would have had dogs, which would have reflected not only northern dog populations but also movements of people and their dogs from other regions into eastern Siberia. If dogs were present in an isolated Beringia, different dog lineages should have developed there. At minimum, one can expect that there were different waves of dogs entering the Americas with different founding human populations, although most of the discussions of dogs in the Americas have treated them as a collective. Jennifer Leonard et al. have proposed that at least five founding dog lineages entered the Americas (2002:1615; see van Asch et al. 2013:8; Crockford 2005). Even today, some limited genetic evidence exists for the original American dogs, based on preliminary research; it has not all been lost by decimation of original dog populations or hybridization with European dogs after 1492 (van Asch 2013; Weidensaul and Richardson 1999; Brisbin and Risch n.d.; Castroviejo-Fisher et al. 2011). In the North, there has been interest in Eskimoan dogs, but no one has yet researched the genetics of the modern Subarctic dogs or what may be the single extant dog from the Mackenzie Basin (or perhaps the entire Subarctic), a Hare Indian Dog specimen sent to the Smithsonian Institution in the mid nineteenth century (discussed below).

What is known about indigenous dogs of the western Subarctic?

The earliest observations may be those of James Isham, Andrew Graham, and Samuel Hearne, all Hudson's Bay Company servants from the mid eighteenth century, before the company began to establish inland posts. Isham served the Hudson's Bay Company at York Fort (Factory) and Fort Churchill from 1732 to 1761. He noted the Cree term for dog – *at tim* (Rich 1949:21), and included a brief note about them in his *Observations on Hudsons Bay, 1743*:

> Dog's are of great service to the Natives in hawlg. Sleds, and carrying of Burthen's also[.] …these Dogs are also of great service to the English in hawling provision's when they Lye abroad from the fort, one Dog being able to hawle a fortnights provision's for 2 men &c.
>
> Rich 1949:164[10]

Andrew Graham, another long-term servant who served under Isham, wrote about the "Wechepowuck Nation" – Chipewyans or Northern Indians – using "Dogs…loaded like packhorses" (Rich 1949:311–12). Samuel Hearne, who travelled with Chipewyans and Yellowknives in the early 1770s, provided the first known description of the northern Indian dogs themselves, as "…of various sizes and colours, but all of the fox and wolf breed, with sharp noses, full brushy tails, and sharp ears standing erect…" (Hearne 1958:207). He said that they were used for both carrying (packing) and hauling sleds, though less often for the latter:

> These [deer-skin] tents, as also their kettles, and some other lumber, are always carried by dogs, which are trained to that service, and are very docile and tractable. ... These dogs are equally willing to haul in a sledge, but as few of the men will be at the trouble of making sledges for them, the poor women are obliged to content themselves with lessening the bulk of their load, more than the weight, by making the dogs carry these articles only, which are always lashed on their backs, much after the same manner as are, or used formerly to be, on packhorses.
> Hearne 1958:207–8

> [Wolves] are great enemies to the Indian dogs, and frequently kill and eat those that are heavily loaded, and cannot keep up with the main body.
> ibid.:232

In the pre-fur trade days, it was mostly women and girls, not dogs, who hauled the sleds. Alexander Mackenzie wrote that women were "accustomed to drag sledges of a weight from two to four hundred pounds" (in Lamb 1970:151), although it is hard to imagine what they were hauling that weighed so much, unless it was meat provisions for the post. The sleighs themselves were light, possibly as little as eight to ten pounds for the smallest Chipewyan sleighs described by Samuel Hearne (Hearne 1958:208–9; calculations by Greg McCormack, email communication, 17 March 2017). When dogs were used, it was one dog or at most two dogs hitched together, in tandem – one in front of the other. There were no long dog "trains" or teams. Thus, analysis of dog team evolution needs to unpack information from discussions of the post-contact world, men, and dog teams. It also brings into question statements about the symbolic meanings and economic uses of dogs.

Using dogs as pack animals did not involve any sophisticated behavior on the part of the dog, other than a willingness to carry a pack, and which can be easily conditioned by placing small packs on puppies. Once dogs are loaded up, they are turned loose and simply follow their people. Hauling a sled involves a harness, but it is still not difficult if a single dog is hitched to a sleigh in the company of his/her people. As with dogs that are packing, the dog will simply follow the people, though the dog may occasionally need to be untangled from the harness. Harnessing a dog to a second dog represents a small step up in difficulty, with a greater possibility of tangling in the harness. The actual "driving" of dogs by someone riding on the back of the sleigh was a complex change that occurred in the late nineteenth century; it was not pre-contact or early fur trade-related.

Sharp has contended that in the modern world, when people relied on dog teams for transport, that "sled dogs are basically things of male concern,

[and] pet dogs are more things of family, women, or children" (2001:87). If one removes fur trade transport, in the pre-contact/early contact times dogs were evidently within the domain of women and secondarily of children, especially girls. Women looked after transport, and if dogs carried packs or hauled sleds, women, not men, managed them. Women were also the primary care-givers for children, and they would have looked after both children and puppies. Dogs continued to fall into the woman's domain among Plains Cree into the later nineteenth century, possibly because men began using horses. The Plains Cree derived from Woodland Crees in the late eighteenth century, so their customs about dogs probably stem from their northern origins. Mandelbaum pointed out that among the Cree, "women cared for [dogs] and owned them. ... When a dog was sold [e.g., to the Hudson's Bay Company], the husband arranged the terms of the sale, but he had to secure his wife's permission and handed over the proceeds to her" (1979:66). Women taught dogs to answer to their names by feeding them individually with strips of meat (ibid.:67). They made them "small rawhide shoes" to protect their feet from sharp ice (ibid.). Presumably it was the women who owned the dogs who had to agree to their being used as ceremonial sacrifices. These complex roles resonate with what Gala Argent has called an "interspecies apprenticeship process" (2013:178).

Dr. John Richardson provided the first formal and detailed description of the indigenous dogs of the western Subarctic, in his *Fauna Boreali-Americana*, after travelling into the western Subarctic with the two Northern Land Expeditions led by John Franklin between 1819 and 1827 (Richardson 1829:xi; Franklin 1928; Franklin 1969 [orig. 1823]). He identified four types of indigenous dogs and provided each with a varietal name: the Esquimaux Dog (*Canis familiaris var. A. borealis*), the Hare Indian Dog (*Canis f. var. B. lagopus*), the North American Dog (*Canis f. var. C. canadensis*), and the Carrier Indian Dog (*Canis f. var. D. Novae Caledoniae*) (Richardson 1829:75–83).[11] Only the Hare Indian Dog and the North American Dog are discussed here. The rapid disappearance of indigenous dogs (see below) after the arrival of Europeans means that Richardson's work has remained the authoritative source for these early dogs in later works (e.g., Allen 1920; Cummins 2002).[12]

Richardson and other writers pointed out the "great resemblance" between domestic dogs and wolves (e.g., 1829:75). Richardson believed that in appearance, they differed only in size and strength (ibid.:64). The Hare Indian Dog and the North American Dog were both spitz-type dogs whose genetic legacy involved occasional interbreeding with wolves, both deliberate and incidental (e.g., Franklin 1969:90, 172). According to Richardson (1829:64), Indians wanted such crosses to improve them as "sledge-dogs," but that would have been a post-contact motive, inspired by people's involvement in the fur trade in the early to mid nineteenth century. The distribution of the Hare Indian Dog seems to have corresponded broadly with that of Athapaskan peoples, and the North American Dog, with Algonquian and Siouan peoples to the east and south.

Figure 7.1 Hare Indian Dog
Source: Sketch from Richardson (1829).

Richardson was especially interested in the Hare Indian Dog, which he described as playful and affectionate. These dogs howled and vocalized rather than barked (1829:80), just as modern huskies do today. He purchased a puppy from the Hare Indians and noted that his dog "became greatly attached to me" (ibid.:80, 79). He provided a drawing of this type of dog (Figure 7.1), perhaps based on his own dog, as well as a detailed textual description:

> The Hare Indian Dog has a mild countenance, with, at times, an expression of demureness. It has a small head, slender muzzle; erect, thickish ears; somewhat oblique eyes; rather slender legs, and a broad hairy foot, with a bushy tail, which it usually carries curled over its right hip. It is covered with long hair, particularly about the shoulders, and at the roots of the hair, both on the body and tail, there is a thick wool. The hair on the top of the head is long, and on the posterior part of the cheek it is not only long, but being also directed backwards, it gives the animals, when the fur is in prime order, the appearance of having a ruff round the neck. Its face, muzzle, belly, and legs, are of a pure white colour, and there is a white central line passing over the crown of the head and the occiput. The anterior surface of the ear is white, the posterior yellowish-gray or

fawn-colour. The end of the nose, the eye-lashes, the roof of the mouth, and part of the gums, are black. There is a dark patch over the eye. On the back and sides there are larger patches of dark blackish-gray or lead-colour mixed with fawn-colour and white, not definite in form, but running into each other. The tail is bushy, white beneath and at the tip. The feet are covered with hair which almost conceals the claws. Some long hairs between the toes project over the soles, but there are naked callous protuberances at the root of the toes and on the soles, even in the winter time, as in all the wolves described in the preceding pages. ... Its ears are proportionably nearer each other than those of the Esquimaux dog.

Richardson 1829:79

Another description was provided in 1861 by Bernard Rogan Ross, an Hudson's Bay Company Chief Trader and naturalist who had extensive northern experience. He was stationed at Fort Norman, in the Hare lands, from 1852–54, and was the Chief Trader in Fort Simpson on the Mackenzie River from 1858 to 1862 (Bowsfield 1972; Hudson's Bay Company Archives n.d.).

The Hare Indian dog, *var. Lagopus* is the race domesticated among the Indians of the Mackenzie River District. It is characterized by a narrow, elongated and pointed muzzle, by erect sharp ears, and by a bushy tail not carried erect but only slightly curved upwards, as well as by a fine silky hair mixed with thick under fur. Its colour is tolerably varied in the shades of brown, grey, black, and white. Of these tints the darkest are the most rare. A white or greyish white being the most usual shade. Some writers have supposed this animal to be a domesticated white fox but the thing is highly improbable. The Indian dog, though there are great differences in its size, has on an average more than treble the proportions of this species of fox, moreover it will not have connection [mate] with this or any other branch of the sub-family *Vulpinoe*, while its varied shades of colour are never seen in the pure white pelt of the arctic fox; with wolves on the contrary, not only will they cohabit but will also produce a hybrid offspring that will for several generations procreate one with another. This fact manifests the close connection that both these varieties of dogs have to the wolves, and would almost prove them identical.

Ross 1861b:13–14

From these two descriptions and Richardson's illustration, the Hare Indian Dog may have resembled a small Siberian Husky or very small Alaskan Malemute. Richardson described it as being smaller than a prairie wolf but larger than a fox.

Ross also commented on First Nations relationships with their dogs, pointing out that the Slave "tribes," which included the Dogribs and probably Hares, "...are kind in their treatment of their women and dogs...," unlike the Beavers, Chipewyans, and Yellowknives (1859:194). That points to the close relationship described later by Savishinsky (1974, 1975) between people and their puppies, a relationship that may have remained relatively happy in the days before dogs hauled sleds. Richardson claimed that this dog was used "...solely in the chase, being too small to be useful as a beast of burthen or draught" (1829:78). However, by Ross' time, if not earlier, they were being used for hauling: "They are the only beasts of burthen, and although they have not the strength of the fort dogs, still a train or team of three good ones, will haul a load of upwards of three hundred pounds, five hundred being considered a good load for the others" (Ross 1861b:14–15). That is, an indigenous dog could pull about 100 pounds; a hybrid dog, about 160 pounds.

While Richardson described the Hare Indian Dog as found among the First Nations of the Great Bear Lake and Mackenzie River region, he opined that it had been found more widely "amongst the Indian tribes north of the Great Lakes" (1829:79). This was guesswork, probably based on what he was told about the indigenous dogs. When Richardson travelled through the Fort Chipewyan-Lake Athabasca region, there was a dearth of dogs among the Chipewyans and Yellowknives, due to their having killed all their dogs as part of a religious movement in or about 1814 (Franklin 1969:160–1; 1828:303; see discussion below). The only dogs surviving were those attached to people of the post, which had already been interbred to some extent with European dogs. The decimation of dogs in the Athabasca region created a significant genetic bottleneck: the later dog population probably had a much larger European dog component than did the earlier indigenous dog population. Some additional information is available about the Hare Indian Dog. William Youatt referred to an address about the Hare Indian Dog given to the Zoological Society of London in 1835 by its secretary, Mr. Bennett, that was based on information from both Richardson and Franklin, though the latter said nothing about them in his publications.[13] Three Hare Indian Dogs were obtained for the Zoological Society of London by a Colonel H. Smith; they subsequently produced two litters (Youatt 1852:50; Cummins 2002:160). It may have been one of these dogs that was painted by John Woodhouse Audubon, who included a lithograph in his book with the annotation, "Drawn from Nature" (Figure 7.2). Its markings are quite different from those of Richardson's image.

Richardson travelled to the Mackenzie region a third time in 1848, in company with Dr. John Rae, on an expedition searching for John Franklin (Richardson 1852). He referred to the Hare and Dogrib women dragging the sledges "alone or aided by dogs" (ibid.:250), which may reflect what he describes as "a stouter race of dogs" than was present 28 years earlier (ibid.:260).

Finally, delving into the primary literature has revealed an extant Hare Indian Dog specimen that until now has remained unknown. In 1858, Sir George Simpson, the Governor of the Hudson's Bay Company, sent a letter to the post factors on behalf of the Smithsonian Institution, which wanted

Figure 7.2 Hare Indian Dog
Source: Illustration by J.W. Audubon, 1845–48.

to complete its "collection of North American Animals" (letter from Ross to Joseph Henry, 28 Nov. 1858, in Lindsay 1991:10–11). Ross was eager to comply. Although he had earlier written about wanting to offer "a just tribute to the affectionate disposition, and kindly habits of this poor and ill-used 'friend of man'" (1861b:15), he did not hesitate to condemn one to a painful death for the Smithsonian's collection, probably selected from the dogs at Fort Simpson:

> Wishing to preserve a specimen of the Hare-Indian dog for the Smithsonian Institution, I resolved to kill the animal by poisoning. Two grains of strychnia of the first strength were administered in a piece of fresh meat, at the end of two hours the animal was as well as ever. I then administered one grain more mixed with grease, in two minutes the spasms began, and in five the animal was dead. [This description was followed by a graphic description of the death of the animal].
>
> Ross 1861b:20

Aboriginal people greatly feared strychnine, and they must have been appalled to see this dog killed in a way they would have considered cruel, "without pity," as northern people would have termed it (on the fear of poison, see McCormack 2010:93).

Ross wrote to Spencer Baird at the Smithsonian on 20 June 1860 describing his preparation of six cases of specimens he was sending, which included the dog. He had used "corrosive sublimate" (mercury chloride) to preserve the dog (Lindsay 1991:49–50). The dog's skull and skin were sent to the Smithsonian, which still has them in its collection (accession numbers are USNM 4291 for the skull and USNM 4397 for the skin) (Craig Ludwig, email communication, 29 Nov. 2016). It is hoped that this specimen can in the future provide both genetic and morphological evidence about these dogs.[14]

Richardson claimed that the North American Dog was the one "most generally cultivated by the native tribes of Canada, and the Hudson's Bay countries" (1829:80). It was undoubtedly the dog he encountered as he traveled westward and probably corresponded to the dogs of the northern Plains and the southern portions of the Subarctic, what Allen (1920) called the "Plains Indian Dog" (also, Olsen 1974:343). He called it "intermediate in size and form" between the Esquimaux and Hare Indian dogs, but not as strong as the former and less "affectionate and playful" than the latter (ibid.:80–1). His description was perfunctory:

> The fur of the North American Dog is similar to that of the Esquimaux breed and of the wolves. The prevailing colours are black and gray, mixed with white. Some of them are entirely black. Their thick woolly coat forms an admirable protection against the cold…
>
> ibid.:81

This dog was used to haul sleds and to carry loads, it was occasionally eaten by Canadian voyageurs and various First Nations (ibid.:81–2), and it was also used for ceremonial purposes.

It seems likely that this dog was genetically similar to those found in archaeological sites and burials in the northern Great Basin, the northern Plains, and the early Holocene Midwest, although to date only morphological evidence is available (Morey 1986; 1992a; Grayson 1988). However, thousands of years of genetic evolution separated those archaeological dogs from the dogs described by early Europeans visiting those regions.

Hybridization with European dogs began very early, as soon as Europeans began to bring their own dogs with them to the Americas. Richardson referred to "the mongrel breed which the Canadian voyagers rear for draught" (1829:81), and Ross (above) distinguished between the larger, stronger post dogs and the Aboriginal dogs. Mason said that the sled dogs were known as "'giddès,' being of a different strain from and somewhat inferior to the Eskimo 'husky'"(1946:24).[15] He also believed that there continued to be regular breeding of these dogs, which were "allowed to run partly wild," with wolves (ibid.). Europeans dogs were brought very early into western Canada from posts on Hudson's Bay and from Quebec, both of which served as intermediary fur trade centers between Europe and Aboriginal regions, as well as from the United States. Occasional snippets can be found in the literature about European dogs brought into the country, which were probably mostly unneutered males.[16] For example, Alexander Mackenzie had a large dog with him – referred to only as "Our Dog" – when he journeyed to the Pacific Ocean in 1793 (Lamb 1970).[17] In 1811, Alexander Henry the Younger, writing from the northern Plains, said that he had purchased from a "Fall Indian" (Gros Ventre) "a stout Black Dog, of a breed between a Hound and Newfoundland Dog" that had been seized from a party of Americans whom they had killed the previous year (Gough 1992:545). John Franklin referred to "two English bull-dogs and a terrier, which had been brought into the country this season" (1819) (Franklin 1969:47).[18] The second Franklin Expedition had with it "a little Scotch terrier" (Richardson 1829:81). In 1865, Hudson's Bay Company trader Willie Traill, then stationed at Fort Ellice in the Swan River District, west of modern-day Winnipeg, was given "a very pretty little pointer dog from Mr. McKay. His [the dog's] name is Frank. I call him Frank Traill" (Munro 2006:54).

Importing European dogs may also have introduced new dog diseases: new parasites and bacterial and viral diseases, including rabies, or new varieties of these (see Elton 1931). These paralleled the better-known introduction of human diseases.[19] However, little is known about either pre-contact or post-contact canid or other animal illnesses in the Americas, including the North, until relatively recently. A few glimpses exist. Cree elder Louis Bird tells a story about a time when "the wolves seem to have a crazy sickness, …and they were very dangerous. There were stories that wolves would kill a man by himself when he hunt. The wolves would hunt the human instead of being hunted" (Bird 2005:55). While Bird thought that this illness occurred before the arrival of Europeans, it is possible that it was a European disease such as rabies that spread at an early date to dogs at a post on Hudson's Bay and from there to wolves. David Thompson was told that after the first tragic smallpox epidemic of 1781, "[a]ll the Wolves and Dogs that fed on the bodies of those that died of the Small Pox lost their hair, especially on the sides and belly, and even for six years after many Wolves were found in this condition and their fur useless. The Dogs were mostly killed" (Moreau 2009:286). In the Mackenzie River region c. 1805–06, "a distemper [that] reached epidemic proportions among large game animals" was reported (Keith 2001:58).[20] Animals were said to be dying "in great numbers…The Dogs who had feasted upon them died also" (ibid.: 300). Humans, too, died after eating the dead animals.

The expansion of hybrid dog populations in the Athabasca region and elsewhere in the western Subarctic would have been facilitated by the genetic bottleneck created by the slaughter of dogs, to which John Franklin referred to around 1814, and by smaller bottlenecks created every time local dogs died of starvation and had to be replaced from neighboring populations. When Franklin returned to the region in 1825, he mentioned that the Chipewyans and Yellowknives again had dogs, which they were using "to drag their sledges" (1828:303). The recovery of the local dog population occurred within a period of a decade, presumably by acquiring dogs from the local fur trade posts, many of them indigenous-European hybrids, and from the neighboring nations that had not destroyed their dogs.

What were the early Aboriginal traditions about wolves and dogs?

There was a wide range of early Aboriginal traditions and beliefs about dogs, most of which are imperfectly known today only in glimpses afforded by primary sources. However, the context for these beliefs is well known and broadly similar across the Subarctic and Arctic. It is the widespread cultural understanding about the world as a place filled with spiritual power and entities which/who can transform between animal and human forms, engage with humans, and influence and even determine the ability of people to hunt and fish successfully. It is a world that combines trust, autonomy, and dependency, according to Tim Ingold (1994:13), which relates to Mary Douglas' argument that the categories humans use for animals reflect their own social principles (1994:33). Robert Losey et al. have called this cosmology "the animistic interpretive model" in their discussion of canid burials in Siberia:

> This model posits that Northern indigenous peoples (and others) both act in and know a world that is full of persons. These persons, namely sentient, willful beings with souls, include not just humans but also implements, plants, weather phenomena, landscapes, and particularly animals. The souls of these beings cycle through the cosmos, returning to the plane of the living to inhabit a newly formed person. An essential part of this process is the proper treatment of the remains of the person, human or otherwise, following their death.
>
> Losey et al. 2011:175; see also Nadasdy 2007

In such systems, humans and non-human persons have parallel social lives that mirror one another; they may also cross the human–non-human boundary to marry one another and have children. Bird-David (1999) interprets these beliefs as an up-dated animism stripped of its derogatory implications of primitivism and superstition (see Gittins 2013:124).

Scholars of northern Canadian Aboriginal cultures have moved away from the concept of animism *per se* to address basic forms of ontology by Athapaskan and Algonquian peoples. It is beyond the scope of this paper to provide a detailed description of these beliefs, which vary somewhat in their details from region to region, or a complete bibliography. For both Athapaskans and Algonquians, these beliefs are well summarized by David Smith in his discussion on Chipewyan ontology, which he calls "their intellections and feelings concerning the nature of being" (1998:412). He writes:

Their thought categories are open-ended; implicitness, indeterminacy, and mystery are accepted as matters of course...

The most fundamental assumption of bush sensibility is that all beings, human and nonhuman, are inextricably engaged in a complex communicative interrelationship. Success in life demands actively maintaining harmony in these interrelationships, especially among human beings, and among human and animal persons. Maintaining harmony requires empirical, experiential, holistic knowledge. But it also means having supraempirically derived knowledge – *inkonze* – that, while never separated by the Chipewyan from pragmatic everyday knowledge, comes as a gift from animal persons, most commonly in dreams. Beneficial, life-enhancing inkonze comes only to those individuals who display respectful attitudes and actions toward human and animal persons and requires being active in the bush, the quintessential realm of the animal people.

Smith 1998:412–13; citations in quotation omitted

That means, as Robert Brightman (2002:1886) has pointed out for northern Crees, that hunting is a "spiritualized" activity, in that it involves humans interacting with animals in advance of a hunt, especially in dreams, resulting in the animal being willing to be killed. Animals and people both cycle if they are treated properly. Animals, including dogs, will be reborn as members of the same species, while humans will be reborn as specific individuals whose personal ancestry can be identified and who sometimes remember events of former lives (e.g., Lamb 1970:150; Wentzel in Masson 1889:88; Blondin 1990:68, 110). For Chipewyans, at least, reincarnation can also occur between humans and animals, especially wolves (Sharp 1976:31; 2001:81). Animals and humans engage in multiple relationships with one another, especially in dreams but also in the "ordinary" lives which people live when they are in the "bush," the lands beyond their camps and settlements. In the past, these relationships sometimes included marriages. It is the power of animal persons that allow people to heal illness and hunt and fish successfully. There is also a darker side: power from animal persons can be used to harm people, and the animals may refuse to offer themselves to be killed by people who have not followed rules about proper behavior and have therefore offended the animals (e.g., Ingold 1994:13).

Henry Sharp has argued that "Chipewyan knowledge transcends Western knowledge," because Dene peoples:

have interacted with the animals of this land since time immemorial, and their experience of that interaction has helped them develop an extensive practical knowledge of them. For all those thousands of years animals have been more than food; they have been a dominant passion of Dene life. The People have thought long and deeply about animals even as they have observed them with intensity, perception, and sensitivity. They have learned their habits and characteristics in often minute detail, but The People have watched and thought about animals not just to prey upon them but with a passion to understand them.

Sharp 2001:66

Nadasdy has pointed out that Aboriginal concepts of animals have typically been interpreted as Aboriginal "cultural constructions" or projections of their own worlds (e.g., Douglas 1994) rather than reflections of physical realities, or how the world actually works: "very few Euro-American scholars are willing to accept the proposition that animals might qualify as conscious actors capable of engaging in social relations with humans" (Nadasdy 2007:26, 29). Recent work has opened an intellectual door to abandoning traditional European distinctions between humans and all other animals in order to consider animals as genuinely sentient beings which exercise their own agency (e.g., Ingold 2011, 2015; Sanders 2007; Balcombe 2009; see Nadasdy 2007:30–3).[21] And, scholars such as Henry Sharp and David Smith have been willing to share their own very personal experiences about animal persons and alternate realities (e.g., Sharp 1996; 2001:chp. 1; Smith 1998). Either way, these beliefs relate to boundaries between persons who are humans and those who are not, to ambiguities about these boundaries and transformations across them, and to related taboos or prohibitions on certain behaviors (e.g., see Leach 1964). Edmund Leach has argued that moral rules are linked with categories of normal-abnormal, and "what we need to know about *the other* – whether animal or human – is where he, she or it *fits in*" (1972:17; see Raier and Rofel 2014:371). Given the widespread geographical distribution of such systems of belief, they were undoubtedly present among the humans who occupied Beringia and provided a cultural foundation for later cultural development of hunting peoples in both Siberia and the Americas.

This ontological and moral context gives rise to questions about differences in northern Aboriginal beliefs between wolves and dogs. In the past, and even today, wolves were animals of the bush *and* non-human persons. It is difficult to know how much to generalize from Henry Sharp's analysis (1976, 2001) about dogs and wolves to other Dene peoples or to the pre-contact world (but see discussion below). However, it is reasonable to assume that at least some Chipewyan understandings would have been shared by other Dene peoples. To Sharp, "Dog and Wolf are metaphorical categories that have a multiple role, particularly of a sexual reference, in expressing certain Chipewyan ideas about nature and culture, ideas that express ambivalence about Man's role as a cultural being" (1976:25), or, as Leach would frame it, where Chipewyans "fit in" to the broader world in which they live/d. Chipewyans and other northern Aboriginal people were well-acquainted with wolves and their habits. They had none of the European fear of wolves, which developed from agrarian cultural and historic circumstances, and possibly even different levels of aggressiveness among populations of wolves elsewhere in the North (e.g., see Mech 1970:289–90). Sir John Richardson called the northern wolves "timid," despite their "large" size. They would "...follow the hunter, and lurk in his neighborhood, to share in the produce of his gun" (1852:292).

Sharp has looked at how Chipewyans conceived of differences and similarities between themselves and wolves, both cooperative hunters of caribou. Differences include the fact that unlike wolves, who like other animals of the bush *know* how to survive and thus obviously have power and knowledge, humans cannot survive "unaided. Humans must be taught; they are not complete unto themselves" (Sharp 2001:66).[22] Similarities included parallels in annual demographic cycle, in abandoning their camps/dens after babies/pups were born, and in eating cooked food (Sharp 1976:31; 2001:75), which Hearne mentioned as something wolves did, though mysteriously *sans* fire (1958:232). Chipewyans regard wolves as being "exceptionally intelligent" and serving "as a model of what Man was and should be" (Sharp 1976:31). Chipewyans traveled widely and were familiar with wolf denning sites, where they would interact with wolf pups, a practice reported by Hearne in the 1770s:

> I have frequently seen the Indians go to their dens, and take out the young ones and play with them. I never knew a Northern Indian hurt one of them: on the contrary, they always put them carefully into the den again; and I have sometimes seen them paint the faces of the young Wolves with vermillion, or red ochre [a mineral with spiritual significance for Aboriginal people].
>
> Hearne 1958:232[23]

This interest has persisted, at least among Chipewyans, who by the late nineteenth century would finally hunt wolves, but "often quite reluctantly" (Sharp and Sharp 2015:14; see Sharp 1996:177). Chipewyans still believe that men and wolves can reincarnate as one another (e.g., Sharp 1976:31; 2001:81), which was one reason that they did not hunt or kill wolves into the twentieth century (or wolverines either; see Hearne 1958:135, 220). Such reluctance was a frequent complaint of both fur traders and game officials; the former wanted the pelts in trade, while the latter shared European understandings about wolves as a scourge: they feared them, believed that they wreaked havoc on game animals, and hoped that Aboriginal hunters would kill them in order to exterminate them (e.g., McCormack 2010:235–41).[24]

For Crees and Ojibwas, wolves can also be animal persons and have power, and there are oral traditions about them. One of the common themes of their stories is that humans must behave properly in order to possess and keep power. In the 1930s, William Berens told several stories to A. Irving Hallowell that featured wolves in some way (Brown and Gray 2009:125). "Wisakedjak and the Water Lions" (Brown and Gray 2009:135–41) is particularly interesting in the way it goes back and forth in its references to wolves and dogs. It is the wolf-persons that have power, but when they behave in ways considered inappropriate or asocial they are called dogs, suggesting not only the cognitive boundary between the two but also the use of this boundary in maintaining cultural values.[25] In this story, the trickster Wisakedjak encounters four wolves. He asks to become a wolf himself and travel with them, presumably to take advantage of their superior abilities to locate game. The old wolf agrees and calls the young wolves – his sons – Wisakedjak's "step-sons" (i.e., Wisakedjak's brother's sons). This kinship reference also paints the old wolf and Wisakedjak as brothers who are hunting together. It is the wolf – the older brother – who has the greater power. The old wolf gives direction several times to Wisakedjak, which he regularly ignores in a disrespectful manner that violates Cree values about respect of younger siblings for their elders. When the young wolf keeping him warm at night would fart, Wisakedjak called him a "Stinking Dog." He is punished by having his food – pemmican – disappear. Later, he is told to carry some wolf dung but refuses to do, calling it "dog dung"; however, it turns out to be "a fine blanket." The old wolf calls a wolf's tooth stuck in a tree the young wolf's arrow, but Wisakedjak calls it "a dog's tooth," only to find that the tooth becomes "a fine arrow." Wasakedjak loses out each time. When they find a place where a moose has been killed, but no moose or moose meat is found there, Wisakedjak refers to "the greedy dogs." When they finally part ways, the old wolf gives Wisakedjak one of his sons to be his step-son, and they travel together like father and son. Later, Wisakedjak dreams about his step-son and in the morning tells him not to jump over any creek or lake if he tracks a moose. The young wolf fails to follow this direction and is killed by a Great Lynx. The story is the preface for the great flood, after which Wisakedjak recreates the world (an earth-diver story). Once the world is made again, Wisakedjak kills the Great Lynx and bring his wolf step-son back to life.

Wolves provided the moral and behavioral template against which dogs were evaluated and defined in traditional Dene and northern Algonquian societies. People must have found it truly wondrous when wolves first began to associate and then to live with them. Creating a place for *dogs* in the world of human society involved cultural shifts toward ambivalence and even disdain that presumably developed at some point during the lengthy process of domestication, as dog ecology and behavior changed. Conceiving of dogs and wolves as different was reflected in terminology, as shown in Table 7.1, which contrasts terms in the two language families spoken in the western Subarctic. A reasonable hypothesis would be that proto-dogs/early dogs would have been

Table 7.1 Terms for wolves and dogs.

	Wolf	*Dog*
Chipewyan (Athapaskan language family)	nuniɛ	łi
Cree (Algonquian language family, y dialect)	mahēkun	ātim

(Anderson 1975; Elford and Elford 1981)

called by terms deriving from terms for wolf, but the terms shown here bear no resemblance at all to one another, suggesting great antiquity in the human concepts of wolves and dogs as distinct from one another. And, at some point in their history together, humans began to give dogs personal names, while wolf-persons who interacted with humans were referred to only by kinship terms, as in the story above.

To the Rock Crees of northern Manitoba, "dogs occupy a multiply ambiguous position in the Cree social universe, possessing neither the sanctity of the wild animal nor the privileges of the house pet" (Brightman 2002:133). These Crees explain that wolves and dogs are enemies because "Wolf envies Dog's protected status as human servant" (ibid.:59). And,

> Before Crees ever saw dogs in sled harnesses, the category "dog" encompassed disparate meanings as the most socialized animal – and hence a logical gift to the spirits who had none – and also as a "dirty" animal who copulates in public, eats feces, and insults the bones of game animals.
> Brightman 2002:184

Dogs were previously "the staple of sacred and sacrificial feasts" (ibid.; see also Mandelbaum 1976:212–13, 216, 224).[26] For example, in 1819 George Back reported about a group of Crees at Muddy Lake, between Norway House and the Pas:

> At our arrival some ceremony of conjuring was going on, for the relief of some sick companion, they had killed a dog for the purpose, and were making certain mixtures with its blood. The measles and hooping cough are so prevalent amongst them that they are constantly perishing.
> in Houston 1994:22; also, Lamb 1970:136; John McDonnell from the mid 1790s in Masson 1889:277; Franklin 1969:47

Crees also handled animal bones carefully. From Cumberland House, Franklin reported:

> Many of the Cree hunters are careful to prevent a woman from partaking of the head of a moose-deer, lest it should spoil their future hunts; and for the same reason they avoid bringing it to a fort, fearing lest the white people should give the bones to the dogs.
> 1969:72

Sharp called the dog a "liminal creature" for Chipewyans, mainly due to its willingness to eat anything, including foods that humans would not (especially feces), and thus become a camp scavenger, counter to Chipewyan ideas of what constitutes proper food (Sharp 1976:27–8). Further, this liminal status is "enhanced by its multiple level use as a metaphor in parts of the Chipewyan symbolic system, in which it functions primarily as a metaphor for women and female sexuality" (1976:28). In Chipewyan, the word for dog is interchangeable with the word for daughter. Dogs are symbolic of "illegitimate sexual intercourse, based on deception and outside of marriage" (ibid.:29), a theme that emerges in several versions of the "Dog Husband" narrative (e.g., Sheppard 1983). This meaning may stem from both the promiscuous mating of dogs in public and from the unconfined bleeding of female dogs when they are in estrus, which probably resonates with menstrual blood, although Sharp did not address this second dimension. Even today, menstruating women may restrict their activities spatially, and in the past they typically retired to a separate structure during their menstrual periods, while dogs roamed everywhere within a camp, and followed separate trails in the bush. That also suggests differential agency and a boundary between women and female dogs, in that women managed their sexuality responsibly, while dogs did not or could not.

Dog sexuality is implicated in the widespread Dene tradition about the woman who married a dog, or the Dog Husband tale. Sheppard collected 11 versions of this story, recorded over a period of 100 years (1983:89). Samuel Hearne's version may be the earliest version:

> They [Chipewyans and Yellowknives] have a tradition among them, that the first person upon earth was a woman, who, after having been some time alone, in her researches for berries, which was then her only food, found an animal like a dog, which followed her to the cave where she lived, and soon grew fond and domestic. This dog, they say, had the art of transforming itself into the shape of a handsome young man, which it frequently did at night, but as the day approached, always resumed its former shape; so that the woman looked on all that passed on those occasions as dreams and delusions. These transformations were soon productive of the consequences which at present generally follow such intimate connexions between the two sexes, and the mother of the world began to advance in her pregnancy.
>
> Hearne 1958:219–20

A giant figure who had earlier marked out all the lakes and waterways killed the dog and:

> …tore it to pieces; the guts he threw into the lakes and rivers, commanding them to become the different kinds of fish; the flesh he dispersed over the land, commanding it to become different kinds of beasts and land-animals; the skin he also tore in small pieces, and threw it into the air, commanding it to become all kinds of birds…
>
> Hearne 1958:220

Hearne's version is part of a much longer and more complex story that is told by all the Dene people in the Mackenzie Basin (e.g., Franklin 1828:294).

In the remaining part of the narrative, the pregnant woman gives birth to puppies, which she discovers can remove their puppy skins during the day and thereby transform into human children. She is able to destroy the skins, or some of the skins, and force those puppies to remain humans. That is, the woman becomes the mother of humans, while the dog becomes the father of the animals. Both were generative, after they mated. In some versions, the dog ancestry is a serious moral indiscretion that taints the children, even after they have a fixed human form (Sheppard 1983). The Chipewyans of the eastern Lake Athabasca region believe that fighting among kin, especially brothers, is the result of the sexual relations between the woman and the dog (Sharp 1976:30). The Dogrib version stands out as one of the few positive stories, in which the transformed puppies are the ancestors of the people, but in a story twist that involves incest, the brothers marrying their sisters (Helm 2000:289–90; Sheppard 1983:96). Thanks to their dog ancestry, "those two boys that she raised were the finest hunters and the bravest fighters and the best medicine men that ever lived" (Helm 2000:290). The Dogrib story resonates more with the marriages between humans and animal persons than do the other Dog Husband stories, in which the dog, even though he can transform, is not fully equivalent to other animal persons. Yet he still plays a pivotal kinship role in Dene mythology and should not be eaten.

Among Chipewyans, dogs and women were restricted from eating some animal parts, including male and female "parts of generation," for it would ruin the hunting (Hearne 1958:205). Alexander Mackenzie said that women were not allowed to touch the skins of bears or wolves (Lamb 1970:153). Bernard Ross reported that women and dogs should not eat moose-nose or animal hearts, or "the hunters would lose their skill" (1859:195). Even in the twentieth century, the Hare did not allow dogs to eat animal bones or parts of certain animals (Savishinsky 1975:486). If meat was not abundant, dogs receive "only the odds and ends of butchering…, or meat that is unfit [or not preferred?] for human consumption (Sharp 1976:27), what Leonard Plotnicov has termed "trash food" (2008). The restrictions occurred even though the difficulties of feeding dogs adequately is a theme that runs throughout the northern literature. If people ran short of food, it was dogs that went hungry first, and died of starvation, before humans did. Northern people considered it more important to show the proper respect to animal prey, which could choose whether or not to make themselves available to the hunters, than to feed inappropriate items even to starving dogs.

Women also had/have the power to harm dogs in ways that reflected their power to harm men and their hunting abilities. Among the Chipewyan, "if a woman had stepped over one's dog harnesses, the dogs would grow weak, perhaps even die if the services of a person with *inkonze* [spiritual power] were not employed" (Smith 1973:13), a clear allusion to women's menstrual powers. The Hare also believed that women should avoid stepping over a dog harness, or the family's female dog might bear only the less desired female pups (Savishinsky 1975:485). People with spiritual power could harm other people's dogs (ibid.:17). At the same time, dogs that are abused have the power to "bring retribution" on the abuser, though it is visited upon someone with a sexual connection to the abuser, not the abuser him(her)self. While Sharp does not consider this power to be *inkonze*, he admits it is a form of power nevertheless (2001:88, 90).

A third factor is also at play. Unlike wolves, northern dogs cannot survive independently, which Chipewyans consider to be evidence that dogs lack the *power – inkonze –* of the wolves from which they are descended and which are self-sufficient. Dogs need "substantial" food and care which are provided by humans (Sharp 2001:85, 88). Another aspect of dependency that contributes to the boundary between dogs and humans is the persistent dependence of puppies/dogs on humans psychologically. As Mech has pointed out, even among wolves the extension of "friendliness… seems to be a reward in itself" (1970:134), and that is certainly the case for dog puppies. Part of the appeal of puppies is their ability and eagerness to establish social and emotional bonds with their owners. While puppies and children parallel one another in this ability, dogs, unlike children, remain dependent for their entire lives. They are like children who never learn proper behaviors or become fully functioning adults.[27] There may also be some resonance between the way humans regard adult dog dependence and the lack of respect for old age and how those "past labor" were neglected in the past in some Dene societies, including the Chipewyans (e.g., Hearne 1958:221).

Issues of dependence and autonomy were addressed by Joel Savishinsky in his work about the roles of dogs within Hare society, especially the emotional ties between dogs and their humans (1974; 1975). The Hare and other northern hunting societies are characterized by what he termed "features of affective restraint and containment" (Savishinsky 1975:476; see also Cohen and VanStone 1964). However, adults engaged emotionally with children and puppies. Both were "spoiled," "played with," and indulged in multiple ways (Savishinsky 1975:476). Puppies and children were named and understood to have individual personalities. Children learned about adult dogs by raising puppies. As Savishinsky explained, the "pups become the children's children," or "the child is father [mother] to the dog" (ibid.:485). That explains why an adult without children or whose children were grown might be referred to teknonymously by the name of his favorite dog, a practice with great antiquity (ibid.:484; cf. Ross 1859:194). Dogs, which could be reincarnated as newly born puppies, learned about humans from their close relationships with children and their parents.

As children reached the age of 5–6 years, and puppies 6–7 months, both began to learn new roles, which involved "discipline, commands, and reprimands" (Savishinsky 1975:480–1; compare with Orr 2016:69). By then, children were expected to begin to contribute economically to their households, and puppies were mostly full-grown in size. It was a difficult adjustment for both pups and children. While children traditionally learned skills and emotional restraint by experience, observation, and listening to oral traditions, it would have been far harder for dogs, in the absence of formal training, which undoubtedly led to frustrations among their human owners/keepers even in the days when there were few dogs and they had fewer responsibilities in the pre-fur trade hunting economy. In the post-contact era, if not earlier, such frustration was demonstrated in verbal and physical abuse visited on dogs in all the northern societies. Dogs were also a surrogate for the venting of human anger and aggression. That is, dogs were yelled at and beaten, often savagely. At the same time, people cared for their dogs, talked about them, watched them, and took special care of sick or injured dogs (e.g., Savishinsky 1975:485). They would go to great lengths to avoid having to kill an old or sick dog, which signified that dogs were a markedly different type of animal from those of the bush (ibid.:486; Sharp 1976). That also speaks to persistent emotional connections between people and their dogs.

Savishinsky argued that boys are given a longer period of carefree childhood than are girls, who are expected to take on adult responsibilities more rapidly. In the past, if there were a shortage of food, it was girls who were more likely to suffer than boys. Even Bernard Ross wrote in the mid 1800s that boys "are invariably more cherished and cared for than females," and girls are subordinated to their brothers (1872:310; see also Richardson 1852:250). Evidence also exists for preferential female infanticide (Wentzel in Masson 1889:86; Helm 1980; Krech 1978:715). Similarly, female dogs were less valued, and female puppies were sometimes killed at birth, because female dogs were considered smaller and less useful and as adults were disruptive when in heat (Savishinsky 1975:483). These cultural and social traditions almost certainly pre-dated contact with Europeans and provided the basic substrate for post-contact treatment of dogs.

While anthropologists have tended to emphasise the economic roles of dogs in human society (e.g., Clutton-Brock 1994), there is little evidence that dogs played *substantial* economic roles in northern Athapaskan and Algonquian societies at contact and in early post-contact times, other than assisting in transport. Dogs are frequently presumed to have helped in hunting, but such uses may have been limited. For example, W. F. Wentzel, at the Forks of the Mackenzie River in 1807, said that "In summer and winter, they pursue them [elk and caribou] with dogs into snares" (in Masson 1889:81; see also George Keith in Masson 1890:66).[28] Similarly, Richardson wrote about "a small breed of dogs" helping to hunt moose in the Mackenzie River region in the spring. "The dogs run lightly over the crusted snow, and hold the animal at bay until the Indian comes up in his snowshoes" (Richardson 1852:257; see also Ross 1861a:436). These were undoubtedly Richardson's Hare Indian Dogs. It is difficult to train dogs not to bark or vocalize when they see game, which might be useful in driving but would otherwise frighten game away from the hunters, including animals that have been wounded and might settle nearby if not disturbed. James Isham described Aboriginal people, probably Crees, using dogs to hunt beavers in the mid 1700s:

> [W]hen they are hunting Beaver they turn the Dogs into the house [beaver lodge], who wurries the Beaver into the Vaults, imagining the Dogs can not come at them their [there], by which means the Indians open's the Vault's and Catches them.
>
> Rich 1949:164

David Thompson also wrote about Crees hunting with dogs, by using dogs to locate "the weakest part of the Beaver House, and the park where they lie," and to locate bear dens in winter (Moreau 2009:193, 123).

The inherent territoriality of dogs would have helped them guard a camp by announcing strangers, but their barking could also reveal its location to enemies. For example, in the early nineteenth century Hare Indians hid from strangers arriving in boats on the river (Richardson 1852:131), a strategy that worked only if they could keep the dogs silent.

In the past, even as late as c. 1900, there were few dogs at best in First Nations camps; most dogs were at the posts, where men and their families were tasked with putting up food to feed both the post occupants and their dogs. Some groups may have lacked dogs completely. When starvation killed people on the Mackenzie River in the winter of 1810–11, it almost certainly meant that most if not all of the dogs in the region also died (Wentzel in Masson 1889:106–7). Starvation sometimes affected the posts as well, especially in earlier times, and they too lost dogs during periods of privation.

It is difficult to assess the pre-contact importance of dogs in transport. Before the advent of the fur trade, people moved less and had fewer possessions. Sleighs were small, and hauling sleighs was undertaken by women and girls. Dogs were mostly used for packing. Thus, it seems likely that there was less demand for dogs to assist in transport before people committed to the fur trade. One consequence of the eventual commitment to trapping in the mid nineteenth century would be a great expansion in the economic role of dogs.

It does not seem to be much of a stretch to say that dogs may have been as important to these northern hunting societies for emotional and symbolic reasons as for economic reasons, even if today it is difficult to identify those reasons. Dogs may have been valued because they brought companionship and pleasure to northern men, women, and their children. While dogs may still not have been "pets" in the sense described by Sharp (2001:87), they probably led somewhat different lives than later in the fur trade. Before dogs increased in number, and the resource base declined, dogs should have been fed more regularly, though they would still have been camp scavengers. Dogs may also have played other roles that have not made it into the primary literature.[29] Dogs and humans living together involved a form of interspecies communication and intersubjectivity that produced benefits for both species and led humans to want to have dogs living with them and to care for them, physically and emotionally.

How did the early fur trade affect Aboriginal people and their dogs?

The context for this discussion is the development of the commercial fur trade in northern and western Canada by French, English, and Scottish enterprises. The companies that operated in the western Subarctic were dominated by the North West Company, whose headquarters and center of operations were in Montreal, and the Hudson's Bay Company, whose headquarters were in London but ran its business in the western Subarctic from York Factory, a major depôt on the west side of Hudson's Bay (e.g., Innis 1964; Payne 1989). Each company had subsidiary posts and outposts, organized in a descending hierarchy of size and responsibility. In the western Subarctic, the major posts were Île-à-la-Crosse (on Lac Île-à-la-Crosse, near the Methye Portage, the major route to the Mackenzie Basin), Fort Chipewyan (Lake Athabasca), Fort Resolution (Great Slave Lake), and Fort Simpson (Mackenzie River).[30] Traders relied on combinations of water and overland transport to import trade goods and get them to the consumers (the Aboriginal population and their own workers), to export furs, and to look after their own provisioning needs (fur trade posts were responsible for virtually all of their food until the mid twentieth century). The traders and their employees used dogs to haul sleighs until the advent of the Ski-Doo in 1959 and its rapid spread throughout the Subarctic (Ski-Doo 2003–2017).[31]

The fur trade was a form of merchant capitalism that incorporated Aboriginal people into the marketplace as producers and consumers. However, even those people who became heavily involved in the fur trade continued to produce most of their own food from bush resources until the years that followed World War II. This production for use represented the persistence of the pre-contact domestic mode of production, which now became one component of a new mixed economy that I have called a "fur trade mode of production" (McCormack 2010:chp. 3; 1984). It featured two new economic components: production for exchange, or independent (petty) commodity production, and wage labor, reimbursed until the twentieth century by exchange credits.[32] The fur traders themselves and especially their employees also entered into this new fur trade mode of production (McCormack 2010:chp. 3).

The increase in the scale of the fur trade during the nineteenth century was predicated on two factors: first, the willingness of Aboriginal people (then, "Indians"; now, First Nations)[33] to commit to regular *trapping* as opposed to the casual collection of furs, and second, a new complex of material goods that was used in sled technology and in producing food for dogs. Sled technology and dog accoutrements were a synthesis of Aboriginal and European – especially Quebecois – material culture and ideas. It was this post-contact complex invoked by Savishinsky (1974; 1975) and Sharp (1976) when they talked about how Dene men were "dependent" on dogs for travel. The dogs themselves changed due to hybridization with European dogs and undoubtedly some selective breeding to produce the larger, stronger dogs that were more suitable for hauling sleds than were the indigenous dogs. And, more dogs were needed, both by the post for its operations and by Aboriginal trappers, so the number of dogs increased substantially.

The fact that European goods were available and that Aboriginal people wanted at least some of them does not mean that they wanted to become *trappers*.[34] Much was written by European traders and travellers about the "indolence" of the Indians, including those living in the Mackenzie Basin, whom they believed should have become busy at trapping fur-bearers and producing provisions. They were perplexed when Indians actually produced *less* if prices paid for furs (exchange values) increased. Many Indians were reluctant to become involved in the fur trade in any major way.

Even Samuel Hearne was conflicted about this point:

> It is undoubtedly the duty of every one of the Company's servants to encourage a spirit of industry among the natives, and to use every means in their power to induce them to procure furs and other commodities for trade... But I must at the same time confess, that such conduct is by no means for the real benefit of the poor Indians; it being well known that those who have the least intercourse with the Factories are by far the happiest.
>
> Hearne 1958:52

He pointed out that Chipewyans lived more easily by following their traditional way of life, because they had few "real wants," while at the same time he bemoaned how it "...is too apt to occasion a habitual indolence in the young and active" (ibid.:51). By the early 1770s, only the "aged and infirm, the women and children, a few of the more indolent and unambitious part of them [men], will submit to remain in the parts where food and clothing are procured in this easy manner, because no animals are produced there whose furrs are valuable." Yet "...those who endeavour to possess more, are always the most unhappy" and likely to starve when they made the long trek to Fort Prince of Wales (also, Fort Churchill) (Hearne 1958:51, 52, 212–13; also, see Wentzel from 1807, in Masson 1889:95). He believed that the fur trade could fill the gap: "...those who do not get their livelihood at so easy a rate, generally procure furrs enough during the Winter to purchase a sufficient supply of ammunition, and other European goods, to last them another year" (ibid.:51).

The pre-contact/early post-contact economy was based on animal populations that were inherently unstable and sometimes cyclical (e.g., Waisberg 1975).[35] Nevertheless, it still allowed people to produce good, reliable livelihoods when they organized their activities and annual cycle mainly for subsistence. If they committed to trapping, they became vulnerable to the market for furs, also inherently unstable, and were forced to re-organize their annual cycles to feed themselves *and* to obtain furs – rarely an easy balance. Contrary to Hearne, it was not always enough to have access to fur trade goods.

By Hearne's time, Chipewyans had begun to move further south to the Slave River and the lands surrounding the western end of Lake Athabasca (e.g., Gillespie 1975). This process was still underway in 1778, when Peter Pond and his men became the first Europeans to visit the region (e.g., Innis 1964:152, 196; Parker 1987:6, 28), when they discovered that the Athabasca region was amazingly rich in both fur and food resources, which contributed to the formation of the North West Company. Pond made subsequent trips, one of which was in 1781, the same year that Chipewyans and Crees suffered the ravages of the first major epidemic in the western Subarctic, a smallpox epidemic that spread north from the Saskatchewan River (e.g., Lamb 1970:76; Innis 1964:152; Ray 1974:105–6; Parker 1987:6–7).[36] The Hudson's Bay Company sent competing traders to Lake Athabasca in 1791–92 and 1802–06, when Peter Fidler ran Nottingham House. Competition there and elsewhere triggered often-vicious conflict between the two companies that continued until the amalgamation of the two companies in 1821 under the Hudson's Bay Company name. While Chipewyans and Crees trading at Fort Chipewyan took advantage of the seller's market, they had not yet become committed to trapping and a fur trade-focused way of life (see Wentzel in Masson 1889:96). Many Aboriginal groups also continued in conflict with one another, engaging in trade and/or raids as a way to obtain furs from other groups.[37] Outright warfare and enmity continued until at least 1822–25, when the Dogribs finally rose up against their Yellowknife oppressors (e.g., Helm 1981:294).

The conflicts of this period were directly implicated in the extraordinary events of 1814, when the Chipewyans and Yellowknives killed all their dogs. A number of factors were responsible, though it may never be clear how they all intersected.

First, at Fort Chipewyan, the gateway to the Mackenzie Basin, some North West Company men resorted to savage methods to force Chipewyans to trap. They seized wives of Chipewyan men for their own uses, sometimes holding them hostage so that the men would be forced to trap. For example, Wenzel wrote about a "Canadian beast" who "pillaged" a native of his wife (Krech 1983). They violated local cultural precepts about sharing and reciprocity. On 14 February 1788, Alexander Mackenzie wrote to his North West Company partners: "'The men who have remained with the Indians last summer were, and still are, of great injury to the concern by their vicious example and influence'" (quoted by MacKenzie in Masson 1889:29). At least some of the Indians were worried about having to repay credit – their "debts" – that had been extended to them, which would have been a culturally novel and unpalatable concept (e.g., Wentzel in Keith 2001:108).

Second, infectious diseases had spread to the North and continued to do so with regularity. Many were virgin soil epidemics, in which extensive sickness and high mortality undermined social networks, with starvation a common result (Crosby 1976; McCormack 1996). The 1781 smallpox epidemic probably reached Lake Athabasca and was reported to have affected even the wolves and dogs that preyed on the dead. Once the human bodies had been consumed, many dogs would have died from starvation as well. It was in 1807 that Wentzel reported the "distemper" that was killing animals "in great numbers," along with the dogs and humans that ate those animals (in Keith 2001:300, 303, 305, 314). In 1808, James Keith reported sickness killing several people at Mackenzie's River (in Masson 1890:79).[38] If disease was present in the Mackenzie River region, it almost certainly passed through Fort Chipewyan, even if there are no reports about it in the extant literature. Starvation occurred at other times, such as the "disastrous" winter of 1810–11 and again in 1811–12, due to the disappearance of hares and the scarcity of large game (Wentzel in Masson 1889:106–7; Keith in Masson 1890:96). The fact that people typically destroyed their personal property following deaths in their families may have contributed to more extensive starvation from both diseases and resource scarcity.

Third, the animal resources diminished. In 1814, Wentzel claimed that "Athabaska itself is in fact dwindling down to nothing. The Indians complain of the want of beaver, (the Iroquois having ruined the country)…" (in Masson 1889:109; see Ferguson 1993). The North West Company had recruited Iroquois and Ojibwas (Saulteaux) to the area because the local Indians were not trapping as intensively as the company wished (that is, they had not yet become *trappers*). David Thompson claimed that the Natives of the country believed that there was a spiritual relationship between disease affecting people and animal decrease. Specifically, before they were attacked by the first smallpox epidemic of 1781–82, "…all the animals of every species were also very numerous and more so in comparison of the number of Natives at present," while the animals in the years after had declined in number, but without any "disorder" that might have killed them (Moreau 2009:119, also p. 186). Instead, diminished animal numbers was a "calamity" brought on by the "Great Spirit," who had taken away the animals "in the same proportion as they were not wanted…and if there were no Men there would be no Animals" (ibid.:287). Thus, "…it might justly be supposed the destruction of Mankind would allow the animals to increase…" (ibid.:120). There is nothing to suggest that Thompson meant to include dogs in his statements, but certainly people would have seen the deaths of dogs as an empirical reality consequent to both infectious diseases and human starvation.

We should not underestimate the emotional and existential trauma that must have followed in the wake of the deaths of entire social communities and the need to reconstitute those communities, along with the conjectures by local people about the causes of these diseases, which usually pointed to the malicious intent of people with *power*. When food was in short supply, or absent altogether, the less productive members of the society were the first to perish, and that included dogs too. Among Crees, the incidence of the *wīhtikōw*, in which humans begin to crave human flesh, may have increased dramatically, due both to occasional cannibalism following starvation and to ideological fears as the entrenchment of the fur trade meant that a new social order with new values was being constructed. Neal McLeod (2002:37) has speculated about the "narrative holes" that emerged after contact, when oral traditions could not longer fully "explain the world." Joel Robbins (2007) has conjectured about a philosophical rupture as the world changed for local people that would facilitate later conversion to Christianity.

Unrest had been building in the Fort Chipewyan region since at least 1812, due to all these factors, when a tower was erected at Fort Chipewyan "...for the purpose of watching the motions of the Indians, who intended, as it was then reported, to destroy the house and all its inhabitants" (Franklin 1969:152). Local Aboriginal people may have been influenced by some earlier events. At the beginning of the nineteenth century, some Chipewyans at Lake Athabasca killed four North West Company traders, which Peter Fidler claimed was "richly merited" (Krech 1983:35). In the winter of 1812–13, Slaveys killed Alexander Henry, his family, and *engagés* at Fort Nelson, a total of 16–18 in all (Rich 1938:394; Keith 2001:65; Krech 1983:35–6). Although George Keith deplored the massacre, he acknowledged it may have been justified "'by the motive of self-existence or preservation as they have subsequently loudly proclaimed... Distress reduced to *absolute despair* for want of ammunition exclusive of other grievances brought on our awful misfortunate'" (Keith 2001:65; emphasis added). There were threats of violence elsewhere (ibid.:66), though remarkably little real violence by Aboriginal people was visited on fur traders. In 1815, Wentzel commented on the general state of unrest:

> I cannot account for it, but, by some fatality or other, the Natives had taken a dislike to the Whites, and the reductions of the returns may perhaps be as much attributed to this unfortunate circumstance as it may be to the pretended ruined state of the country.
>
> in Masson 1889:114

It was also in this year that the North West Company abandoned the Mackenzie River posts (Keith 2001:66), even though by this time the Dene people had begun to shift to firearms, ammunition, and other imported material goods. It must have seemed catastrophic to the Dene who no longer had access to some now-important trade items, and it would bring them to heel – to be more accommodating of the needs and desires of the fur traders – when the posts returned.

The events at Fort Chipewyan must be understood within this broader picture of Dene (and Cree?) unhappiness, fear, and desperation. In 1813, Wentzel wrote:

> They [the Indians] formed a conspiracy last Spring [1813] to massacre all the whites of Fort Chipewyan and Big Island, in the Peace River, as well

as Moose Deer Island Establishment at Slave Lake. The Chipewean tribe appears to have been the first instigators, and altho' the affair seems to have been laid aside and forgotten, still we are alive to the most painful apprehensions for the safety of our lives.

in Masson 1889:109–10

Sir John Franklin reported on what he heard about this "conspiracy" while on his trip through the area in 1819–22 (1969). They had been instigated by a "prophet," an Indian skilled in "necromancy" who:

> ...prophesied that there would soon be a complete change in the face of their country; that fertility and plenty would succeed to the present sterility; and that the present race of white inhabitants, unless they became subservient to the Indians, would be removed, and their place be filled by other traders, who would supply their wants in every possible manner.
>
> Franklin 1969:152

> ...the northern Indians had cherished a belief for some years that a great change was about to take place in the natural order of things, and that among other advantages arising from it, their own condition of life was to be materially bettered.
>
> Franklin 1828:305

In his 1828 *Narrative*, based on travels from 1825 to 1827, Franklin wrote that this story "originated with a woman," but not necessarily one from the Athabasca region (1828:305). With specific reference to their dogs:

> The Northern Indians suppose that they originally sprang from a dog; and, about five years ago, a superstitious fanatic [the prophet, above?] so strongly pressed upon their minds the impropriety of employing these animals, *to which they were related*, for purposes of labour, that they universally resolved against using them any more, and, strange as it may seem, destroyed them.
>
> Franklin 1969:160, emphasis added

How can Franklin's account be interpreted? It is tempting to look to the Dene oral tradition that death of the Dog Husband had produced the animals of the world; perhaps sacrificing their dogs was an attempt to re-enact this story. Also, the prophet may have been influenced by Cree traditions about sacrificing dogs, which could be construed as a point of confluence with the Dene story.[39] And, inasmuch as the dogs were kinsmen of a kind, Chipewyans may not have seen it as right to direct or force them to work in the same ways that the traders were trying to force the people to work. Chipewyans were almost certainly put off by the practice by the fur traders of eating dogs, anathema to Chipewyans and other Dene peoples.

In the end, the enormous sacrifice that Chipewyans and Yellowknives made when they killed their dogs did not produce the "great change" that their prophet had predicted. The failure put an end to this millennial movement, which was succeeded by the eventual commitment of Chipewyans and Crees to the fur trade, probably in the second quarter of the nineteenth century, as peace was coming to the entire region, and the development of a new culture of dog use. By the time of the second Franklin Overland Expedition, Chipewyan and Copper (Yellowknife) women were again "employing dogs to drag their sledges," which Franklin considered "a most happy relief" for these women (1828:303).

A multi-species ethnohistory

For the most part, both Aboriginal people and their dogs would suffer in the years that followed, when people became committed to trapping. To be a *sled dog* was a highly specialized role for which little or no formal training seems to have been provided. Looking at dogs and humans as part of the same society – a multi-species study – during the era of the fur trade will lead to what Sherry Ortner has termed "dark anthropology," but with a peculiar twist on the species that humans exploited for their own purposes, often in "harsh and brutal" ways (2016). Previously, dogs had enjoyed some autonomy, despite their overall dependence; once they were forced into fur trade-related transport, they could be and were dominated more extensively by their human keepers/care-givers/owners, whether those were First Nations living in small camps or settlements on the land or fur trade employees who lived at the post. Dogs would increase in numbers and shift from female to male domains.

That story will be told in the second half of this ethnohistory, which will feature *Canadien* workers from Quebec who came to the Canadian Northwest after having developed their own traditions of horse and dog winter transport to adapt to snow-filled winters, based on a synthesis of earlier European traditions and practices of Quebec Indians (Ferland and Fournier 2007). It was those new forms of dog sleds, dog teams, and even the dogs themselves that would come to dominate the lives of the posts and of Aboriginal people too, and provide the bases for the stereotypes and mythologies summarized earlier in the paper. These developments were already occurring in the northern Plains and Parkland by 1800. The new complex of dogs, technology, and dog-related behavior, dominated by men, moved rapidly into the North in the early nineteenth century to serve the fur traders and the posts and eventually was adopted by First Nations living in their own social communities in the bush. The dogs themselves, along with their Aboriginal owners, would often live lives of tragedy and sorrow, despite becoming some of Canada's foremost romantic images.

Tim Ingold contends that "...every living being is a line, or, better, a bundle of lines" (2015), and that the living beings that interact are entangled into a "meshwork." Humans "grow themselves and, since their growth is conditioned by the presence and actions of others, they grow one another" (ibid.:120). To survive, they must attend "to the trajectories of these non-human lives" – the plants, animals, and materials (ibid.:155). Humans and non-human animals each have knowledge, which "...consists not in propositions about the world but in the skills of perception and capacities of judgement that develop in the course of direct, practical and sensuous engagements with the beings and things with whom, and with which, we share our lives" (ibid.:157). His argument easily encompasses domestic dogs and the other animals with whom humans interact, both domestic and "wild." It relates to Gala Argent's quest for "...an approach which considers animals as 'minded and self-aware participants in collective action with their human associates'" and that can be "...mutually cooperative rather than unilaterally exploitative..." (2013:179). Similarly, Clinton Sanders has argued that non-human animals are "authentic" social actors:

> The animal self...is constituted by the animal-actor's recognizing he or she is distinct from others and can engage in volitional behavior; that moods and feelings are connected to experiences, places, and relationships; and that past events are relevant to the emotional experience of and physical response to current situations.
>
> Sanders 2007:327

The lives of humans and dogs have been intimately intertwined for millennia.[40] The relations they have with one another are inherently social, and the boundaries between them are fluid and diverse. Those boundaries are regularly redefined, crossed, and in conflict (Mullin 1999).[41] Brian Hare has argued that dogs have lived successfully with humans because dogs *use* humans to solve problems. "Dogs excel, relative to other animals, at using human behaviors to learn about the world and modify their own behavior" (2004:277). He goes so far as to propose that "many dogs can even be characterized as human tool users because they intentionally elicit help from humans if they are unable to solve a problem by themselves" (ibid.). In short, he is talking about the *agency* of dogs. Human societies do not consist of humans alone but involve an interspecies sociality in which dogs, other animals, and non-human persons may be present, sentient, exercise agency, and play roles in human lives. These are lived relations that are co-constitutive and mutually affective (see Latimer 2013:80; Latimer and Miele 2013; Maurstad et al. 2013; Fuentes 2010).

Thus, dogs are implicated in the construction of humans as a special kind of animal and of human societies. As Brightman has pointed out for the Rock Cree, the boundaries between human and animal categories are "continuous rather than discrete" (2002:3; also in Mullin 1999:209). In northern

Aboriginal societies, dogs were a liminal animal, sharing in both the worlds of wolves and of humans. Traditional Dene oral traditions resonate with the theme of dogs as founding members, both good and bad. Dogs may not be as powerful as the animals of the bush, but they have retained some measure of power nevertheless. In northern Algonquian societies, dogs could make appeals on the behalf of humans to non-human powers. Dogs were parts of northern Aboriginal families and the local bands in which they lived, and the raising of puppies parallelled the raising of children. Each had different but related adult roles, which included economic roles vis-à-vis one another.

In short, the joint societies of humans and dogs in the western Subarctic involved a form of intersubjectivity in which both dogs and humans engaged in learning so that they could interact successfully with one another. Dogs *aligned* themselves with humans, and the minds of both were "the outcome of social interaction and social experience" (Sanders 2007:323). This recognition is at the heart of the new idea of multi-species ethnography – Kohn's "anthropology beyond the human" – and it serves to collapse an artificial dichotomy between "nature" and "culture." Some scholars are using the new term "natureculture" "to suggest that nature and culture are not two different things, but a matrix of contrasts" and that "...humans – and everything that humans are and do – are always in connection with the other non-humans that make up the world at any one time" (Latimer and Miele 2013:11, 16).

As Donna Haraway has pointed out about her dog, and by implication about other dogs, "We are training each other in acts of communication we barely understand. We are, constitutively, companion species" (2003). When wolves in Eurasia thousands of years ago learned to "get on together" with humans (Haraway 2003:7), that relationship produced dogs, which then co-evolved with humans. As Haraway sees it, dogs are "partners in the crime of human evolution, they are in the garden from the get-go, wily as Coyote" (ibid.:5). Thus, most human societies, and certainly all those deriving from the North, are historically composite societies featuring a Mitochondrial Bitch and a Mitochondrial Eve (ibid.:5).

The dogs and people of the western Subarctic are both directly descended from the dogs and people of Beringia. This paper has sought to read the data closely in the context of my own background as an ethnohistorian of this region to expand on the complex history of northern dogs as integral parts of western Subarctic societies for the *longue durée* before those relationships were altered by the new economic, political, and social realities of European fur traders and the capitalist economy they brought to the Canadian Northwest.

Notes

1 Aboriginal people are often reluctant or unwilling to talk about such beliefs with others, knowing well about non-Aboriginal scepticism and not wishing to be the victims of scorn or ridicule.

2 Formal breeds and breed registration are a development since the mid-nineteenth century that have produced highly inbred lines of dogs. Some types of dogs have been "reconstructed" for particular phenotypes, but without reconstructing original genotypes (Parker et al. 2004).

3 Similarly, there seem to have been few dogs in the Arctic region during Paleoeskimo times and even into the contact-era Neoeskimo or Inuit world (e.g., Savelle et al. 2014:140).

4 For a discussion of *which* humans those may have been, there is much discussion about whether pre-modern *Homo sapiens* populations were distinctive species or simply "archaic *Homo sapiens*" that evolved into modern *H. sapiens* (i.e., subspecies) (e.g., Clark 2002). The literatures about evolving humans and wolves evolving into dogs seem to exist in separate silos.

5 This new nomenclature seems to have been imposed for terminological and genetic reasons but without any other consideration of whether or not dogs should be considered a separate species. A series of articles about "Case 3010" in the *Bulletin of Zoological Nomenclature* addressed issues relating to "15 mammal specific names based on wild species which are antedated by or contemporary with those based on domestic animals." The case was proposed in 1996 and a formal opinion issued in March 2003 (Gentry et al. 1996; International Commission on Zoological Nomenclature 2003). It would be interesting to compare the discourse surrounding wolf and dog evolution, though beyond the scope of this paper, to issues surrounding the discourse about human evolution (e.g., Marks 2012).

6 Another potential line of genetic information that to date has not been used is the investigation of parasites that are pandemic among dogs, such as roundworms and tapeworms, and that can also be transmitted to humans. *Toxacara canis*, the dog roundworm, is an especially likely candidate. It passes through the placenta to puppies, which means that one might look for correspondences between the evolutionary histories of mtDNAs of both species. It could also lead to hypotheses for diseases spread by dogs – zoonoses – prior to the arrival of European dogs, which would have brought different genetic strains to the Americas. Such research would parallel current investigations into the co-evolution of humans and body lice (e.g., Boutellis et al. 2014; Toups et al. 2011).

7 Dogs are also able to bond with individuals from other species as well, although the articles about dog cognition and social skills do not address that ability.

8 This section does not attempt to review the large literature on the peopling of the Americas.

9 In the papers cited, evolutionary dates are typically given with various kinds of qualification, such as "calibrated" or "calendar" years before present (BP), which are omitted here. The earlier date presumes a route down the west coast; the later date would be down a newly viable ice-free corridor formed by the retreating glaciers.

10 For Crees further west, there is some later anecdotal evidence from Alexander Mackenzie about dogs hauling loads on sleds (Lamb 1970:135), but he also wrote about how the Canadians who replaced the French in the fur trade themselves dragged their property using sledges (ibid.:71). Among Crees of the northern Plains, whose origins lie in the Subarctic, dogs were used to haul travois, but according to Fine-day, an elder born c. 1850, they never pulled toboggans (sleds) until they saw men from the Hudson's Bay Company use dogs in this way. "As soon as we saw the toboggans we all began to make them because otherwise we

could only pack a little on a dog" (Mandelbaum 1979:67). Wentzel referred to "sleighs," which he wrote as "Slays" (Keith 2001:221), so this term must have been in common use.

11 Today, zoological nomenclature does not have a rank of "variety," which exists only in botanical classifications. Names published before 1961 as "varieties" might today be considered subspecies (Wikipedia 2017).

12 Stanley Olsen's "Early Domestic Dogs in North America" (1974) only looked at dogs in the United States.

13 Sarah Broadhurst, the Archivist and Records Manager of the Zoological Society of London, looked unsuccessfully for this address; it was evidently not published in the Transactions. While it is possible that the bones of the dogs that were placed in the zoo were retained for the Natural History Museum, full record of which bones were deposited there does not exist (Sarah Broadhurst, email communication, 17 March 2017).

14 Email correspondence is underway with the Smithsonian Institution and scholars about these possibilities.

15 So far, I have not been able to locate a back translation of this term into English; it was probably a unique term in the so-called "rababou" mixture of languages spoken in the Northwest.

16 It might be revealing to test northern Aboriginal dogs today for mtDNA and Y-chromosomes. If it was mostly male dogs that were imported, the two lines of evidence may tell different stories about ancestry.

17 A charming children's book by Ainslie Manson, *A Dog Came, Too*, tells the story of "Our Dog" (1992). Similarly, Gail Karwoski wrote about Seaman, a large black dog who accompanied Lewis and Clark in 1803 on their western trip to the Pacific (1999).

18 It is interesting that the term "bulldog" is commonly used in the North for a very large and aggressive biting fly, although the age of this term is unknown. George Keith, a trader for the North West Company, referred to the "horse fly" in 1812 (in Masson 1890:102). The emergence of a new term suggests that northern Aboriginal people had a chance to see bulldogs fight. While I gloss bulldog and horsefly as the same kind of biting insect, the Chipewyan language distinguishes between them. A bulldog is *tl'izi*, and a horsefly, *tl'izaze*, or a small bulldog (Elford and Elford 1981:9). Sharp and Sharp describe bulldogs, which they calls a large deer fly, found in Chipewyan lands as being the size of a man's thumb (2015:129–30).

19 Wolves and dogs take some instinctive measures to avoid disease pathogens (Hart 2011), but indigenous dogs can be expected to have been overwhelmed by newly introduced infectious diseases, perhaps even more than humans were, given their often-malnourished conditions.

20 The use of the term "distemper" was intended to mean an illness or disorder, not the set of viral diseases known formally today as distemper.

21 Like humans (Ingold 2010), dogs and other animals engage with the world directly and therefore become "knowledgeable." However, each species has its own unique senses and will therefore learn different things. Dogs, for example, have a much keener sense of smell than do humans. In the world of animism, which Philippe Descola calls one kind "of inference about the identities of beings in the world" (2014:277), this approach is one in which there are "identical internal essences… lodged in different types of bodies," which means that each kind of being will have its own perspective on the world (ibid.:275).

22 Contrary to this belief, wolf studies have shown that even wolf pups do not survive by instinct alone; they are actively taught skills critical for survival by adult members of the pack.
23 The fur trade term "Northern Indian" was usually equated with Chipewyans, but Hearne's use might also include the Yellowknives; he travelled with people from both cultural traditions in his journeys in the early 1770s.
24 Even today, Alberta game managers have a policy to kill wolves, ostensibly for game conservation reasons. They also allow the private payment of wolf bounties. Lurking in the background of these decisions is the long history of attempts to eradicate wolves.
25 Similarly, among Chipewyans "*Chi-pai-uk-tim*" – you dead dog – was "a most opprobrious epithet," according to Richardson (1852:246).
26 French and mixed ancestry fur trade employees (proto-Métis and Métis), were fond of eating dogs. For example, Alexander Henry the Younger wrote that "My people prefer eating Fat Dogs from the Indians to eat than to live upon lean Buffalo Meat" (Gough 1992:488).
27 Harald Broch has pointed out that the Matinen in East Indonesia "…say that is of no use to punish dogs because they are like children; they do not understand when they misbehave" (2008:60). Northern Aboriginal peoples did not share this sentiment but expected their dogs to learn from observing and doing.
28 However, caribou snares were frequently set into caribou "fences," and there is little evidence of dogs being used in that hunting.
29 For example, I was told in Fort Chipewyan that sores on the faces of children (such as those caused by impetigo, a bacterial skin infection) can be treated by putting grease on their faces and then letting the family dogs lick it off.
30 Posts were normally located on lakes or rivers to facilitate travel and access to fish for human and dog food. The posts at these key locations had complex histories and names.
31 There was some limited use of horses in the North in the early nineteenth century at posts in the Peace River region and by the mid nineteenth century at the Methye Portage (Portage La Loche) and later at some of the major posts. Horses were important at the posts in the parkland, although dogs were also used there in winter. No one has yet done an ethnohistory of horses in the fur trade.
32 Even if they had wanted to do so – which they did not – Aboriginal people, whether local First Nations or Métis workers living at the posts, could not have supported themselves from their sales of fur and food provisions or from their wage labor, or even from both together. Although the fur trade is normally considered a distinctive economy, *structurally* its operation was not greatly different from herring fishermen in northern Scotland or homesteaders in Alberta, both of whom supported themselves by means of a mixed economy that included local food production.
33 Terminology for Aboriginal people has changed since 1982, when the terms "Indian, Inuit, and Métis" were enshrined in Section 35(2) of Canada's *Constitution Act*, 1982. "First Nations" has become a preferred term, although it does not always have the same meanings historically and is not necessarily appropriate when using information from older primary sources. I find it helpful to use "Indian" for people of the past, in part to distinguish them from other Aboriginal people with mixed-ancestries who mostly lived at or near the posts and who did not necessarily possess an "Indian" identity. Also, Indian is the term used consistently in the primary sources. The term "Native" has fallen out of favor, and

even the term "Aboriginal" is being replaced by "Indigenous," perhaps to invoke the similarities they share with Indigenous peoples elsewhere in their colonial histories. Sometimes (though not always) these terms are used to include people with distinctive mixed ancestry identities – "Half-breeds" or "Métis." The former is today seen as pejorative, even though it was common parlance in the western Subarctic until at least World War II. It has been supplanted by Métis in both legal and popular uses. This paper strives to respect these various usages.

34 Word about the usefulness of European goods spread rapidly among northern peoples and was even part of the story of Thanadelthur, the first Dene woman to discover the fur traders (Hearne 1958:172; McCormack 2003:349). See McCormack 2010:41 for a brief discussion of the concept of "dependence" with respect to imported material culture.

35 In many parts of the Subarctic, animal habitats were managed and enriched by the practice of controlled burning, which contributed to larger and predictable animal populations and thus reduced much uncertainty (e.g., McCormack 2007). Even today, the historic roles of controlled burning by Aboriginal people are little appreciated and do not factor into provincial game and fire management.

36 This tragic epidemic may not have reached Great Slave Lake or points farther north, but stories would have been told about it even in areas not directly affected.

37 In 1786, the Chipewyans who visited Great Slave Lake were reported as "…being somewhat lazy to hunt [i.e., to trap and/or produce food provisions for exchange], went in quest of strange nations with whom they would trade an old knife or a worn out axe, which they had got for little or nothing, for double or triple its value…" (Wentzel in Masson 1889:94).

38 Krech has focused on constant epidemics and starvation in the Mackenzie region in the two decades beginning in the 1820s (1978).

39 Cree "medicine" or spiritual power has always been considered very strong among Dene peoples.

40 For example, Donna Haraway has pointed out that she undoubtedly shares elements of her dog's microbiome (2003:1), a continuity at a highly personal level. Dogs and humans that live together typically exchange both micro-organisms and parasites.

41 Interest in human–animal boundaries has extended to many other animal species, including non-human primates and horses, as well as plants (Mullin 1999; Latimer 2013; Latimer and Birke 2009; Maurstad et al. 2013; Argent 2013).

Bibliography

Allen, G.M. 1920. "Dogs of the American Aborigines." *Bulletin of the Museum of Comparative Zoology, Harvard University,* 73(9): 433–517.

Anderson, A. 1975. *Plains Cree Dictionary in the "y" Dialect.* Rev. ed. Edmonton: Anne Anderson.

Argent, G. 2013. "Inked: Human-Horse Apprenticeship, Tattoos, and Time in the Pazyryk World." *Society & Animals,* 21: 178–193.

Balcombe, J. 2009. "Animal Pleasure and Its Moral Significance." *Applied Animal Behaviour Science,* 118(3–4): 208–216.

Bird, L. 2005. "Telling our Stories." In *Omushkego Legends & Histories from Hudson Bay.* Edited by J.S.H. Brown, P.W. DePasquale, and M.F. Ruml. Peterborough, ON: Broadview Press.

Bird-David, N. 1999. "'Animism' Revisited." *Current Anthropology*, 40 (Supplement): S67–S91.

Blondin, G. 1990. *When the World was New. Stories of the Sahtú Dene*. Yellowknife: Outcrop.

Boutellis, A., A.-R. Laurent, and D. Raoult. 2014. "The Origin and Distribution of Human Lice in the World." *Infection, Genetics, and Evolution*, 23: 209–217.

Bowsfield, H. 1972. "Bernard Rogan Ross." *Dictionary of Canadian Biography Online*. Vol. 10. www.biographi.ca/en/bio/ross_bernard_rogan_10E.html (Accessed 18 Nov. 2016).

Brightman, R. 2002 [Orig. 1973]. *Grateful Prey: Rock Cree Human–Animal Relationships*. Regina: Canadian Plains Research Center.

Brisbin, I.L. and T.S. Risch. n.d. *Primitive Dogs, Their Ecology and Behavior: The Carolina Dog*. www.carolinadogs.org/geninfo/primative.html (Accessed 7 Feb. 2017).

Broch, H.B. 2008. "Gender and Matinen dogs." *Asian Anthropology*, 7: 55–77.

Brown, J. and S.E. Gray (eds.). 2009. *Memories Myths and Dreams of an Ojibwa Leader. William Berens, as told to A. Irving Hallowell*. Montreal: McGill-Queen's University Press.

Castroviejo-Fisher, S., P. Skoglund, R. Valadez, C. Vilà, and J.A. Leonard. 2011. "Vanishing Native American Dog Lineages." *BMC Evolutionary Biology*, 11(73). www.biomedcentral.com/1471–2148/11/73.

Clark, G.A. 2002. "Neandertal Archaeology – Implications For Our Origins." *American Anthropologist*, 104(1): 50–67.

Clutton-Brock, J. 1994. "The Unnatural World: Behavioural Aspects of Humans and Animals in the Process of Domestication." In *Animals and Human Society: Changing Perspectives*. Edited by A. Manning and J. Serpell, 23–35. New York: Routledge.

Cohen, R. and J.W. VanStone. 1964. *Dependency and Self-sufficiency in Chipewyan Stories. Contributions to Anthropology 1961062. Part 2*. National Museum of Canada Bulletin No. 194. Anthropological Series No. 62, 29–55. Ottawa: Department of the Secretary of State.

Crockford, S.J. 2005. Native Dog Types in North America Before Arrival of European dogs. World Small Animal Veterinary Association World Congress Proceedings, 2005. www.vin.com/apputil/content/defaultadv1.aspx?meta=generic&Id=11196&catID=30764&id=3854290&print=1 (Accessed 4 Feb. 2017).

Crosby, A.W. 1976. "Virgin Soil Epidemics as a Factor in the Aboriginal Depopulation in America." *The William and Mary Quarterley*, 33(2): 289–299.

Cummins, B.D. 2002. *First Nations, First Dogs*. Calgary, AB: Detselig Enterprises Ltd.

Descola, P. 2014. "Modes of Being and Forms of Predication." *HAU: Journal of Ethnographic Theory*, 4(1): 271–280.

DogsReviewed. n.d. Dog Breed Information & Reviews. DogsReviewed. www.dogsreviewed.com/dog-groupsspitz-dog-breeds (Accessed 1 Dec. 2016).

Douglas, M. 1994. "The Pangolin Revisited: A New Approach to Animal Symbolism." In *Signifying Animals. Human Meaning in the Natural World*. Edited by R. Willis, 25–36. London: Routledge.

Edwards, T. 2015. "The North by Dogsled." Up Here. 1 January 2015. https://uphere.ca/articles/north-dogsled (Accessed 3 Dec. 2016).

Elford, L.W. and M. Elford. 1981. *English-Chipewyan Dictionary*. Prince Albert, SK: Northern Canada Evangelical Mission.

Elton, C. 1931. "Epidemics Among Sledge Dogs in the Canadian Arctic and Their Relation to Disease in the Arctic Fox." *Canadian Journal of Research*, 5(6): 673–692.

Ferguson, T.A. 1993. "Wood Bison and the Early Fur Trade." In *The Uncovered Past: Roots of Northern Alberta Societies*. Edited by P.A. McCormack and R.G. Ironside, 63–79. Circumpolar Research Series No. 3. Edmonton: Canadian Circumpolar Institute, University of Alberta.

Ferland, C. and M. Fournier. 2007. "Adapting to Winter: Transportation." *Encyclopedia of French Cultural Heritage in North America*. www.ameriquefrancaise.org/en/article-714/Adapting%20to%20Winter:%20Transportation (Accessed 5 March 2017).

Franklin, J. 1828. *Narrative of a Second Expedition to the Shores of the Polar Sea in the Years 1825, 1826, and 1827*. London: John Murray.

Franklin, J. 1969 [1823]. *Narrative of a Journey to the Shores of the Polar Sea in the Years 1819, 20, 21, and 22*. Edmonton: M.G. Hurtig. (Facsimile ed.; orig. 1823).

Freedman, A.H., I. Gronau, R.M. Schweizer, D. Ortega-Del Vecchyo, E. Han, P.M. Silva, et al. 2014. "Genome Sequencing Highlights the Dynamic Early History of Dogs." *PLoS Genetics*, 10(1): e1004016.

Fuentes, A. 2010. "Naturalcultural Encounters in Bali: Monkeys, Temples, Tourists, and Ethnoprimatology." *Cultural Anthropology*, 25(4): 600–624.

Gentry, A., J. Clutton-Brock, and C.P. Groves. 1996. "Case 3010. Proposed Conservation of Usage of 15 Mammal Specific Names Based on Wild Species Which Are Antedated by or Contemporary with Those Based on Domestic Animals." *Bulletin of Zoological Nomenclature*, 53(1): 28–37.

Gillespie, B.C. 1975. "Territorial Expansion of the Chipewyan in the Eighteenth Century." In *Proceedings: Northern Athapaskan Conference, 1971 (Volume 2)*. Edited by A. McFadyen Clark, 350–388. Canadian Ethnology Service Paper No. 27. National Museum of Man Mercury Series. Ottawa: National Museums of Canada.

Gittins, E. 2013. "The Archaeology of Becoming the Human Animal." *Society & Animals*, 21: 120–133.

Gough, B.M. (ed.). 1992. *The Journal of Alexander Henry the Younger, 1799–1814*. Vols. 1, 2. Toronto: The Champlain Society.

Grayson, D.K. 1988. "Danger Cave, Last Supper Cave, and Hanging Rock Shelter: The Faunas." *Anthropological Papers of the American Museum of Natural History*, 66(1): 1–130.

Haraway, D. 2003. *The Companion Species Manifesto: Dogs, People, and Significant Otherness*. Chicago: Prickly Paradigm Press.

Hare, B. 2004. "Cognition: Domestic Dogs Use Humans as Tools." In *Encyclopedia of Human Behavior (Volume 1)*. Edited by M. Bekoff, 277–285. Westport, Conn.: Greenwood Press.

Hare, B., M. Brown, C. Williamson, and M. Tomasello. 2002. "The Domestication of Social Cognition in Dogs." *Science*, 298: 1634–1636.

Hare, B. and M. Tomasello. 2006. "Behavioral Genetics of Dog Cognition: Human-Like Social Skills in Dogs are Heritable and Derived." In *The Dog and its Genome*. Edited by E. Ostrander, U. Giger, and K. Lindblad-Toh, 497–514. New York: Cold Spring Harbor Laboratory Press.

Hart, B.L. 2011. "Behavioural Defences in Animals Against Pathogens and Parasites: Parallels with the Pillars of Medicine in Humans." *Philosophical Transactions of the Royal Society B*. 366: 3406–3417.

Hearne, S. 1958. *A Journey to the Northern Ocean*. Edited by R. Glover. Toronto: The Macmillan Company of Canada Limited.

Helm, J. 1980. "Female Infanticide, European Diseases, and Population Levels among the Mackenzie Dene." *American Ethnologist*, 7(2): 259–295.

Helm, J. 1981. "Dogrib." In *Subarctic: Handbook of North American Indians*, 6: 291–309. Washington, DC: Smithsonian Institution.

Helm, J. 2000. *The People of Denendeh: Ethnohistory of the Indians of Canada's Northwest Territories*. Iowa City: University of Iowa Press.

Hoffecker, J.F., S.A. Elias, D.H. O'Rourke, G.R. Scott, and N.H. Bigelow. 2016. "Beringia and the Global Dispersal of Modern Humans." *Evolutionary Anthropology*, 25: 64–78.

Houston, C.S., with commentary by I.S. MacLaren. 1994. *Arctic Artist: The Journal and Paintings of George Back, Midshipman with Franklin, 1819–1822*. Montreal: McGill-Queen's University Press.

Hudson's Bay Company Archives (HBCA). n.d. Biographical Sheet, Bernard Rogan Ross. www.gov.mb.ca/cgi-bin/print_hit_bold.pl/chc/archives/hbca/biographical/r/ross_bernard-rogan.pdf (Accessed 19 Jan. 2017).

Huson, H.J., H.G. Pasrker, J. Runstadler, and E.A. Ostrander. 2010. "A Genetic Dissection of Breed Composition and Performance Enhancement in the Alaskan Sled Dog." *BMC Genetics*, 11:71. www.biomedcentral.com/1471–2156/11/71.

Ingold, T. 1994. "From Trust to Domination: An Alternative History of Human–Animal Relations." In *Animals and Human Society: Changing Perspectives*. Edited by A. Manning and J. Serpell, 1–22. New York: Routledge.

Ingold, T. 2010. "Footprints Through the Weather-World: Walking, Breathing, Knowing." *Journal of the Royal Anthropological Institute*, 16(Supplement): S121–S139.

Ingold, T. 2011 [Orig. 2000]. *The Perception of the Environment. Essays on Livelihood, Dwelling and Skill*. New York: Routledge.

Ingold, T. 2015. *The Life of Lines*. New York: Routledge.

Innis, H.A. 1964 [Orig. 1956]. *The Fur Trade in Canada. Rev. ed.* New Haven: Yale University Press.

International Commission on Zoological Nomenclature. 2003. "Opinion 2027 (Case 3010)." *Bulletin of Zoological Nomenclature*, 60(1):81–84.

Karwoski, G.L. 1999. *Seaman: The Dog who Explored the West with Lewis & Clark*. Atlanta, Georgia: Peachtree Publishers.

Keith, L (ed.). 2001. *North of Athabasca: Slave Lake and Mackenzie River Documents of the North West Company, 1800–1821*. Rupert's Land Record Society Series, 6. Montreal: McGill-Queen's University Press.

Kirksey, E. and S. Helmreich. 2010. "The Emergence of Multispecies Ethnography." *Cultural Anthropology*, 25(4): 545–576.

Kohn, E. 2007. "How Dogs Dream: Amazonian Natures and the Politics of Transspecies Engagement." *American Ethnologist*, 34(1): 3–24.

Kohn, E. 2013. *How Forests Think: Toward an Anthropology Beyond the Human*. Berkeley: University of California Press.

Krech III., S., 1978. "Disease, Starvation, and Northern Athapaskan Social Organization." *American Ethnologist*, 5(4): 710–732.

Krech III., S., 1983. "The Beaver Indians and the Hostilities at Fort St. John's." *Arctic Anthropology*, 20(2): 35–45.

Lamb, W.K. (ed.). 1970. *The Journals and Letters of Sir Alexander Mackenzie*. Cambridge: Published for the Hakluyt Society at the University Press.

Larson, G., E. Karlsson, A. Perri, M.T. Webster, S.Y.W. Ho, J. Peters, P.W. Stahl, P.J. Piper, F. Lingaas, M. Fredholm, K.E. Comstock, J.F. Modiano, C. Schelling, A.I. Agoulnik, P.A. Leegwater, K. Dobney, J.-D. Vigne, C. Vilà, L. Andersson, and K. Lindblad-Toh. 2012. "Rethinking Dog Domestication by Integrating Genetics, Archeology, and Biogeography." *Proceedings of the National Academy of Sciences USA*, 109(23): 8878–8883.

Latimer, J. 2013. "Being Alongside: Rethinking Relations Amongst Different Kinds." *Theory, Culture & Society*, 30(78): 77–104.

Latimer, J. and L. Birke. 2009. "Natural Relations: Horses, Knowledge, Technology." *The Sociological Review*, 57(1): 1–27.

Latimer, J. and M. Miele. 2013. "Naturecultures? Science, Affect and the Non-Human." *Theory, Culture & Society*, 30(78): 5–31.

Leach, E. 1964. "Anthropological Aspects of Language: Animal Categories and Verbal Abuse." In *New Directions in the Study of Language*. Edited by E.H. Lenneberg, 39–67. Cambridge, MA: MIT Press.

Leach, E. 1972. *Humanity and Animality: 54th Conway Memorial Lecture, 28 Nov. 1972*. London: South Place Ethical Society

Leonard, J.A., R.K. Wayne, J. Wheeler, R. Valadez, S. Guillén, and C. Vilà. 2002. "Ancient DNA Evidence of Old World Origin of New World Dogs." *Science*, 298: 1613–1616.

Lindsay, D. 1991. *The Modern Beginnings of Subarctic Ornithology: Northern Correspondence with the Smithsonian Institution, 1856–68*. The Manitoba Record Society Publications, 10. Winnipeg: The Manitoba Record Society.

Losey, R.J., V.I. Bazaliiskii, S. Garvie-Lok, M. Germonpré, J.A. Leonard, A.L. Allen, M.A. Kjatzenberg, and M.V. Sablin. 2011. "Canids as Persons: Early Neolithic Dogs and Wolf Burials, Cis-Baikal, Siberia." *Journal of Anthropological Archaeology*, 30: 174–189.

McCormack, P.A. 1984. "Becoming Trappers: the Transformation to a Fur Trade Mode of Production at Fort Chipewyan." In *Rendezvous: Selected Papers of the Fourth North American Fur Trade Conference, 1981*. Edited by Thomas C. Buckley, 155–173. St. Paul, MN: North American Fur Trade Conference.

McCormack, P.A. 1996. "The Athabasca Influenza Epidemic of 1835." In *Issues in the North*. Edited by J. Oakes and R. Riewe, 33–42. Occasional Publication No. 40. Edmonton: Canadian Circumpolar Institute in cooperation with the Department of Human Ecology, University of Alberta, and Department of Native Studies, University of Manitoba.

McCormack, P.A. 2003. "The Many Faces of Thanadelthur: Documents, Stories, and Images." In *Reading Beyond Words: Contexts for Native History*. 2nd. ed. J.S.H. Brown and E. Vibert, 329–364. Peterborough, ON: Broadview Press.

McCormack, P.A. 2007. Deconstructing Canadian Subarctic Grasslands. Paper presented at the European Environmental History Conference, Amsterdam, 5–9 June 2007.

McCormack, P.A. 2010. *Fort Chipewyan and the Shaping of Canadian History, 1788–1920s*. Vancouver: UBC Press.

McCormack, P.A. 2014a. "Evolving Accommodations: The Sled Dog in the Canadian Fur Trade." In *Une Bête parmi Les Hommes: Le Chien*. Edited by F. Guizard and C. Beck, 129–148. Amiens, France: Encrage University.

McCormack, P.A. 2014b. "The Canadian Fur Trade, Dr. John Rae, and Evolving Dog Teams." *New Orkney Antiquarian Journal*. Special edition: John Rae 200 Conference Proceedings, 7: 106–118.

McLeod, N. 2002. "*Nēhiyāwiwin* and Modernity." In *Plain Speaking: Essays on Aboriginal Peoples and the Prairie*. Edited by P.C. Douard and B.W. Dawson, 35–53. Regina: Canadian Plains Research Center.

Mandelbaum, D.G. 1979 [Part 1 orig. 1940]. *The Plains Cree: An Ethnographic, Historical, and Comparative Study*. Canadian Plains Studies No. 9. Regina: Canadian Plains Research Center, University of Regina.

Manson, A. 1992. *A Dog Came, Too*. Toronto: Groundwork.

Marks, J. 2012. "The Origin of Anthropological Genetics." *Current Anthropology*, 53(S5): S161–S172.

Mason, J.A. 1946. *Notes on the Indians of the Great Slave Lake Area*. Yale University Publications in Anthropology No. 34. New Haven: Yale University Press.

Masson, L.R. (ed.). 1889. *Les Bourgeois de la Compagnie du Nord-Ouest (Volume. 1)*. Quebec: De L'Imprimerie Générale A. Coté et Cie.

Masson, L.R. (ed.). 1890. *Les Bourgeois de la Compagnie du Nord-Ouest (Volume. 2)*. Quebec: De L'Imprimerie Générale A. Coté et Cie.

Maurstad, A., D. Davis, and S. Cowles. 2013. "Co-Being and Intra-Action in Horse-Human Relationships: A Multi-Species Ethnography of Be(com)ing Human and Be(com) Horse." *Social Anthropology*, 21(3): 322–335.

Mech, L.D. 1970. *The Wolf*. Garden City, NY: The American Museum of Natural History, the Natural History Press.

Miklósi, Á. and J. Topál. 2013. "What Does It Take to Become 'Best Friends'? Evolutionary changes in canine social competence." *Trends in Cognitive Science*, 17(6): 287–294.

Moreau, W.E. (ed.). 2009. *The Writings of David Thompson (Volume 1): The Travels, 1850 Version*. Montreal: McGill-Queen's University Press, in association with the Centre for Rupert's Land Studies at the University of Winnipeg.

Morey, D.F. 1986. "Studies on Amerindian Dogs: Taxonomic Analysis of Canid Crania from the Northern Plains." *Journal of Archaeological Science*, 13: 119–145.

Morey, D.F. 1992a. "Early Holocene Domestic Dog Burials From the North American Midwest." *Current Anthropology*, 33(2): 224–229.

Morey, D.F. 1992b. "Size, Shape and Development in the Evolution of the Domestic Dog." *Journal of Archaeological Science*, 19: 181–204.

Morey, D.F. 2006. "Burying Key Evidence: The Social Bond Between Dogs and People." *Journal of Archaeological Science*, 33: 158–175.

Morey, D.F. 2014. "In Search of Paleolithic Dogs: A Quest with Mixed Results." *Journal of Archaeological Science*, 52: 300–307.

Morey, D.F. and R. Jeger. 2015. "Paleolithic Dogs: Why Sustained Domestication Then?" *Journal of Archaeological Science: Reports*, 3: 420–428.

Mullin, M.H. 1999. "Mirrors and Windows: Sociocultural Studies of Human–Animal Relationships." *Annual Review of Anthropology*, 28: 201–224.

Munro, K.D. (ed.). 2006. *Fur Trade Letters of Willie Traill, 1864–1894*. Edmonton: University of Alberta Press.

Nadasdy, P. 2007. "The Gift in the Animal: The Ontology of Hunting and Human–Animal Sociality." *American Ethnologist*, 34(1): 25–43.

Olsen, S.J. 1974. "Early Domestic Dogs in North America and Their Origins." *Journal of Field Archaeology*, 1(3–4): 343–345.

Orr, Y. 2016. "Interspecies Semiotics and the Specter of Taboo: The Perception and Interpretation of Dogs and Rabies in Bali, Indonesia." *American Anthropologist*, 118(1): 67–77.

Ortner, S.B. 2016. "Dark Anthropology and Its Others. Theory Since the Eighties." *HAU: Journal of Ethnographic Theory*, 6(1): 47–73.

Parker, H.G., L.V. Kim, N.B. Sutter, S. Carlson, T.D. Lorentzen, T.B. Malek, G.S. Johnson, H.B. DeFrance, E.A. Ostrader, and L. Kruglyak. 2004. "Genetic Structure of the Purebred Domestic Dog." *Science*, 304: 1160–1164.

Parker, J.M. 1987. *Emporium of the North: Fort Chipewyan and the Fur Trade to 1835*. Edmonton: Alberta Culture and Multiculturalism.

Payne, M. 1989. *The Most Respectable Place in the Territory: Everyday Life in Hudson's Bay Company Service York Factory, 1788 to 1870*. Studies in Archaeology Architecture and History, National Historic Parks and Sites, Canadian Parks Service, Environment Canada. Hull, QC: Minister of Supply and Services Canada.

Pedersen, M.W., A. Ruter, C. Schweger, H. Friebe, R.A. Staff, K.K. Kjeldsen, M.L.Z. Mendoza, A.B. Beaudoin, C. Zutter, N.K. Larsen, B.A. Potter, R. Nielsen, R.A. Rainville, L. Orlando, D.J. Meltzer, J.H. Kjaer, and E. Willerslev. 2016. "Postglacial Viability and Colonization in North America's Ice-Free Corridor." *Nature*, 537(7618): 45–49.

Plotnicov, L. 2008. "Introduction. Special Issue: 'Trash' Food: Polygyny." *Ethnology*, 47(2–3): 85–88.

Raier, L. and L. Rofel 2014. "Ethnographies of Encounter." *Annual Review of Anthropology*, 43: 363–377.

Ray, A.J. 1974. *Indians in the Fur Trade: Their Role as Hunters, Trappers and Middlemen in the Lands Southwest of Hudson Bay 1660–1870*. Toronto: University of Toronto Press.

Rich, E.E. (ed.). 1938. *Journal of Occurrences in the Athabasca Department by George Simpson, 1820 and 182a, and Report*. Toronto: The Champlain Society.

Rich, E.E. 1949. *James Isham's Observations on Hudsons Bay, 1743*. Toronto: The Champlain Society.

Richardson, J. 1829. *Fauna Boreali-Americana; or the Zoology of the Northern Parts of British America*. London: John Murray.

Richardson, J. 1852. *Arctic Searching Expedition*. New York: Harper & Brothers, Publishers.

Robbins, J. 2007. "Continuity Thinking and the Problem of Christian Culture." *Current Anthropology*, 48(1): 5–37.

Ross, B.R. 1859. "On the Indian Tribes of the McKenzie River District and the Arctic Coast; From a Correspondent." *Canadian Naturalist and Geologist*, 4(3): 190–197.

Ross, B.R. 1861a "An Account of the Animals Useful in an Economic Point of View to the Various Chipewyan Tribes." *Canadian Naturalist and Geologist*, 6(6): 433–444.

Ross, B.R. 1861b. "A Popular Treatise on the Fur-Bearing Animals of the Mackenzie Valley District." *Canadian Naturalist and Geologist*, 6: 5–36.

Ross, B.R. 1872. "The Eastern Tinneh." In *Notes on the Tinneh or Chepewyan Indians of British and Russian America*. Edited by G. Gibbs, 303–311. Annual Report of the Smithsonian Institution for 1866. Washington, DC: Smithsonian Institution.

Saetre, P., J. Lindberg, J.A. Leonard, K. Olsson, U. Pettersson, H. Ellegren, T.F. Bergström, C. Vilà, and E. Jazin. 2004. "From Wild Wolf to Domestic Dog: Gene Expression Changes in the Brain." *Molecular Brain Research*, 126: 198–206.

Sanders, C.R. 2007. "Mind, Self, and Human–Animal Joint Action." *Sociological Focus*, 40(3): 320–336.

Savelle, J.M., A.S. Dyke, and N. Giguèrevh. 2014. "Prehistoric Neoeskimo Komatiks, Victoria Island, Arctic Canada." *Arctic*, 67(2): 135–142.

Savishinsky, J.S. 1974. *The Trail of the Hare: Life and Stress in an Arctic Community*. New York.: Gordon and Breach Science Publishers.

Savishinsky, J.S. 1975. "The Dog and the Hare: Canine Culture in an Athapaskan band." In *Proceedings: Northern Ahapaskan Conference, 1971 (Volume Two)*. Edited by A. McFadyen Clark. Pp. 462–515. Canadian Ethnology Service Paper No. 27. National Museum of Man Mercury Series. Ottawa: National Museums of Canada.

Savolainen, P., Y.-P. Zhang, J. Luo, J. Lundeberg, and T. Leitner. 2002. "Genetic Evidence for an East Asian Origin of Domestic Dogs." *Science*, 298(5598): 1610–1613.

Sharp, H.S. 1976. "Man:Wolf: Woman:Dog." *Arctic Anthropology*, 13(1): 25–34.

Sharp, H.S. 1996. "Experiencing Meaning." *Anthropology and Humanism*, 21(2): 171–186.

Sharp, H.S. 2001. *Loon: Memory, Meaning, and Reality in a Northern Dene Community*. Lincoln, NE: University of Nebraska Press.

Sharp, H.S., and K. Sharp. 2015. *Hunting Caribou: Subsistence Hunting along the Northern Edge of the Boreal Forest*. Lincoln: University of Nebraska Press.

Sheppard, J.R. 1983. "The Dog Husband: Structural Identity and Emotional Specificity in Northern Athapaskan Oral Narrative." *Arctic Anthropology*, 20(1): 89–101.

Shields, G.F., A.M. Schmiechen, B.L. Frazier, A. Redd, M.I. Voevoda, J.K. Reed, and R.H. Ward. 1993. "mtDNA Sequences Suggest a Recent Evolutionary Divergence for Beringian and Northern North American Populations." *American Journal of Human Genetics*, 53(3): 549–562.

Ski-Doo. 2003–2017. About Ski-Doo. www.ski-doo.com/ca/about-skidoo.html (Accessed 23 Feb. 2017).

Smith, D.M. 1973. *Inkonze: Magico-religious beliefs of contact-traditional Chipewyan trading at Fort Resolution, NWT, Canada*. Mercury Series, Ethnology Division Paper No. 6. Ottawa: National Museum of Man, National Museums of Canada.

Smith, D.M. 1998. "An Athapaskan Way of Knowing: Chipewyan Ontology." *American Ethnologist*, 25(3): 412–432.

Tamm, E., T. Kivisild, M. Reidla, M. Metspalu, D. Glenn Smith, C.J. Mulligan, et al. 2007. "Beringian Standstill and Spread of Native American Founders." *PLOS ONE*, 2(9): e829.

Torroni, A., T.G. Schurr, M.F. Cabell, M.D. Brown, J.V. Neel, M. Larsen, D.G. Smith, C.M. Vullo, and D.C. Wallace. 1993. "Asian Affinities and Continental Radiation of the Four Founding Native American mtDNAs." *American Journal of Human Genetics*, 53(3): 563–590.

Torroni, A., R.I. Sukernik, T.G. Schurr, Y.B. Starikovskaya, M.F. Cabell, M.H. Crawford, A.G. Comuzzie, and D.C. Wallace. 1993. "mtDNA Variation of Aboriginal Siberians Reveals Distinct Genetic Affinities with Native Americans." *American Journal of Human Genetics*, 53(3): 591–608.

Toups, M.A., A. Kitchen, J.E. Light, and D.L. Reed. 2011. "Origin of Clothing Lice Indicates Early Clothing Use by Anatomically Modern Humans in Africa." *Molecular Biology and Evolution*, 28(1): 29–31.

van Asch, B., A.-B. Zhang, M.C.R. Oskarsson, C.F.C. Klütsch, A. Amorim, and P. Savolainen 2013. "Pre-Columbian Origins of Native American Dog Breeds, with Only Limited Replacement by European Dogs, Confirmed by mtDNA Analysis." *Proceedings of the Royal Society B*, 280: 20131142.

Vilà, C., P. Savolainen, J.E. Maldonado, I.R. Amorim, J.E. Rice, R.L. Honeycutt, K.A. Crandall, J. Lundeberg, and R.K. Wayne. 1997. "Multiple and Ancient Origins of the Domestic Dog." *Science*, 276 (5319): 1687–1689.

Waisberg, L.G. 1975. "Boreal Forest Subsistence and the Windigo: Fluctuation of Animal Populations." *Anthropologica*, 17(2): 169–185.

Wayne, R.K. and E.A. Ostrander. 2007. "Lessons Learned From the Dog genome." *Trends in Genetics*, 23(11): 557–567.

Weidensaul, S. and L. Richardson. 1999. "Tracking America's First Dog." *Smithsonian*, 29(12): 44–57.

Wikipedia. 2017. Variety (botany). https://en-wikipedia.org/wiki/Variety_(botany) (Accessed 25 Feb. 2017).

Witt, K.E., K. Judd, A. Kitchen, C. Grier, T.A. Kohler, S.G. Ortman, B.M. Kemp, and R.S. Malhi. 2015. "DNA Analysis of Ancient Dogs of the Americas: Identifying Possible Founding Haplotypes and Reconstructing Population Histories." *Journal of Human Evolution*, 79: 105–118.

Youatt, W., with editing and additions by E.J. Lewis. 1852. *The Dog*. Philadelphia: Blanchard and Lea.

8 The police and dogs during the early patrol years in the Western Canadian Subarctic
An inter-species colonial cooperation?

Robert P. Wishart

Introduction

The history of dogs in the North includes a variety of inter-species relationships and various working roles. This chapter seeks to shed light on the relationships and roles dogs had in the "opening" of the Canadian North-West during the late nineteenth and early twentieth centuries by examining the use of dogs by the North West Mounted Police (NWMP), Royal North West Mounted Police (RNWMP), and the Royal Canadian Mounted Police (RCMP).[1] During this period, the Canadian government was actively debating and setting policy about the settling of the North (Oliver 1910).[2] The police had a large role in enforcing and shaping these policies. Many, including myself, have written about the impacts of these policy shifts on northern Indigenous peoples and the effects on the human–animal relationships in this region (e.g., Nadasdy 2004, Piper 2009, Sandlos 2007, Wishart 2004). Until recently, dogs have been marginal to these studies (Loovers 2015), as were the species which were to become the main diet of sled dogs: fish (Wishart 2014). The marginalisation of dogs in the history of the North perhaps has something to do with the way dogs figure as an outlier in the master narrative of the domestic-wild dichotomy (Anderson et al. 2017) and the manner in which "wild" things served a political purpose in Canadian legal parlance so much so that the recognition of a domestic relationship between Indigenous people and the animals on which they relied would fundamentally change the legal landscape (Asch 1989). In shifting attention back onto dogs I also want to shift the focus onto the settler authorities. By expanding upon our knowledge of the mechanisms of surveillance and control in this part of the world at this crucial point in history, I want to call attention to the multiple possible roles that dogs had in their cooperation with human actors. Using the letters, orders, reports, and observations of the police themselves, I demonstrate the inter-species unfolding of this colonial history, the limitations on knowing about the dogs used by the police, and the challenges which developed out of a precarious balance between police officer and dog team.

Dogs as historical partners

Recently in human–animal studies there has been a move to re-interpret historical events through the inclusion or recognition of the experiences of other animal participants (e.g., Nance 2015, Few and Tortorici 2013). This move of inclusion follows a longer history of animal recognition that reaches back in academia at least as far as writings on the role of animals in society in the work of Jeremy Bentham (1789). He makes an equivalence between the rights of the politically voiceless human slave and that of the physically voiceless other animals, arguing that neither should be denied rights under legislation and it is an act of tyranny to do so. Providing a voice attesting to the suffering of animals certainly follows from this original argument. At the same time, the move to be more inclusive in the history of world events to consider human actors left out of the dominant narrative has been the goal of many in the social sciences and humanities. For example, the American Society for Ethnohistory makes this inclusionary goal into their mission statement: "The unifying factor is a commitment to the mission of our association—professionals from a variety of backgrounds who are helping to create a more inclusive picture of the histories of native groups in the Americas" (www.ethnohistory.org). Following from previous moves on the ethical treatment of animals, it is not surprising to find dissatisfaction with maintaining a species barrier when it comes to history. At the same time others have argued convincingly that humans have never been alone in the world and our history, both personal and inter-generational, is really one of hybrid animal communities (Haraway 2007, Lestel 1996).

At conferences and discussions on the animal turn in anthropology, more than one scholar has asked if we can think about Europe and the People without History (Wolf 1982), why not humans and the animals without history? The goal is to provide, once again, a voice for their historical participation and suffering, to bring them back as historical actors. Animals have figured in historical texts, even taking a centre role, such as in Kurlansky's *Cod: A Biography of the Fish That Changed the World* (1997) where animals as resources become the driver of human history. Such works, however, do not necessarily tell the story from the animal's perspective. Is it ever possible to accomplish this noble but difficult inclusionary goal? Companion animals, and particularly dogs (Haraway 2003, 2007) would seem to be the best candidates for such a pursuit. To begin with their long history of living in mutual community with humans raises the serious question of who domesticated who (Hare and Woods 2013, Coppinger and Coppinger 2001). Already individualised within Western consciousness, they are certainly part of the personal history of many people; their relationships with us makes it easy to discuss these animals' motivations and desires as they are in fact entwined with our own. Moreover, dogs have served multiple roles that are sometimes embedded within social control and their service roles make their lives part of our own politics.

Take, for example, police dogs. Today the dogs of canine units (sometimes written K9 unit) work closely together with their human partners in multiple roles. Their keen sense of smell makes them invaluable for the detection of smuggled goods and explosives, discovering evidence, finding people both living and dead, and tracking. Their strength and agility makes them a powerful deterrent and they are able to tackle and bring those fleeing the law into submission. While the intentional killing or maiming of any dog is subject to the pertinent laws of humane animal treatment, in most jurisdictions it is a felony to kill or harm a police dog because of their status as a member of a law enforcement team. Today we encounter stories of individual police dogs being mourned by their human working partners and being given memorials to their heroism and service. A quick search on the internet using the terms "police dog funeral" brings forth multiple stories of police dogs being memorialised for their work—particularly if they died in the line of duty. Typically the dogs are cherished for their service to society and spoken about as being akin to a fallen human officer. The human partner is often depicted mourning the loss of the dog and language of good overcoming evil is frequently employed. The dog becomes a symbol for the never ending battle of protecting society against those who would seek to destroy it. It is an uncomplicated depiction which ignores the potential abuse of authority and how the dogs do not have much choice in accepting or rejecting the actions of their human partners and the force which they serve.

In December 2015 an article appeared in the journal *Totalitarianism and Democracy* written by Christiane Schulte, and academia got a glimpse of the type of work that might be possible in the history of joint human–dog political complexities. It was a fascinating story of a dog named Rex, an Alsatian police dog patrolling the Berlin Wall who became an early victim of the harsh political segregation between East and West Germany following World War II. The story of Rex went on to explain that he had been born into a tradition of violence and totalitarianism as he was a direct descendant of Alsatians who patrolled the Nazi concentration camps during World War II. Citing all the relevant theoretical literature in post-human studies, it was a compelling story of how these animals became part of the history of almost unimaginable human brutality and how in some ways Rex died for our sins and should be commemorated along with the human victims of the wall. It was also a complete fabrication, including the name of the author and the dog; a hoax perpetrated by a group of academics[3] calling themselves Christiane Schulte and friends who are critical of conformity, particularly in human–animal studies and the animal turn in philosophy which calls for post-human, hybrid species attentions. The original article has since been retracted but it serves as a cautionary note, not only of the problems of academic peer review, but also of the possibility of fabricating a compelling history from the perspective of the voiceless animal companions—how far is it possible to be inclusive, particularly when the records are admittedly fragmentary when it comes to the recording of the dogs' own histories?

Sometimes the story is too good to be true and we must question the authority of the human author to provide the history and voice for other beings. At the same time, it would be an omission to simply ignore the various roles dogs played in history, including that of the development of human environmental relations and domestication as illustrated in other papers in this collection, but also in the way control has been exercised by government authorities. Dogs were used in concentration camps to further Nazi control (Trautman 1964: 135) and police dogs did patrol the Berlin Wall with their human partners (Major 2010: 149, 243). Would history have unfolded differently without these hybrid units? It is a question we perhaps can never fully answer, but we can be fairly certain that the North would be significantly different without the cooperation of dogs.

Dogs in the North had different roles. Elsewhere I have presented historical evidence for the importance of dogs in creating a fur trade economy in the Canadian Subarctic that relied on a meshwork of indigenous subsistence activities and technologies as well as cooperation between traders, trappers, and other animals (Wishart 2014). Dogs became crucial to this economic adventure because they solved, or at least alleviated, a problem of transportation. Prior to snowmobiles, even though technically possible to run a trap line without a dog team it was extremely difficult. I have been told many stories of tough old trappers who would walk their lines on snowshoes even when they had a dog team so as to break the trail and allow the dogs to follow more easily, but the real problem is transportation when one considers the weight of moving animal bodies and then, after being processed, their furs, in addition to that of provisions, traps, and camp materials. The dog team and sled became so crucial to life in this region that it was almost impossible to imagine or remember that there had been a time before the fur trade in the Subarctic when dogs were present in far lower numbers and did not work as a team with a sled (Slobodin 1962: 26, McCormack 2014). Travel and transportation during the long winter months between camps, the centres of trade, and the further distant trade networks which brought fur to the world economy were made possible because of the labour of dogs which also resulted in unique relationships between Indigenous people and their personified canine partners (e.g., Loovers 2015, Shannon 1997). The work done on these relationships is crucial to our understanding of the way dogs figured as part of history in the North, but they also served as partners to different actors in the history of the region.

The problems of transportation and travel also affected non-Indigenous lives in the North and led to other relationships with the dogs who solved these overarching problems. The fur trading companies and their employees were perhaps even more dependent on dog labour. Not only did the companies need to transport trade goods and provisions into the posts, but they also needed to move fur bales to central locations for outward transport.

This was described in the reports as the problem of moving freight. While boats were part of the transportation mix, the times of the year when the posts were ice-bound required dog sleds. In the diary of R. George Cowley in 1866, he describes the overland journey from Peel's River Fort (now Fort McPherson) to "Fort Youcon" where he was to be stationed as a Hudson's Bay Company fur trader. The late summer journey is marked by hardship and wonder at the capabilities of his Gwich'in guides carrying heavy loads while traversing what he describes to be a country dominated by "Tetes de femmes":

> I cannot better describe than by calling them thick tufts of grass growing at intervals in abominable bogs—they resemble what I would imagine the hair of an old hag unkempt, unshorn, would be like [September 17, 1866].
> British Columbia Archives 1866–1867

Once at the "Youcon" he traded in his walking boots for a dog sled and wrote daily of his easy travel to provisioning stations, camps, woodlots etc. He no longer described the crushing weight of loads but instead lauded his "four very good dogs" (November 5, 1866) and highlighted the size of the sled loads of materials coming into the fort (BC Archives 1866–1867). Krech III (1976: 222) notes that the same tortuous journey made by Cowley on foot prior to freeze-up could be made in the winter in four days using just a few dogs and a sled, while transporting about 100 kilograms of freight.

The police, their mission, and their dogs

The relationship between the fur traders and their dogs in some ways matches those of the Indigenous trappers in that they were all involved, albeit in differing roles, in an economy of trade. However, with a shift in Canadian policy regarding the northern territories at the end of the nineteenth century, a new set of actors appeared in the North whose mission was not necessarily to further the trapping economy but to assist in the settling of these lands in Ottawa's image, the extension of Canadian sovereignty and governance (Schledermann 2003), and then the settling of Indigenous peoples. In short, the colonisation of the North. Canada has its share of iconic symbols: beaver, maple leaves, ice hockey, and "Mounties". The Royal Canadian Mounted Police (RCMP), or "Mounties", at that time titled the North West Mounted Police (NWMP), began their patrolling of the North in 1893. They were the "medium through which the central government…changed the history of the Canadian north" (Morrison 2011: xviii) and brought the North under central government control and authority. Steele (1936: i) refers to the role—using triumphant language—as the "conquest of the arctic". In a letter dated December 4, 1896, the Comptroller of the NWMP writes in regards to a request made by Police Commissioner Herchemer with a suggestion for policing the Athabaska District:[4]

Sir,

The Commissioner suggests that an officer of the Force, who is to spend the Winter in the Northern part of the District of Athabaska, with a view to the suppression of illegal traffic in liquor and the enforcement of certain other laws in these parts, should, when called upon to act as a Justice of the Peace, be permitted to accept furs in payment of fines, or to give time if payment must be made in money.

You observe that there are no places in the District where money could be obtained; that the officer will travel by dog-sled and endeavour to visit the camps of all trappers and hunters, and that he will not have facilities either for confining prisoners in default of payment of fines or for sending them to Edmonton under escort; and you say that you would strongly suggest the desirability, if possible, of permitting him to exercise his own discretion as to the collection of any fines which may be imposed by him.
       Library and Archives Canada. RCMP fonds 1896, nos. 23–27

In developing their footholds in the North, the NWMP were thus acting not only as police but as judge, jury, and fine collector for any transgression they witnessed or possibly imagined. The arrival of the NWMP in the Subarctic and their new authority to control was met with resistance and a realisation that the police were not like the traders who came before. On February 25, 1897, Inspector A.M. Jarvis sent a package of reports and letters from Fort Chipewyan to "The officer commanding, N.W.M.Police". Contained in this package was a report on the progress of the orders to implement and police new Canadian game laws and controlling unruly trade, but the package also contained a letter dictated by Alicksand Levillot, "an Indian", regarding what his people thought of the new arrivals:

February 3, 1897

Dear Sir,

Who told you to come out here. I would like to know that. Am sure it isn't God. God let this Country free, and we like to be free in this Country. I don't want any of you people to come and bother us in this Country. The Company was here from long ago and can stay as long as they like. Because we he[a]r about the wrough about the country we don't want any of that business out here. About that rifle you brought it is not for people and there is no mutton in this country. I think myself a man, same as you, and would not step back for your gun. Not you will scare me. It is not because I am down on you. I suppose you want to hear about our Country… It is no use to stop us to kill anything in this Country. It is not you that grows anything in this Country. I don't care if I have a cent in my hand. God never made money for me, anything alive, that is my money for just now.

Library and Archives Canada. RCMP fonds 1897a, nos. 36–62

Levillot ends his letter with an invitation for the commanding officer to come see his people in the spring so that he might better understand. Whether the letter had any effect is unclear but it certainly is not evidenced by the intensification of government control with the policing of game laws and the implementation of The Indian Act (1876) throughout the northern territories.

Early NWMP reports, such as those collected by Jarvis, indicate that there were a distinct set of priorities for the new police force. These priorities included the enforcement of the game laws and to educate people about the proper use of the Crown's resources,[5] to enforce The Indian Act primarily through controlling access to illegal goods like alcohol, to stop the indigenous practice of burning the country[6] or stopping "bush fires", to police miscellaneous law and order issues, and to establish a way of patrolling the North to make the authority of Ottawa felt by all.

Despite the role of dogs in the enforcement of these colonial transformations in the Western Canadian Subarctic, the closest association between the RCMP, dogs, and colonial authority in the historical and anthropological literature pertains to the Eastern Canadian Arctic where the police slaughtered Inuit sled dogs in the 1950's and 1960's under the authority of An Ordinance Respecting Dogs 1929. Ostensibly the killing of dogs was for health and safety reasons, but it has also been suggested and then debated that it was actually a direct attempt to force Inuit to assimilate by destroying Inuit dog sociality and thus removing their mode of transport (Tester 2010, Lévesque 2011; see Lévesque, this volume). The ordinance and the actions which followed occurred after the RCMP had already established themselves as the Canadian authority in the North by patrolling the territories using dogs.

The image of the Mountie patrol is of course tied up with another animal partner, the horse. In southern Canada the relationship between the RCMP and horses is still championed, and it finds its way into kitsch souvenirs (Dawson 2008). What could possibly be more Canadian than the image of the Mountie on patrol wearing The Red Serge and sitting atop a trusted steed? The Mounties, who found themselves assigned to the North to regulate the region according to the desires of Ottawa, would not have arrived during the winter on horseback but most likely would have had their appearance announced by the barking, yipping, whining, and howling of dogs, and they would have been wearing fur-trimmed parkas. While the image of the Mountie working in partnership with a dog team is memorialised in the RCMP Heritage Centre in Regina, Saskatchewan, and did make its way onto a collector's silver dollar coin, it is a coin few ever use or see.[7]

Starting in the late nineteenth century and continuing until the late 1960's, the RCMP patrolled the northern territories and delivered mail using dogs and sleds along routes between centres and the trading forts, small settlements, and trap lines of the vast territory now under their supervision. The geographical difficulties (Longstreth 1929) of policing the North using manned patrols lasting months and traversing thousands of kilometres made the use of dogs a simple necessity until a reliable alternative came along. A dog team at this point in history was made up of four or five dogs, a sled, and a human dog-driver. Multiple teams would travel together in what were sometimes referred to as trains.[8] Snow machines and airplanes eventually made dog-teams redundant, but this was not a sudden shift as Shackleton notes:

> the introduction of the snowmobile into the North forever changed the way the RCMP did their work. In the early 1960s the "ski-dogs," as they were originally called by the Bombardier Company, were recreation vehicles. Unreliable and dangerous in the Arctic environment, they were prone to break down far from home and, unlike the sled dogs, the snowmobile could not find its way home in a blizzard. By the end of the 1960s, however, technology had improved the reliability and speed of the machines. The RCMP increasingly relied on the snowmobile for local patrols. The RCMP Commissioner's report of 1967 signalled the end of the dog sled era when it announced that "motorized toboggans can safely replace sleigh dogs at most detachments, promoting efficiency and economy.
>
> Shackleton 2012: 18

For the authorities making decisions on how to police the North, dogs were a necessity until something better came along. From the standpoint of economics, speed of travel, and efficiency, dogs presented many challenges for the force doing the government's work in transforming the North.

The police and their dogs: health, procurement, and drivers

Dogs were the most efficient, economical, and reliable mode of transport available but the practice of keeping dogs and working with dog teams is fraught with many difficulties that the RCMP had to overcome. Keeping the dogs healthy was difficult enough, and division heads would include a section on the health of the dogs in their monthly reports. For example, in the monthly report for August 1908 the Inspector commanding B Division[9] notes:

> Dogs: All dogs on charge are in good condition. Three have been destroyed at Forty Mile, having been found useless for further police work.
> Library and Archives Canada. RCMP fonds 1908, nos. 184–186

What made these three particular dogs unsuitable for police work is not mentioned but it is interesting that the health and condition of the dogs is listed just before the health of the men in the division, and the men's health receives the same terse treatment. It would be unreasonable to assume that the importance of the health of the dogs came first, but that men and dogs were listed alongside each other as reportable assets does indicate some acknowledgement of cooperation.

If reality followed the fiction of writers such as Jack London, then surely there was a heroic and sometimes tragic place for the dog actors in the unfolding of RCMP history in the North. However, unlike now with the memorialisation of police dogs, if they ever mourned or thought of their dogs as partners during the early patrol years, it was not reported in the official documents. We do know that the dogs had names[10] and that they were differently valued. For example in the accounts of the NWMP for 1897 there is a list of dogs purchased either in trade or by cash from the Hudson's Bay Company (HBC) for the purpose of establishing the Northern Patrol. Between January and March of that year eight dogs were bought (enough for two teams); the cheapest was $3.50 and the most expensive was $9. Given an average historical rate of inflation of 2.5% per annum we can estimate that $1 is now equivalent to about $30. This would make the most expensive dog worth $270 in today's money, which is not a high value for a well-trained dog. The price would inflate rapidly during the Klondike Gold Rush. By 1899, $500 was not considered to be an unusual price for a good dog and some dogs sold for as much as $1000, which would be $30 000 today, and the price of dogs made headlines in southern newspapers (The New York Times 1899). It is most likely that these particular police dogs were supplemental animals being used to fill the gaps in already existing teams or perhaps to act as breeding stock. The latter is suggested by the fact that the police were occasionally trading their own "worn out" dogs for others from the HBC. Perhaps these worn out dogs could still be traded as breeding stock and not all were instantly destroyed, but the rationale is not directly mentioned. There is mention in reports of how buying dogs from the HBC was necessary because of the poor quality of some of the dogs brought north from Edmonton. These Edmonton dogs did not survive the winter (Library and Archives Canada. RCMP fonds 1897b, nos. 36–62).

In these early years, getting enough dogs was always a problem and the police attempted to alleviate shortages of dogs by importing them from other areas of Canada. Outbreaks of canine diseases would occasionally devastate local populations of sled dogs throughout the Subarctic, and competition from traders and gold miners also created a high demand for dogs. Early observers noted the short life-span of sled dogs; harsh conditions and hard work meant that they would only be useful for a couple of seasons before needing to be replaced (Kane 1859: 100). Those without a national network were often left in a difficult situation by such shortages, but the police could rely on other areas, both near and far, to supply new dogs.

In 1898 the western Subarctic was facing a shortage of dogs due to disease and the demand of the Klondike Gold Rush, so the police went exceptionally far afield to secure both new working dogs and hire dog-drivers. In all, 140 dogs (enough for 35 teams) were secured from the coast of Labrador and sent overland to the Yukon accompanied by dog-drivers, stopping en route so as to be inspected in teams by the authorities (Library and Archives Canada. RCMP fonds 1899a, no. 115). Loovers (2015: 400) argues that the importation of these particular dogs was an exceptional case of bringing new breeds to the North and to fill in the gap of insufficient dogs for the NWMP to operate their policing, but it was also a continuation of the gradual breeding of larger, stronger dog types into the economic adventure of using dog teams to move freight and people.

The fate of individual dogs is mostly unknown. The possibility of dogs being suddenly injured beyond use or killed, coupled with the more gradual wearing out of dogs due to their heavy workload, meant a rapid turn-over of dogs and possibly a lack of any sort of ceremony or much thought about their departure from service.

In the early years of the establishment of the NWMP, it was also necessary to hire additional dog-drivers to assist with the training, working, and shipping of goods and officers across the country. The dog-drivers were well paid and even then the force had difficulty in keeping the drivers under contract. The lure of working the freight lines in the gold rush regions made it even more difficult to keep these highly skilled men attached to the divisions (Library and Archives Canada. RCMP fonds. 1899b, no. 115). This problem was eventually alleviated for the most part by contracting out freight duties to the HBC and by instructing the officers in the breeding, training, and working with dogs. The role of Indigenous people in teaching the police how to do many of these things is not commented upon in their reports, but we know from oral history that Indigenous dog skills were relied upon to some extent by the police and that dogs were being bred and sold to the police by Indigenous people.

Over the first few decades, the police became skilled with dogs, enough so that when Ernest Shackleton was planning his Imperial Antarctic Expedition[11] in 1914 he wrote to the Commanding Officer, R.N.W.M. Police, stating that he needed to purchase 100 of the "best dogs obtainable" and one man to serve as an experienced dog-driver. Despite the North being full of experienced and skilled dog-drivers Shackleton demanded that the driver be "a white man to be depended on both in sudden emergency and in times of anxiety and monotony" (Library and Archives Canada. RCMP fonds. 1914a, nos. 255–276). Even though Shackleton had the backing of the British Empire to organise and commandeer resources, the RCMP immediately declined (the same day that the cablegram was received from Shackleton) to participate in this adventure passing the opportunity to the London-based HBC instead. Their rationale was that their dogs were too valuable in the field, getting them to London by the deadline would be next to impossible because of the dogs being dispersed amongst various divisions throughout the North, and that a good dog-driver and police officer were too valuable to their true mission (Library and Archives Canada. RCMP fonds 1914b, nos. 255–276). By this point, the relationship between the police in this region and the dogs had become one of a mostly dependable working unit. The individual dogs came and went but for the most part the bugs had been worked out of the system and the police became more efficient in their mission. However they still faced the biggest challenge in working with dog teams in the North: the problem of feeding them.

The big problem: provisions

The problem of provisioning both people and dogs haunted both the fur trade and the opening of the North to colonial authorities. In the early fur trade, one of the problems encountered by North West Company traders was that they were not able to sufficiently provision themselves so as to make trade profitable over the long term (Asch with Wishart 2004). An attempt to alleviate the conditions of this problem was to locate trading posts in places where the traders could feed themselves with fish (Keith 2001: 42). When fishing did not provide an adequate supply of provisions for the traders, the posts would have to be moved and trade restarted in a new location. For example, the trader James Porter noted in his journal (in Keith 2001: 19) that the location of a post had to be linked to the availability of fish to both provision themselves and to supply the post. The problem of reliable provisions to feed the traders was endemic to the fur trade in the Mackenzie District due to supply problems and faunal cycles (Yerbury 1986: 126). This situation resulted in times when traders would be forced to expend their trade goods in order to purchase provisions from Indigenous hunters. Forts on the shores of Great Slave Lake brought in hired fishers whose sole occupation was to capture and store fish to last through the winter months with the possibility of selling the surplus to missionaries (Piper 2009: 171) and then later to government agents like the NWMP.

Provisioning men was difficult enough but they also needed to feed their dogs, including during the months when they were not working. Just as today, where the infrastructure of our mechanised transportation and supply systems requires fuel in the form of petroleum, in that time similar demands were being made of dogs which also require a dependable supply of fuel. If the NWMP were to be successful in creating and maintaining a presence throughout the North the simple economics of transport and provisions required that they solve the fuel problem for their dogs. Certainly in the early years and until provisioning networks were better established, that fuel more often than not came in the form of fish (Wishart 2004). In the letters sent between the divisions and the commanding officers almost as much is written on the provision problem as on actual police work. For example, in a letter from Inspector Jarvis on April 24, 1897 to the Officer commanding, NWMP, Fort Saskatchewan, he explains his failure to complete his patrol:

> Another reason for this action was the impossibility of carrying enough fish for the dogs from Lac La Biche to Grand Rapids and then on to Fort

McMurray, as it was on arrival there expecting to get food. I was told I could get none and therefore it was necessary for me to go sixty miles down the river to get fish to carry me to Fort Chipewyan, had I at this time gone to Grand Rapids I should most certainly have lost all my dogs and probably my men and self.
Library and Archives Canada. RCMP fonds 1897d, nos. 28–37

Policing by dog team required vast amounts of fish to supply the dogs. It was at times difficult to directly acquire this themselves, although they did try at first to do so. Reports of meagre catches are fairly common in the reports. On Great Slave Lake, a report by S. Hetherington on the dog food fishery reported a disappointing catch of only 400 fish to feed the division's dogs, which was all they could catch due to a lack of nets (Library and Archives Canada. RCMP fonds 1897c, nos 28–37). The demand for fishing nets by everyone in the North to fish for dog feed was difficult to meet, and this meant that supplies sometimes ran short and the NWMP were forced to buy fish directly from the Hudson's Bay Company supplies. Alternatively the police could hire people to fish for them and considerable sums were spent by divisions to buy fish. So much so that letters from the officers in charge demanded that divisions put in nets to catch the fish themselves and the amounts spent on fish for the NWMP were debated in Parliament. For example, in a lengthy set of exchanges between the Dawson division, Members of Parliament in Ottawa, and the quarter master for the NWMP, Col. White, a dispute regarding monies owed to a fisherman named Mr. Gauthier is described. Mr. Gauthier was hired to supply fish for the Dawson division and he felt cheated out of money owed to him for one shipment of fish in October 1898. The quartermaster only made monies available for fish weighed upon entry into the stores while the police promised to pay Mr. Gauthier for the weight upon capture. Individual fish lose weight between these steps due to desiccation. The difference was 121 lb in total which left Mr. Gauthier demanding $62 from the division that they could not pay (Library and Archives Canada. RCMP fonds 1911, nos. 317–324). This amounts to about $1800 in today's money, which is no small figure for 120 lb of dog food, and this is just the disputed amount, not the total cost for the shipment. The Dawson division paid $532 for this one shipment, or about $16 000 today. Put quite simply, there were good pay cheques to be made in supplying the NWMP dogs if the police could not do it themselves. In 1900, the NWMP put out notices in northern British Columbia for the provision of dried salmon for dog food. They needed 50 000 lb for the winter patrols in that region (Library and Archives Canada. RCMP 1900, nos. 78–80). The call does not list a value per pound, but if Gauthier was being paid 50 cents per pound of fish eleven years later and after the gold rush, it is not unreasonable to assume at least an equal sum for dried fish at the turn of the century. It was a massive expenditure for the police and the government was keen to reduce these costs by any means possible.

The need to fish to feed their dogs sometimes put the RCMP in a difficult conundrum depending on where they were located. The RCMP were in the North to enforce game laws, which included those of various valuable commercial fisheries, especially when located along the rivers in the west where salmon spawned. The Canadian government was busy in the early twentieth century creating fisheries laws for these stocks including a ban on fishing with nets in some of the spawning rivers. These laws had an enormous impact on Indigenous people who needed to feed themselves and their dogs, but it also left the RCMP in a bind. They could neither ship enough food nor afford to buy dog food to meet their needs. The only possibility to purchase fish would be from the dried salmon merchants either in Canada or across the border in Alaska as described by Andersen (1992: 10):

> In some upriver communities... which had become regional freighting and trading centers, the demand for dried salmon frequently exceeded the capacity of local fishermen and bales of dried fish were shipped in from premier fishing locations along the Yukon... and were warehoused for winter use.

This left the RCMP in a position where they had to ask to set aside the law for their own purposes. On April 16, 1903 Superintendent A. E. Snyder of the White Horse Division wrote a letter to the Assistant Commissioner, NWMP, Dawson, Yukon Territory demanding a resolution to this problem:

> Sir,
>
> I forward you herewith a communication received by the Wells Detachment re fishing in the Chilcat river above tidal waters and within British Colombia, in the Modus Vivendi.[12]
>
> I would draw your attention to the necessity of obtaining from the Minister of Fisheries a permit, as provided for in Section 8, sub-section 5, under which we should be able to secure a permit.
>
> I would draw your attention to the fact that within 200 yards of where this fishing could be carried on and where we have been in the habit of fishing, lies American territory and where enormous numbers of fish are caught.
>
> If we cannot do this fishing, we will have to purchase our dog feed from the U.S. Indians, which will entail great expense, which we last year avoided by putting up our own fish.
>
> Library and Archives Canada. RCMP fonds 1903, nos. 512–532

A permit was granted on June 9th that year by the minister of Marine and Fisheries to the NWMP to use nets to provide dog feed. It is unknown what the effects of this relaxation of the rules governing fishing for the police were, but from evidence presented elsewhere (Harris 2001), it is likely that there was a realisation of the hypocrisy of one set of rules for the police and another for the people residing in the area. In 1905 Snyder followed up with a demand for $60 plus rations to hire a man for two months to fish for the supply of dog food under the permit which was anticipated to provide all the food they need for the following winter (Library and Archives Canada. RCMP fonds 1905 nos. 622–648). This contract would have saved the RCMP money but would also have affected the dog food supply economy in that area.

The lost patrol

Few stories of the police and their dogs made any sort of impact in other regions of Canada but the case of the lost Dawson–Fort McPherson Patrol made headlines throughout the nation. It is also a story that illustrates the challenges of working with dogs, finding good drivers, and provisions. In December, 1910, Inspector Fitzgerald led a group of two constables and a special constable (who was to guide them) on the return leg of a patrol carrying mail and reports from Fort McPherson to Dawson City. They took with them three sleds powered by five dogs each, which Reverend Whittaker of Fort McPherson would later refer to as "not of the best". They declined to hire a Gwich'in guide and dog-driver, and they were lightly provisioned (Library and Archives Canada. RCMP fonds 1913a, no. 400 part I). Their patrol never reached Dawson and on February 27, 1911, Corporal Dempster was ordered to lead a search mission for the missing patrol by Superintendent Snyder (Library and Archives Canada. RCMP fonds 1913b, no. 400 part I). Not making the same errors as Fitzgerald, Dempster was well provisioned, employed a Gwich'in guide, and he described working his fifteen dogs in a way that gradually broke them into their role and got them used to the harder work to come. Fitzgerald and his men did not give their dogs this sort of forethought. Over the next few weeks, Dempster discovered the fate of the missing patrol.

The story is tragic and well documented by Fitzgerald's own diary, discovered next to the bodies of the two constables who perished first. This story was also publicised in various newspaper articles of the time and in later histories (North 1978). It is also still told throughout this part of the Mackenzie region albeit giving different reasons for the cause of Fitzgerald's lack of preparation and poor judgement. The patrol did indeed leave Fort McPherson ill-prepared and provisioned,[13] the officer serving as guide had only been over the route once before, four years earlier, and Fitzgerald made the fatal decision to try to break the time record for this trip by further lightening his load, which included the removal of a shotgun and ammunition that would have supplemented their diet through the hunting of ptarmigan which were reported to be plentiful that year. The patrol made slow progress either because of the quality of the dogs or how they were being worked.

The snow was unusually heavy and this made the dogs' work much more difficult. They soon got lost after leaving the Peel River and spent nine days searching for the route over the divide to Dawson. With provisions running dangerously low, Fitzgerald decided to turn back to Fort McPherson. At this point they began to eat their dogs and tried to feed the other dogs with the same meat. Fitzgerald writes that the dogs refused to eat their own kind so he made a decision to feed the men on dog meat and the dogs with the dwindling provisions. As the dogs were consumed they made slower progress until they could move no more and died within a normal day's dog sled journey from Fort McPherson. Dempster remarks that he can say nothing of the dogs because he never saw them, but even if they were good dogs, the patrol did not take enough provisions to safely make the journey (Library and Archives Canada. RCMP fonds 1913b, no. 400 part I).

Inquiries were made into the cause of the loss of the patrol and some newspapers picked up on the statement by Whittaker about the quality of the animals, blaming the dogs while lauding the officers for their heroic struggle against the elements (e.g., The Edmonton Journal 1912). What is apparent in the unfolding of this story is that a delicate balance existed between the reliability of dogs to take people and goods to places and the need to provision them properly that Fitzgerald either ignored or chose to gamble against. Dogs and people worked together to make these patrols possible, but it took considerable forethought and planning to make this collaboration successful. In striking this balance the police faced the same problem as the traders who went to the North before them and when the balance was upset, the problem of dogs became the central focus, and perhaps like a piece of technology that failed its user the dogs became the scapegoats.

Conclusion

The role of dogs in the colonisation of the Canadian North has tended to focus on adoption of sled dog technology by Indigenous people during the fur trade. It is a compelling and complex story of shifting economies and changing sensibilities about the role of dogs in society, but the use of dogs by the force put in place to govern the North has not been well examined. In the case presented here, did the police consider and treat their dogs as mere machines to be used and abused in the carrying out of their mission in the North or was the relationship more akin to a mutually dependant working unit? It is possible to tease information out of the archives to try to bring the dogs who made colonial control in this region a reality back into the story but like many stories of human–animal cooperation it is told from the human point of view. In the diary of Fitzgerald there is no mention of the names of the dogs, nor is there any sentiment displayed in the choice of which to eat first. The RCMP never memorialised the dogs in their epic struggle nor in recognition of their flesh which kept the men alive during their last days of struggle. Instead they were reported to be a problem or an obstacle which needed to be guarded against. The cold, clinical language that police were trained to use in all reports and correspondence may simply disallow any recognition of the character of inter-dependence between police and dogs with which we are more familiar with today's canine units. We do know that the police had to work hard for their dogs and that lack of care for them could be disastrous. It was also in the interest of the dogs themselves to work and thus be fed and bred during their short lives. Certainly by the beginning of the twentieth century the skill of police in working with dogs and creating good teams was recognised in the centres of colonial power. In the end, the relationship between police and dogs in this region fell victim to the same policy of control that the police were in the North to enforce. While dogs are no longer necessary for transportation, they have continued to play a significant role in Northern Indigenous communities, but the police for the most part have had to abandon the dogs in the same way that they need to surrender other obsolete equipment when something new and seemingly better comes along.

Notes

1 The Royal Canadian Mounted Police is the last and current title for Canada's national police force, but its name changed over the years to better describe the force's mission. For the sake of simplicity I will be referring to the police force in general terms as the RCMP while maintaining the other titles when citing directly from the primary source materials.
2 Frank Oliver was Minister of the Interior during the Senate hearings of 1887–1888 where the fate of the Mackenzie district was being decided: "The work of transforming the virgin prairies of Manitoba and southern Saskatchewan and Alberta into productive grain fields and pastures is rapidly approaching completion, and places which up to 1880 had never been visited by a white man, are now the sites of large and prosperous cities.

While the work of developing the southern portion of the new western provinces was yet in its infancy the claim of the resources of the great northland to national attention began to assert itself." *Hon. Frank Oliver, Minister of the Interior, Canada* (1910: 7).
3 (www.heise.de/tp/features/Kommissar-Rex-an-der-Mauer-erschossen-3378291.html) (Accessed 15 April 2017).
4 The Athabasca District—sometimes spelled Athabaska—at this time was composed of the northern third of what is now the Provinces of Alberta and Saskatchewan but also intruded into Manitoba. It was the gateway to the Northwest Territories and was considered to be crucial in establishing a police foothold.
5 There were times when the policing of game laws was supposed to be for the benefit of the Indigenous people. In a letter to Wilfrid Laurier, the Prime Minister of Canada in 1896 justifies the police presence in the North by claiming that they are there to stop the destructive practices of "whites" who use poison to capture game and destroy not only the stocks of animals but also the "valuable sled-dogs of the Indians" (Library and Archives Canada. RCMP fonds 1896, no. 54).

6 See Lewis and Ferguson (1988) for a detailed description on the social-ecological importance of this practice and the problems which banning the practice had in maintaining the resources the RCMP believed they were protecting.
7 The 1994 silver $1 Queen Elizabeth II commemorative coin has an image of an RCMP dog team on the tail side to mark the 25th anniversary of the last RCMP dog team patrol.
8 Trains of dogs vs. teams is a confusing word choice in the historical documents. Both could be used to refer to singular sled plus dogs or a plural of sleds plus dogs.
9 The structural organisation of the RCMP in the north is beyond the scope of this article. See Morrison (2011) for these details.
10 While it is difficult to read into the names assigned to the dogs the purchase list does give us insight into the casual racism of the time and possibly the subservient roles they played. Of the eight dogs, two are named "Nigger" and one is named "Darkey." Perhaps the names suggest a position in the hierarchy of a team or they might be descriptive names given to dogs for their behaviour or coat colour, or they might just be random names that the breeder assigned to the puppies from a limited repertoire.
11 Later came to be known as the Trans-Antarctica Expedition 1914–1917, or the Endurance Expedition.
12 The Fisheries Act of 1886 made it unlawful to fish with nets for salmon in British Columbia except in tidal waters.
13 Fitzgerald took 900 lb of dried fish with him to feed his dog teams, an amount that Dempster considered to be insufficient for the jouney.

References

Andersen, D. 1992. *The use of dog teams and the use of subsistence caught fish for feeding sled dogs in the Yukon River drainage, Alaska*. Juneau: Alaska Department of Fish and Game.
Anderson, D.G., J.P.L. Loovers, S.A. Schroer and R.P. Wishart. 2017. "Architectures of domestication: on emplacing human–animal relations in the North." *Journal of the Anthropological Institute*, 23 (2): 398–416.
Asch, M.I. 1989. "Wildlife: Defining the Animals the Dene Hunt and the Settlement of Aboriginal Rights Claims." *Canadian Public Policy*, 15 (2): 205–219.
Asch, M.I. with R. Wishart. 2004. "The Slavey Indians: the relevance of ethnohistory to development." In *Native Peoples: The Canadian Experience*. Edited by Morrison, R.B. and C.R. Wilson, 178–197. Oxford: Oxford University Press.
Bentham, J. 1789. *An Introduction to the Principles of Morals and Legislation*. Oxford: Clarendon Press
British Columbia Archives. 1866–1867. Diary of R. George Cowley. R. George Cowley fonds. PR-1538.
Coppinger, R. and L. Coppinger. 2001. *Dogs: A Startling New Understanding of Canine Origin, Behavior & Evolution*. New York: Scribner.
Dawson, M. 2008. *The Mountie: From Dime Novel to Disney*. Toronto: Between the Lines.
Few, M. and Z. Tortorici. 2013. *Centering Animals in Latin American History*. Durham: Duke University Press.

Haraway, D. 2003 *The Companion Species Manifesto: Dogs, People, and Significant Otherness*. Chicago: Prickly Paradigm Press.
Haraway, D. 2007. *When Species Meet*. Minneapolis: University of Minnesota Press.
Hare, B. and V. Woods. 2013. *The Genius of Dogs*. London: Oneworld.
Harris, D.C. 2001. *Fish, Law, and Colonialism: The Legal Capture of Salmon in British Columbia*. Toronto: University of Toronto Press.
Kane, P. 1859. *Wanderings of an Artist among the Indians of North America*. London: Longman, Brown, Green, Longmans, and Roberts.
Keith, L. 2001. *North of Athabasca: Slave Lake and Mackenzie River Documents of the North West Company, 1800–1821*. Montreal: McGill Queen's University Press.
Krech, III., S. 1976. "The Eastern Kutchin and the Fur Trade, 1800–1860." *Ethnohistory*, 23: 213–235.
Kurlansky, M. 1997. *Cod: A Biography of the Fish That Changed the World*. Ottawa: Knoph.
Lestel, D. 1996. *L'animalité*. Paris: Hatier.
Lévesque, F. 2011. "An Ordinance Respecting Dogs: How Creating Secure Communities in the Northwest Territories Made Inuit Insecure." In *Humanizing Security in the Arctic*. Edited by M. Daveluy, F. LéVesque and J. Fergusson, 73–90. Edmonton: CCI Press
Lewis, H.T. and T.A. Ferguson. 1988. "Yards, Corridors, and Mosaics: How to Burn a Boreal Forest." *Human Ecology*, 16 (1): 57–77.
Library and Archives Canada. September 11, 1896. Letter from the Officer in Charge NWMP to Hon. Wilfred Laurier. RCMP fonds 1896, no. 54.
Library and Archives Canada. December 4, 1896. Letter from the Comptroller NWMP to Commissioner Herchemer. RCMP fonds, nos. 23–27.
Library and Archives Canada. February 3, 1897a. Letter from Alicksand Levillot to the Officer in Charge NWMP. RCMP fonds 1897, nos. 36–62.
Library and Archives Canada. 1897b. Report on the purchase of dogs for the Slave Lake region with receipt from HBC. RCMP fonds, nos. 36–62.
Library and Archives Canada. February 25, 1897c. Report by S. Hetherington to the Officer Commanding RNMP Athabasca detachment. RCMP fonds 1897, nos. 36–62.
Library and Archives Canada. April 24, 1897d. Letter from Inspector Jarvis to the Officer commanding, NWMP, Fort Saskatchewan. RCMP fonds 1897, nos. 36–62.
Library and Archives Canada. 1899a. Various reports on the import of dogs from the coast of Labrador to the Yukon Territory. RCMP fonds 1899, no. 115.
Library and Archives Canada. 1899b. Various reports on the shortage of dog-drivers and demands of drivers for more pay. RCMP fonds 1899, no. 115.
Library and Archives Canada. 1900. Notice for the purchase of dried fish for dog food. RCMP fonds 1900, nos. 78–80.
Library and Archives Canada. April 16, 1903. Letter from Superintendent A.E. Snyder of the White Horse Division to the Assistant Commissioner, NWMP, Dawson, Y.T. Re. Permit to fish. RCMP fonds 1903, nos. 512–532.
Library and Archives Canada. 1905. Letter from Superintendent A.E. Snyder. Re. hiring men to fish. RCMP fonds 1905, nos. 622–648.
Library and Archives Canada. August 1908. Report from Inspector Commanding B. Division. Dawson, to The Assistant Commissioner R.N.W.M. Police, Yukon Territory. RCMP fonds 1908, nos. 184–186.

Library and Archives Canada. 1911. Various letters regarding money owed to Mr. Gauthier in regards to the supply of fish for dog food. RCMP fonds 1911, nos. 317–324.

Library and Archives Canada. 1913a. Extract of letter from Reverend Whittaker, Fort McPherson to Bishop Stringer, Dawson. RCMP fonds 1913, no. 400, part I.

Library and Archives Canada. 1913b. Report by Corporal Dempster on the search for the lost Fitzgerald patrol. RCMP fonds 1913, no. 400, part I.

Library and Archives Canada. April 13, 1914a. Cablegram from Ernest Shackleton to The Commanding Officer R.N.W.M. Police. RCMP fonds 1914, nos. 255–276.

Library and Archives Canada. April 13, 1914b. Lettergram from A.B. Perry Commissioner R.N.W.M Police to Comptroller R.N.W.M police. RCMP fonds 1914, nos. 255–276.

Longstreth, T.M. 1929. "Some Geographical Difficulties of the R.C.M.P." *The Police Journal*, 2(1): 37–50.

Loovers, J.P.L. 2015. "Dog-craft: a history of Gwich'in and dogs in the Canadian North." *Hunter-Gatherer Research*, 1(4): 387–419.

McCormack, P. 2014. "Evolving Accommodations: The Sled Dog in the Canadian Fur Trade." In *Une Bête Parmi les Hommes; Le Chien: De la domestication à l'anthropomorphisme*. Edited by F. Guizard and C. Beck, 130–147. Valenciennes: Distribution Les Belles Lettres.

Major, P. 2010. *Behind the Berlin Wall: East Germany and the Frontiers of Power*. Oxford: Oxford University Press

Morrison, W.R. 2011. *Showing the Flag: The Mounted Police and Canadian Sovereignty in the North, 1894–1925*. Vancouver: UBC Press.

Nadasdy, P. 2004. *Hunters and Bureaucrats: Power, Knowledge, and Aboriginal-State Relations in the Southwest Yukon*. Vancouver: UBC Press.

Nance, S. 2015 *The Historical Animal*. Syracuse: Syracuse University Press.

North, D. 1978. *The Lost Patrol*. Anchorage: Alaska Northwest Books.

Oliver, F. 1910. *The Great Mackenzie Basin: The Senate Reports of 1887–1888*. Ottawa: C.H. Parmelee, Printer to the King's Most Excellent Majesty.

Piper, L. 2009. *The Industrial Transformation of SubArctic Canada*. Vancouver: UBC Press.

Sandlos, J. 2007. *Hunters at the Margin: Native People and Wildlife Conservation in the Northwest Territories*. Vancouver: UBC Press.

Schledermann, P. 2003. "The Muskox Patrol: High Arctic Sovereignty Revisited." *Arctic*, 56(1): 101–106.

Shackleton, R. 2012. "'Not Just Givers of Welfare': The Changing Role of the RCMP in the Baffin Region, 1920–1970." *Northern Review*, 36: 5–26.

Shannon, K.A. 1997. The Unique Role of Sled Dogs in Inuit Culture: An Examination of the Relationship between Inuit and Sled Dogs in the Changing North. Unpublished MA thesis. Edmonton: The University of Alberta.

Slobodin, R. 1962. *Band organization of the Peel River Kutchin*. Ottawa: National Museum of Canada Bulletin 179.

Steele, H. 1936. *Policing the Arctic: The Story of the Conquest of the Arctic by the Royal Canadian (formerly North-West) Mounted Police*. Toronto: Ryerson Press.

Tester, Frank J. 2010. "Mad dogs and (mostly) Englishmen: Colonial relations, commodities, and the fate of Inuit sled dogs." *Études/Inuit/Studies*, 34 (2): 129–147.

The Edmonton Journal. 1912. *Memorial for The Lost Patrol*. April 1, 1912.

The New York Times. 1899. *Dogs in the Klondike*. January 1, 1899.

Trautman, E.C. 1964. "Fear and Panic in Nazi Concentration Camps: a Biosocial Evaluation of the Chronic Anxiety Syndrome." *International Journal of Social Psychiatry*, 10 (2): 134–141.

Wishart, R.P. 2004. Living "On the Land": Teetl'it Gwich'in Perspectives on Continuities. Unpublished PhD Thesis. Edmonton: The University of Alberta, Department of Anthropology.

Wishart, R.P. 2014. "'We Ate Lots of Fish Back Then': The Forgotten Importance of Fishing in Gwich'in Country." *Polar Record*, 50 (4): 343–353.

Wolf, E.R. 1982. *Europe and the People Without History*. Berkeley: University of California Press.

Yerbury, C. 1986. *SubArctic Indians and the Fur Trade, 1680–1860*. Vancouver: UBC Press.

9 Threatening the fantasy of an Arctic welfare state
Canada, Quebec and Inuit dogs in Qikiqtaaluk and Nunavik between 1957 and 1968

Francis Lévesque

Introduction

Between 1957 and 1968, dogs of the Eastern Arctic Inuit were killed by colonial agents (members of police forces, civil servants, citizens, teachers, citizens, and even by Inuit hired to do so) in many Qikiqtaaluk (Baffin Island) communities and Nunavik (Northern Quebec) villages (Figure 9.1). These killings, which Inuit elders call *qimmijaqtauniq* ("being deprived of one's dogs repeatedly") are commonly known as the "dog slaughter". They took place alongside the migration of Inuit to newly created settlements throughout both territories. In the early 2000s, little was known about what had taken place: not only were Inuit elders reluctant to talk, but the Canadian and the Quebec governments and their respective police forces denied any wrongdoing. Moreover, no research had been done on the topic (see Lévesque 2008: 68–109 for more details). More than a decade later, the dog slaughter has become "a flashpoint in Inuit memories of the changes imposed on their lives by outsiders" (QTC 2013a: 416), and has been studied by several researchers (Lévesque 2010, 2011, 2015; McHugh 2013; Tester 2010a, 2010b; Zahara and Hird 2015). Documentaries have also been made on the topic (Makivik Corporation 2005; Gjerstad and Sanguya 2010). More significantly, it has been the object of an independent inquiry commissioned by Nunavik Inuit (Croteau 2010) as well as of a truth and reconciliation commission established by Qikiqtaaluk Inuit (Qikiqtani Truth Commission (QTC) 2013a, 2013b).

All of these publications have contributed to increasing our knowledge of what took place and have shown that the slaughter of dogs was an inevitable consequence of Canadian colonialism. Yet, the narrative proposed by most of them either (a) ignores events that seem to contradict the very existence of the slaughter, like the continuous efforts made by governments to feed and vaccinate dogs, or (b) ignores local specificities. A close look at historical archives and oral records shows that although dogs were killed throughout the Eastern Arctic between 1957 and 1968, the killings took different shapes, involved a great many actors, and were

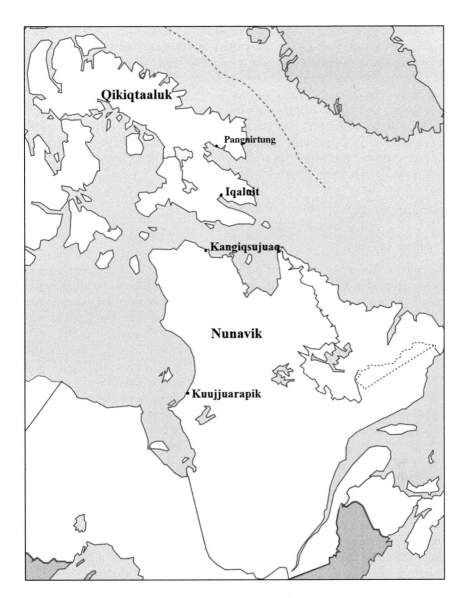

Figure 9.1 Map of Qikiqtaaluk and Nunavik, Canada
Map created by F. Lévesque.

justified through separate sets of laws: those of Quebec in Nunavik and those of the Northwest Territories for the Qikiqtaaluk. It also shows that while some dogs were killed, there were many attempts to keep others alive by feeding or vaccinating them. This chapter will present a narrative that pays attention to local specificities, contradictions and territorial differences. It will seek to determine whether the thesis that claims that the slaughter of dogs was the consequence of Canadian colonialism still holds true once specificities and contradictions are taken into account. Using archival material from Library and Archives Canada (Ottawa) and the Prince of Wales Northern Heritage Centre (Yellowknife) as well as testimonies from Nunavut and Nunavik Inuit, this chapter follows Haraway who mentions that understanding dogs requires raising questions of histories, politics and ethics (Haraway 2003). This chapter will thus focus on the historical, political and ethical issues surrounding the killing of dogs in four different locations: Kuujjuarapik and Kangiqsujuaq (Nunavik), as well as Pangnirtung and Iqaluit (Qikiqtaaluk).

Qimmijaqtauniq

Northern Quebec

Kuujjuarapik is a half-Inuit, half-Cree village (known as Whapmagoostui in Cree) situated at the mouth of Grande rivière de la Baleine on the Eastern shores of Hudson's Bay. Following the establishment of the Hudson's Bay Company (HBC) in 1853, Great-Whale-River, as it was then known, was visited by many Inuit families who came to hunt belugas and trade Arctic fox and seal pelts for goods (tea, flour, guns, ammunition, etc.). The post did not become a permanent settlement until the US Air Force (USAF) decided it was a suitable location to establish a radar station in the 1950s.[1] Following World War II, the USAF, with the collaboration of the Canadian government, decided to build a series of radar stations (known as the DEW Line) throughout the Arctic in order to detect Soviet bombers attacking North America. Kuujjuarapik was part of the Mid-Canada Line, which stretched from Northern British Columbia to Labrador. The construction of radar stations attracted Inuit, many of whom were looking for new sources of income after the value of white fox pelts crashed following WW II (Gagnon 1999; Gagnon and Inuit Elders 2002; Bégin 2004).

Up until the 1950s, the Canadian government remained virtually absent from the Arctic. Apart from the Royal Canadian Mounted Police (RCMP), the government had no civil servants in the region. Inuit, Arctic administrators believed, were better off on their own. Yet, the USAF was very critical of the Canadian administration for not taking care of Inuit (Diubaldo 1985); so was the RCMP.[2] These critics,[3] coupled with the aforementioned crash of the value of white fox pelts and the collapse of caribou herds throughout the Arctic, forced the Canadian government to reverse its stance and start establishing programmes to care for the well-being of Inuit. This policy reversal, which has been well documented (Damas 1993, 2002; Zaslow 1988; Tester and Kulchisky 1994; Lesage 1955; Robertson 1960, 1961, 2002), was introduced in *The Canadian Eskimo Problem*,[4] a document that encouraged Inuit who were unable to hunt to come near construction sites to find work. It also introduced the idea that Inuit should send their children to school as was mandatory for First Nations since 1920.

In the 1960s, Quebec also started to claim its sovereignty over its Arctic territory. Jean Lesage, who, as the federal minister of the North and National Resources between 1953 and 1957, played an instrumental role in the policy reversal toward Inuit, became Quebec's Premier in 1960. He decided that the North should become one of Quebec's priorities and that the province should also offer services to Inuit (education, health, etc.). In 1963, the Direction générale du Nouveau-Québec was created to coordinate the administrative efforts of the Quebec government. The Sûreté du Québec (Quebec's provincial police, thereafter SQ) replaced the RCMP in larger settlements (Kuujjuarapik, Kuujjuaq, Inukjuak, Puvirnituq), schools were built throughout the territory (Lévesque, Jubinville and Rodon 2016) and civil servants were sent to Puvirnituq, Inukjuak and Kangiqsujuaq.

At the end of the 1950s, Kuujjuarapik was an Arctic boom-town with an economy that revolved around the trading post and the construction sites. At that time Inuit came to Kuujjuarapik to find jobs; most thought the move was temporary. They therefore came with their whole families as well as their dogs, which they still relied on to travel, hunt and trap. At that point in time, Inuit dogs still occupied a peculiar place in Inuit society. Like humans, dogs had names (sg. *atiq*, pl. *atiit*). For the Inuit, *atiit* are autonomous entities that possess their own kinship relations. For example, a woman that named her baby girl after her deceased father would call her daughter "father" and act with her as if she were her father (i.e., raising her to be a hunter, asking her questions about her own youth, etc.). Thus dogs shared kinship relations with Inuit. They could be fathers, grandfathers, mothers, grandmothers, uncles, aunts and so forth (Mitiarjuk 1994). Hence, dogs were full-fledged members of the community. In fact "the community as a whole consist[ed] not only of people but also of the dogs they own[ed]" (Laugrand and Oosten 2002: 101; Laugrand and Oosten 2014).

Kuujjuarapik had few amenities at the end of the 1950s. Apart from the infrastructures being built for the radar station, the settlement had a federal day school built in 1958, an Anglican mission, a RCMP station and a HBC post. The settlement also had a single Northern Service Officer (NSO), the federal civil servant whose job it was to administer federal programmes and to encourage "the Eskimos to take responsibility for local decisions to as great an extent as possible" (Lesage 1955: 8). Most Inuit lived in tents, surrounded by their dogs, which they refused to tie up. Indeed, they said that loose dogs were better socialized, in better shape because they could exercise and were able to feed themselves.

In March of 1957, the daughter of the local Anglican missionary and a local Cree girl were both attacked by dogs that belonged to Inuit. Furious, the Bishop of the Arctic, Donald B. Marsh, wrote a letter to Gordon Robertson, who was Commissioner of the Northwest Territories (NWT), in which he asked him to force Inuit to tie up their animals.[5] Robertson answered that there was nothing he could do.⁶ First, Kuujjuarapik was under Quebec's jurisdiction, not that of the NWT, and second, section 11 of the provincial *Agricultural Abuse Act*,⁷ prevented the killing of loose dogs between December 15th and April 30th in unorganized territories (the law did force owners to tie up their animals between May 1st and December 14th and allowed anyone to kill loose dogs). Nevertheless, Robertson asked the local NSO, R.L. Kennedy, to tell him what happened. After mentioning that he had already brought the topic up with the provincial police, Kennedy mentioned that the dog that attacked the girls was tied up and that they had got too close. According to him, dogs were less dangerous when not tied, so he recommended that Inuit be allowed to keep them loose.⁸ Nevertheless, Kennedy called a meeting with local hunters to remind them that whenever possible, they should be tying their dogs up to please the government.

In early September 1957, loose dogs destroyed the radar station's food warehouse. All of them were killed on the spot by the man in charge of the station, the manager of the Bell Telephone Section Plant and by a RCMP member (who claims to have killed at least eight of them). Inuit were angered by this action. On September 8th 1957, Kennedy convened a meeting where the local RCMP member explained that according to the Agricultural Abuse Act, dog owners were forced to tie up their dogs between May 1st and December 14th. Following the meeting, the RCMP member wrote to his superiors stating that "[a]t this time all those who complained of having had dogs destroyed readily admitted they had been told to keep their dogs tied or they would be shot […]".⁹ Inuit were thus made responsible for the loss of their own dogs. Worse, they started to believe that they were responsible for their death. According to a Kuujjuarapik Inuk interviewed by Makivik Corporation in 1999, "[t]he Inuit only blamed themselves whenever their dogs got killed" (M-015[10]). Nevertheless, the irony of this measure was not lost on the Inuit, one of whom remarked that although the killing of dogs was supposed to make the community more secure, "it became dangerous to have dogs being loose in the middle of the community as they were automatically shot whenever they were sighted" (M-096).[11]

In 1958, a young Inuit girl was attacked by dogs in a camp north of Kuujjuarapik. Despite being medivacked to Val-d'Or; she passed away the next day. This accident, added to those that occurred in previous years, worried R.A.J. Phillips, head of the Arctic Division. In a memorandum sent to the new Kuujjuarapik NSO, J. G. Walton, Phillips required that measures be taken to prevent accidents. Walton replied that Inuit still continued to let their dogs loose, especially in camps. He also emphasized that they accepted the risks associated with living among dogs, the same way Canadians accept the dangers of traffic.[12] In 1959, Deputy Sergeant (D/Sgt.) Tourville of the Quebec provincial police came to Kuujjuarapik and told dog owners they had 24 hours to tie up their animals. After the delay expired, he killed at least six dogs himself.

On July 22nd 1959, S., an employee of the radar station, who had lost a daughter to a dog in Puvirnituq in 1955 (RCMP 2006: 356),[13] killed two loose dogs. Upset with him, several Inuit gathered around his camp and threatened him with their guns. S., frightened, called Walton for help and told him he did not understand why Inuit were furious at him. Later, Walton explained to his superior that:

> Mr. [S.] was very hasty in not taking care when shooting through the settlement. I think that the few shots which went through the tents caused the actual resentment and not the fact that some dogs were killed. This is not the first time loose dogs have been shot at Great Whale River but it was the first time that the Eskimos have been so concerned, and they had good cause to be alarmed.[14]

The next day, S. sent a telegram to the Premier of Quebec, Maurice Duplessis, to inform him that stray dogs were a serious threat to the local population. Three weeks later, D/Sgt. Edgar Anderson of the provincial police investigated the case.[15] The *Montreal Gazette* reported the event:

> *Mad Dogs "Terrorize" North, Police to Probe Shooting*
>
> A detective of the provincial Police homicide squad is scheduled to fly to Quebec's North country tomorrow morning to investigate reports that wild dogs are terrorizing the area and residents who have shot them have been threatened by armed Eskimos.
>
> The report which came to QPP headquarters here from Churchill, Great Whale River, claims two girls and a boy have been killed by roaming dogs in recent years.
>
> Det.- Sgt. Nick (*sic*) Anderson said he will investigate the situation there and, if necessary, warn Eskimos a provincial law requires all dogs be tied or leashed between May 1 and December 15 in "unorganized" territory.
>
> It is estimated that between 500 and 550 dogs are loose in the district" Sgt. Anderson said last night, "and the Eskimo population is 352. The dogs apparently have turned loose and ran short of food in the summer months. […]
>
> Anonymous 1959a

Time Magazine also reported on the story following a letter sent by S.: "starving huskies, set loose by the Eskimos to scavenge for themselves through the lean summer months, were terrorizing the village. When [S.] took his rifle in hand to protect his family, Eskimos loosed a volley of gunshot at his wood-frame shack " (Anonymous 1959b). Not everyone in town saw loose dogs as a problem. P.J. M., an employee of the Canadian Marconi Company working in Kuujjuarapik, responded to the *Time Magazine* article with the following letter, reproduced here in its entirety:

> Dear Sirs:
>
> The residents of Great Whale River would be greatly indebted to the Editors of *Time Magazine* if a collection was undertaken to purchase large willow sticks, to beat off the alleged 500 mad dogs roaming at will in this region.
>
> Not having previously realized the grave dangers we faced each time we stepped outdoors, we are truly thankful to your publication for having enlightened us of the feat that such a dreaded situation exists.[16]

Canadian Arctic administrators, all of whom were based in Ottawa and seldom went up North, were worried about emerging conflicts between Inuit and non-Inuit. On one hand, they wanted to find solutions to reduce conflicts among Kuujjuarapik inhabitants, and on the other, they recognized that dogs were "an important part of their [Inuit] culture, both as a mean of transportation and as a symbol of prestige and success".[17] The mass shooting of loose dogs was thus not a solution they envisioned:

> The long-term solution to the problem of dogs running loose is to convince their owners to keep them tied up. Indiscriminate shooting reduce the number of dogs, but will certainly increase hostility toward the person who does the shooting, and any group he is identified with. It will also make it more difficult to convince the dog owners that dogs should be tied up.[18]

At the end of the 1950s, dogs were still the only mean of transportation in the Arctic for most of the year. The federal government wanted Inuit to make a decent living, and that meant they needed to be able to travel on the land.

In 1961, the community faced a new threat: an epidemic of Canine Distemper[19] killed between forty and fifty dogs. In order to control the spread disease, Quebec's department of Agriculture recommended that dogs be tied up at all times and vaccinated.[20] In 1962, some dogs believed to be rabid were killed by a SQ[21] policeman. In the note accompanying the carcass sent for analysis, David Neve, the administrator responsible for Kuujjuarapik, mentioned that "these dogs are extremely valuable to the Eskimos in this community and I am anxious to take every precaution to prevent a spread of the disease as soon as possible".[22] It was then decided to send a veterinary, Dr. Toupin, to the community. He realized dogs were not infected with rabies, but rather by canine hepatitis, which killed about forty of them in December of that year. To prevent the spread of the disease, 250 dogs were vaccinated in 1962 (RCMP 2006: 240). Nevertheless, dogs continued to fall victim of various diseases, thus 2350 doses of vaccines had to be sent to the community in 1963 (RCMP 2006: 245), and 550 more in 1964.[23] In 1966, rabies struck and killed dogs again; 300 doses of vaccines were sent to prevent the spread of the disease. Alongside these epidemics, Kuujjuarapik Inuit started using snowmobiles instead of dogs. Snowmobiles had appeared in the Arctic in 1962 and were commonplace in 1968 (Honigmann and Honigmann 1965: 16, 44; Pelto 1973: 67–75). By 1970, dogs had all but disappeared from Kuujjuarapik and other settlements in the Canadian Eastern Arctic.

Kuujjuarapik shares many similar features with other Northern Quebec villages. However, as a fairly large village, its story is distinctive from that of smaller settlements where dogs were also killed, but where patterns differ significantly. One of these small settlements is Kangiqsujuaq which, in the early 1960s, was inhabited by 176 Inuit and 11 non-Inuit who worked at the federal school and the provincial school. There was one catholic missionary as well as one mechanic. Every year, a nurse would come to the community to make sure everybody was OK.[24] But there was no SQ detachment. Inuit elders remember that that one day, in 1964 or 1965,[25] a plane landed and a SQ policeman accompanied by an Inuk got off. An elder interviewed by Makivik Corporation in 1999 remembers:

> [The policeman] told us that the dogs were to be killed, since they were a danger to people and they could carry rabies. There was a small meeting held about this, with no feedback from the Inuit. [The policeman] was working with [Inuk] of Kuujjuaq. Everyone had to bring their dogs, even if they didn't want to. They took the dogs to an island and killed them. My father's dogs were killed. I can still remember the pile of dead dogs on the ice. I don't know exactly how many there were, but it was a very big pile.
>
> M-019

Another adds that "half of the population of dogs were killed. Even though the men cherished their dogs, they tried picking the ones they cherished less than others and brought them down to the sea ice to be put to death" (M-034). Many dog owners felt they had no choice: "We just accepted it as we were persuaded. Nobody said that they should not be killed. Everyone was told and was not given any choice, no way to say no" (M-041). The Inuk man who assisted the SQ policeman mentions that he thought Inuit wanted their dogs to be killed because "people brought dogs that they didn't want". Nevertheless, he also claims that the policeman and him "got shot at when we just finished shooting dogs" (Croteau 2010: 71), meaning Kangiqsujuaq Inuit were furious at them for having killed dogs. Dogs' carcasses were put on the ice and burned. This episode was traumatic for many Inuit of the region: "our children were crying learning that our dogs were to be killed

[...] They cried and asked, are they going to kill them? [...] We really did love them, some of the people really loved their dogs, as though it was their human companion, and the dogs were comprehensive to their masters" (M-030). Even the Inuk man who assisted the SQ policeman said that "All those dead dogs that piled up. I will never forget that in Kangiqsujuaq" (Croteau 2010: 71).

This traumatic event may have several causes. First, dogs had been sick the previous year and the Canadian government had vaccinated 250 of them (RCMP 2006: 247). The fact that carcasses were burned also seems to indicate that authorities were afraid of sickness, as it was their privileged technique to kill sick dogs (RCMP 2006: 99–125). Secondly, two young women had been attacked by dogs in Quaqtaq just months before, which may have prompted the Quebec government to seek a solution. Being a new administration with little knowledge of how the federal government dealt with dogs, the Quebec administration developed its own strategies. It first started by amending the Agriculture Abuse Act and making it legal for anyone to kill stray dogs at any moment of the year in Nunavik villages (Order in Council 332). It then decided that the killing of dogs would be its main strategy to control the inherent risk associated with the large population of dogs in Nunavik villages. However, the practice of killing dogs to keep the community secure ceased in 1967 to "prevent antagonizing the Eskimos".[26] Nevertheless, dogs disappeared from the community in the late 1960s and early 1970s, replaced by snowmobiles.

Northwest Territories[27]

Iqaluit, then known as Frobisher Bay, was another community built around a military site operated by the USAF and the Royal Canadian Air Force (RCAF) during and after WW II as a base of operation to construct the Distant Early Warning (DEW) Line. In the 1950s, Iqaluit was an Arctic boom-town that attracted Inuit from all over south Baffin Island and southern workers. Between 1951 and 1961, the population went from 298 to 1162. Of those, 950 were Inuit who came to look for work. They came with their dogs, which they let loose. Since 1928, the Northwest Territories (NWT) had a Dog Ordinance (DO) that forced dog owners to tie up their animals at all times. The DO did not permit the killing of loose dogs. A Dog Officer, named by the Commissioner of the NWT, was responsible of catching dogs, keeping them for five days (in case their owner would want to pay the fee to get them back), and then auctioning them. Dogs were killed only when no one bought them (Lévesque 2011).

Although the ordinance had force of law at the air base, it did not in the makeshift settlement where Inuit established themselves close to the base. The fact that Inuit brought all their dogs with them actually forced local and federal authorities to rethink this state of affairs. In 1956, local and federal administrators discussed at length the pros and cons of applying the DO to the settlement. While on one side they wanted to get rid of loose dogs, on the other, they were aware that:

> many Eskimos have been employed during the past two years and it is likely that some of these will be laid off this winter. If so, they will need to hunt and they have no dogs. Van [Norman, RCMP Corporal in Iqaluit] recommended that we refrain from having the dog population reduced in the interval. I agreed, expressing the hope that the dogs would be chained.[28]

Nevertheless, in 1956, it was decided to apply the DO to the settlement. By 1955, the DO had been amended to allow Dog Officers, most of whom were RCMP members, to kill loose dogs on the spot instead of catching them. Although the DO still prevented them from killing dogs that were tied up, the amendment gave a lot of power to Dog Officers. The RCMP's implementation strategy was fairly simple:

> …members of this detachment propose to catch about a dozen loose dogs and place them in the pound: also prosecute the owners. It is believed that this will result in owners of remaining loose dogs taking the necessary action to secure their animals. Then, if owners are prosecuted from time to time, there will result a minimum of loose dogs in the community.
> RCMP 2006: 364

In the first two months of 1957, "Some twenty dogs have been impounded, two men have been fined for allowing their dogs to run loose, and three or four dogs have been shot after being impounded for the legal limit of five days" (RCMP 2006: 214).

The DO did not deter Inuit from letting their dogs run loose. As the local NSO observed, "the men who are obeying the new rules, tying their dogs and attempting to feed them dog meal, are the ones who have suffered losses by freezing and whose teams are poor and thin. The others who still allow their dogs to roam the garbage dumps have fat sleek animals ready for the trail at any time" (RCMP 2006: 214). For months thereafter, Inuit continued to leave their dogs running at large while the RCMP caught some and killed others. In 1959, the situation degenerated in Iqaluit when police started killing more dogs than ever before and leaving carcasses where the dogs had died. J.F. Delaute, the regional administrator, wrote a vivid account of the situation:

> The practice of the R.C.M. Police here is occasionally to go either to Apex Hill, or the air base, or Ikaluit [different areas of town] and shoot two or three dogs not tied to a leash or chain. Presumably they do this after convicting the owner of an infraction of the Dog Ordinance or after being unable to seize the stray dogs. In any event the method used

causes resentment on the part, not only of the owners, but also of other residents in a populated area like Frobisher Bay. It is regarded as indiscriminate and senseless, although it is realized that the Police do so to set an example and warn owners that the law must be observed. Within the last few months dogs have been shot outside people's front doors at Apex Hill and along one road close to the airbase D.N.A. quarters; the carcasses, left to lie there, unclaimed. From a sanitation point of view the Engineering Division here has arranged for the garbage collectors to pick up the carcasses and dispose of them. Since the Dog Ordinance says nothing as to disposal of a carcass, the Police, of course, in the strict legal sense, have no responsibility–but the practice nevertheless causes resentment everywhere.

RCMP 2006: 223–224

Many eye-witnesses agree with Delaute's account. Long-time resident of the area Brian Pearson remembers that in "1959 I recall vividly seeing squads of cars going out on Sunday afternoon in particular with shotguns shooting dogs and in October of 1959 the RCMP in that month alone shot 280 dogs". (RCMP 2006: 273). Yatsushiro, an anthropologist who spent the summers of 1958 and 1959 in Iqaluit recalls that "the 1958 dog population of nearly 500 was reduced to less than half that number by 1959" (Yatsushiro 1960: 16). A witness met in 2004 also remembers:

> [I]n [1959], we were having something to eat at lunch time suddenly we heard there was shooting outside. So we ran out and we saw two RCMP with shotgun rifles and shoot our thirteen dogs. All of them! They were in a chain, they don't roam around. And suddenly, we went out and all of them were dead. When we got out, two of them were still alive but they shot them again. All tied up. Now, they never tell us, not even once, that they are going to shoot our dog team. They never say that to my grandfather, my father, my uncles or anybody in this town. They just come and start shooting. About five yards from our home. The building my father built. Our porch was full of harnesses and ropes and everything, the qamutik, and everything. The RCMP never removed the dead dogs. The dogs were rotting after one week.

E-014

The reasons behind this sudden increase in the number of killed dogs in 1959 remains unknown, although it could be linked to the large increase in the number of loose dogs in town following the continual arrival of new Inuit families. It could also be linked to the arrival of new RCMP members that had this task more at heart than others. But no one knows for sure.

In the early 1960s, efforts were made to put notices on various buildings in town to remind dog owners they needed to tie their dogs up. Radio was also used by the authorities for the same purpose (Honigmann and Honigmann

1965: 134). In 1961, the RCMP noted that there were 950 Inuit in town, but that "[t]here [were] probably only about 3 to 6 dog teams in Frobisher Bay owned by Eskimos. Many families have one or two dogs, but as they get further away from their old ways they do not attend the animals as they should. During the summer months particularly there are always a few dogs running loose".[29] In 1961, the RCMP also asked the territorial authorities to name Dog Officers, so that they would not have to kill dogs anymore. This led to the nomination of John Eksinak, an Inuk, as the first civil Dog Officer in Iqaluit's history.[30] From his nomination on, the situation seems to have calmed down and very few dog killings were reported after. However, as it did elsewhere in the Arctic, sickness struck the dogs in the early 1960s (Graburn 1969: 44) and snowmobiles appeared in 1963. In 1965, Iqaluit Inuit owned 30 snowmobiles and there were only about seven to nine dog teams left,[31] which amounts to less than 100 dogs.

While all of this was going on in Iqaluit, the situation differed dramatically in Cumberland Sound. In the early 1960s, Cumberland Sound Inuit still lived in camps. What would eventually become Pangnirtung only had a HBC post, a nursery and a RCMP detachment. In December of 1961, an epidemic of canine hepatitis, probably the same that had struck Frobisher Bay earlier that year (Duffy 1985: 4), killed hundreds of dogs in the Sound. For the Inuit, this was a turning point (QTC 2013b: 322–328). Corporal C.B. Alexander of the local RCMP reported that "a contagious disease had broken out among the dogs of Kingmilksoon [Kingmiksoo] camp on the south shore of Cumberland Sound. This disease spread rapidly to all thirteen camps on Cumberland Sound" (RCMP 2006: 399). Despite the severity of the epidemic, the RCMP did not see fit to tell the Federal authorities in Iqaluit. R.J. Orange, the administrator in charge of Iqaluit and the Sound, learned about the epidemic only on January 29th 1962 and was bitter about it:

> […] unless further information leads us to different conclusions, the R.C.M. Police will bear a large measure of responsibility in the delay and resulting hardships which will inevitably occur. At this stage, we sometimes wonder about the effectiveness of the Force in the North, other than to round up the odd occasional drunk, always Eskimo, or to inspect at regular intervals the two or three rifles assigned to station chiefs along the DEW Line. I recognize that the foregoing are bitter remarks, and the facts as they are uncovered may not bear me out in this situation, however, I doubt it at this stage.
>
> RCMP 2006: 231

As soon as he was made aware of the gravity of the situation, Orange sent Peter Murdoch, a RCMP agent, to visit all the camps. He estimated that the number of dogs in all the 13 camps went from 900 to 273 in less than two months (RCMP 2006: 399; Duffy 1985: 10–13). For Orange and the Canadian administration, this situation put Inuit at risk. It was then decided to do something that had never been done before: "[a]fter some discussion among local [Pangnirtung] whites, the suggestion of taking food to the people in camps was rejected in favour of moving them to Pangnirtung as the only practical solution" (Damas 2002: 142). Between March 3rd and 5th, a plane flew to all the camps and evacuated 217 people to Pangnirtung where they stayed in tents for several months. This was a shocking experience for many Inuit. As a witness met in 2004 recalls, policemen came out of the plane, told people to gather their stuff as quickly as possible, and shot the remaining dogs before taking off. Inuit were not told why they were brought to Pangnirtung (E-010; see also QTC 2013b: 322–328 for other testimonies). In May, after the disease had passed, Inuit were told to go back to their camps, although very few of them still had dogs. For this reason, 69 dogs were brought from other regions of the Arctic, mainly from North Baffin Island and the Mackenzie. In 1963, there were eleven camps in the Sound, only two less than before the epidemic (Damas 2002: 142). By the summer of 1964, "most teams were up to strength again" (QTC 2013b: 326).

Discussion

Justice Croteau, who was appointed by Nunavik Inuit, and Justice Igloliorte, who was president of the Qikiqtani Truth Commission (QTC), came to the conclusion that the killing of dogs was linked to the expansion of Canada into the Arctic. For Croteau, dogs were killed only after Inuit moved to villages for reasons of public health and security (2010: 154). For Igloliorte, the killings were "completely consistent with standard government policy that Inuit must, at their own expense, accommodate newcomers' needs and wants" (QTC 2013a: 419). Most researchers who have studied this issue push the logic further by asserting that the killing of dogs was not only a consequence of Canadian colonialism, but that it was inevitable. For Zahara and Hird (2015), "the colonial rhetoric of safety and security" employed to legitimize Canada's expansion throughout the North transformed Inuit dogs into trash animals that were killed both as a colonial strategy to change the Inuit relationship with the environment and because Qallunaat (white people) were afraid of them. Tester claims that the imposition of the welfare state in the Canadian Arctic, which was "a totalization with capital accumulation at its core" (Tester 2010a: 11), made dogs unwelcomed in settlements for they were "seen as menace to health and safety" (Tester 2010a: 17). McHugh (2013), whose reflection draws heavily on the conclusion of the Qikiktani Truth Commission (2013a, 2013b), describes dogs as a threat to the Canadian colonial project.

Claiming that dogs represented a menace to the colonial project and were killed to favour Canada's expansion is compelling and mostly true. However, it fails to explain why the killing of dogs took many different shapes, involved a great many actors and could take place in two territories operating on two distinct set of laws. How can one claim that what took place in the

Cumberland Sound, where dogs were shot to prevent the spread of diseases and Inuit given new dogs, has similar justifications from the killing of stray dogs in Kuujjuarapik by a radio station operator? How can the mass killing of dogs in Kangiqsujuaq in 1964, a Nunavik community that had no police force and a very small population, be compared to the killing of more than 250 dogs in Iqaluit Bay in 1959, a NWT community of more than a thousand inhabitants with a RCMP detachment? If there had been a global plan to kill dogs for the sake of imposing Canadian institutions in the North, why were dogs killed even before the imposition of centralizing policies? Why were dogs that were tied up seldom killed? Furthermore, if dogs needed to be killed to secure communities why were local civil servants and administrators telling their superiors in Ottawa to let Inuit untie their dogs? Why did Ottawa and Quebec set up vaccination campaigns? Why did the Canadian government send dog food so that Inuit could feed their animals? Why did they import dogs into regions where they were too few? In other words, claiming that dogs represented a menace to the colonial project and were killed to favour Canada's expansion is compelling but cannot explain contradictions and local specificities.

In order to make sense of what happened, one needs to stop looking at contradictions as contradictions. They are not. All of them, the killing of dogs, their vaccination, their importation into regions where there were too few, the shipping of dog food, etc., are actually perfectly coherent with Canada's colonialism. The same goes for regional specificities, which only highlight the stages where the colonial project was at different moments and locations. What John and Jean Comaroff have shown for Africa actually applies in the Canadian Arctic as well: colonialism is not a linear process which takes on similar forms in time and space, it is a project full of contradictions both in its form and in its substance (Comaroff and Comaroff 1992: 211).

In order to understand everything that was done to dogs between 1957 and 1968, a brief description of Canada's colonial history in the Arctic is in order. In the mid-twentieth century, Canada went through deep changes that involved the imposition of the welfare state throughout the territories. It is during that period that the universal healthcare system was instituted, the secularization of schools took place, family allowances introduced, and housing norms increased to the point where whole neighbourhoods in large cities were destroyed to make room for new housing projects. In many ways, Canada was not different from most Western countries: following a rapid industrialization period and a demographic explosion, it was looking at governing over biological processes (life, death, reproduction, etc.) by trying to control external occurrences (accidents, sicknesses, filthiness, natural disaster, unforeseen turn of events, deficiencies, etc.) that threatened the lives of its populations (Foucault 1991). At the same time, Canada became interested in the Arctic to assert its own sovereignty (Pigott 2011) and exploit resources (McPherson 2003).

As we have seen earlier, Canada was interested in the land but did not give second thoughts about the Arctic inhabitants until it was heavily criticized by the RCMP and the USAF. So when they decided to administer over the Inuit, Canadian policy makers, politicians and civil servants decided to do what all colonial powers do and impose the same policies and administrative structures that were in place in the homeland (Comaroff and Comaroff 1992). Starting in the 1950s, Canadian authorities tried to create an Arctic welfare state where inhabitants could live fulfilling lives in a secure context (Damas 2002; Lévesque 2011; Robertson 2000; Zaslow 1988). However, dogs threatened that fantasy of an Arctic welfare state because they were a "menace to health and safety" (Tester 2010a: 17). They caused havoc, injured or killed people, destroyed warehouses, etc. Yet, at the same time, before the adoption of the snowmobile in 1965, dogs were essential for Inuit to make a living, a fact administrators were well aware of. Therefore, they needed to find solutions that would mitigate risks and allow Inuit to hunt and trap. The easy solution, from the point of view of the administration, was to force Inuit to tie up their dogs and kill stray ones. Following the same logic, the government vaccinated healthy dogs, but did not hesitate to kill dogs that showed symptoms of sickness. When dogs were missing, or when they were hungry, they were replaced and fed.[32] Indeed, when a dog was hungry or sick, it represented a threat to the imposition of the welfare state because it could pose risks, but also because it prevented Inuit from earning a living. What the welfare state required were healthy and well-fed dogs that would not obstruct public peace and that would continue to accompany Inuit in their daily activities. These dogs were not only kept, they were well taken care of. However, those that represented potential risks were killed regardless of what Inuit thought.

Thus, every time dogs were threatening the fantasy of the Arctic welfare state by being loose, sick, hungry or even already dead (as in the Cumberland Sound), administrators would take actions to attenuate the threat, by killing loose and sick ones, but also by feeding hungry ones and importing some where there were none. Whereas most researchers who have worked on this issue claim that dogs were killed because they represented a threat to colonial expansion, I propose to add that dogs were also vaccinated, fed and replaced for the same reason. In fact, there are no contradictions between the killing of dogs and the other things that were done to them. All of them are part of the same logic of governance that looks over biological processes and seeks to control external occurrences that threaten the lives of populations.

Notes

1 PWNHC, Alexander Stevenson Fonds, Box File 35-16, *Communities – Great-Whale-River, Quebec 1955–1958*, "Great-Whale-River (Poste-de-la-baleine) P.Q.", December 1967.
2 PWNHC, Alexander Stevenson Fonds, Box File 42-5, *Royal Canadian Mounted Police 1949–1973*, "Responsibility, Care and Supervision of Eskimos", October 30, 1951.

3 Farley Mowat's first book, *People of the Deer*, which was extremely critical of the government for letting Ihalmiut starve, was also instrumental in forcing the government to act.
4 PWNHC, Alexander Stevenson Fonds, Box File 17-7, *Policy – Inuit 1935–1959*, "The Canadian Eskimo Problem", 1954.
5 LAC RG22, volume 1332, file 40-2-170, *Letter from M. Marsh to M. Robertson*, April 12 1957.
6 LAC RG22, volume 1332, file 40-2-170, *Letter from M. Robertson to M. Marsh*, May 10 1957.
7 Agriculture Abuse Act [L.R.Q. Chapter A-2, 1964, C. 130, s. 11]. Retrieved from http://legisquebec.gouv.qc.ca/en/ShowDoc/cs/A-2.
8 LAC RG85, deposit 1997–98/076, volume 159, file 1006-8-1, *Memorandum for Mr. Kennedy*, May 17 1957.
9 LAC RG85, deposit 1997–98/076, volume 159, file 1006-8-1, *Control of dogs running loose in Northern Quebec*, October 8 1957.
10 In order to protect respondents, interviews have been anonymized. "M" signifies that the interview was done by Makivik Corporation and "E" that it was made by the author.
11 According to Kennedy, Crees were responsible for most of the dog killings in Kuujjuarapik in the late 1950s (LAC RG85, deposit 1999-98/076, volume 159, file 1006-8-1, *Dogs – Great Whale River*, May 25 1957).
12 LAC RG85, deposit 1997–98/076, volume 159, file 1006-8-1, *Memorandum for the Chief, Arctic Division*, October 3 and 4 1958.
13 In 2006, the RCMP produced a report about Inuit dogs that includes hundreds of archival records. However, none of them are properly referenced. The only way to use these records is to cite the report and the page number. For a critical assessment of the RCMP report, see QTC 2013a: 17–65.
14 LAC RG85, deposit 1997–98/076, volume 159, file 1006-8-1, *Memorandum for the Administrator of the Arctic*, October 6 1959.
15 LAC RG85, deposit 1997–98/076, volume 159, file 1006-8-1, *Memorandum to the Arctic Administration*, September 4 1959.
16 LAC RG85, deposit 1997–98/076, volume 159, file 1006-8-1.
17 LAC RG85, deposit 1997–98/076, volume 159, file 1006-8-1, *Memorandum for Mr. J.G. Walton*, September 1 1959.
18 *Ibid.*
19 Canine Distemper is a viral and contagious disease with no known cure that attacks the respiratory and nervous systems of dogs. In later stages, the disease can lead to fits, seizures, paralysis, and attack of hysteria (www.petmd.com/dog/conditions/respiratory/c_dg_canine_distemper) (Accessed 1 April 2017).
20 LAC RG85, volume 1959, file A-1006-8-1, part 1, *Memorandum for the Area Administrator*, March 27 1961.
21 The Sûreté du Québec had replaced the Royal Canadian Mounted Police in Kuujjuarapik in 1961.
22 LAC RG85, volume 1959, file A-1006-8-1, part 1, *Lettre de David C. Neve à l'Officier en charge de l'Institut de recherche sur les maladies animales de Hull*, December 11 1962.
23 All in all, more than 3,600 doses of vaccines were sent to 12 Nunavik villages in 1964 in an effort to control diseases affecting dogs. LAC RG85, volume 1959, file A-1006-8-1, part 1, *Memorandum for the administrator of the Arctic*, April 29 1963.

24 PWNHC, Alexander Stevenson Fonds, Box File 35-19, *Communities – Arctic Quebec 1955–1972*, "Wakeham Bay, P.Q."
25 The following account comes entirely from oral accounts told to Makivik Corporation researchers by elders in 1999. Although there is confusion as to the exact date the event took place, everyone agrees about the event.
26 LAC, RG85, deposit 1997–98/076, box 159, file: 1006-8-1, *Control of Dogs*, October 17 1967.
27 The Northwest Territories (NWT) is a territory in northern Canada. In 1999, it was subdivided in two distinct parts: the western part remained the NWT and the eastern part became Nunavut. Baffin Island (Qikiqtaaluk) is situated in the eastern part of Nunavut. In the 1950s and 1960s, Qikiqtaaluk Inuit were under the jurisdiction of the administration of the NWT.
28 LAC, RG85, deposit 1997–98/076, box 159, file: 1006-8-1, *Control of Dogs*, October 17 1967.
29 LAC RG18, deposit 1985–86/048, volume 55, file TA 500-8-1-8, *Annual Report Year Ending December 1961*.
30 LAC RG85, volume 1220, file 530-25-2, *Appointment of Dog Officers – Frobisher Bay*, September 15 1961.
31 LAC RG18, deposit 1985–86/048, volume 55, file TA 500-8-1-8, *Annual Report Year Ending December 1964* and *Annual Report Year Ending December 1965*.
32 None of these interventions made any sense to Inuit, most of whom resisted by refusing to tie up their dogs or even to give them the food that was given to them by civil servants (Lévesque 2008, 2010 and 2011).

Archival references

Library and Archives Canada (LAC)

RG18: Deposit 1985–86-048, volume 55, file TA 500-8-1-8, Conditions of Eskimo Frobisher Bay, 1947–1968.
RG22: Volume 1332, file 40-2-170, Dog Ordinance – NWT.
RG85: Deposit 1997–98-076, volume 159, file 1006-8-1, Control of dogs in Quebec Province.
Volume 1220, file 530-25-2, Dog Officer – NWT (appointments).
Volume 1959, file A-1006-8-1 part 1.

Prince of Wales Northern Heritage Centre (PWNHC)

Alexander Stevenson Record Group: Box Files 17-7, 35-16, 35-19, and 42-5.

References

Anonymous. 1959a. "Mad Dogs 'Terrorize' North, Police to Probe Shooting." *Montreal Gazette*, Montréal, August 19.
Anonymous. 1959b. "Husky Terror." *Time Magazine*, New York, August 31, 8.
Bégin, M.S. 2004. Des radars et des hommes: mémoires inuit de la station Fox Main de la DEW Line (Hall Beach, Nunavut), Quebec City. Masters Degree Thesis. Department of Anthropology, Université Laval.

Comaroff, J. and J. Comaroff. 1992. *Ethnography and the Historical Imagination*. San Francisco: Westview Press.

Croteau, J.-J. 2010. *Rapport final de l'Honorable Jean-Jacques Croteau, juge retraité de la Cour supérieure relativement à son mandat d'examen des allégations d'abattage de chiens de traîneau inuits au Nunavik (1950 – 1970)*. Montréal: Société Makivik.

Diubaldo, R. 1985. *The Government of Canada and the Inuit, 1900–1967*. Ottawa: Department of Indian and Northern Affairs Canada. Research Branch, Corporate Policy.

Damas, D. 1993. "Shifting Relations in the Administration of the Inuit: The Hudson's Bay Company and the Canadian Government." *Études-Inuit-Studies*, 17(2): 5–28.

Damas, D. 2002. *Arctic Migrants/Arctic Villagers. The Transformation of Inuit Settlement in the Central Arctic*. Montréal & Kingston: McGill-Queen's University Press.

Duffy, R. 1985. "Une épidémie décime les chiens d'attelage de la baie Cumberland." *North*, 31(1): 4–15.

Foucault, M. 1991. "Faire vivre et laisser mourir: La naissance du racisme." *Les Temps Modernes*, 535: 37–61.

Gagnon, M. 1999. Les militaires américains à Crystal 2 (Frobisher Bay) dans les années 1940: perspectives inuit. Masters Thesis, Department of Anthropology, Université Laval, Québec.

Gagnon, M. and Iqaluit Elders. 2002. *Inuit Recollections on the Military Presence in Iqaluit*. Iqaluit: Nunavut Arctic College.

Gjerstad, O. and J. Sanguya. 2010. A Clash of Two Truths. National Film Board of Canada and Piksuk Media. 1 h 8 min.

Graburn, N. 1969. *Eskimos Without Igloos: Social and Economic Development in Sugluk*. Boston: Brown and Company.

Haraway, D.J. 2003. *The Companion Species Manifesto: Dogs, People, and Significant Otherness*. Prickly Paradigm Press.

Honigmann, J.J. and I. Honigmann. 1965. *Eskimo Townsmen*. Ottawa: Canadian Research Centre for Anthropology, University of Ottawa.

Jenness, D. 1964. *Eskimo Administration: II. Canada*, Montréal: Arctic Institute of North America.

Laugrand, F. and J. Oosten. 2002. "Canicide and Healing: the Position of the Dog in the Inuit Cultures of the Canadian Arctic." *Anthropos*, 97(1): 89–105.

Laugrand, F. and J. Oosten. 2014. *Hunters, Predators and Prey: Inuit Perceptions of Animals*. New York and Oxford: Berghahn Books.

Lesage, J. 1955. "Enter the European: Among the Eskimos." *Beaver*, 285: 3–9.

Lévesque, F. 2008. Les Inuit, leurs chiens et l'administration nordique, de 1950 à 2007. Anthropologie d'une revendication inuit contemporaine. Ph.D. thesis. Québec: Université Laval, Département d'anthropologie.

Lévesque, F. 2010. "Le contrôle des chiens dans trois communautés du Nunavik au milieu du 20e siècle." *Études/Inuit/Studies*, 34(2): 149–166.

Lévesque, F. 2011. "An Ordinance Respecting Dogs: How Creating Secure Communities in the Northwest Territories Made Inuit Insecure." In *Humanizing Security in the Arctic*. Edited by M. Daveluy, F. Lévesque and J. Ferguson, 73–90. Edmonton: CCI Press.

Lévesque, F. 2015. "Là où le bât blesse : soixante ans de gestion des chiens au Nunavik." In *Visions du monde animal*. Edited by M. Cros, J. Bondaz and F. Laugrand, 65–85. Paris: Éditions des Archives contemporaines.

Lévesque, F., M. Jubinville and. T. Rodon. 2016. "En compétition pour construire des écoles: l'éducation des Inuit du Nunavik de 1939–1976." *Recherches amérindiennes au Québec*, XLVI(2–3): 145–154.

McHugh, S. 2013. "'A Flash Point in Inuit Memories': Endangered Knowledges in the Mountie Sled Dog Massacre." *ESC: English Studies in Canada*, 39(1): 149–175.

McPherson, R. 2003. *New Owners in the Own Land. Minerals and Inuit Land Claims*. Calgary: University of Calgary Press.

Makivik Corporation. 2005. Echo of the Last Howl. Kuujjuaq: Makivik Corporation.

Mitiarjuk. 1994. "Encyclopédie inuit de Mitiarjuk. Sauniq – les homonymes." *Tumivut*, 5: 73–80.

Pelto, P. 1973. *The Snowmobile Revolution. Technology and Social Change in the Arctic*. Prospect Heights: University of Connecticut.

Pigott, P. 2011. *From Far and Wide. A Complete History of Canada's Arctic Sovereignty*. Toronto: Dundurn.

Qikiqtani Truth Commission (QTC). 2013a. *Qikiqtani Truth Commission. Thematic Reports and Special Studies 1950–1975*. Iqaluit: Qikiqtani Inuit Association.

Qikiqtani Truth Commission (QTC). 2013b. *Community Histories: 1950–1975*. Iqaluit: Qikiqtani Inuit Association.

Robertson, G. 1960. "Administration for Development in Northern Canada: The Growth and Evolution of Government." *Canadian Public Administration*, 3(4): 354–362.

Robertson, G. 1961. "The Future of the North." *North*, 8(2): 37–40.

Robertson, G. 2000. *Memoirs of a Very Civil Servant. Mackenzie King to Pierre Trudeau*. Toronto: Toronto University Press.

Royal Canadian Mounted Police (RCMP). 2006. *The RCMP and the Inuit Sled Dogs (Nunavut and Northern Quebec: 1950–1970)*. Ottawa: Royal Canadian Mounted Police.

Tester, F. 2010a. "Can the Sled Dog Sleep? Postcolonialism, Cultural Transformation and Consumption of Inuit Culture." *New Proposals: Journal of Marxism and Interdisciplinary Inquiry*, 3(3): 7–19.

Tester, F. 2010b. "Mad Dogs and (mostly) Englishmen: Colonial Relations, commodities, and the fate of Inuit Sled Dogs". *Études/Inuit/Studies*, 34(2): 129–147.

Tester, F. and P. Kulchyski. 1994. *Tammarniit (mistakes): Inuit Relocation in the Eastern Arctic, 1939–63*. Vancouver: UBC Press.

Yatsushiro, T. 1960. *Eskimo Attitudes Toward Wage Employment and Related Considerations*. Montréal: McGill University Press.

Zahara, A.R.D. and M.J. Hird. 2015. "Raven, Dog, Human: Inhuman Colonialism and Unsettling Cosmologies." *Environmental Humanities*, 7: 169–190.

Zaslow, M. 1988. *The Northward Expansion of Canada 1914–1967*. Toronto: McClelland and Stewart.

10 'Hard times are coming'
Indeterminacy, prophecies, apocalypse, and dogs

Jan Peter Laurens Loovers

Building on Gwich'in elaborations on the Biblical *End of the World*, the frequently expressed statement 'hard times are coming' – by Gwich'in (elders) in northern Canada – provides different insights into human–animal relations. Incorporating vernacular prophecies of such indeterminate ending, the understanding of an apocalypse is twofold: both as the spiritual meaning of the Biblical End of the World and as the literal Greek meaning as a revelation. 'Working dogs', and the current revitalisation of such dogs, play a pivotal entanglement to counteract the 'hard times that are coming' as widely revealed by Gwich'in elders. Gwich'in argue that while snowmobiles depend on monetary funds for gas and mechanical parts, the 'working dogs' – and subsequently Gwich'in themselves – can live off the land without dependency on the broader economic system. In this sense it is crucial for Gwich'in to maintain relations with *working dogs*, other animal species (such as fish and caribou), and the land, to remain ready and prepared when there are increasing ruptures in life as we know it. To a certain extent I follow Henry Sharp's notion of indeterminacy. He states that 'indeterminacy means that the outcome of an event is determined by the observation/measurement of the event though the event may occur before or after the observation/measurement has taken place' (Sharp 2001: 29).

Indeterminacy, revelations, and manifestations

Several decades ago, a late Teetł'it Gwich'in elder (Annie G. Robert) dreamt about the changing land. In her dream she saw how the Peel River had dried up and was turned into a small creek. What to make of this dream? How does it relate to hard times coming that prelude the Apocalypse or the end of the world?

Apocalyptic dreams of Gwich'in elders, such as those above, are part of a much wider nexus of dreaming and imagination. Indeed, as other scholars who have worked with indigenous people have documented, dreams are an integral part in the lives of indigenous people (Hirt 2012). Dreams can reveal events to happen: e.g. successful hunting, fishing or trapping, death and hardship, and other matters. The revelation, taking up the original Greek meaning of apocalypse, offers a path to future events. Gaston Bachelard considers dreaming as a 'movement of imagination', a 'kinetic activity' where 'imaginary is immanent to the real, ... a continuous path [that] leads from the real to the imaginary' (1988: 2–4, original emphasis). While Bachelard is concerned with poetic imagination, his understanding of dreams as journeys offers room to consider the dreaming as paths running between past, present, and future. Thus, perhaps journeying on the trail of dreams, one can go back and forth in time with speed and rest (following Deleuze and Guattari 2003). Other anthropologists have already come to a similar conclusion, thus Lohmann (2003) speaks of dream travellers. Watson and Goulet consider dreams and vision by Dene Tha as constitutive to Dene Tha reality (Watson and Goulet 1992: 216). 'A prediction is not about the inevitable, but about the probable' (ibid: 218) where reality is socially constructed. Through dreams one can experience the 'other world' and gain knowledge. This is similar to Petra Rethmann's observation that 'for many Koriaks..., dreams were not a reflection of the past. Dreams did not belong to the realm of the ethereal and vague. Instead they showed the concreteness of the future' (2001: 83).

Sigmund Freud (1920) was very much concerned with dreaming imbued with desire, reflections of the unconscious, and symbolism. Dreams, for Freud, are physical manifestations of the past shaped inside the mind. Subsequently, according to Freud, dream interpretation allows for an understanding of a person's psychic apparatus in which the concealed unconscious is partially revealed. Psychiatrist and analytical psychologist Carl Jung, at one stage Freud's protégé, moved away from (sexual) desires to further the analysis of the unconscious through dreams. He built on some of his own 'fantasies' or dreams that preceded, but seemingly prophesied, World War I. Amongst the dreams were visions of seas of blood and destructions made by war. While initially fearing that he had fallen upon a neurosis, Jung came to consider his dreams as part of the 'collective unconsciousness' after the outbreak of war (in Shamdasani 2009). Jung's student Marie-Louise von Franz elaborated that the 'unconscious *knows* things; it knows the past and future' (Franz 1980: 39, original emphasis). The spirit, or 'anima', is '*the dynamic aspect of the unconscious*' in which Jung identifies three characteristics: 'it is spontaneously active, it freely creates images beyond sensual perceptions, and it autonomously and in a sovereign manner manipulates those images' (ibid: 20–1, original emphasis). Furthering this idea of the spirit, Franz set out to investigate the relation between divination, synchronicity, chance, and predictability building on the mathematics and Chinese *I Ching* among other examples. The 'absolute knowledge' of the spirit, situated in the unconscious, can shed insights of synchronistic events (those of the future) through dreams. Such occurrences of synchronic events have also been the interest of more recent works such as philosopher of science Olivier Costa de Beauregard (1987). Arguing for a four-dimensional time, he illustrates through geometrical calculations how past, present, and future collide. Anthropologist Alfred Gell, in his book *The Anthropology of Time*, provides a brief overview of sociological, philosophical, and anthropological theories on time. Bringing together Husserl and Nessier, he speaks of 'protentions' as projections of the future experienced in the present but guided by the past (Gell 1992: 233–4).

Annie George Robert's dream continues to be recounted by Teetł'it Gwich'in. The transformations of the river have become very vivid with the appearance of willowed sandbars and the river's channel shifting. Another Gwich'in elder, Jane Charlie Snr, recalls how her mother and other Gwich'in elders (notably, women) have been warning of the 'hard times [that] are coming' and that the end of the world or Judgement Day draws near. Local atmospheric happenstances, such as an increase of lightning and stormy weather, as well as global phenomena such as earthquakes, tsunamis, tornadoes, cyclones, or hurricanes are preludes as described in the Biblical Book of Revelation. The 'hard times' further makes a reference to the era where all the comforts and luxuries of the present day disappear, with the grocery stores having no products and no gas being available.

The Bible, dreams, and Gwich'in

> Reached [Peel River] Fort at 4 p.m. Received hearty welcome from some Yukon [sic.] Indians, who are to cross come goods; also a few Lapierre's House ... Held evening prayers with the Tukudh [Gwich'in]
> (McDonald, 8 September 1862, Yukon Archives, 85/97, 1862, MSS195)

It is 8th of September 1862 when the Métis Anglican missionary Robert McDonald arrives in the northwestern-most Hudson's Bay Company (HBC) post at that time. Peel Post, or Fort McPherson as it would come to be known, was established along the Peel River in 1840. The post was founded to commence fur trade between the HBC and Teetł'it Gwich'in and other northern Dene people. The HBC, a London-based fur trading conglomerate, had exclusive trading rights over a vast portion of Canada. Within several years, another trading post (Fort Yukon) and a distribution post (LaPierre House) were built to accommodate the expansion of the HBC trade with Gwich'in and other Aboriginal people in the Northwest. During the first two decades of HBC posts in the Northwest, there were no Christian institutions that could accommodate the spiritual needs of the HBC men or indeed to convert the Aboriginal people into Christians. By the end of the 1850s, a change occurred with Anglican and Catholic missionaries travelling on the HBC flotilla to the North. The Missionary Oblates of Mary Immaculate, a French Catholic order created in the aftermath of the Napoleonic era, had established missionary posts in the Athabasca-Mackenzie region in the 1840s. The Church Mission Society of the Anglican Church, a British movement of activist evangelic Christians created at the end of the eighteenth century, followed the Oblate order into the North (Choquette 1995). Craig Mishler (1990) and Robert Choquette (1995) provide an insightful overview of the movement of the Christian faith into the Northwest and how there were ongoing tensions and confrontations between the Catholics and Anglicans. As Mishler argues, on several occasions the Gwich'in played a role in orchestrating such 'collisions' to discover which Church (leader) had a stronger *medicine*. In Fort McPherson, LaPierre House, and Fort Yukon, Robert McDonald was instrumental for converting Gwich'in into Anglicans. Through his meticulous consistency in keeping a diary and religious textual work for more than forty years, McDonald provides a glimpse into the formation of these texts, his relations with Gwich'in people, and his personal experiences of travelling and living in Gwich'in country. Both being a linguistic prodigy and receiving the help of Gwich'in women including his wife Julia Kuttug, McDonald transcribed the entire Bible as well as hymns and Anglican ceremonies into the Gwich'in language. While there are elements of colonial practices woven into the expansion of the Christian faith into the North, Gwich'in became actively involved in spreading God's word (Fafard and Kritsch 2005; McDonald 1862–1911; Mishler 1990; Moore 2007; Sax and Linklater 1990). Gwich'in lay-readers, for example, would hold services in McDonald's absence and study the Bible and other religious texts. The incoming Anglican faith with God, Jesus, the Devil, and Angels also led to a creolisation, synthesis, or amalgamation of Gwich'in notions of dreams and medicine and the Anglican religion. Gwich'in were already aware of God or *Vittekwichanyo* as a Supreme Being (McDonald diary: 6 January, 1865; also Petitot 1970: 78; Jones 1867: 325), of the Devil or *Tritrin* (McDonald diary: 6 January, 1865; also Petitot 1970: 80–1; but contested by Jones 1867: 325), and of angels (McDonald diary: 6 January, 1865; also Hardisty 1867: 318 [Boy in the Moon, which Petitot indicates as the Supreme Being]), but also dealt with animal guardian spirits, celestial beings, Giant beings, and Bushmen.

On several occasions, Gwich'in who had been taught by McDonald, or had been introduced to the Anglican faith by other Gwich'in, started to have dreams or visions of Heaven. During these visions they claimed to communicate directly with God to receive particular instructions or prophecies (see also McClellan 1975: 553–63, for other Aboriginal people). Thus, in June 1863, some Teetł'it Gwich'in had had divine communication through dreams and were instructed not to kill foxes and martens (McDonald 1863; Mishler 1990: 124). Other Gwich'in dreamed and received hymns from Heaven that they would teach to other Gwich'in (Mishler 1990: 124). McDonald strongly criticised and opposed these claims, and he writes on different occasions his denouncement of these 'false prophecies' in his own words (see also Moore 2007: 36–7). For example, he writes about Gwichya Gwich'in Tiujito as 'making extravagant pretension to prophecy … being favoured with divine revelations', but even Tiujito starts to wonder whether these revelations are perhaps not 'suggestions of the evil spirit' (diary 12 January 1865). As linguist Patrick Moore (2007: 37) points out, and as can be read through McDonald's accounts and Oblate priest Émile Petitot's work, the Romanists (Catholics or Oblates) were less radical and gave room for the incorporation of these amalgamations. Christianity continued to be contested by medicine men. McDonald recounts one episode in which Neguitsyik and Nulato people are led by medicine men 'to neglect the [C]hristian instruction' after a winter filled with death is blamed on Christianity (diary: June 4, 1877). Thus, some Gwich'in incorporated the Christian faith through local notions of medicine, prophecies, personal experiences, and practices in being. Other Gwich'in, on the contrary, denounced the Christian faith and continued to build upon their traditional understandings.

Fur trade, gold rush, and whaling

Dogs played a significant part in the lives of the missionaries. The Anglican and Catholic missionaries would travel with dogs in winter to visit hunting camps and spread and teach God's word (see also Eber 1989: 151). Elsewhere I have employed the notion of 'dog-craft' to address how dogs and related artefacts have been crafted by the Gwich'in and improvised in connection with expansion of capitalist markets (Loovers 2015). Prior to the HBC-era, certain Gwich'in had Hare Indian dogs that were kept as guards and hunting companions. These dogs, similar to collies but with brushy tails, were further used for packing goods and, arguably, for pulling moose-skin sleds that were otherwise drawn by women. There were relatively few dogs in these communities, with those households that kept them typically having only one or two (Heine et al. 2007: 113–14; Schwartz 1997: 33; see also Cummins 2002: 155–7; Richardson 1829: 78–80, for Hare Indian dogs). Besides the Hare Indian dog, there is also evidence that there were Larger or Common Indian dogs (Allen 1920: 459; also Cummins 2002: 37–8). These dogs, larger than the Hare Indian dogs with short-haired bodies and pointy faces, were spread throughout Canada. Both types of dogs were gradually replaced or interbred with dogs that HBC-men brought in. Bundles of fur, meat, and trading goods were moved across the mountains between Fort Yukon, LaPierre House, and Fort McPherson. As the fur trade intensified, there were changes made to sleds. Furthermore, the crafting of different breeds of dogs emerged that were larger and stronger than the Hare Indian and Common Indian dogs, or at least better equipped for hauling more freight. Allegedly, the Common Indian dog was already widely used for draught (Allen 1920: 463). Such practices of interbreeding between 'aboriginal' dogs and 'European' dogs had become rather common in the southern HBC posts. For example, 'Eskimo dogs' were being interbred with 'large English dogs' or 'pointers' (Allen 1920: 442–3).

Pat McCormack provides an eloquent analysis of the relation between changes in the dogs, sleds, and gender roles during the HBC period (McCormack 2014). Whereas Aboriginal women had been handling dogs, the masculine-oriented HBC shifted the handling and subsequent driving of dogs to men. At this stage in time, the men would predominantly run or walk alongside the sleds and perhaps occasionally sit on the freight. As McCormack illuminates, the addition of back-boards and wrappers on the sleds enabled heavier loads (ibid: 142–3). This improvisation also allowed men and women to stand behind the sled rather than running or walking alongside it for greater part of the journey. This adjustment further altered the composition of the dog team and dogs. More and stronger dogs were needed to haul the heavy-loaded sleds (Osgood 1936: 132–3). The dogs, however, remained relatively small compared to those that would enter in the late 1800s. A significant change in the variety and crafting of dog breeds occurred with the Klondike Gold Rush at the end of the nineteenth century. As the influential author Jack London observes, '[t]housands of men were rushing to the frozen Northland. These men needed dogs. They wanted heavy dogs with strong muscles and furry coats. Big dogs would be able to work hard. And their furry coats would protect them from the cold' (1990: 5). The infamous Klondike Gold Rush, commencing in 1896, brought numerous different breeds of dogs besides thousands of fortune-seekers to the Northwest. The labour that awaited the dogs was hauling goods, travelling across the mountains, and working in the mining camps. Alongside dogs and newcomers, the Royal North West Mounted Police (RNWMP, now the Royal Canadian Mounted Police) moved into the North (see Wishart, this volume). Like the miners, they were highly dependent on dogs. The RNWMP used teams of five to seven dogs to patrol the vast northern regions. The Dawson Patrol, for example, ran between Fort McPherson and Dawson City (roughly 650 kilometres) to monitor the movement of miners, govern the area, and deliver mail. Ann Chandler (2009; see also Loovers 2015) provides a graphic account of one episode in which the police bought and shipped Labrador dogs from the east coast of Canada to Dawson City. Not all dogs survived the six-week journey and those that did were soon to be found unfit for the freighting jobs of the miners and the harsh travelling conditions. Indeed, within three months only 21 dogs remained of the initial 140. While this particular experiment was a failure, the police continued bringing in German Shepherds and Labradors. Subsequently these breeds became part of Gwich'in dog teams and dog patrols. The unsuccessful and cumbersome attempts of bringing dogs from the South, however, led the RNWMP to instigate dog-breeding stations in the area. Not only miners were of a concern to the RNWMP and missionaries, as at around the same time whaling increased in the Beaufort Sea. Similar to the gold rush in which Southerners envisioned unforeseen riches, the whaling era likewise found masses of outsiders travelling to the North to hunt bowhead whales for the profitable baleen in 1887. For the next six years the whalers made disproportional profits from the baleen trade, but the industry decreased after 1895 and would eventually stop by 1908 (Morrison 2003). Where the trade in baleen had collapsed, the former fur trade re-intensified, and some whalers and Inuvialuit became actively engaged in the fur trade, competing with the HBC. The whalers, too, brought dogs with them. Gwich'in became involved in both resource extraction projects by trading meat to the outsiders or taking up specific jobs.

The Muskrat Period

By 1910 the Klondike Gold Rush and the Beaufort Sea Whaling had petered out. Both Gwich'in and Inuvialuit had obtained new tools such as iron stoves, different kinds of guns, canvas, European-style clothing, and sewing machines. Furthermore, they had become engaged with the monetary market rather than the HBC barter system. Whereas many of the miners and whalers had left the North, they were soon replaced by numerous and often impoverished Southerners who would take up trapping. Richard Slobodin (1962: 36–41) named the period between 1917 and 1947 the 'Muskrat Period', marking the era in which trapping of muskrats, amongst other animals, became the predominant economy in the Mackenzie Delta. The price for one muskrat skin rose from 40 cents in 1914, to a staggering $1.50 in 1920. These prices further increased in the 1920s. Such extravagant prices, like those for baleen a few decades earlier, came to attention of fortune-seekers. For example, in 1920–21 there were around 140 white trappers in the Delta which increased to around 500 in 1926–27 (Bromley 1986: 16). Historian Arthur Ray demonstrates that the fur markets shifted from Leipzig and London to New York, St. Louis, and Montreal during World War I, placing significant pressure on the Hudson's Bay Company. This also influenced the North. Trading company Lamson and Hubbard, for example, played a significant role in 'flooding' the North with white trappers to break the HBC and Aboriginal people's hegemony (Ray 1990: 111). Many of these men were former miners and were merely interested in quick-return profits, giving little attention to the long-term effects of their activities on the environment. Whereas the HBC had a near monopoly in the North before the 1910s, the influx of trappers had led to an increase of competing trading posts.

The number of trappers entering the Northwest also brought further adjustments in the dog teams. The increased trapping of muskrats, and other fur-bearing animals such as foxes and marten, required the establishment of longer traplines and use of greater numbers of steel traps. The traplines for marten could be tens of kilometres long with different camps along the line. With the arrival of the RNWMP (RCMP), miners, whalers, and white trappers, there was also the influx of different dog breeds. This mix of dogs is exemplified in Gwich'in narratives. German Shepherds, border collies, Labradors among other breeds became parts of the teams. Other dogs also reached the region, including among the Chipewyan, who included poodles in their teams (Sharp 2001: 85). There were further adjustments, with the three to five dogs in the HBC teams increasing to eight (or more) dogs. A plausible cause, besides the trade in meat and the longer traplines with iron traps, could be that there were changes in the transport with arrival of steamboats in the 1880s. These boats, together with the incorporation of new products such as iron stoves, enabled the movement of larger goods to the region, which in turn required some means of over-ground transport.

By 1912, Aklavik had been established and emerged as a trading and Government nexus in the Mackenzie Delta. With the Roman Catholic and Anglican boarding schools, a hospital, a RCMP detachment, hotels, bars, and Government offices, Aklavik would draw in Gwich'in, Inuvialuit, and 'Southerners'. Located in the Mackenzie Delta, Aklavik thus became the 'transportation, commercial, and administrative capital of the North' (Morrison and Kolausok 2003: 117). Aklavik was prone to flooding and lacked space to expand, and the Canadian Government decided to move this administrative and political centre to Inuvik in the 1950s (Stoneman-McNichol 1983: 5). A number of Gwich'in men and women would participate in the building of Inuvik. The location was chosen in part for its more favourable weather conditions and proximity to the Beaufort region where oil exploration had started. By the 1960s oil had been struck near Inuvik and in other northern regions, and the era of oil and mine exploration commenced in the Canadian North. While both Inuvik and Aklavik attracted Gwich'in and Inuvialuit to settle, many Teetł'it Gwich'in continued to live in their bush camps to trap. In similar vein, a number of white trappers stayed out in their bush camps most of the year, only making visits to town for trading and socialising.

Peter Usher (1971) shows that the arrival of Alaskan Inuit and white trappers had significant impact on animals, with over-harvesting evident even in the early 1920s.[1] The Great Depression of the 1930s that struck in the more southern parts of North America did not reach the North directly, but did bring another flow of newcomers into the North. Lisa Piper's insightful book *The Industrial Transformation of Subarctic Canada* touches on this. She argues that while the Depression destroyed many prairie farmsteads, quite the opposite occurred in the North (Piper 2009: 81–2). In Subarctic Canada, instead of a collapse there was a flourishing of industry, particularly those related to so-called natural resources and mineral extraction. In the Mackenzie Delta and Crow Flats, the Great Depression brought Southerners into the area to trap the fur-bearing 'natural resources' (VGFN and Smith 2009: 161, 226, 233–4, 247). The late Woodie Elias, for example, recounted how Southerners escaped and anticipated the hardships in their own places and came North. The Gwichya Gwich'in, around Arctic Red River, likewise found a number of white trappers who came at the peak of the fur prizes in the 1930s. They would set up competing trading posts and would trap alone or with other white trappers who had come to the Mackenzie Delta (see Heine et al. 2007: 191–8). Teetł'it Gwich'in Gladys Alexie mentioned how a Gwich'in elder recounted the famine that happened in the Prairies with the drought at the time of the Depression and that this has been a warning for being prepared, for keeping up tradition. Gladys adds 'The elder said that the old people at that time said that we need to always be prepared as the north will one day experience a famine. But they don't know when or the type (sort) of famine' (personal correspondence, 17 November 2017).

Preparing for the hard times

The statement 'hard times are coming' is frequently followed by 'the elders have said that you need to be prepared'. Perhaps one could situate these statements in the larger discourse of the Anthropocene, though Gwich'in have not addressed such a concept with me and rather phrase it in apocalyptic terms as stated above. The preparation for these times, though, comes in the form of maintaining knowledge/skills to live out on the land. Hence, rather than placing preparation in the realm of habitus or cultural frameworks, the preparation is something to actively work for and at. The emphasis on 'tradition', then, has to be situated in this dialogue. So, what do the Gwich'in elders infer with these 'hard times'? How should one get prepared? The Gwich'in elders to whom I have listened and learned from, explain that a moment will arise in the near, indeterminate future in which the two grocery stores have empty shells and the 'gas-bars' (gas stations) have run out of fuel. To understand the implications of both these statements we need to address the role that store-bought food and fuel play in the community. Since the 1950s and 1960s, Fort McPherson has increasingly become a more structured settlement with pre-fabricated houses (see also Wishart and Loovers 2013) that have fuel tanks for heating and a water boiler. In a number of houses this has also meant that the stoves for burning wood have been replaced by central heating, or stoves were not incorporated into the original housing design. Occurrences of power shortage have illustrated the importance of having wood-burning stoves to ensure survival in the midst of winter when temperatures can drop to -40 or -50 degrees Celsius. Fuel is also being used for more obvious reasons: e.g. trucks, snowmobiles, four-wheelers, outboard motors, and generators are regularly being operated. The Gwich'in, as noted before, rely heavily on motorised vehicles for travelling on the land and continuing traditional activities such as hunting, fishing, trapping, and gathering in addition to travelling to other cities for visiting. In similar vein, fuel further enables the movement of goods from the South to the North via large trucks or airplanes. Gwich'in, like other Indigenous people across North America incorporate both traditional food with store-bought food. The stores have many of the products that can be found in urban supermarkets, and Gwich'in are keen to eat steaks, chicken, pork chops, canned and 'fresh' vegetables, crisps, pop, Kraft dinner (macaroni-cheese), pizza, rice, potatoes, 'Klik' [canned meat], ice-cream, and so on together with traditional food. Hence, the absence of fuel in the North would bring forth a series of life-alternating changes: no more products from the South, and no possibility to use motorised vehicles for travelling, including for traditional activities. This is precisely the moment to which the elders allude, when Gwich'in will be unable to heat their houses with fuel, use their electric stoves for cooking, and to travel on the land to procure food, furs, and traditional medicines. At the same time, without fuel there is no possibility to bring in store-bought food. Thus we arrive at the 'hard times' that the elders predict. Without store-bought foods and without the ability to travel on the land with motorised vehicles, life will become very dire in the North. This is precisely why the late Gwich'in elders have warned their children and grandchildren to be prepared.

Gwich'in elder Rosalie Ross, during an interview at the Fort McPherson Hamlet talking about dogs, turns to prophecies of the 'hard times' and how this affects the animals. She recounts teachings she and her siblings received from her renowned parents: 'And they taught us about the land, the water, the animals, just everything. And what's going to happen today with our land, our animals, you know like the caribou is disappearing now. My dad talked to us about it. He said it is coming. I don't know how they knew all this but it's true. What's happening now, I never seen caribou all winter and even animals. Fish can't breathe'. She goes on to say that 'everything changed you know. It's [the animals] getting less of everything around here, you know'.

Preparations entail a twofold process. First, one should continue participating in traditional activities, and second, one should have dogs. The first is rather straightforward but crucial in understanding the pivotal importance that Gwich'in place on continuing and emphasising hunting, fishing, trapping, berry picking, and practising traditional medicine. Not only do they address this in terms of well-being, but they also explain that children need to know how to survive out on the land for the reasons just described above. Secondly, dogs are fundamental for being able to travel on the land when there is a lack of fuel, and will be critical for obtaining essential foods and materials. However, dogs and people need to share in their preparations for 'hard' times, which I now turn to.

Abe Stewart Junior's and Georgie Moses' dog teams

Abe Stewart Junior has been one of the few who had started taking up such preparations when I met him again in January 2013. When I came to his house, he showed me his female and male dog. The female dog was in heat, and he explained that he was going to breed her with the male, in the bush away from all the loose dogs. Elaborating on his grand scheme, he addressed the 'hard times' that the elders have predicted, and stated that he wanted to build up a dog team again. There are a few themes that emerge from this initial encounter with my befriended Gwich'in teacher: re-building dog teams, breeding dogs, and loose dogs. In order to understand the themes or events to which Abe Stewart Junior refers, we need to address the construction of a gravel road that connects the South with Fort McPherson.

By the early 1980s, the Dempster Highway was constructed and connected southern Canada with Fort McPherson and onwards to Inuvik. The Dempster Highway was part of the 1950s *Roads to Resources* initiatives catalysed by then premier John Diefenbaker (Abele 1987; Diefenbaker 1958; Loovers 2010). Upon completion, the gravelled road brought significant changes to the lives of the Teetł'it Gwich'in. Abe Stewart Junior recalled during a lengthy interview over two days that 'lots of dog teams disappeared'. Another Gwich'in man (Charlie Kaye), who had been away from the community working from 1964–79, recounts: 'when I came back to the community [in 1979] I noticed there was fewer dogs and people start going to the oil fields and buying skidoos and all the dog teams starts disappearing'. Other Gwich'in have echoed this change. They have emphasised that once the road was built, and motorised vehicles such as trucks and snowmobiles came into the community, the dogs were either shot or given away. From Gwich'in perspective, the shooting of the dogs (while being a very difficult and emotional event) made sense. As Gwich'in elders have explained, the dogs stopped working, and keeping them tied up in the community would have been cruel. With snowmobiles taking over their jobs, the large, broad-shouldered, strong dogs became obsolete in the community and were replaced by smaller 'racing-dogs' kept for racing in several annual festive occasions, or by pet dogs ('lap-dogs', in Abe Stewart's words) who were kept inside the house. Recall that the working dogs were sturdy and able to haul large freight on sleds, and some were also used for carrying dog-packs. Speaking with Gwich'in, and having observed Abe Stewart Junior building up his team, both the disappearance of working dogs and appearance of pet dogs have had important impacts on the anticipation of the 'hard times'. To put it bluntly, as the Gwich'in have told me, pet dogs cannot pull sleds. First, they are too weak to pull heavy loads of meat, wood, or ice, and second, they do not have the skills or knowledge to do so. Georgie Moses and Abe Stewart Junior, among many other Gwich'in with whom I have spoken, underscored how much work it takes to set up a dog team. It begins with looking for the right kind of dogs to breed: e.g. those with broad shoulders, good character, and strong bloodlines.

Breeding dogs

Speaking with Gwich'in who keep dogs, they make a further difference between 'working dogs' and 'breeding dogs'. The 'breeding dogs' are treated more delicately and not used (intensively) for hauling freight. The dogs are intermittently kept for extended periods depending on the breeder and the dog. Abe Stewart Junior, for example, kept his young female dog Oscar just for giving birth to the proper litter and then he got rid of her. Georgie Moses, on the other hand, had been keeping his 'breeding dogs' for a longer period and was more articulate about them: 'these guys [referring to his six dogs, excluding the collie that was tied separate from his racing/working dogs] are breeding dogs and I wouldn't run them, like work too hard, you know. I have something in there so I have to look after them good. You can injure them. I want them to be pure dogs'. In another case, Georgie kept one of his favourite dogs, Spirit, who was in the middle of the dog team, as working dog and only bred her in the later stage of her life when she was unable to work anymore. Reminiscing about Spirit, Georgie explains how she was tough and happy with the right attitude for working together with Georgie and the other dogs in the team.

Georgie Moses continued to elaborate on crafting the right dog body through breeding and selection. During one of our daily 'feeding the dogs' routine, Georgie stopped at one of them and told me to look at the dog's shoulders. He mentioned that good working dogs can be defined by their shoulder blades. As measurement he used his thumb, which he placed between the shoulder blades. During the earlier-mentioned lengthy conversation, he turned back to the shoulders:

> So you see when you go on, this dog, his shoulders are out you see. Simple thing. But if your dog is kind of, his blades are up here, it's not good. He's going to have problems with his top shoulder up here. Because it's going to be hard for him right here. And you can tell your dog blades are close together then they are going to get tired and he's not going to do the job for you. He's going to get tired and it's important you know you've got a good shouldered dog. Right here. You can put your thumb in between it. All the way up. It's about this wide. But some dogs are too narrow and get tired too quick. I guess all that is down to breeding. The breed-line and performance. Bloodline and performance. Body and how it performs. So, if your dog's shoulders are good, your guys are just going to be good.

Besides the shoulders, Georgie comments that he is looking and breeding for dogs with big chests so that they got their 'first wind, their second wind (breath/stamina)'. As the Vuntut Gwich'in recounted his four, memorable round-trips with dog teams across the mountains from Old Crow to Fort McPherson, he mentioned that dogs need to have sufficient 'wind' (lung capacity, breath) in order to sometimes run continuously for many kilometres. Stretches of 30 km a day are not uncommon. Another set of body parts that has been emphasised is the legs and paws, which need to be respectively long and broad. For the reasons above, this is why certain Gwich'in have been breeding their dogs with wolves, which always possess these qualities.

The breeding of dogs, then, is not as straightforward as it seems and takes time. Obviously one first needs to find the right kind of male and female dog with the right body proportions and wit. Then one 'experiments' with *crafting* dogs and sees what kinds of pups are born out of specific male and female pairings. There are different philosophies about first litters in the North. As we drove on the Dempster Highway to a gravel pit to check on Abe's male dog Snowball and female dog Oscar, Abe mentioned that some Gwich'in had stated that 'the first-born litter is no good, especially when female [dog] gets them young'. This first litter from a young female would therefore be given away or killed. One of the explanations that the elders gave Abe is that the young mother does not yet know how to care for her litter and subsequently

Figure 10.1 Breeding dogs: Abe Stewart Junior with Oscar
Photograph by P. Loovers.

the pups grow up relatively weak. The second litter, however, is the one that brings forth strong dogs. These thoughts/teachings kept Abe Stewart Junior occupied as we travelled the few kilometres to the place where he had his two young dogs tied up for breeding. The killing of first litters is not practised by all Gwich'in and Vuntut Gwich'in. Georgie Moses stated that first litters can be excellent for dog teams.

Henry Sharp, working with Denésuliné in northern Canada, explains: '[n]ot only do Dene feel affection for sled dogs, they see white attitudes toward dogs as producing unreliable and lazy dog teams whose incompetence ... becomes a hazard to life and limb under the harsh conditions of the Dene homeland' (Sharp 2001: 86). Hence it is not just enough to have working dogs, one has to work in *crafting* working dogs to know the land, and life in the bush, as well as knowing how to work pulling a sled or pack meat. The late Georgie Moses has been perhaps the most articulate about dogs that are brought up in the bush, and are able to see the country, and dogs that live inside the house in town (see also Anderson et al. 2017). Spending time with him at his camp, during a long conversation, I ask him to tell me more about the importance of keeping dogs in the bush in open areas. Georgie states: '[The dogs] want to know what's going on. They need a view. They got to have that view. If you tie the dog in the bushes and he's going to be stubborn. He's going to be bad, yes. Dogs are smart. And living in the bush with your dogs, they see the view, the animals and things go by them'. Later on during the conversation, Georgie Moses returns to the theme of dogs in the bush. He elaborates that the dogs in town are noisy and bark for nothing. He then turns to one of his dogs, who is a small, bushy dog: 'This little guy here was supposed to be a pet dog. Last year he was nothing. This year he's right up there. He just fit in with everybody. And right now, he barks and last year he bark at Caribou – he didn't know what's that. Now, phew. The bush'. While Georgie Moses articulated the importance of raising dogs in the bush, like him most other Gwich'in have also discussed the work that goes into training dogs.

Training dogs

By summer 2015, Abe Stewart's puppies of the second litter had grown quite a bit and he decided to begin training them to be in harness. At his new camp near *Nitainlaii* (Eight Miles), where he kept his dogs in the bush, he walked over to Snowball (the male dog with whom he started breeding) and tried to put him into a harness. Snowball was not yet familiar with harnesses and Abe was wrestling and struggling to get him into one. Sam, the male puppy that Abe wanted to train as leader, was taken and also put into a harness. It soon became apparent that the old harnesses that Abe had laying around at his house were too big for Sam, but nonetheless Abe eventually managed to get him into one. He then tied a rope from Snowball's harness to Sam's harness in order to 'force' Sam to keep pace with his dad. As the dogs started pulling on the brushy meadow, Abe was watching and commenting on the dogs. It was soon obvious that there was a surprising difference between Sam and Snowball. Rather than Snowball being a good lead dog and teaching Sam, it was Sam who was pulling the sled consistently and constantly with little distraction. Snowball, on the other hand, seemed to be confused and at times got tangled up as he stopped and got off the track. Abe, at times standing behind the sled or running alongside or behind it, said: 'I knew he [Sam] would be a good leader, do you see how he pulls the sled!'

During the interview with Abe Stewart Junior, he articulated in some detail how he went about training his dogs. First of all, he stated, one needs to train a leader. Thus, Snowball was assigned as leader since particular aspects in Snowball's movements (e.g. staying in front of the ski-doo when running and having good endurance) hinted that he could become a good leader.[2] Explaining how he trained Snowball, Abe let him run on the lakes in front or behind the ski-doo and started putting him in a harness attached to a sled, and gradually increased its load. Not everybody is able to train (good) leaders, and Abe prized himself for having such an ability, which was also acknowledged by late Gwich'in elders. Upon asking whether he also trained wheel dogs, Abe stated that one cannot train them, but rather they train themselves. The same seems to count for the working dogs in the middle of the team. Having the lead dog and the other dogs sorted, the next part involves training them to work as a team and how to pull heavy freight. During this part of training a dog team, the dogs start to travel longer distances and over different terrain, such as hills. At the same time, it seems that this also entails letting the dogs get to know the 'country'. One of the things dogs need to learn is how to haul freight across the mountains as a team, or as Abe exemplifies:

> If you going to come to a hill, they gonna go up, but before you get that hill with a load you, you whoop (hook?) them any one of them. And they just pull with all their might on top the hill, they climb on top of the hill, they get on top. Every time, and pretty soon you do not have to do that again and they are just going to be trotting around and there is going to be hill there huh, they finally going to pull with all their might instead of getting stuck all the way. Right up they gonna go, no stuck and then they go again. When they climb a hill they pull with all their might, they work hard until level again. But that is how we train dogs how to pull, they know that they going to climb that hill and don't want to get whooped. They make effort to go. And the wheel dog, the wheel dog he eventually learn when you have your wheel dog, your toboggan is right here huh and the wheel dog is right there. Well the sled will go like this and that way and will pull him around huh, you gotta keep, hit him a little bit and he learns. Every time he goes sideways, he pull it, he pull on this way, I seen dogs doing that, the way that sled pull him, he pull. He know how to do it, you know. The rest of the dogs, they just go.

Abe continues that the training of dogs takes a long time:

> Actually, your dog team they all learn how to work together. When they work together, you have no problem. Yeah, it takes more than one or two years you know. Lot of times … in the past we had dog teams you know for five, six years. Same dogs, they don't, they travel just the same. Because when they are young they get better all the time, stronger too.

Other Gwich'in, too, mention that it takes considerable time and effort to have a good dog team that is able to work together. One of the ways of training the different dogs – lead dogs, working dogs in the middle, and wheel dogs – in a team is to take them on a frozen lake or existing trails. The training itself, especially when it comes to racing dogs, is often imbued with a certain degree of secrecy. While the specifics differ, generally speaking, lead dogs are trained alongside another more experienced dog as described above. It is on the lakes, for example, that the commands 'gee' (for right turn)[3] and 'haw' (for left turn), which are more broadly used by dog mushers across North America, are taught to young pups while they pull alongside a more experienced leader. Particularly, lead dogs need to know and are taught these commands as they guide the team. Besides these vocal directions, Abe Stewart Junior also makes use of a stick to make gentle correctional hits to teach the novice dog in the team something like take the right turn. He explains that during these initial stages of teaching dogs the commands, one discovers whether the young dog indeed has leader qualities or not.

Figure 10.2 Training dogs: Abe Stewart Junior with his dog team
Photograph by P. Loovers.

Georgie Moses, too, elaborated in great detail how he set up a dog team in the late 1990s. During our conversation he is somewhat more reserved about the practices of training dogs as to not reveal the secrets of his trade as dog musher. Like Abe, he would put a young puppy alongside a more experienced dog to teach him. He exemplifies how his first trip across the mountains from Old Crow to Fort McPherson was particularly challenging as the dogs were not completely attuned to working with each other and with him. In order to get them ready for the long trip, he was running them all winter and walking with snowshoes and having the puppies run alongside or in front or back. It was during the first lengthy trips with his new dog team that he found a leader:

> Well, we were way out without a leader. We had no leader. A brand new team. We were looking for a leader and we were trying hard. They follow trail good. We came down the trail. When we came down Crow River, it drifted. You know, deep snow. They did not want to go. So I walked ahead: got to walk all the way down the river. But not more. I wanted to make a shortcut. And I had no snowshoe too and I went to walk in deep snow you know. Walking ahead. I am so tired. I had to go to my Thermos and said what the hell am I doing round here in the first place. But God, I made a commitment. And when I said that they all come over and they just all licked my face. You know, like they exactly knew what I meant. So they kind of licked my face and I thought are you guys just trying to make me happy or what. You know. So I kept going. We came across the lake and I was walking. I thought I'm going to walk all the way down and here they went right by me. Grabbed that sleigh and jumped on. I made a leader that day. That night, I made a leader. Holy, I should say. I got home. I told my wife I made a leader today. Breaking through the trail. Holy smokes. Made a leader right there. Got it home. No more problem right there. Hooked it up and on. Before that I'd have to go push up like that and go huh. No more of that. Just go huh now. See, mission accomplished and we are on our way right there. And she trained all the other ones. Trained them all too. Really amazing all attached to your dog team and seeing them and who's who and what they can do. Really sensitive to their mood.

The making of a leader, thus, not only depends on the actions of the musher but furthermore on how particular dogs take up this position in relation to the musher and the other dogs. Like Abe, he too would take the dogs out on the lakes to teach them to listen well to commands. As the conversation progresses, Georgie rebukes claims that training dogs is easy:

> [I]t's not easy. Spend lots of time with your dogs. I remember when my grandpa [the late Vuntut Gwich'in Chief Peter Moses] came home from Crow Flats or somewhere with his dogs. And I'm back there. I'm putting

branches under them. I'm playing with them you see. He came home from trips and when it came to me being a dog musher, I use all that to learn what to do. What my grandpa teached me. So I'm out there training and talking way out there and pick it up quick. Hey this guy is alright so let's go. I learnt a lot from my dogs. I learn a real lot!

Conclusion

In this chapter I have outlined the amount of work that goes into getting ready for the 'hard times that are coming'. The setting up of dog team cannot be done overnight and requires a lot of dedication, searching, and breeding for proper dogs, as well as the training of the leader and other dogs. With this in mind, the warning to be prepared for the hardships implies being able to revitalise dog teams. I have further considered the notion of indeterminacy and dreaming as a trail in which one can move in a non-linear way. Time, thus, in the examples of the dreaming, is an embroidery with past, present, and future. The apocalyptic ending of the world, as preluded in the Bible as well as Gwich'in prophecies, is not fixed in time but rather is revealed through events that currently take place and herald the nearing of such an ending. Before that, though, the Gwich'in elders have emphasised that one needs to continue with traditional activities and practices, and know the land as well as having working dogs in order to counteract the time when fuel and groceries no longer exist in the community.

Acknowledgements

I want to acknowledge Ingrid Kritsch, Alestine Andre, Sharon Snowshoe, Mary Jane Moses, Abraham Stewart Junior, Rosalie Ross, and Georgie Moses as well as other many other Gwich'in for their teachings. I thank Rob Losey, Rob Wishart, and David G. Anderson for commenting on this paper. This chapter has been made possible through the financial support of ERC Advanced Grant (295458) Arctic Domus. I dedicate this chapter in memory of the late Georgie Moses and his passion for dogs.

Notes

1 The entry of white trappers into indigenous lands was not solely confined to the Gwich'in and Inuvialuit; other Aboriginal people experienced similar things.
2 When it comes to puppies and leaders, Abe Stewart Junior mentions that he observes puppies to discover the characteristics of future lead dogs: that is, the bossy puppy that is always first with eating.
3 The etymological roots of 'gee' come from Scotland and was first recorded in 1622 (see online etymology dictionary). The command was related with driving horses and I would assume that it came overseas with the Scottish fur traders and incorporated as a command in the dog teams.

Bibliography

Abele, F. 1987. "Canadian Contradictions: Forty Years of Northern Political Development." *Arctic*, 40(4): 310–320.

Allen, G. 1920. "Dogs of American Aborigines." *Bulletin of the Museum of Comparative Zoology at Harvard College, in Cambridge*, LXIII: 429–517.

Anderson, D.G., J.P.L. Loovers, S.A. Schroer, and R.P. Wishart. 2017. "Architectures of Domestication: On Emplacing Human–Animal Relations in the North." *Journal of the Royal Anthropological Institute*, 23(2): 398–423.

Bachelard, G. 1988. *Air and Dreams: An Essay On the Imagination of Movement.* (E. Farrell, and F. Farrell, Translators). Dallas: The Dallas Institute Publications.

Bromley, M. 1986. "'Fur Trade in the Northwest Territories: From the Earliest days to the Present Time." In *A Way of Life*. Edited by E. Hall, 7–29. Yellowknife: Department of Renewable Resources, Government of the Northwest Territories.

Chandler, A. 2009. "Black Dogs of the Gold Rush." *The Beaver* (August-September), 42–45.

Choquette, R. 1995. *The Oblate Assault on Canada's Northwest*. Ottawa: University of Ottawa Press.

Costa de Beauregard, O. 1987. *Time, The Physical Magnitude*. Dordrecht: D. Reidel Publishing Company.

Cummins, B.D. 2002. *First Nations, First Dogs: Canadian Aboriginal Ethnocynology*. Calgary: Detselig Enterprises Ltd.

Deleuze, G. and F. Guattari. 2003. *A Thousand Plateaus: Capitalism and Schizophrenia*. London: Continuum.

Diefenbaker, J. 1958. *A New Vision*. Winnipeg: Civic Auditorium. Available at webpage of Canada History: The History Project at www.canadahistory.com/sections/documents/Primeministers/diefenbaker/docs-diefenbaker.htm (Accessed 14.01.2009).

Eber, D.H. 1989. *When the Whalers Were Up North: Inuit Memories from the Eastern Arctic*. Montreal and Kingston: McGill-Queen's University Press.

Fafard, M. and I. Kritsch. 2005. *Yeenoo Dai' Gwatsat Teetł'it Zheh Googwandak: The History and Archeology of Fort McPherson*. Yellowknife: Outcrop Communications Ltd.

Franz, M.-L. von. 1980. *On Divination and Synchronicity: The Psychology of Meaningful Chance*. Toronto: Inner City Books.

Freud, S. 1920. *Dream Psychology*. www.feedbooks.com: http://krishnamurti.abundanthope.org/index_htm_files/Dream-Psychology-Sigmund-Freud Psychoanalysis-for-Beginners.pdf (Accessed 31.05.2017).

Gell, A. 1992. *The Anthropology of Time: Cultural Constructions of Temporal Maps and Images*. Oxford: Berg.

Hardisty, W. 1867. "The Loucheux Indians." In *Notes on the Tinneh or Chepewyan Indians of British and Russian America*. Edited by G. Gibbs, 311–320. Washington: Smithsonian Institute.

Heine, M., A. Andre, I. Kritsch, and A. Cardinal. 2007. *Gwichya Gwich'in Googwandak: The History and Stories of the Gwichya Gwich'in* (2nd ed.). Tsiigehtshik and Fort McPherson, NT: Gwich'in Social and Cultural Institute.

Hirt, I. 2012. "Mapping Dreams/Dreaming Maps: Bridging Indigenous and Western Geographical Knowledge." *Cartographica: The International Journal for Geographic Information and Geovisualization,* 47(2): 105–120.

Jones, S. 1867. "The Kutchin Tribes." In *Notes on the Tinneh or Chepewyan Indians of British and Russian America*, Edited by G. Gibbs, 320–327. Washington: Smithsonian Institute.

Lohman, R.I. 2003. "Introduction: Dream Travels and Anthropology." In *Dream Travellers: Sleep Experiences and Culture in the Western Pacific*. Edited by R.I. Lohman, 1–18. New York: Palgrave Macmillan.

London, J. 1990. *The Call of the Wild, White Fang, and Other Stories*. Oxford: Oxford University Press.

Loovers, J.P.L. 2010. 'You Have to Live It': Pedagogy and Literacy with Teetł'it Gwich'in. PhD dissertation. Aberdeen: University of Aberdeen.

Loovers, J.P.L. 2015. "Dog Craft: A History of Gwich'in and Dogs in the Canadian North." *Hunter Gatherer Research*, 1(4): 387–419.

McClellan, C. 1975. *My Old People Say: An Ethnographic Survey of Southern Yukon Territory (Part 2)*. Publications in Ethnology Vol. 6(2). Ottawa: National Museum of Canada.

McCormack, P. 2014. "Evolving Accommodations: The Sled Dog in the Canadian Fur Trade." In *Une Bête Parmi les Hommes; Le Chien: De la domestication à l'anthropomorphisme*. Edited by F. Guizard and C. Beck, 130–147. Valenciennes: Distribution Les Belles Lettres.

McDonald, R. n.d. *Diaries of 1862–1911*. Yukon Archives, Robert McDonald Fonds, 85/97, MSS195.

Mishler, C. 1990. "Missionaries in Collision: Anglicans and Oblates among the Gwich'in, 1861–65." *Arctic*, 43(2): 121–126.

Moore, P. 2007. "Archdeacon Robert McDonald and Gwich'in Literacy." *Anthropological Linguistics*, 49(1): 27–53.

Morrison, D. 2003. "The Winds of Change Blow Hard: The Whaling Era, 1890–1910." In *Across Time and Tundra: The Inuvialuit of the Western Arctic*. Edited by I. Alunik, E.D. Kolausok, and D. Morrison, 79–112. Vancouver: Raincoast Books.

Morrison, D. and E.D. Kolausok. 2003. "Trappers, Traders and Herders, 1906 –." In *Across Time and Tundra: The Inuvialuit of the Western Arctic*. Edited by I. Alunik, E.D. Kolausok, and D. Morrison, 113–137. Vancouver: Raincoast Books.

Osgood, C. 1936. *Contributions to the Ethnography of the Kutchin*. New Haven: Yale University Press.

Petitot, É. 1970. *The Amerindians of the North-West Canada in the 19th Century*. (D. Savoie, Translator). Ottawa: Department of Indian Affairs and Northern Development.

Piper, L. 2009. *The Industrial Transformation of Subarctic Canada*. Vancouver: UBC Press.

Ray, A.J. 1990. *The Canadian Fur Trade in the Industrial Age*. Toronto: University of Toronto Press.

Rethmann, P. 2001. *Tundra Passages: History and Gender in the Russian Far East*. University Park, Pennsylvania: The Pennsylvania State University Press.

Richardson, J. 1829. *Fauna Boreali-Americana; or the Zoology of the Northern Parts of the British America*, London: John Murray.

Sax, L. and E. Linklater. 1990. *Gikhyi: The One Who Speaks the Word of God*. Whitehorse: Diocese of Yukon.

Schwartz, M. 1997. *A History of Dogs in Early Americas*. New Haven and London: Yale University Press.

Shamdasani, S. 2009. "Liber Novus: The "Red Book" of C.G. Jung." In *The Red Book: Liber Novus*. Edited by C. Jung and S. Shamdasani (M. Kyburz, J. Peck, and S. Shamdasani, Translators), 193–221. New York and London: Philemon Series, W.W. Norton & Company.

Sharp, H. 2001. *Loon: Memory, Meaning, and Reality in a Northern Dene Community*. Lincoln and London: University of Nebraska Press.

Slobodin, R. 1962. *Band Organization of the Peel River Kutchin*. Ottawa: Department of Indian Affairs and Northern Development.

Stoneman-McNichol, J. 1983. *On Blue Ice: The Inuvik Adventure*. Yellowknife: Outcrop–The Northern Publishers Ltd.

Usher, P.J. 1971. *Fur Trade Posts of the Northwest Territories 1870–1970*. Ottawa: Northern Research Group, Department of Indian Affairs and Northern Development.

Vuntut Gwitchin First Nation (VGFN) and S. Smith. 2009. *People of the Lakes: Stories of Our Van Tat Gwich'in Elders/Googwandak Nakhwach'anjoo Van Tat Gwich'in*. Edmonton: University of Alberta Press.

Watson, G. and J.-G. Goulet. 1992. "Gold In, Gold Out: The Objectification of Dene Tha Accounts of Dreams and Visions." *Journal of Anthropological Research*, 48(3): 215–230.

Wishart, R.P. and J.P.L. Loovers. 2013. "Building Logs Cabins in Teetł'it Gwich'in Country: Vernacular Architecture and Articulations of Presence." In *About the Hearth: Perspectives on the Home, Hearth and Household in the Circumpolar North*. Edited by D.G. Anderson, R.P. Wishart, and V. Vaté, 54–68. New York and Oxford: Berghahn.

11 Dogs among others
Inughuit companions in Northwest Greenland

Kirsten Hastrup

Once upon a time, a dog took a woman as his wife; from that union came the white people. This fragment of a tale recorded by Knud Rasmussen from the Polar Eskimos in 1903 (Rasmussen 1908: 15, 85–86), comes in more or less elaborated variants, and has parallels among other indigenous people of the American Arctic. This serves as a first indication of the ambiguous relationship between dogs and humans in the Arctic, including Northwest Greenland, known as either the Thule region, named from the trading station established by Knud Rasmussen and others in 1910, or Avanersuaq – the 'Big North' in Greenlandic. In both cases it is more than a name; it is also a set of places and people, of experiences and imaginations (Hastrup 2014).

The High Arctic landscape of Avanersuaq carries its own connotations of permafrost, sea-ice, sparse vegetation, long winters and equal summers, and a scant human population living off marine mammals in particular. This still holds true, yet otherwise there is nothing inherently still or stable about this deep-frozen region, having been subjected to both long and short-term changes in climate and living conditions. Among these are the Medieval Warm Period (ninth to twelfth centuries) and the Little Ice Age (fourteenth to eighteenth centuries), but also short-term shifts and lasting uncertainties often relating to the outer world. Today, global warming deeply affects both the region and the people living there, undermining their access to parts of their ancient hunting grounds.

The inhabitants number some 700 people, of whom c. 600 live in the town of Qaanaaq and the rest in the remaining three settlements elsewhere in the region. They descend from the Thule Culture (so named by archaeologists) making its way from America to Northwest Greenland around 1200 CE. In the literature, the natives of the region have been known as Eskimos, Arctic Highlanders, Polar Eskimos, Thule Eskimos or the Thule people in historical times. Today they refer to themselves as Inughuit, if they must have a name apart from Greenlanders. While the inhabitants of the region have been isolated in some periods, they have also moved in or out, intermarried, and been educated elsewhere in Greenland or Denmark. The name Inughuit is mostly used as a political gesture since the 1970s, when it got coinage along with vague attempts at getting recognized as an indigenous people – which they did not really have to fight for, as it turned out. Truly, the inhabitants of Avanersuaq are far apart from the rest of the Greenlanders, in terms of both kilometres and access. Yet the development in communication technologies over the past ten years now connect them directly with family, friends, or acquaintances elsewhere in Greenland and the rest of the world. What remains exceptional for the region is that hunting is still the predominant source of income; in fact there are few alternatives, making the community vulnerable to the current environmental challenges.

The hunt is mainly a hunt for marine mammals from the sea-ice, and not least by the ice edge of the North Water, the polynya making both human and animal life possible (Hastrup 2016). Dogs and dog sledges are essential for this, entailing a close relationship between dogs and humans, which shall be unpacked in the following pages showing how they can be seen as companion species. It is a term launched by Donna Haraway (2003, 2008) to address the fact that human life depends on relations to other species. For her, it is not a matter of discarding the human perspective but to broaden it. She says: "The reason I go to companion species is to get away from posthumanism" (Haraway, in Gane and Haraway 2006: 140). Posthumanism has been claimed to acknowledge humanity's responsibility for the ecological crisis. Yet, it seems not to be the right word, if it is still for humans to take action on behalf of the many. This is one reason why I would go along with Haraway and opt for the notion of companion species implying a relational definition of species. This makes a case for expanding ethnography beyond the human as suggested by Kohn (2007: 5). The claim may not be as novel as it seems, if we recall for instance Evans-Pritchard's detailed analysis of the Nuer cattle and their place in an ecological system that included the herders (Evans-Pritchard 1940). This was indeed "an anthropology of life" as the one Kohn calls for, and which is a kind of anthropology that situates all-too-human worlds within a larger series of processes and relations (Kohn 2007: 6). We are in difficult terrain here, of course, because we (humans) always have to tell the story, even when we acknowledge the presence and significance of 'others'. As Anna Tsing says:

> Species are not always the right units for telling the life of the forest. The term 'multispecies' is only a stand-in for moving beyond human exceptionalism. Sometimes individual organisms make drastic interventions. And sometimes much larger units are more able to show us this historical action. This is the case, I find, for oaks and pines as well as matsutake. Oaks, which interbreed readily and with fertile results across species lines, confuse our dedication to species. *But of course what units one uses depends on the story one wants to tell.*
>
> Tsing 2015: 162 (emphasis added)

Both history and geography enter into this relationship, pointing to a particular assemblage of human, animal, and material agents, the latter including the sea-ice. The hunt itself involves different animal species, either as game, or as hunting companions in the case of the dog. Dogs are in focus here, but they are so through their relations to both humans and their prey. This is where the concept of assemblage presents itself as helpful, in the sense suggested by Tsing:

> Ecologists turned to assemblages to get around sometimes fixed and bounded notions of ecological 'community'. The question of how varied species in a species assemblage influence each other – if at all – is never settled: some thwart (or eat) each other; others work together to make life possible; still others just happen to find themselves in the same place. Assemblages are open-ended gatherings. They allow us to ask about communal effects without assuming them. They show us potential histories in the making.
>
> Tsing 2015: 22–23

This is the point, even if we assume that people, dogs, and other animals form a kind of assemblage, affecting each other more or less at certain times, the configuration is always emergent. With the dogs in particular, their relation to other species is inherently unstable. They may be co-hunters, helping their masters to get meat, or they may themselves be meat, enabling people to survive a meagre period. In the following we shall see how dogs become part of different assemblages at different points in time; these inevitably are described through human knowledge practices, our only access to the non-human companions (Tsing 2014: 34). First, we shall see the dogs as a kind of social engineers – holding the community together; next, we shall unpack the shifting positions of dogs and men in the history of exploration; and third, we shall use the notion of companion species as an analytical device to get closer to the dogs within our own anthropological interests of capturing a multifaceted community, always in the making.

The refrain: dogs as territorial engineers

When walking around in Qaanaaq or one of the three small settlements in the region, the voices of dogs are often heard well above the voice of humans. Dogs barking or howling do not simply signpost their own presence but also that of their human companions; dogs are present only as part of a larger social community. Once, in the field, it struck me how the sounds of dogs invariably revealed human presence and activity also well outside of your vision, and I was reminded of the notion of *the refrain*, suggested by Deleuze and Guattari as "any aggregate of matters of expression that draws a territory and develops into territorial motifs and landscapes" (Deleuze and Guattari 2004: 356). It points to territories made by sound, such as the singing of birds, or the ringing of church-bells, or the voices flowing out of minarets at particular times – but refrains can also be optical, gestural, architectural, and much more, including combinations of them all. The general point is that the refrain 'holds together' the heterogeneous elements of a territory, by bestowing it with a sense of consistency. This is why we experience it as a territory in the first place, and not simply as a boundless and unmarked world. Through their concerts, the dogs *make* the territory in that sense.

In Thule, dogs certainly hold together the inhabited part of what is otherwise an unmarked region (see also Hastrup 2010). If out on a sledge on the ice-covered fjord during a grey day with bad visibility, hearing other dogs gives one a sense of assurance about friends nearby. And if indoors, say in late April when there is light, while one may still be weather-bound by a snowstorm, the refrain takes on a new literal meaning, when one hears the chorus of (chained) sledge dogs singing their sad songs at certain moments of the day, longing for movement. Often one pack will set off the neighbouring one, and thus the song may spring from one place to the next – except when feeding has them all howling at the same time. This sonorous reminder of the relationship between people and their means of transport and hunting is a significant part of the refrain that marks the human terrain in Avanersuaq, which the ethnographer learns to appreciate and interpret.

If we expand this beyond sound, there is no doubt that dogs by their labour and skills can be seen to hold together the entire region in a rather literal sense as well. They have been co-defining the Thule Culture since its arrival in Northwest Greenland from the American Arctic c. 1200 CE, in their capacity as sledge dogs. These were the first Inuit in the region and they gradually overran or subsumed the previous inhabitants, known as the (late) Dorset people (c. 800–1200 CE). For the Dorset people, the technologies were different:

> There is no archaeological evidence ... to indicate that the Dorset people used dogsleds. We can be sure [however] that at least some Dorset groups must have had dogs. The pact between humans and dogs was made during the last Ice Age, and the two species have been inseparable ever since.
> McGhee 1997: 145

Since the first Palaeo-Eskimos moved from Siberia to North America some 12000 years ago and brought dogs with them, "the descendants of these animals would have continued to earn their keep as hunting companions, camp guards, and scavengers" (ibid.). When it comes to the late Dorset people, arriving in Thule some centuries before the Thule Inuit, there is no evidence of the complex harness needed for proper sledge driving for long-distance travel, yet the dogs may occasionally have been hitched to small sleds, of which there is some evidence in the shape of small sledge shoes (Holtved 1944), by a simple leather line. In general, McGhee argues, "the scarcity of finds relating to dogs suggests that most Dorset camps possessed few of the animals and that they were not an essential element of transportation" (McGhee 1997: 146). There was a pact, indeed, but it was one that (probably) also meant that in case of general food shortage, the dogs were the first to go (ibid.). It takes a relatively strong hunting economy to feed dogs, eating off the same resources as people. There is truly a balance to maintain.

With the Thule Inuit, rapidly moving east from the Bering Strait, the pact changed. What made these people superior to the Dorset people was not their numbers, but mainly their transportation technologies. These included both dog sledges and the large skin-covered umiaks for travelling on sea, which allowed them to travel together in great numbers; the Inuit were also equipped with strong bows that could be used against humans and animals alike, and "could be deadly at a much greater range than the spears and harpoons of Dorset hunters" (McGhee 1997: 223). These quick and well-equipped Thule hunters crossed Smith Sound c. 1200 CE and entered into Northwest Greenland, where the remnants of the Dorset people soon disappeared. The ensemble of the Thule technologies was first identified in excavations of "Comer's midden" in 1916. This was close to the Thule Station and to the ancient Uummannaq settlement; the culture, accordingly, was named the Thule Culture and it was later to be traced 'back' and identified also in America, first by Therkel Mathiassen (1927) – and the name persisted. It was then left to the Thule immigrants to repopulate all of western Greenland, where at the time only a small group of Norsemen lived in the south, having settled there in the tenth century to disappear again around 1400. As the original Thule Inuit moved south, they gradually shed some of the defining features of the Thule Culture, and were to be known as the Inugsuk Culture, relying more on seals than on whales (Mathiassen 1930; Holtved 1944).

The story of the emblematic Thule dog sledge thus begins with a particular assemblage of technologies that have survived until this day in the Thule region (McGhee 1997: 233; see also Hill, this volume). This can be seen as a technological refrain, connecting past and present within a territory that once was much larger than now, when it is left only in the Thule region proper. The technologies, both of transport and of hunting, were to define the Thule Culture for centuries to come. Only the dogs and the sledges survived the cooling of the Little Ice Age. This closed the waters for sea-borne travel and prevented driftwood from reaching the far northern shores to where it would previously have been borne on the warm West Greenlandic current, and thus put a temporary end to umiaks, kayaks, and bows. It also cut off communication with the southerly kinsmen of the Thule Inuit until the sea opened again and allowed European and American explorers to reach the High Arctic shores fairly regularly and write the first reports of the Inughuit and their dogs in the nineteenth century.

Among the early visitors was Elisha Kent Kane, who spent the years 1853–55 in the region and came to know and appreciate the people, who at the time seemed rather destitute and numbering only 140 souls, according to a census made by Kane and his local helpers. Still, their sense of community was remarkable, as was their keeping track of each other. Kane writes:

> The narrow belt subjected to their nomadic range cannot be less than six hundred miles long; and throughout this extent of country every man knows every man. There is not a marriage or a birth or a death that is not talked over and mentally registered by all. I have a census, exactly confirmed by three separate informants, which enables me to count by name about one hundred and forty souls, scattered along from Kosoak, the Great River at the base of a glacier near Cape Melville, to the wind-loved hut of Anoatok.
>
> Destitute as they are, they exist both in love and community of resources as a single family. The sites of their huts – for they are so few in number as to not bear the name of villages – are arranged with reference to the length of a dog-march and the seat of the hunt; and thus, when winter has built her highway and cemented into one the sea, the islands, and the main, they interchange with each other the sympathies and social communion of man, and diffuse through the darkness a knowledge of the resources and condition of all.
>
> Kane 1856, II: 211

This is a clear example of how dogs and sledges make community possible over such vast stretches of coastland and hold it together, by enabling people to move, to meet, and to hunt wherever there is game. While the tides are changing these years, and the winter highway between the settlements, of which there are also much fewer, is far less reliable than in the nineteenth century, I would argue that the dogs are still needed for maintaining a sense of territory, or a sense of sharing a particular landscape. This is how they become the moving refrain of the Thule territory.

In that sense, focussing on dogs as I do here, also makes the field – holding past and present together and incorporating voices from the nineteenth century onwards, until today where the fieldworker not only senses the deep roots of present hunting life but also hears the barking of an ancient companion species. In the process, the anthropologist notes the plasticity of the field and the need to scale the attention to particular concerns (Hastrup 2013a). The Thule dogs engineer both a particular territory and a specific analytical field, into which we shall now delve a bit further.

Exploring Thule: mad dogs and wild men

When the people living in secluded Avanersuaq came to the explorers' attention, they were immediately deemed savage. One reason was their being totally clad in fur, on which John Ross, the first explorer to bring the Arctic Highlanders (as he called them) to European knowledge, appreciatively comments (Ross 1819: 125). In a manner of speaking, they presented themselves in all their interspecies engagement, as has likewise been suggested for the Fuegians when they were first 'discovered' (Dransart 2013). There was also the matter of their mobile lifestyle made possible by the dog sledges, which was also of great interest to Ross. Explorers not only came from an unmarked 'south', they hailed from temperate zones and sedentary societies, setting the frame for proper social life. As Hugh Brody has it:

> The gulf between hunter and peasant consciousness that is revealed by so many opposing ideas, ideals and social habits is reinforced, in the case of the hunters of the far north by climate. In all peasant-originated systems, soil and warmth define a framework of human well-being. Late frosts and early winters are the enemy. Cold is a symbol of lovelessness, poverty and fear. A world without summer becomes a world without possibility of human existence.
>
> Brody 1987: 15

What is now happening in the Arctic is a form of sedentarization; people are drawn into villages and settle down in the vicinity of modern institutions. In the process, dogs have become more or less redundant, and in some places in Canada this has resulted in new mechanisms of control and in the killing of stray (and other) dogs (Lévesque 2010; see Lévesque, this volume). Not surprisingly, this has entailed some misgivings on the part of the dog-owners, losing their mobility. Stray dogs may be truly dangerous, but this gets a twist when it becomes associated more generally with the mobile life that has marked proper social life in the North. Also in Greenland, including Avanersuaq, dogs have to be chained when not in use, and while this makes practical sense, the implications are more than practical. As suggested for northern Canada, apart from being a matter of safety and health, it is a token also of a more or less forced change from a mobile to an increasingly sedentary life in line with the modern world (Tester 2010).

Meanwhile, safety remains an issue in Thule, and it has become even more so due to the current environmental changes and the new difficulties in procuring enough food for the dogs through winter; one could argue that the process of sedentarization is accompanied by a process of 'summering' – being kinder to human existence if seen from the South, but certainly adverse to proper hunting life in the High Arctic. Dogs sometimes starve and become 'mad' – that is, becoming unreliable. One January a couple of years ago, when darkness prevailed and the ice would not settle on the fjord outside Qaanaaq and no meat was available, I saw some young children playing on the ground just outside their house, and I was worried, knowing how starved the dogs were, and how they would sometimes break loose of their harness. I discussed this with an elderly friend of mine, and she shuddered and said that "young mothers do not know what they are doing; they have no experience of what dogs may do to children". She knew, one of her sons having been attacked at a young age and badly scarred for life. Now people had forgotten this, even though (or maybe because) the police made rounds in the town every two hours to look out for stray dogs – and polar bears, roaming in the area. The following year a young girl was actually killed by a dog in one of the settlements; a sad lesson of their ferocity, indeed. Mad dogs are not only starving dogs, but sometimes also sick dogs, to which we shall return.

John Ross not only took an interest in the people, but also in their sledges and dogs. His first report on the dogs runs like this:

> It being proposed that they should drive close to the ship on their sledges, for this purpose the eldest got into his sledge, and we had thus an opportunity of witnessing the mode in which he managed his dogs. These were six in number, each having a collar of seal skin, two inches wide, to which the one end of a thong, made of strong hide, about three yards long, was tied. The other end being fastened to the fore part of the sledge: thus they all stood nearly abreast, each drawing by a single trace without reins. No sooner did they hear the crack of the whip, than they set off at full speed, while he seemed to manage them with the greatest ease, guiding them partly by his voice, and partly by the sound of the whip. On approaching our sailors, however, they became so terrified, that it was with some difficulty they could be stopped.
>
> Ross 1819: 102

Not surprisingly (to us), the unknown people from the south with their military uniforms and strange hats terrified the dogs, all while Ross noted how the savages were totally clad in fur and – by implication – were of one piece with the animals they hunted. Yet, he was impressed, not least by their technical ingenuity, and he immediately bought a sledge (now in the British Museum) built almost entirely from bone material from whale and walrus, and with sealskin runners (Ross 1819: 102). Having described the formidable piece of technology he continues:

> I also purchased from them a dog, but with some difficulty, as they seem very adverse to part with it. I chose the one which appeared to Mr Parry and me the handsomest. In examining them we found that three of them had lost each an eye; these, as the natives informed us, having been accidents from the lash of the whip. The dog was bound, and led on by one of the sailors, and an excellent portrait was made of him by Mr. Skene ... The animal was sometime afterwards, unfortunately, washed overboard in a gale.
>
> Ross 1819: 103

When Ross wanted to buy a second dog, this was not granted him (1819: 107); the natives had no more to spare, badly needing their dogs to remain mobile. Ross mostly wanted to study them in the manner of a naturalist making an inventory of life in the region, and clearly the dogs were understood within two different registers, implying distinct relations between dogs and humans. Ross writes about the dogs:

> The dogs which are the only animals that have been domesticated by the Arctic Highlanders, are of various colours, but chiefly resembling that given on the plate; they are of the size of a shepherd's dog, they have a head like a wolf, and a tail like a fox; their bark resembles the latter, but they also have a howl like the former.
>
> Ross 1819: 133

What is striking here is the ambiguous classification of the dog; while domesticated it still bears the mark of wildness. Just like the human inhabitants of the region defied facile definition in relation to their sedentary and temperate cousins elsewhere so also the dogs. They howled like wolves, and were not to be entirely trusted.

Kane, who came to the region a quarter of a century later on a search expedition sent out for John Franklin, already knew that dogs would be an advantage and he brought his own, both from Newfoundland and from South Greenland, so that he would not depend on the semi-wild dogs in the North, yet it turned out to be a nightmare in many ways. Early in his report, after a successful crossing of the North Water, he writes:

> It may be noted among our little miseries that we have more than fifty dogs on board, the majority of whom might rather be characterized as 'ravening wolves.' To feed this family, upon whose strength our progress and success depend, is really a difficult matter. The absence of shore or land ice to the south in Baffin's Bay has prevented our rifles for contributing any material aid to our commissariat. Our two bears lasted our cormorants but eight days; and to feed them on the meagre allowance of two pound of raw flesh every other day is an almost impossible necessity.
>
> Kane 1856, I: 55–56

This is an indication of men and dogs competing about the resources; in the process of intensifying competition, the dogs are increasingly seen as wild. A week after the outburst above, Kane gives vent to this, when he again describes the dogs as a major nuisance, this time destroying the expedition's sample of specimens on account of them being famished.

> More bother with these wretched dogs! Worse than a street of Constantinople emptied upon our decks; the unruly, thieving, wild-beast pack! Not a bear's paw, or an Eskimo cranium, or basket of mosses, or any specimen whatever, can leave your hands for a moment without their making a rush for it, and, after a yelping scramble, swallowing it at a gulp.
>
> Kane 1856, I: 65

The parallels Kane draws are quite powerful; Constantinople on the deck – uncultured indeed. The images testify to Kane's experience of foreignness and unpredictability when dealing with the dogs. He soon loses some of his hard-won samples of naturalist value to the unruly pack, always prepared to turn their backs to the gentleman explorer. "When we reach a floe, or berg, or temporary harbour, they start out in a body, neither voice nor lash restraining them, and scamper off like a drove of hogs in an Illinois oak-opening" (Kane 1856, I: 65). Kane goes on to tell how they had had to send a boat to a rescue of two dogs, having made it from floe to floe for more than eight miles until they were found "fat and saucy, beside the carcass of a dead narwhal" (ibid.). They succeeded in catching only one of them, while "the other suicidal scamp had to be left to his fate" (ibid.).

Starving dogs are no fun, but at least Kane understands their desperation and knows the remedy, even if it is not easily available. It was another matter when in the dead of winter darkness, the dogs became badly afflicted by depression – like the men. "Even our dogs, although the greater part of them were natives to the Arctic circle, were unable to withstand it. Most of them died from an anomalous form of disease, to which, I am satisfied, the absence of light contributed as much as the extreme cold" (Kane 1856, I: 156). Spelling out the affliction, he quotes an entry in his diary (dated 25 January 1853):

> The mouse-colored dogs, the leaders of my Newfoundland team, have for the past fortnight been nursed like babies. No one can tell how anxiously I watch them. They are kept below, tended, fed, cleansed, caressed, and *doctored*, to the infinite discomfort of all hands. To-day I give up the last hope of saving them. Their disease is as clearly mental as in the case of any human being. The more material functions of the poor brutes go on without interruption; they eat voraciously, retain their strength, and sleep well. But all the indications beyond this go to prove that the original epilepsy, which was the first manifestation of brain disease among them, has been followed by a true lunacy. They bark frenziedly at nothing, and walk in straight and curved lines with anxious and unwearying perseverance.
>
> Kane 1856, I: 158

We are offered more details about individual dogs and their demise, but these snippets suffice to give a sense of the challenge posed by the dogs on the one hand, and of the ambiguous relationship between the men and the dogs on the other. The dogs are not quite companions, it seems, and they can only be comprehended in a human vocabulary deeming them mad and miserable. Kane's winter also tolled among his men, deeply affecting the morale of the crew, and the expedition was pretty desperate until they finally met some local inhabitants. Having at first been rather careful inviting them on board, Kane gives in and seeks to establish a kind of exchange-relation with them. He still believes himself to be the master of the situation, but he is not; he is the one who needs them, not the other way round. He immediately "bought all the walrus-meat they had to spare, and four of their dogs, enriching them in return with needles and beads and a treasure of old cask-staves" (Kane 1856, I: 209). This marks the beginning of a long and productive collaboration with both dogs and people, even if Kane remained a relatively distant observer of the inhabitants. While he learnt to appreciate the skills of both people and dogs in the region, and actually began wearing fur-clothes along with his men, he never really felt equal to them; both dogs and humans remained *others*.

Isaac Hayes, the next in line to report from the region, gets much closer to the dogs. He writes:

> These dogs are singular animals, and are a curious study. They have their leader and their sub-leaders – the rulers and the ruled – like any other community desiring good government. The governed get what rights they can, and the governors bully them continually in order that they may enjoy security against rebellion, and live in peace. And a community of dogs is really organized on the basis of correct principles.
>
> Hayes 1867: 119

What transpires in this note is an appreciation of the dogs as human-like. Significantly, this goes together with a growing admiration for the little tribe of 'Eskimaux', who now (in the mid 1860s) are on the verge of extinction, numbering only one hundred souls and badly hit by sickness (Hayes 1867: 386). This was probably owed to epidemics brought by foreign sailors and whalers to Cape York, the southern promontory of the Thule region, where people eagerly awaited them each summer for bartering (Hastrup 2017). At the time the local population had no resistance against any introduced diseases.

This also applied to the dogs. In the interest of taking his own dogs with him to Avanersuaq, Hayes had brought fine specimens with him from the Danish settlements in the more southerly parts of Greenland. Recalling Kane's troubles with the dogs (Hayes had been part of Kane's expedition), Hayes had been meticulous in his choice of dogs on his way, knowing that a disease had affected some populations and being told that if he removed healthy dogs from contagion, they would remain so. He took a lot of time choosing the best among non-affected packs, and brought thirty-six animals with him to the North picked up among the best packs (Hayes 1867: 195ff.). The dogs remained in good health until December, when he received news from the region of Whale Sound about heavy losses of dogs, due to the dog-disease also known in Southern Greenland. His dogs were amply fed with fresh meat, and he thought himself in the clear. Yet, the dreaded disease was not to be avoided.

> My hopeful anticipations were, however, not realized. One day in early December Jensen reported to me that one of the finest animals had been attacked with the disease, and recommended that it should be shot, to

prevent the disease spreading; and this was accordingly done. A few hours afterwards another one was seized in the same manner. The symptoms were at first those of great restlessness ...

The disease ran its course in a few hours. Weakness and prostration followed the excitement, and the poor animal staggered around the vessel, apparently unable to see its way, and finally fell over in a fit.

Hayes 1867: 196

We need no more details about the agony of the afflicted dogs, but we note how Hayes gradually lost a good number of his splendid dogs. Among them was a "superb beast", the "best draught animal of my best team" – Karsuk. "I have never seen such expression of ferocity and mad strength exhibited by any living creature, as he manifested two hours after the first symptoms were observed" (Hayes 1867: 197). Hayes goes on, describing the development and his attempts at isolating the sick animals, yet to no avail. After a few weeks, his team was down to nine dogs. This greatly affected his plans, and he considered his options, and hoped that somewhere further north, there would be families with healthy dogs that he could enlist in his endeavour of exploration.

We now know that the dreaded dog-disease, sometimes called distemper, which largely remains unspecified in the region, affects the dog-teams from time to time. People are extremely observant of their dogs, and wary of bringing in non-local teams. Yet sometimes it is necessary. Thus, in the 1980s the Thule dogs were badly hit by the disease, annihilating all of the dogs in particular villages, and leaving people at a great loss – literally. It is still talked about, when one converses with the hunters of Savissivik, for instance, living on the southern outskirts of the region, and increasingly cut off from the rest – if now re-opening old ties with the Upernavik region on the southerly fringe of the Melville Bay. With no dogs, the hunters of Savissivik could not do what they do best – hunt bears – for a couple of years. Mad or dead dogs are of no use in the emblematic bear-hunt, where dogs are not only dragging the sledges but also encircling and thus stopping the bear in its tracks. This, again, resulted in some very hard years, with people on the brink of starvation, because without the dogs they could not go anywhere else either. Now the dwindling sea-ice also contributes to a sense of being stuck.

The dog-disease is a latent threat, and people watch their dogs closely. Only last year there was an outbreak of the disease further south in West Greenland and people worried about its spreading; it did not, fortunately. Another threat is posed by rabies, always attributed to polar foxes 'gone mad' and walking into the settlements (probably for food), where they are closely watched by people. One dark day in January, 2013, I suddenly heard a lot of commotion outside and looked out of my window to see a group of children running after and shouting at a meagre white fox in the street. When under the streetlights, it was easy to see that the fox was not well, and according to my host the children were trying to push it out of town to protect the dogs from (possible) rabies. Like the bears coming into town – or rather to the dump – during winter, the fox could have been simply hungry, but no chances were taken, and it was eventually shot by the vigilant policeman on the outskirts of the village. Whatever madness it carried, it would not be allowed to spread. It was a winter also of starvation among the dogs themselves, as I related above, and which already had the police making rounds. Eventually, the hunters made a plea to the authorities down south to help with dog feed, and they answered by supplying the shop with dog-pellets by airplane, and while it did make a difference, it was still considered a very sad situation. Feeding a dog pellets (and having to purchase it in the first place) does not make anyone, human or dog, happy. It becomes yet another token of the hard times that the community is facing, including also the dwindling of the sea-ice, and the increasingly difficult access to familiar hunting grounds. The community in many ways is on thin ice (Hastrup 2013b).

Hard times are not new, as we have heard also from Hayes' report. When taking his leave from the Eskimos, Hayes made the following parting note, where humans and dogs are somehow co-mingled in their lot. He greets his Eskimo partners, who had helped him out with dogs among many other things, in the following way:

> They have all been faithful, each in his way, and they have done me most important service. The alacrity with which they have placed their dogs at my disposal (and without these dogs I could have done absolutely nothing) is the strongest proof that they would give me of their devotion and regard; for their dogs are to them invaluable treasures, without which they have no security against want and starvation, to themselves and their wives and children. True, I have done them some good, and have given them presents of great value, yet nothing can supply the place of a lost dog; and out of all that I obtained from them, there were but two animals that survived the hardship of my journey. These I have returned to their original owners. I have given them high hopes of my speedy return, and in this prospect they appear to take consolation.
>
> Hayes 1867: 414

Reaching Godhavn, his last port of call in Greenland and the administrative centre of North Greenland, Hayes gathered the latest news. He learnt that the American Civil War had broken out in his absence and he decided to travel back to the States to enlist. When finally reaching Boston he offered his own service and that of his schooner to the President. He never returned to Thule, being caught up in another kind of madness – war. He never returned.

Companion species: a shifty space of relations

In present day Thule, dogs are still very prominent. The barking, howling, smelling, sudden emergence of young dogs from under the houses built on stilts reaching down in the permafrost, and the temporary placement of a whelping female dog in a special dog-house along with her pups, she being tied up of course – all of this forms an under-life in the towns and settlements, hardly noticed because it is so obviously part of the everyday. In Thule as elsewhere in Greenland, dogs must be tied up when they are six months old; in the Thule-law, established in 1929 and governing the proceedings of the Hunters' Council, the hunters' responsibility for their dogs and their damages are clearly stated, adding that this does not apply to young dogs that are still going loose. Clearly, it is an old rule that mature dogs should be kept tied up to prevent damages; what is relatively new are the designated areas for tying up the packs on the outskirts of the villages. Among the designated areas, the hunters choose whatever is most convenient in relation to their houses and their having to feed the dogs regularly also when they are not in use. Mostly, when they are going hunting on the ice, they will take down the sledge and the dogs to the beach separately and only connect them when on the ice. If they know they will soon be going out again, they may leave the dogs tied on the ice next to the sledge.

The ice is also the primary hunting ground, and it attracts hunters whenever it is stable enough to drag out the sledge. Whether going for *uttoq*-hunting (seals basking in the sun beside their breathing holes, and approached from behind a shooting screen), or for bigger game such as narwhal or walrus, the hunter mostly directs his dogs from the sledge. He has two instruments for this: the voice and the whip. He tells, sometimes loudly, when to go left and when to go right, or whether to speed up and prepare for a long jump over a rift in the ice. As a passenger, one gradually learns this particular language well enough to brace oneself for the manoeuvres. Eduardo Kohn (2013: 144–145) speaks of a "trans-species pidgin" in the case of the Amazonian Runa with whom he worked and suggests that it both instantiates and blurs the distinction between people and dogs. This is an evocative term, and while in the Inughuit case the pidgin is actually rather more simplified than seems to be the case in Ávila, there is definitely a kind of two-way communication going on, upon which the success of the hunt may hinge; the dogs seem to have a degree of ice-literacy of their own. In an interesting article from 1928, Elmer Ekblaw underscores how the "dogs of Thule are not only gentle, but loyal to their team, their driver, and their village" (Ekblaw 1928: 16), and he offers the following observation on the dogs that tallies with my claim to a trans-species understanding of the ice:

> Their sense of ice conditions is almost uncanny. They realize the danger the moment they venture upon uncertain ice, and pick their way cautiously. They will not sledge out upon unsafe ice unless their driver forces them to do so. They are unerring in finding their way through darkness and storm if they have once been over the trail.
>
> Ekblaw 1928: 17

The whip is mostly used to keep the dogs in place before starting, to get going in the first place, and to make them speed up if they begin to lose their stamina after a long trip. The latter stops some of the dogs falling behind and leaving their braces to slacken and getting entangled with each other. A lot depend on the hunter's skill at breeding and training the dogs; some teams are just better than others, and some hunters more attentive to their dogs' expressions than others, and having more or less patience with their companions, and using the whip more or less. In general, the hunters respect their dogs, but they are not adverse to shouting at them and using the whip in having it their way.

Only once have I been out with a hunter who truly lost patience with his dog team (implicitly with me, too, possibly), shouting and whipping violently, and even driving over dogs that had laid down to lick their bleeding feet – a result of the ice condition. While never commented upon (at least not to an outsider; or, for that matter, *by* an outsider depending on future collaborations with other hunters), the locals have a clear sense of some dog-owners ranking higher than others, and readily praise the good teams. In a case like the one related above, other hunters might have chosen to reduce speed, maybe to stop and put dog-kamiks on his companions' sore feet, as described by Holtved (1967: 67) and as witnessed by myself. It is not always easy to put them on the dogs, or to keep them there, but it is an important practice in keeping the dogs healthy. Part of the reason for the loss of temper in the case related above was a rather dramatic change of the ice conditions. On our return, the ice had changed so much that the eight-hour relatively smooth outward trip became a cumbersome fourteen-hour home trip, where we had to negotiate new cracks, and eventually cross over a belt of unstable hummocks to get onto the ice foot. It was pretty tough, and the driver lost patience when the dogs slowed down. In their turn, the dogs went 'on strike' due to the working conditions, and we were left with only four dogs dragging the sledge. The other four were left at various points along the route, lying down, visibly battered, and with bleeding paws. They returned to town over the next days.

Even though dogs blend into the everyday, there is a lot of attention and pride invested in the teams of individual hunters, who breed and name them and place them at particular places in the fan-shaped team in front of the sledge according to their strength and character. Once, I had been out with a hunter from one of the small settlements, who had only five dogs left at the time, and it was a matter of great importance and pride to him that next time I came, he could boast of fifteen when we met. He had acquired pups from others and started a concerted effort at breeding a new team. Before, he had largely given up on dogs, because the hunt had become very poor, but with the new opportunities to catch halibut (by long line from the ice), he once again needed a strong team to drag his sledge, loaded with his gear and his catch. There is no infrastructure apart from the ice, and if the fish is not brought to the freezing plant in time, it will fall through the ice when it cracks up, and months of effort will have been wasted; it has happened. Being successful always requires good transportation. Snow-mobiles on the sea-ice are allowed only very sparingly and under well-defined circumstances, as their noise makes *uttoq*-hunting impossible. There are very few of them in Qaanaaq and none elsewhere, as access to spare parts is almost non-existent.

Dogs have always been important even if they have played varying roles at different times and in different seasons. For example, Erik Holtved, an archaeologist working in Thule in the late 1930s and again in the 1940s when he sojourned mainly at the Thule Station and excavated parts of the Uummannaq settlement, importantly notes:

> The dogs take up a goodly part of the existence of the Polar Eskimos. A good dog team is necessary in order to keep up what, according to Polar Eskimo conditions, is considered a high standard of living: and losing one's dog team is a very serious matter, which among other things entails greater dependency on others. The number of dogs in a team varies from time to time, but it is generally between 7 and 15. However, a great deal of meat is naturally required for dog food so only the most efficient hunters can afford to keep the really big teams. To understand the great importance of the dogs, one must keep in mind that the hunting trips of the Polar Eskimos often extend over hundreds of kilometres from home and may last for months. An existence without dogs is a toilsome existence. Nevertheless, times are recalled when the dogs for some reason had died, and people had to push the sledges themselves by the upstanders.
>
> Holtved 1967: 69–70

Many would understand this as a description of yesteryear but it certainly is still a valid observation. Once again we are reminded of the continuity of the Thule community, always implying a partnership with dogs. In interesting ways, there again seems to be a parallel between the dogs in focus here, and the dogs belonging to Runa with whom Kohn worked. Kohn writes that in many ways people and dogs live separate lives, and he continues:

> And yet their lives are also deeply entangled with those of their human masters. This entanglement does not just involve the circumscribed context of the home or the village. It is also the product of the interactions that dogs and people have with the biotic world of the forest as well as the socio-political world beyond Ávila through which both species are linked by the legacy of a colonial history.
>
> Kohn 2013: 135

What is at play here is a claim that over the generations, human and non-human histories have become entangled. In both Ávila and Avanersuaq, the dogs are fellow-hunters in one sense or another. Apart from dragging the sledge, the dogs in Thule are fellow-hunters in the polar-bear-hunt; the dogs are often the first to sense the bears, and when close enough the pack is let loose from their braces and sent off to encircle and keep the bear in place until the hunter can catch up with his gun. At other points in time, dogs may be eaten (in the North); Ross even suggests that: "Dogs are also esteemed excellent food, and are bred as live stock, as well as to draw the sledge; but they are only eaten in winter, in times when no other food can be obtained" (Ross 1819: 131). It is doubtful that the dogs were ever bred as livestock, although it is perfectly true that they would sometimes be eaten (as they still may, if surreptitiously); as we know, they were always in danger once food became scarce. The problem was that they competed for the same resources. They still do, if to a lesser extent. The problem intensified with the forced tying-up of the packs; Holtved explains why:

> There are undoubted advantages in having the team tied up at all times. No time is lost getting the dogs together again when they are to be used, and the risk of their eating straps and skin things is at least somewhat reduced. But the dogs are in this way prevented from getting some food for themselves and have to be fed regularly. If there is nothing to give them it is necessary therefore to let them loose. At Thule this was usually the case at a certain time of the summer (July), when hunting was normally slack, and nothing was safe from the roaming dogs, which could be dangerous, not least to the children.
>
> Holtved 1967: 71

While it is forbidden to let adult dogs loose, the above is otherwise still a valid observation, as we saw above, and it bears witness to the many, sometimes contradictory, ways in which dogs and humans are companion species. Focussing on the companionship of humans and dogs in the North, I recognize my sorting through observations and readings in the interest of this particular perspective. Within this framework, I also acknowledge Kohn's attribution of subjectivity to both people and dogs; forgetting this may be disastrous (Kohn 2007: 9). Dogs are never just that – they are dog-subjects in particular story, as lived *and* told.

What we should also not forget is how people and dogs are surrounded by other companion species on which their life depends. In Avanersuaq, the dogs are invaluable co-hunters for the bear-hunt and highly valued for that. "Bear hunting is one of the subjects that most strongly occupy the mind of the Polar Eskimo, and having good bear dogs is a matter of great pride" (Holtved 1967: 105), and, one would like to add, a precondition for success. Not everybody has the skill or the economy to aspire to the bear-hunt, and it demands a well fed and trained dog team. Having never participated in a bear-hunt myself, the stories I have heard still tally with Holtved's description. Especially in Savissivik, people are still prominent bear-hunters in the Melville Bay, yet in actual fact it is only a small group who have the skills, the dogs, and the stamina to really make it. For the Inughuit community as a whole the current waning of the bear-hunt (especially in the northern part of the region, tapping into the Kane Basin bear population) is part of a larger vicious circle of dwindling ice, destabilization of the walrus hunt, famished dogs, and strict quotas on the bear. In turn, this has led to a lack of bearskin for trousers that have been the uniform of a proper Inughuit hunter.

When the Arctic Highlanders refused to part with a second dog, and when they flatly refused to part with any of their fur dress on Ross' request (1819: 125), this was an expression of their need for these things to hunt and survive in the region, and they had nothing to spare. The fur-clothes connected the hunters directly to other species, but they were also instrumental to survival on these latitudes. Humans, bears, and dogs unite in making life possible, even if their interrelations differ according to time and place, and to modes of action. As agents, all of them are mobile and constantly shifting places in the larger assemblage of agents, including other companions such as seals, walruses, narwhals, little auks, and multiple smaller animal and vegetal life forms – and their collective dependence on particular sea currents and ice conditions.

Conclusion: the historicity of interspecies relations

In many ways, anthropology is beyond the call for a multispecies anthropology (Kirksey and Helmreich 2010). It seems that we are already there, and have always been, even if the emphasis on interspecies relations may have changed over time. Clearly, no species is ever self-sufficient, but there are many ways of describing this. As anthropologists, we are bound to use the language of humans. We may recognize our being enmeshed in all sorts of relations to other species, yet it is for us to show how these relations are historically embedded, and may be valued in many different ways. The species 'become' with one another, but not in fixed ways. "The open beckons; the next speculative proposition lures; the world is not finished" (Haraway 2008: 244). In the High Arctic, hunting, killing, eating, and dressing may be read in different ways, but they all testify to deep-seated interspecies relationships. We may return to Tsing, who suggested:

> Interspecies relations draw evolution back into history because they depend on the contingency of encounter. They do not form an internally self-replicating system. Instead, interspecies encounters are always events, 'things that happen,' the units of history. Events can lead to relatively stable situations, but they cannot be counted on in the way self-replicating units can; they are always framed by contingency and time.
>
> Tsing 2015: 142

This goes to stress, once again, that the human/non-human relations, like the ones between the Inughuit and their dogs, 'happen' and become units in the making of history. If, in this case, we may find continuity back in time, it still has shifted from encounter to encounter. The very volatility of the human, animal, and material relations that make up the lived landscape installs a particular emotional topography in people, and even a set of mobile emotions (Hastrup 2010; Elixhauser 2015).

We are back to the notion of assemblage left undefined since the introduction, and now seen as a way to grapple with the multiple and shifty relations between agents. Jane Bennett suggests:

> Assemblages are ad hoc groupings of diverse elements, of vibrant materials of all sorts. Assemblages are living, throbbing confederations that are able to function despite the persistent presence of energies that confound them from within. They have uneven topographies, because some of the points at which the various affects and bodies cross paths are more heavily trafficked than others, and so power is not distributed equally across its surface.
>
> Bennett 2010: 23–24

In other words, even if we adopt the notion of companion species, it would be ill advised to treat the relationships between the companions as fixed once and for all. When dogs are bear-hunting they stand in a different relationship to their companion hunter than when they are dragging the sledge home from the seal hunt, or when they are tied up and barely fed during winters with little game. These three positions that the dogs may take in their relation to humans are all of them defined by humans, in both practice and description. Being a companion species it not necessarily a matter of having an equal say.

As anthropologists we need not take sides for or against interspecies dynamics. It is a fact, which may or may not be worth highlighting in particular analyses. Even if all landscapes are assembled from material, animal, and human agents, there is still a particular place for anthropology, describing how assemblages are marked by shifting relations between the agents. Anthropology itself is a relational practice, not a self-replicating field of knowledge; it is based on anthropologists' encounters with other real people and their companions, and written into a long pedigree of deep interest in their lives and a will to make the rest of the world know about it.

Acknowledgements

The author wants to thank Peter Loovers and Robert Wishart for their astute comments to the early draft of this article, which helped me clarify the argument. Thanks are also due to the European Research Council (ERC AdG no. 229459), The Carlsberg Foundation, and the Velux Foundations for making recurrent research in Avanersuaq possible.

Bibliography

Bennett, J. 2010. *Vibrant Matter. A Political Ecology of Things*. Durham and London: Duke University Press.

Brody, H. 1987. *Living Arctic. Hunters of the Canadian North*. London and Boston: Faber & Faber.
Deleuze, G. and F. Guattari. 2004. *A Thousand Plateaus: Capitalism and Schizophrenia*. London: Continuum.
Dransart, P. 2013. "Dressed in Furs: Clothing and Yaghan Multispecies Engagements in Tierra del Fuego." In *Living Beings. Perspectives on Interspecies Engagements*. Edited by P. Dransart, 183–204. London: Bloomsbury (ASA Monographs 50).
Ekblaw, W.E. 1928. "The Material Response of the Polar Eskimo to Their Far Arctic Environment." *Annals of the Association of the American Geographers*, 18 (1): 1–24.
Elixhauser, S.C. 2015. "Travelling the East Greenlandic Sea- and Landscape: Encounters, Places and Stories." *Mobilities*, 10 (4): 531–551.
Evans-Pritchard, E.E. 1940. *The Nuer. A Description of the Modes of Livelihood and Political Institutions of a Nilotic People*. Oxford: Clarendon Press.
Gane, N. and D. Haraway. 2006. "When We Have Never Been Human, What Is To Be Done? Interview with Donna Haraway." *Theory, Culture & Society*, 23 (7–8): 135–158.
Haraway, D. 2003. *The Companion Species Manifesto: Dogs, People, and Significant Otherness*. Chicago: Prickly Paradigm Press.
Haraway, D. 2008. *When Species Meet*. Minneapolis: University of Minnesota Press.
Hastrup, K. 2010. "Emotional Topographies: The Sense of Place in the North." In *Emotions in the Field*. Edited by J. Davies and D. Spencer, 191–212. Palo Alto: Stanford University Press.
Hastrup, K. 2013a. "Scales of Attention in Fieldwork. Global Connections and Local Concerns in the Arctic." *Ethnography*, 14 (2): 145–164.
Hastrup, K. 2013b. "Anticipation on Thin Ice. Diagrammatic Reasoning in the High Arctic." In *The Social Life of Climate Change Models. Anticipating Nature*. Edited by K. Hastrup and M. Skrydstrup, 77–99. London and New York: Routledge.
Hastrup, K. 2014. "Of Maps and Men. Making Places and Peoples in the Arctic." In *Anthropology and Nature*. Edited by K. Hastrup, 211–232. London and New York: Routledge.
Hastrup, K. 2016. "The North Water. Life on the Ice Edge in the High Arctic." In *Waterworlds: Anthropology in Fluid Environments*. Edited by K. Hastrup and F. Hastrup, 279–299. Oxford and New York: Berghahn.
Hastrup, K. 2017. "The Viability of a High Arctic Community: A Historical Perspective." In *The Anthropology of Sustainability*. Edited by M. Brightman and J. Lewis, 145–163. New York: Palgrave Macmillan.
Hayes, I.I. 1867. *The Open Polar Sea. A Narrative of a Voyage of Discovery towards the North Pole, in the Schooner United States*. London: Sampson Low, Son and Marston.
Holtved, E. 1944. *Archaeological Investigations in the Thule District, II: Analytical Part*. Copenhagen: C.A. Reitzels Forlag (Meddelelser om Grønland, vol. 141).
Holtved, E. 1967. *Contributions to Polar Eskimo Ethnography*. Copenhagen: C.A. Reitzels Forlag (Meddelelser om Grønland, vol. 182, no. 2).
Kane, E.K. 1856. *Arctic Explorations. The Second Grinnell Expedition in Search of Sir John Franklin, 1853–55*, vols I & II. Philadelphia: Childs & Peterson; London: Trübner & Co.
Kirksey, S.E. and S. Helmreich 2010. "The Emergence of Multispecies Ethnography." *Cultural Anthropology*, 25 (4): 545–576.

Kohn, E. 2007. "How Dogs Dream: Amazonian Natures and the Politics of Transspecies Engagement." *American Ethnologist*, 34 (1): 3–24.
Kohn, E. 2013. *How Forests Think. Toward an Anthropology beyond the Human*. Berkeley and London: University of California Press.
Lévesque, F. 2010. "Le contrôle des chiens dans trois communautés du Nunavik au milieu du 20e siècle." *Études/Inuit/Studies*, 34 (2): 149–166.
McGhee, R. 1997. *Ancient People of the Arctic*. Vancouver: University of British Columbia Press.
Mathiassen, T. 1927. *Archaeology of the Central Eskimos I-II. Report of the 5th Thule Expedition 1921–24*. Vol. IV. Copenhagen: Gyldendal.
Mathiassen, T. 1930. *Inugsuk, a Mediaeval Eskimo Settlement in Upernavik District, West Greenland*. Copenhagen: C.A. Reitzels Forlag (Meddelelser om Grønland, vol. 77).
Rasmussen, K. 1908. *The People of the Polar North. A Record*. (Edited and translated by G. Herring). London: Kegan Paul, Trench, Trübner & Co. Ltd.
Ross, J. 1819. *Voyage of Discovery, made under the orders of Admiralty, in his Majesty's ships Isabelle and Alexander, for the Purpose of Exploring Baffin's Bay, and inquiring into the probability of a North-West Passage*. London: John Murray, Albemarle-Street.
Tester, F.J. 2010. "Mad Dogs and (Mostly) Englishmen: Colonial Relations, Commodities, and the Fate of Inuit Sled Dogs." *Études/Iniut/Studies*, 34 (2): 129–147.
Tsing, A.L. 2014. "More-than-Human Sociality. A Call for Critical Description." In *Anthropology and Nature*. Edited by K. Hastrup, 27–42. London and New York: Routledge.
Tsing, A.L. 2015. *The Mushroom and the End of the World. On the Possibility of Life in Capitalist Ruins*. Princeton: Princeton University Press.

12 Prehistory of dogs in Fennoscandia
A review

Suvi Viranta and Kristiina Mannermaa

Introduction

Dogs are very popular pets in Northern Europe. Besides being important as companions, they serve as service animals such as police dogs. Moreover, Northern Europe, having remained largely forested compared to the rest of Europe, still has a strong hunting culture, and hounds as well as gun dogs continue to be an intimate part of local hunting culture. In prehistory, dogs accompanied people inhabiting the land as it was freed from the last glaciation. Archeological evidence provides a picture of a close and special, but at the same time complex relationship between humans and dogs in prehistory. Ethnographic sources from northern areas suggest different attitudes toward dogs, and the roles and treatment of dogs vary even within a small geographic area. However, the data suggest that dogs have played a role quite different from other wild and domestic animals in human society.

The best evidence of prehistoric dogs comes in the form of bones and teeth preserved in archeological sites: settlements, burials, ritual places, etc. In this chapter we provide a review of the history of the domestic dog based on the literature on osteoarcheological finds, limiting the task to the geographical frame of Fennoscandia. Fennoscandia is a geographic term for an area comprising Finland and Scandinavia (Figure 12.1). Before going to this, we present some key geographical definitions and overview the chronology of Fennoscandian prehistory.

Post-glacial history of Fennoscandia

As a regional term, Scandinavia has two distinct meanings. It may be used as a cultural-linguistic concept meaning the kingdoms of Sweden, Norway, and Denmark. Geographically the Scandinavian Peninsula is made up of two countries, Sweden and Norway. To the south, the Scandinavian Peninsula is separated by a sound from Jutland and the Danish islands, which are the territory of Denmark. Finland is connected to the Scandinavian Peninsula in the North. Scandes is the mountain range that runs through Norway and Sweden.

The prehistories of the southern and central parts of Scandinavian have common features due to close cultural connections to Central Europe.

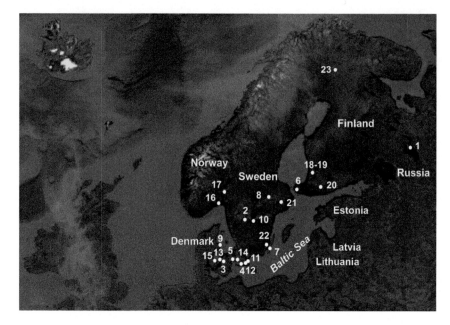

Figure 12.1 Map of the sites mentioned in the chapter: 1. Lake Onega, 2. Almeö, 3. Åmose, 4. Skateholm, 5. Vedbæk, 6. Jettböle, 7. Eketorp, 8. Äs, 9. Kainsbakke, 10. Alvastra, 11. Östra Vemmerlöv, 12. Röekillorna, 13. Næsholm, 14. Uppåkra, 15. Ladby, 16. Gokstad, 17. Oseberg, 18. Luistari, 19. Köyliönjärvi, 20. Rikalanmäki, 21. Spånga, 22. Vibyhögen, 23. Sodankylä

Map created by K.Mannermaa and S. Viranta-Kovanen.

Northern parts of Norway and Sweden as well as the whole area of Finland have a more northern climate and stronger cultural links to the East and Southeast. Lapland is the northernmost part of this region and is situated above the Arctic Circle. It remains a geographically and culturally distinct region, known as Sápmi, and is inhabited by the Sámi, an indigenous Finno-Ugric group. Sápmi comprises the areas of Norway, Sweden, Finland, and Russia (the Kola Peninsula).

During the Weichselian glaciation (c. 115 000–11 500 years ago), continental ice prevented human occupation in Fennoscandia. Southern Scandinavia started to become free from ice c. 14 000 years ago. Animals and plants immigrated northward as soon as routes were established. The first humans entering southern Scandinavia were Paleolithic hunter-gatherers, with wild mountain reindeer (*Rangifer tarandus tarandus*) being their main prey (Larsson 1996; Aaris-Sørensen 2009). Around 12 000 years ago people spread northward along the edge of the retreating ice sheet in areas of Denmark, Sweden, and the Norwegian west coast. These people had origins in Paleolithic Western Europe. The earliest traces of humans in northern Scandinavia are found in Slettnes, Northern Norway (at 9000 cal BC) (Hesjedal et al. 1996).

The first occupants of Finland arrived from the South and East, from the Kunda culture in the Baltic area, the Veretye culture from the eastern part of Lake Onega, and the Butovo culture from the Volga and Oka regions in Russia (Takala 2004; Jussila et al. 2012; Pesonen et al. 2014; Rankama & Kankaanpää 2014). With the warming climate, the open post-glacial landscape soon became forested, resulting in a faunal change. In southern areas the mountain reindeer were replaced by large ungulates such as Eurasian elk (*Alces alces*), red deer (*Cervus elaphus*), and aurochs (*Bos primigenus*). In more northern parts the Eurasian elk (*Alces alces*) and European beaver (*Castor fiber*) were the main hunted species (Ukkonen 1993; Pesonen et al. 2014; Ukkonen & Mannermaa 2017). However, for the early people in Lapland, the wild mountain reindeer was the most important game animal (Halinen 2005; Rankama & Kankaanpää 2008, 2014) although the people were nomadic foragers, spending the summer along the coast hunting seals and fishing, and hunting land mammals inland during winter. Some permanent occupations may have existed along the coastline (Grøndahl et al. 2010; Price 2015).

The Fennoscandian archeological record of dogs

Stone Age hunter-gatherers

Table 12.1 provides a general chronological outline for the prehistory of Fennoscandia. Lapland has many distinct features in prehistory resulting from its unique climate and cultural history. Here the hunter-gatherer lifestyle was never replaced by agriculture: instead, the most significant change in subsistence occurred when people started to herd mountain reindeer (*Rangifer tarandus tarandus*), perhaps beginning c. 3000 years ago (Hansen & Olsen 2004; Røed et al. 2008). Large-scale herding of semi-domesticated reindeer probably emerged only in the Middle Ages (Aikio 1989; Nieminen & Pietilä 1999).

In some parts of Fennoscandia dog remains have been identified in human burials as well as in individual graves (Larsson 1988: 147–153, 1989, 1990), but these are never abundant (Albrethsen & Brinch Petersen 1976; Aaris-Sørensen 1977). The oldest known dog find in Fennoscandia is from Almeö, western Sweden. Remains of five dogs have been found at this site, each buried in a human cemetery located nearby a settlement site. Four of the dogs were buried with humans and covered with red ochre, whereas one was found in a separate grave. The dog in a separate grave is 10 000 years old (Nordqvist 1999).

Several separate dog graves are known from the younger Mesolithic cemeteries of Denmark (Vedbæk Gøngehusvej; Jensen 2001: 226–227; Brinch Petersen 2015: 82) and Sweden (Larsson 1988, 1989). The two cemeteries

Table 12.1 Simplified chronology of prehistory in Scandinavia and Finland. Note that in Finland the start of the Neolithic is marked by pottery use, not by the adoption of agriculture.

Period	Scandinavia	Finland
Late Iron Age and Viking Age	AD 750–1200	500 cal BC–AD 1150 (1300)
Early Iron Age	c. 500 cal BC–AD 750	
Bronze Age	c. 1700–500 cal BC	1700–500 cal BC
Neolithic Stone Age	c. 4000–1500 cal BC	5200–1700 cal BC
Mesolithic Stone Age	c. 9000–4000 cal BC	9000–5200 cal BC

at Skateholm, southern Sweden have several activity phases during c. 7000–5500 years ago. The Skateholm burials probably indicate dog ownership, as entire dogs were buried with the same care as human beings. The dogs were positioned in the graves as if they were sleeping, and were covered with red ochre and grave goods. Some dogs bear signs of a violent death (Larsson 1988).

Ritual interment of dogs in settlement sites seems to have been relatively common in Mesolithic burial customs among hunter-gatherers (Larsson 1990; Storå 2000; Olson & Walther 2007). An indication of domestic dogs in a ritual context in Stone Age Finland comes from the Scandinavian Pitted Ware culture site Jettböle in Åland (Middle Neolithic). Here dog remains were found in two different contexts: scattered among other refuse faunal remains at the site, and in a special area where bones of two dogs were discovered in ritual pits together with remains of at least seven human individuals (Götherström et al. 2002). The distinct ritual character of the pits is indicated by the presence of cut marks, implying meat removal from both human and dog bones (Núñez 1995).

Not all dogs were buried or otherwise ritually treated. Dog teeth, like those of seals and other species, were sometimes drilled for use as pendants. They were also used on headgear, shirts, aprons, and other kinds of clothing that were employed to cover and decorate the deceased. In some Pitted Ware settlement sites and cemeteries on the eastern Swedish coast and islands of Öland and Gotland, isolated dog remains are present in cultural layers and human graves (Janzon 1974; Burenhult 2002, Rainio & Mannermaa 2014). The meanings and uses of these items are unclear.

In Denmark, dogs are represented in almost all osteological collections from settlement sites (Jensen 2001: 199), and some Finnish faunal samples have also yielded dogs (Mannermaa et al. 2014). The presence of dog bones in the same contexts as bones of wild game species indicates that they were probably eaten (Møhl 1979; Aaris-Sørensen 1990; Richter & Noe-Nygaard 2003). At Pitted Ware site Äs, in eastern Sweden, crania and long bones from two dogs were found in an occupation layer. According to Lepiksaar (1974: 146), these were small-sized dogs, probably mainly used as household guards and in small-game hunting. The extremities of the dogs were totally absent, indicating that their furs may have been used and the rest of the bodies deposited near the settlement.

Stone Age farming societies

Studies on carbon and nitrogen stable isotopes (Fischer et al. 2007; Noe-Nygaard 1988) showed that the diets of the Danish dogs were similar to the diets of humans through the transition from a marine and game-based diet to the advent of agriculture. Agriculture spread to Denmark, and southern parts of Norway and Sweden c. 4000 cal BC. These practices were brought to the area by new people arriving from continental Europe (Malmström et al. 2008; Malmström et al. 2009). They probably brought dogs with them (Skoglund et al. 2012). In many areas the local hunter-gatherers also adopted this subsistence economy (Hjelle et al. 2006).

In the northern parts of Fennoscandia, agriculture was adopted much later. Although the first evidence of crops in Finland is from the Early Neolithic at c. 5300 cal BC (Alenius et al. 2013), subsistence practices continued to be based on foraging until at least the final Stone Age (Lahtinen & Rowley-Conwy 2013). So far, in Finland the earliest evidence of animal husbandry dates to the third millennium BC, or the Corded Ware culture period (Cramp et al. 2014; Bläuer & Kantanen 2013).

In some Stone Age farming societies dogs were disposed of with remains of other domestic animals in kitchen middens, as in Kainsbakke, northern Denmark (c. 2200 cal BC) (Richter 1991). However, in some large osteological collections from this general period (e.g., Alvastra in middle Sweden), dog remains are completely absent in such middens (During 1986).

Bronze Age societies

In the Bronze Age dogs continued to be buried and be part of sacrifices, and dog remains continue to be found, although rarely, in settlement sites as part of household waste, probably indicating consumption of dogs (Gräslund 2004: 167; Mannermaa et al. 2014).

In Swedish Bronze Age human cremation graves, dog bones from most parts of the body are found, in contrast with those from livestock, which include only elements from fleshy edible parts of the body (Mattisson 1994; Jennbert 2011). One such a site is Östra Vemmerlöv in southern Sweden, a large cult site in a swamp with large amounts of animal and human remains. Remains from a total of four humans, twenty dogs, and four foxes (*Vulpes vulpes*) were deposited in the swamp (Jennbert 2011: 114). The rest of the animal species present were ungulates, represented only by loose skeletal parts.

In Finland there is very little evidence of dogs in the Bronze Age, but this is mainly due to general poor preservation of osteological materials from this period (Ukkonen 1993; Mannermaa et al. 2014).

Early Iron Age societies

Dogs are sometimes present at Iron Age farms and other settlement sites in Fennoscandia, but they are far more commonly found in graves and other cult sites. Dog burials, either separate or accompanying humans, are known from practically all phases of the Iron Age in cremations and inhumation burials (Wessman 2010; Jennbert 2011: 108; Mannermaa et al. 2014; Gräslund 2004).

Dogs have also been found in special cult deposits or sacrificial places from the Iron Age. Cult deposits with complete dog skeletons or loose dog bones (together with other species) are known, in both Sweden (Röekillorna in Skåne, dating from the Neolithic to Early Iron Age) and Denmark (wetland site Valmose in Jutland, from the fourth and fifth centuries AD) (Jennbert 2011; Gräslund 2004: 167).

An interesting site with dog finds in Finland is Majankangas in central Finland, where cremated bones of at least one human, one dog, one pine marten (*Martes martes*), and several fish were found in an area of 3 m^2 (Ukkonen 2003). All body parts of the dog except the claws are present, indicating that a complete dog was cremated. The pine marten is represented by cranial bones, a mandible, and some front limb bones and claws, and it is possible that they derive from a hide (Vanhatalo 2005). The find probably represents a single cremation burial from the Iron Age, dating to c. AD 200–550/600 (Mannermaa et al. 2014).

Dog remains are found also in Iron Age occupation sites. For example, at the fortified settlement known as Eketorp on the island of Öland (Sweden), remains of at least 98 individual dogs were found in layers dating to c. AD 400–700 and 1000–1300 (Boessneck & von den Driesch 1979). In the Medieval fortress of Næsholm in western Denmark, intact dogs and horses were buried in the rampart of the building (Jennbert 2011: 108).

Late Iron Age and Viking Age societies

Dogs are present in many Late Iron Age sites in Fennoscandia, but most of these finds derive from grave sites. In Finland, half of the sites with dog remains are burials (Mannermaa et al. 2014; Ukkonen & Mannermaa 2017). The most remarkable dog finds of the Late Iron Age are those from Viking sites. In Nordic mythology, the dog is a border medium between the living and the dead (Gräslund 2004: 172–173). Odin, the renowned god, on his way to Hel meets a bloody dog, a guardian. When Vikings sacrificed animals, dogs may have been allowed to consume the carcasses. In this way dogs may have been responsible for the transformation of the animals to the divine (Gräslund 2004). The abundance of dogs in Viking burials also supports the idea of their importance as guides for the deceased.

The number of dog burials increase during Viking Age; most dog burials in the Iron Age date to c. AD 600–1050 (Gräslund 2004). Many Iron Age and

Viking Age occupation sites have also yielded dog bones, such as the regional center of Uppåkra in southern Sweden, which was occupied during the first millennium AD (Nilsson 2001, 2003).

Viking Age ship burials, mainly made for the chiefs, in Norway and Denmark often have one or several complete dogs. Gräslund (2004) lists several high-status graves with dogs. For example, in Ladby (tenth century, island of Fyn in Denmark) the dead chief was accompanied by four dogs, put together on one lead, and each collar gathered together in a bronze ring (Gräslund 2004: 168). In the fabulous Gokstad Viking ship grave in Norway (AD 900), a chief was given at least eight complete dogs, twelve horses, and a peacock (*Pavo cristatus*). The animals were found outside the ship (Sjøvold 1964: 54). In another fabulous ship burial in Oseberg, Norway (AD 834), six dogs, fifteen horses, and two cows were interred together with two women. Among other finds were also the remains of four decorated wooden sleds (Sjøvold 1964: 33–37).

The very special Viking Age burial-ground Luistari in Eura (Finland) contained remains of at least thirteen dogs (Fig. 2) that were buried together with the deceased, who were mainly men (Lehtosalo-Hilander 1982). Dogs were placed in most cases inside the chambers or other constructions near the feet of the deceased (Fortelius 1982). In Finland, dog bones are also regularly found in cremation cemeteries that were created on flat ground during the Merovingian period, c. AD 550/600–800. For example, the dog bones at

Figure 12.2 Dog mandible from the grave at Luistari in Eura, Finland. Most bones in Luistari are poorly preserved and only some skeletal parts have been found

Photograph by Kristiina Mannermaa.

Rikalanmäki in Salo probably represent a complete skeleton or at least most parts of one individual (Mäntylä-Asplund & Storå 2010: 62).

In the Iron Age (500 cal BC–AD 1050) cremation cemeteries in Spånga near Stockholm (Sweden), 43% of cremations included dog remains. In most cases only one individual was found, but sometimes two or three were present (Sigvallius 1994: 67). Gräslund (2004) gives several examples of inhumation burials of women and men buried together with various animal species, including the dog. Dogs are present in graves of high-status people as well as ordinary people. Occurrence of dog bones increases significantly from the Early Iron Age to the Late Iron Age (Sigvallius 1994: 67). However, this trend might be partly due to lack of osteological research for this period rather than an actual historical patterning (Gräslund 2004: 169).

It is possible that in Iron Age burials some of the dog bones represent hides used for wrapping or covering the body. However, in a study of Finnish Iron Age (AD 800–1300) fur and hide materials, no hair was identified as dog (Kirkinen 2015). In the cremation burial mound at Vibyhögen (AD 950) in eastern Sweden, a middle-aged man was probably wrapped in skins of bear (*Ursus arctos*) and lynx (*Lynx lynx*). The grave also had a large number of cremated animals (nineteen species). Among these were remains of seven dogs and six horses, all of which were cremated whole (Sten & Vretemark 1988).

In Lapland, dogs are not among the typical sacrificial animals at Sámi offering sites (*Sieidi*) (Mulk 2009; Äikäs et al. 2009), and they have not been commonly found in prehistoric or historical Sámi graves (e.g., Schanche 2000). One of the rare Sámi sites with dog remains is the summer village Juikenttä in Sodankylä, Finland (AD 1050–1650) (Carpelan 1992).

Evidence of dog types in prehistory and their roles

The fact that dogs have received special treatments at death often indicates a special relationship between the humans and dogs (Losey et al. 2011). Different dogs certainly had different status. Larsson (1990) has suggested that some dogs achieved the status of human beings and were recognized as persons. Fahlander (2012) found indications for a similar kind of status for dogs and children in a Late Mesolithic society in Sweden.

In human graves other animals are represented by edible parts, while dogs (as well as horses) are represented by skulls and mandibles only, or complete bodies (Gräslund 2004). Sten and Vretemark (1988) suggest that dogs, along with horses, represented in Early Iron Age cemeteries had practical functions. Complete dogs in graves could have had roles of companions, transporters, and guardians, but most likely also more complicated ritual associations were involved in such practices. Large dogs in Late Iron Age burials may represent communication and maintaining a social identity and status (Jennbert 2011).

Gräslund (2004) concludes that the dogs in first-millennium AD graves were ascribed with symbolic-mythological meaning surrounding the transformation from life to death.

However, dogs were not kept only for companion and ritual purposes. Dog keeping surely had many practical functions and dogs were utilized in many ways to support livelihood. Many possible roles have been suggested for prehistoric dogs (Manwell & Baker 1984). Occasionally dogs served as food sources but more often they probably participated in hunting and worked as guardians as well as beasts of burden. After the agricultural revolution, dogs became both herders and guardians of livestock. Historically, the Sámi have had special reindeer-herding dogs (e.g., Itkonen 1948:173; Anderson, this volume).

Hunting with dogs is still popular in Northern Europe, and the general assumption is that dogs were hunting companions for prehistoric people (Sablin & Khlopachev 2002). Although hunting dogs come in many sizes and shapes, something can be said based on body size. For example, the early dogs of Fennoscandia were quite variable in size (Aaris-Sørensen 1990). In the Mesolithic, very small and gracile dogs were present, as well as larger dogs, the latter with estimated shoulder heights of 55–60 cm (Richter & Noe-Nygaard, 2003; Forstén 1972). These dogs were probably used to hunt small and large game, respectively. In Finland, dog bones are common on sites that also have seal or squirrel bones, indicating that sealers and small-game hunters were likely to possess dogs (Mannermaa et al. 2014). The rock pictures in Stone Age Norway show dogs as powerful and bold hunting companions, probably capable of protecting their human companion from the attacks of large prey animals. Dogs are depicted in various hunting situations, including confronting a bear (Helskog 2012). There are also two ambiguous dogs in probable hunting scenes of large game in Finnish rock art (e.g., Lahelma 2008; Luho 1970).

Very large dogs (shoulder height > 65 cm) appear in the record in the Neolithic period of southern Fennoscandia, while in the North they are absent until the Iron Age. Most dogs in the North during the Neolithic are small or medium-sized dogs (e.g., Fortelius 1982). Although the material from the Neolithic consists of burnt and fragmentary bone only, it is possible that very large dogs were mostly associated with agriculture and were truly absent in the North where such practices were not occurring.

Beginning in the Iron Age more specialized forms occur. For example, very gracile greyhound-type dogs appear in the southern Fennoscandian record during this period (Jennbert 2011: 169; Öhman 1983). However, these were probably not related to the modern greyhounds (Larson et al. 2012), but could have a similar function to today's sighthounds.

Artifacts related to dogs are collars and sleds. The oldest known possible dog sled in the circumpolar area is from an 8000-year-old site on the island of Zhokhov in northeastern Russia (Pitulko & Kasparov 2017). Equally old evidence of sleds from Fennoscandia does not exist. The oldest evidence is currently the remains of a sled type having a runner with a longitudinal groove dating to the Neolithic Comb Ware period (Itkonen 1935; Luho 1950: 22–23; Mannermaa et al. 2014: 27). This type of sled runner might be used in dog sleds (Itkonen 1948: 410). Occasional findings of prehistoric dog harnesses or sleds for dogs are typically from more recent periods (Mannermaa et al. 2014). Transportation is considered as one of the uses of the early dogs (Fiedel 2005), and this was probably true in Fennoscandia as well.

Modern breeds

Genetic studies show that most modern breeds have very recent origins (Parker et al. 2004). However, in many breeds there may be input or introgression from far older endemic populations. Many dogs in the archeological record resemble modern breeds in shape (Larson et al. 2012). In Scandinavia the first period of admixture probably occurred when agricultural people arrived with their dogs. Ever since, dogs were probably imported from the other parts of Europe and interbred with the indigenous dogs. The Scandinavian dogs have also mixed with local wolves (Klütsch et al. 2011).

Today there are at least fourteen dog breeds originating from Fennoscandia. All three northern countries have their elk hunting dogs (the Norwegian Elkhound, the Jämthund, and the Karelian Bear Dog). The Karelian Bear Dog is a close relative to the Russian Laika. Because of its braveness, it is also used for bear control in many countries. Probably with recent origins (the Vikings may have had similar dogs) are the two tracking types: the Old Danish Bird Dog and the Finnish Hound.

There are also herding dogs (the Norwegian Buhund, Swedish Vallhund), which may have origins (with later admixture) in Viking times. The Sámi have their own reindeer-herding dogs (the Lapp Reindeer Dog (Lapponian Herder), Swedish Lapphund, and Finnish Lapphund). These dogs have been valuable for the reindeer-based economy well into the modern era. Interestingly, the Lappish breeds share a rare haplotype (apparently received from the local wolves) with the Scandinavian herding and hunting dogs. Klütsch et al. (2011) hypothesized that this may indicate dog trade between the Sámi and the south Fennoscandian farmers. On the other hand, in the very southern parts of Sweden the haplotypes of the Neolithic dogs suggest their pure continental European origin (Malmström et al. 2008).

In recent genetic studies (based on the SNP mutations), only the Finnish Spitz has appeared as a truly ancient breed in Fennoscandia (Parker et al. 2004; Larson et al. 2012). The Finnish Spitz is a medium-sized spitz with a red coat. It is known for its intelligence and unique skills in hunting fowl. The

Figure 12.3 The Finnish Spitz. The origins of the Finnish Spitz may extend to the Stone Age. The brave Finnish dog with a red coat is documented in Medieval texts
Photograph by Outi Heikkilä-Toni.

spitz will follow the birds until they settle in a tree, and then attract the bird's attention by wagging his tail, and also barking softly. This way the bird is mesmerized and will not notice the approaching hunter.

The Finnish Spitz-type dogs have been valued as squirrel dogs during the historic period. Linguistics data also emphasize the importance of dogs from Finnish prehistory to today. In the Proto-Finnic language the first word meaning dog was "peni". Peni is still a popular name given to dogs in Finland. It is the oldest known word in Finnish meaning a domestic animal and its roots go back to 6000–4000 years ago (Häkkinen 2013; Pietiläinen 2014: 41–58). The Finnish Spitz type of dog may have been an integral part of the hunting-gathering culture that resisted agriculture until the Middle Ages. (Fig. 3)

Another unique breed is the Norwegian Lundehund. The Lundehund is adapted to hunt puffins on the steep mountainsides of Norway. It is a small spitz with flexible joints and six toes on each paw (polydactyly). It probably is an ancient form kept by coastal people, but the modern breed has a very low genetic variability due to a population crash. All the modern Lundehunds derive from a small population from one village (Melis et al. 2013). A similar

Table 12.2 Some important archeological dog finds in Fennoscandia.

Site	Country	Burial type	Period
Almeö in Hornborgasjön	Sweden	Burial site	Mesolithic
Skateholm	Sweden	Burial site	Mesolithic
Vedbæk	Denmark	Burial site	Mesolithic
Åmose in W-Zealand	Denmark		Mesolithic/Neolithic
Jettböle in Åland	Finland	Settlement/ritual site	Neolithic
Ajvide in Gotland	Sweden	Settlement/ritual site	Neolithic
Äs in Romfartuna	Sweden	Settlement	Neolithic
Alvastra in Östergötland	Sweden		Neolithic
Kainsbakke in Djursland	Denmark		
Vibyhögen in Uppland	Sweden	Burial site	Late Iron Age
Spånga in Stockholm	Sweden	Burial site	Iron Age
Næsholm in Sjælland	Denmark	Fortress	Medieval
Rikalanmäki in Salo	Finland	Burial site	Iron Age/Merovingian period
Röekillorna in Skåne	Sweden	Cult Site	
Ladby in Fyn	Denmark	Burial site	Iron Age
Uppåkra	Sweden	Center	Iron Age
Köyliönjärvi	Finland	Burial site	Viking Age
Oseberg in Slagen	Norway	Ship burial	Viking Age
Gokstad in Slagen	Norway	Ship burial	Viking Age
Luistari in Eura	Finland	Burial site	Viking Age–Early Medieval times
Eketorp in Öland	Sweden	Fortress	Late Iron Age–Early Medieval
Juikenttä in Sodankylä	Finland	Settlement of the forest Sámi	Lapland Iron Age

fate was met by the Finnish seal dogs, which went completely extinct during the Second World War. The breed is now recreated from dogs that resemble the extinct breed.

Conclusions

In this review, we have presented the main aspects of the prehistory of dog in Fennoscandia. We conclude that the archeological data provide evidence for a variety of roles for dogs living with prehistoric people, both practical and symbolic. The bond between humans and their canine companions has been strong, and it still remains as such. Dogs persist as an inseparable part of modern Nordic culture. Although many non-domestic dog breeds are now common, domestic Fennoscandian breeds remain popular and are used in their original roles as hunters and herders. Archeological evidence leaves open the question of the origin of the dog breeds. We do not know how endemic the breeds are and whether they represent the local prehistoric dogs at all. We predict (as already indicated for the Finnish Spitz), that Fennoscandian breeds have maintained genes and adaptations from the local Stone Age dogs that coevolved with the Fennoscandian prehistoric people. Molecular studies on the archeological material are needed to address this question.

Bibliography

Aaris-Sørensen, K. 1977. "Vedbæk-jægeren og hans Hunde." *Søllerødbogen*. Pp. 170–176. Herning: Historisk-Topografisk Selskab for Søllerød Kommune.

Aaris-Sørensen, K. 1990. *Danmarks forhistoriske Dyreverden*. Copenhagen: Gyldendal.

Aaris-Sørensen, K. 2009. "Diversity and Dynamics of the Mammalian Fauna in Denmark Throughout the Last Glacial-Interglacial Cycle, 115-0 Kyr BP." *Fossils and Strata*, 57: 1–58.

Äikäs, T., A.-K. Puputti, M. Núñez, J. Aspi and J. Okkonen. 2009. "Sacred and Profane Livelihood: Animal Bones from Sieidi Sites in Northern Finland." *Norwegian Archaeological Review*, 42(2): 109–122.

Aikio, P. 1989. "Role of Reindeer in the life of the Sámi." In *The Walking larder. Patterns of Domestication, Pastoralism, and Predation*. Edited by J. Clutton-Brock, 169–183. One World Archaeology 2.

Albrethsen, S. E. and E. Brinch Petersen. 1976. "Excavation of a Mesolithic Cemetery at Vedbæk, Denmark." *Acta Archaeologica*, 47: 1–28.

Alenius, T., T. Mökkönen and A. Lahelma. 2013. "Early Farming in the Northern Boreal Zone: Reassessing the History of Land Use in Southeastern Finland through High-Resolution Pollen Analysis." *Geoarchaeology*, 28 (1): 1–24.

Bläuer, A. and J. Kantanen. 2013. "Transition From Hunting to Animal Husbandry in Southern, Western and Eastern Finland: New Dated Osteological Evidence." *Journal of Archaeological Science*, 40: 1646–1666.

Boessneck, J. and A. von den Driesch. 1979. *Eketorp. Befestigung und Siedlung auf Öland/Schweden: Die Fauna*. Stockholm: Almqvist & Wiksell International.

Brinch Petersen, E. 2015. *Diversity of Mesolithic Vedbæk*. Acta Archaeologica, 86 (1). Oxford: Wiley.

Burenhult, G. 2002. "The Grave-Field at Ajvide." In *Remote Sensing: Applied Techniques for the Study of Cultural Resources and the Localization, Identification and Documentation of Sub-surface Prehistoric Remains in Swedish Archaeology 2*. Edited by G. Burenhult, 31–168. Hässleholm: Stockholm University.

Carpelan, C. 1992. "Juikenttä – Näkökulma Saamelaiseen Yhteiskuntaan (Summary: Juikenttä – A Window on the Society of the *Saami*)." *Studia Historica Septentrionalia*, 21: 34–44.

Cramp, L., R. Evershed, M. Lavento, P. Halinen, K. Mannermaa, M. Oinonen, J. Kettunen, M. Perola, P. Onkamo and V. Heyd. 2014. "Neolithic Dairy Farming at the Extreme of Agriculture in Northern Europe." *Proceedings of the Royal Society B: Biological Sciences*, 281: 20140819.

During, E. 1986. *The Fauna of Alvastra. An Osteological Analysis of Animal Bones From a Neolithic Pile Dwelling. Ossa 12, Supplement 1.* Stockholm Studies in Archaeology 6. Stockholm.

Fahlander F. 2012. "Mesolithic Childhoods: Changing life-courses of young hunter-fishers in the stone age of southern Scandinavia." *Childhood in the Past*, 5: 20–34.

Fiedel, S.J. 2005. "Man's Best Friend–Mammoth's Worst Enemy? A Speculative Essay on the Role of Dogs in Paleoindian Colonization and Megafaunal Extinction." *World Archaeology*, 37(1): 11–25.

Fischer, A., J. Olsen, M. Richards, J. Heinemeier, Á.E. Sveinbjörnsdóttir and P. Bennike. 2007. "Coast–Inland Mobility and Diet in the Danish Mesolithic and Neolithic: Evidence From Stable Isotope Values of Humans and Dogs." *Journal of Archaeological Science*, 34(12), 2125–2150.

Forstén, A. 1972. "The refuse fauna of the Mesolithic Suomusjärvi Period in Finland." *Finskt Museum*, 79: 74–84.

Fortelius, M. 1982. "Dogs in Eura." In *Luistari I: The Graves*. Suomen muinaismuistoyhdistyksen aikakauskirja 82(1). Edited by P.-L. Lehtosalo-Hilander, 310–312, Appendix II. Helsinki: Suomen Muinaismuistoyhdistys.

Gräslund, A-S. 2004. "Dogs in Graves – A Question of Symbolism?" In *PECUS. Man and animal in Antiquity. Proceedings of the Conference at the Swedish Institute in Rome, September 9.12, 2002*. Edited by B. Santillo Frizell, 167–176. Rome: The Swedish Institute in Rome.

Grøndahl, F.M., A.K. Hufthammer, S.O. Dahl and J. Rosvold. 2010. "A Preboreal Elk (*Alces alces* L. 1758) Antler From South-Eastern Norway." *Fauna Norvegica*, 30: 9–12.

Götherström, A., N. Stenbäck and J. Storå. 2002. "Jettböle Middle Neolithic Site of the Åland Islands –Human Remains, Ancient DNA and Pottery." *European Journal of Archaeology*, 5: 42–104.

Halinen, P. 2005. *Prehistoric Hunters of Northernmost Lapland. Settlement Patterns and Subsistence Strategies*. Iskos 14. Finnish Antiquarian Society.

Hansen, L.I. and B. Olsen. 2004. *Samenes Historie Fram til 1750*. Oslo: Cappelen.

Helskog, K. 2012. "Bears and Meanings among Hunter-fisher-gatherers in Northern Fennoscandia 9000–2500 BC." *Cambridge Archaeological Journal*, 2282: 209–236.

Hesjedal, A.C., C. Damm, B. Olsen, and I. Storli. 1996. *Arkeologi i Slettnes: dokumentasjon av 11.000 års bosetning*. Tromsø: Universitetet i Tromsø.

Hjelle, K.L., A.K. Hufthammer and K.A. Bergsvik. 2006. "Hesitant Hunters: A Review of the Introduction of Agriculture in Western Norway." *Environmental Archaeology*, 11 (2): 147–170.

Häkkinen, K. 2013. *Nykysuomen Etymologinen Sanakirja*. Helsinki: Sanoma Pro.

Itkonen, T.I. 1935. "Muinaissuksia ja -jalaksia III." *Suomen Museo*, 41: 1–21.

Itkonen, T.I. 1948. *Suomen Lappalaiset Vuoteen 1945*. Helsinki: Toinen osa. WSOY.

Janzon, G.O. 1974. *Gotlands Mellanneolitiska Gravar*. Studies in North-European Archaeology 6. Stockholm: Acta Universitatis Stockholmiensis.

Jennbert, K. 2011. *Animals and Humans. Recurrent Symbiosis in Archaeology and Old Norse Religion- Vägar till Midgård 14*. Lund: Nordic Academic Press.

Jensen, J. 2001. *Danmarks Oldtid. Stenalder 13.000–2.000 f.Kr.* Copenhagen: Gyldendal.

Jussila, T., A. Kriiska and T. Rostedt. 2012. "Saarenoja 2 – An Early Mesolithic Site in South-Eastern Finland: Preliminary Results and Interpretations of Studies Conducted in 2000 and 2008–10." *Fennoscandia Archaeologica*, XXIX: 3–27.

Kirkinen, T. 2015. "The Role of Wild Animals in Death Rituals: Furs and Animal Skins in the Late Iron Age Inhumation Burials in Southeastern Fennoscandia." *Fennoscandia Archaeologia*, XXXII: 101–120.

Klütsch, C.F.C., E.H. Seppälä, T. Fall, M. Uhlén, Å. Hedhammar, H. Lohi and P. Savolainen. 2011. "Regional Occurrence, High Frequency but Low Diversity of Mitochondrial DNA Haplogroup D1 Suggests a Recent Dog–Wolf Hybridization in Scandinavia." *Animal Genetics*, 42(1): 100–103.

Lahelma, A. 2008. *A Touch of Red. Archaeological and Ethnographic Approaches to Interpreting Finnish Rock Paintings*. Iskos 15. Finnish Antiquarian Society.

Lahtinen, M. and Rowley-Conwy, P. 2013. "Early Farming in Finland: Was There Cultivation Before the Iron Age (500 BC)?" *European Journal of Archaeology*, 16: 660–684.

Larson, G., Karlsson, E.K., Perri, A., Webster, M.T., Ho, S.Y., Peters, J., ... and Comstock, K.E. 2012. "Rethinking dog domestication by integrating genetics, archeology, and biogeography." *Proceedings of the National Academy of Sciences*, 109(23): 8878–8883.

Larsson, L. 1988. *Ett Fångstsamhälle för 7000 År Sedan: Boplatser och Graver I Skateholm*. Lund: Signum.

Larsson, L. 1989. "Big Dog and Poor Man: Mortuary Practices in Mesolithic Societies in Southern Sweden." In *Approaches to Swedish Prehistory. A spectrum of problems and perspectives in contemporary research*. BAR International Series S50. Edited by T.B. Larsson and H. Lundmark, 211–223. Oxford: Archaeopress.

Larsson, L. 1990. "Dogs in Fraction – Symbols in Action." In: *Contribution to Mesolithic in Europe. Papers presented at the Fourth International Symposium "The Mesolithic in Europe", Leuven 1990*. Studia Praehistorica Belgica 5. Edited by P.M. Vermeerch and R.P. Van Peer, 153–160.

Larsson, L. 1996. *The earliest settlement of Scandinavia and its relationship with neighbouring areas*. Acta Archaeologica Lundensia, Series in 8 Vols, 24. Stockholm.

Lehtosalo-Hilander, P.-L., 1982. *Luistari III: A Burial Ground Reflecting the Finnish Viking Age Society*. Suomen Muinaismuistoyhdistyksen Aikakauskirja 82(3). Helsinki: Suomen Muinaismuistoyhdistys.

Lepiksaar, J. 1974. "Djurrester Från den Mellanneolitiska (Gropkeramiska) Boplatsen vid Äs, Romfartuna sn, Västmanland." In *Yngre stenålderns kustboplatser*. Edited by L. Löfstrand, 141–156. Uppsala: Aun 1.

Losey, R. J., V.I. Bazaliiskii, S. Garvie-Lok, M. Germonpré, J.A. Leonard, A.L. Allen and M.V. Sablin. 2011. "Canids as Persons: Early Neolithic Dog and Wolf Burials, Cis-Baikal, Siberia." *Journal of Anthropological Archaeology*, 30 (2): 174–189.

Luho, V. 1950. "Kivikautisista Talviliikennevälineistä." *Suomen Museo*, 56: 1–25.

Luho, V. 1970. "Om det förhistoriska hällmålningarna i Finland. " *Finskt Museum 1970*: 5–11.

Malmström, H., C. Vilà, M.T.P. Gilbert, J. Storå, E. Willerslev, G. Holmlund and A. Götherström. 2008. "Barking Up the Wrong Tree: Modern Northern European Dogs Fail to Explain Their Origin." *BMC Evolutionary Biology*, 8(1): 71.

Malmström, H., M.T.P. Gilbert, M.G. Thomas, M. Brandström, J. Storå, P. Molnar, P. and E. Willerslev. 2009. "Ancient DNA Reveals Lack of Continuity Between Neolithic Hunter-Gatherers and Contemporary Scandinavians." *Current Biology*, 19(20): 1758–1762.

Mannermaa, K., P. Ukkonen and S. Viranta. 2014. "Prehistory and Early History of Dogs in Finland." *Fennoscandia Archaeologica*, XXXI: 25–44.

Manwell, C. and C.M. Baker. 1984. "Domestication of the Dog: Hunter, Food, Bed-Warmer, or Emotional Object?" *Zeitschrift für Tierzüchtung und Züchtungsbiologie*, 101(1–5): 241–256.

Mattisson, A. 1994. *Djurben i Gravar Från Yngre Bronsålder*. Fourth term paper, institutionen för arkeologi. Uppsala: Uppsala universitet.

Melis, C., Å.A. Borg, I.S. Espelien and H. Jensen. 2013. "Low Neutral Genetic Variability in a Specialist Puffin Hunter: the Norwegian Lundehund." *Animal Genetics*, 44(3): 348–351.

Mulk, I.-M. 2009. "From Metal to Meat: Continuity and Change in Ritual Practices at a Saami Sacrificial Site, Viddjavarri, Lapland, Northern Sweden." In *Máttut – Máddagat: The Roots of Saami Ethnicities, Societies and Spaces/Places*. Edited by T. Äikäs, 116–133. Publications of Giellagas Institute 12. Oulu: Giellagas Institute.

Møhl, U. 1979. "Aggersund – Bopladsen Zoologisk Belyst. Svanejagt Som Arsag til Bosættelse?" *Kuml*: 57–76.

Mäntylä-Asplund, S. and J. Storå. 2010. "On the archaeology and osteology of the Rikala cremation cemery in Salo, SW Finland." *Fennoscandia Archaeologica*, XXVII: 53–68.

Nieminen, M. and U.A. Pietilä. 1999. *Peurasta poroksi: Paliskuntain yhdistys*. Jyväskylä: Gummerus Kirjapaino Oy.

Nilsson, L. 2001. "Benmaterialet från Uppåkra 98:2 – preliminära resultat." *Uppåkra. Centrum i analys och rapport*. Edited by L. Larsson.Uppåkrastudier 4. Acta Archaeologica Lundensia, Series in 8 Vols, 36. Lund.

Nilsson, L. 2003. "Animal Husbandry in Iron Age Uppåkra." In *Centrality – Regionality: The Social Structure of Southern Sweden During the Iron Age*. Edited by L. Larsson and B. Hårdh, 89–103. Acta Archaeologica Lundensia 40. Lund.

Noe-Nygaard, N. 1988. "δ13C-Values of Dog Bones Reveal the Nature of Changes in Man's Food Resources at the Mesolithic-Neolithic Transition, Denmark." *Chemical Geology: Isotope Geoscience Section*, 73(1): 87–96.

Nordqvist, B. 1999. "The Chronology of the Western Swedish Mesolithic and Late Paleolithic: Old Answers in Spite of New Methods." *The Mesolithic of Central Scandinavia*. Edited by J. Boaz. Oslo: Universitetets Oldsaksamlinges Skrifter 2.

Núñez, M. 1995. "Cannibalism on Pitted Ware Åland?" *Karhunhammas*, 16: 61–68.

Öhman, I. 1983. "The Merovingian Dogs from the Boat Graves at Vendel." In *Vendel period Studies. Transactions of the Boat-grave symposium in Stockholm, February 2–3. 1981. Stockholm*. Edited by J.-P. Lamm and H.-Å. Nordström, 167–182. Stockholm: Museum of National Antiquities.

Olson, C. and C. Walther. 2007. "Neolithic Cod (Gadus morhua) and Herring (Clupea harengus) Fisheries in the Baltic Sea, in the Light of Fine-Mesh Sieving: A Comparative Study of Subfossil Fishbone From the Late Stone Age Sites at Ajvide, Gotland, Sweden and Jettböle, Åland, Finland." *Environmental Archaeology*, 2 (2):175–185.

Parker, H.G., L.V. Kim, N.B. Sutter, S. Carlson, T.D. Lorentzen, T.B Malek, … and L. Kruglyak. 2004. "Genetic Structure of the Purebred Domestic Dog." *Science*, 304(5674): 1160–1164.

Pesonen, P., E. Hertell, L. Simponen, K. Mannermaa, M. Manninen, T. Rostedt, N. Taipale and M. Tallavaara. 2014. "Postglacial Pioneer Settlement in the Lake Sarvinki Area, Eastern Finland." In *Lateglacial and Postglacial Pioneers in Northern Europe*. BAR International Series S2599. Edited by F. Riede and M. Tallavaara, 176–192. Oxford: Archaeopress.

Pietiläinen, P. 2014. *Koirien Suomi. Kansanperinnettä ja historiaa*. Helsinki: Suomalaisen Kirjallisuuden Seura.

Pitulko, V.V. and A.K. Kasparov. 2017 "Archeological Dogs from the Early Holocene Zhokhov Site in Eastern Siberian Arctic." *Journal of Archeological Science*, 13: 491–515.

Price, D.T. 2015. *Ancient Scandinavia. An Archeological History from the First Humans to the Vikings*. Oxford: Oxford University Press.

Rainio, R. and K. Mannermaa. 2014. "Tracing the Rattle of Animal Tooth Pendants from the Middle Neolithic Graves of Ajvide, Gotland, Sweden." *World Archaeology*, 43(3): 332–348.

Rankama, T. and J. Kankaanpää. 2008. "Eastern Arrivals in Post-Glacial Lapland: the Sujala Site 10 000 BP." *Antiquity*, 82: 884–899.

Rankama, T. and J. Kankaanpää. 2014. "Fast or Slow Pioneers? A View from Northern Lapland." In *Lateglacial and Postglacial Pioneers in Northern Europe*. BAR International Series S2599. Edited by F. Riede and M. Tallavaara, 147–159. Oxford: Archaeopress.

Richter, J. 1991. *Kainsbakke. Aspects of the Palaeoecology of Neolithic Man*. Grenaa: Djurslands Museum & Dansk Fiskerimuseum.

Richter, J. and N. Noe-Nygaard. 2003. "A Late Mesolithic hunting station at Agernæs, Fyn, Denmark." *Acta Archaeologica*, 74: 1–64.

Røed K.H., Ø. Flagstad, M. Nieminen, Ø. Holand, M.J. Dwyer, N. Røv and C. Vilà. 2008. "Genetic analyses reveal independent domestication origins of Eurasian reindeer." *Proceedings of the Royal Society B: Biological Sciences*, 275 (1645): 1849–1855.

Sablin, M., and G. Khlopachev. 2002. The Earliest Ice Age Dogs: Evidence from Eliseevichi 11." *Current Anthropology*, 43(5): 795–799.

Schanche A. 2000. *Graver i Ur og Berg. Samisk Gravskikk og Religion fra Forhistorisk til Nyere Tid*. Karasjok: DavviGirji OS. Schefferus J. 1674/1963.

Sigvallius, B. 1994. *Funeral Pyres: Iron Age Cremations in North Spånga*. Theses and Papers in Osteology 1. Stockholm: Stockholm University.

Sjøvold, T. 1964. *Osebergfunnet*. Oslo: Universitetets Oldsaksamling.

Skoglund, P., H. Malmström, M. Raghavan, J. Storå, P. Hall, E. Willerslev, M.T.P. Gilbert, A. Götherström and M. Jakobsson. 2012. "Origins and Genetic Legacy of Neolithic Farmers and Hunter-Gatherers in Europe." *Science*, 336 (6080): 466–469.

Sten, S. and M. Vretemark. 1988. "Storgravsprojektet Osteologiska Analyser av Yngre Järnålderns Benrika Brandgravar." *Fornvännen*, 83(3): 145–156.

Storå, J. 2000. "Sealing and Animal Husbandry in the Ålandic Middle and Late Neolithic." *Fennoscandia Archaeologica*, XVI: 57–81.

Takala, H. 2004. *The Ristola Site in Lahti and the Earliest Postglacial Settlement of South Finland*. Lahti: Lahti City Museum.

Ukkonen, P. 1993. "The Post-Glacial History of the Finnish Mammalian Fauna." *Annales Zoologici Fennici*, 30: 249–264.

Ukkonen, P. 2003. Konnevesi Majakangas (KM 34052). Unpublished osteological report. Helsinki: National Board of Antiquities.
Ukkonen, P. and Mannermaa, K. 2017. *Jääkauden jälkeläiset. Suomen lintujen ja nisäkkäiden leviäminen Suomeen jääkauden jälkeen*. Museoviraston julkaisuja 8. Helsinki: Museovirasto.
Vanhatalo, S. 2005. "Konneveden Majankankaan Rautakautinen Polttohauta." In *Kentältä poimittua 6: Kirjoitelmia arkeologian alalta*. Museoviraston arkeologian osason julkaisuja 11. Edited by H. Ranta, 96–102. Helsinki: National Board of Antiquities, Helsinki.
Wessman, A. 2010. "Death, Destruction and Commemoration. Tracing ritual activities in Finnish late Iron Age cemeteries (AD 550–1150)." *Iskos* 18.

13 "A dog will come and knock at the door, but remember to treat him as a human"
The legend of the dog in Sámi tradition

Nuccio Mazzullo

Introduction

Today, the Sámi are Europe's only indigenous people. According to Sámi parliaments, the Sámi people count about 100,000 members in total, and their languages are divided into nine different groups. Their contemporary homeland, *Sápmi*, covers the northern part of Fennoscandia as well as the Kola Peninsula in Russia. Sámi livelihood is commonly associated with reindeer herding, although this practice has developed alongside other activities. In the case of the Skolt Sámi, for instance, fishing became marginal after relocation to Finland, although hitherto fish had been the most important staple food (see Mazzullo 2017).

Probably around the seventeenth century – the exact time frame is debated among scholars – the Sámi people increased the number of reindeer they kept to tame and train, while also hunting wild reindeer. There is some evidence, as reported by the Norwegian merchant Ottar, that taming had been practised since the ninth century (Magnus 1998 [1555]). First, they used the trained reindeer as decoys and for transport, but as their number increased they started to herd these animals. This developed into a livelihood that is still being practised. As we shall see in the discussion of different sources below, the dog had played an important role in the lives of Sámi people long before this transition from hunting to herding. Near the beginning of the seventeenth century, the dog was co-opted into the new way of life, and has since then kept a central position in reindeer herding.

To introduce the reader who is unfamiliar with the subject of reindeer herding, a good account of Sámi reindeer herding in Finnish Upper Lapland is given by Itkonen (1984:144–145) who describes the practice at the beginning of the twentieth century. In this period, in September, the herding was undertaken in such a way that there were always two people watching the herd. They both had dogs and would stay in a tent (*lávvu*) close to where the herd was 'digging' for food (*guohtut*). The tent would be moved about five kilometres every month. If the pasture was good, then the herd would tend to stay put. After the mating season at the end of September, the herd would move less and less. In the meantime, the snow would have covered the forest, making it easier for the herders to ski. By November, only one herder was needed to move around the herd to keep the wolves away. In December, the herd became quiet and only required two herders to go around it in the morning, one clockwise and the other counter-clockwise. From January onwards, they moved the herd only two or three times until mid-April. Then, one or two weeks before the beginning of May, they drove the herd beyond the pine treeline, to reach the calving ground on the tundra. They stayed there until the end of June. During this period the herd was split into two smaller units, one made up of the bucks, and the other of the does and calves. The two units had to be from one to three kilometres away from each other. Both herds had to be circled, the does once a day, and the bucks twice daily. In mid-June the herd was put back together again and moved towards the high fells. During this period, the herd was observed from afar twice a day until it reached the earmarking corral area. In the last week of June and first two weeks of July, the calves were earmarked. After the earmarking the herd was released back to the summer pasture until the end of summer where they would be monitored less. The mating season started in autumn, and sometime around the end of October to the beginning of November the Sámi organized the first separation and slaughter.

As I shall argue and describe in this chapter, the dog was indispensable in all these activities and hence it has been highly appreciated as a co-worker and companion by Sámi reindeer herders.[1] Up to this day, the dog is considered an autonomous family member rather than a pet, and should not be kept in captivity. "The dog is not only an essential partner to his partner, or *isit* (master), but also an important member of the family, where there may be several such dogs" (Anderson 1986:7). In this article, I will argue along the lines stated by Myrdene Anderson who speaks of a "codomestication framework [that] specifically incorporates the other actors in the coevoluntionary drama, whether human or otherwise. Humans have not stood outside the equation of domestication as they have 'subjugated' plant and animal species through the millennia" (Anderson 1986:4).

At the beginning of the twenty-first century, the picture of reindeer herding includes many new technologies that have been widely adopted since the 1960s. One of the most influential technologies and surely the one that attracted the interests of various researchers was the snowmobile (Pelto 1973; Ingold 1974; Ingold 1978; Paine 1994; Vuojala-Magga et al. 2010). Snowmobiles, motocross bikes, all-terrain vehicles, helicopters and GPS collars for reindeer have replaced several activities in herding, such as the overseeing of the herd's movement on the ground. However, each technology has limitations, and hence requires the presence of humans and their traditional skills. Hugh Beach describes how the helicopter – for its useful features to be able stand still in the air, turn around on the spot and zigzag behind a herd to drive it into the corral – has been termed a "flying dog" by Sámi reindeer herders. "Anyone who has watched a helicopter at work when collecting and driving reindeer to the corral can understand the appreciative but somewhat ironic term for them: 'flying dogs' [...] With a *skilled herder* sitting beside a skilled helicopter pilot, the flying dog can do the job of many in a fraction of the time" (Beach 2013:94 *my italics*). Hence, despite technological advances dogs keep an important place in Sámi culture and society and cannot be substituted by technologies. On the contrary, technologies are adopted only as they turn out to be useful in connection with other actors, including dogs.

The close connection to the dog as a friend and co-worker is evident in the innumerable pictures of Sámi posing with their dogs since the camera was invented. During different periods of my anthropological fieldwork in Finnish Lapland since the 1990s, herders have talked to me at length about their dog's abilities and independent actions. For instance, in one case a herder told me how much his dog had got used to the snowmobile. The dog developed a remarkable sense of balancing on the back of the moving vehicle as well as the skill of jumping on and off when it understood that a reindeer had gone astray. I then witnessed how herder and dog had actually become a work team that required hardly any communication, and how a stray reindeer would be followed independently by the dog while the herder would continue driving his snowmobile behind the herd. The dog still plays a central role across different aspects of everyday life. Centuries of collaboration have also left traces in the language. To give one example, the Sámi term *beanagullan* (Finnish *peninkulma*) refers to the distance that a dog can be heard barking. In practice, one *beanagullan* would be equivalent to about ten kilometres.

During my fieldwork even my own presence in the Sámi community was also commented upon in connection to the social relevance of the dog. I was repeatedly told the following old joke: "What is a Sámi family made of? ... Father, mother, two children, a dog and ... an anthropologist!" The joke epitomizes the spirit with which the Sámi have learned to cope with the substantial number of researchers, both from the south of Finland and from abroad, who have taken an "interest" in their physical characteristics and their culture. At the same time, it emphasizes the social relevance of the dog as it reserves a place in the traditional composition of the Sámi (herder) family.

I shall now turn to describe how in Sámi oral tradition and reindeer-herding practice, the dog has been understood as being an essential and in many ways a better partner than any human worker. Legends and stories have been kept alive over centuries, conveying a code of conduct for the interaction with the dog and other living beings, and a new generation of narratives follows along these lines. In the next section of this chapter I describe how the collaboration between herder and dog has been formulated in terms of a contract. Following this, I juxtapose versions of the "legend of the dog", in which the dog transcends boundaries and enters into a marriage with a Skolt Sámi woman.

The dog as the herder's co-worker, *reaŋga* (Sámi)/*renki* (Finnish)

The dog's long relationship with the Sámi is evident in historical sources. Drawings from the sixteenth century show the dog running along with Sámi hunters on skis (Olaus Magnus 1555, reprinted in Bjørklund 2013). Sámi shaman drums from the seventeenth century depict the dog "so well [...] that one can even speculate as to what breed it is" (Kjellström 1991:129).

Knud Leem's "accidental" ethnographic descriptions[2] of the Sámi in the eighteenth century give an impression of the important role dogs had during the transition from hunting to herding. Four drawings by Leem (Figure 13.1, a–d) depict the dog in its daily activity among the Norwegian Sámi. The first drawing (Figure 13.1a) shows the dog at a winter camp. Two Sámi reindeer herders, each of them with a dog, gather draught reindeer in order to leave the camp. In the tundra (Figure 13.1b) the reindeer dig for food, with one herder watching them and the other taking a rest in a temporary shelter dug into the snow. Both herders are accompanied by their dogs. Figure 13.1c then shows the two herders walking behind the draught animals and their dogs running towards wild, i.e. non-domesticated reindeer to circle them and make them join the herd of trained animals. The fourth table (Figure 13.1d) depicts the herders with the dogs and the reindeer (both wild and trained) arriving at the winter camp.

In this description of herding by Leem, the dog had become an essential part of the herding/hunting activities of the Sámi by the middle 1700s. In his table 46, each dog stays with its owner, one herder and dog pair watches the reindeer, and the other pair rests in the shelter. The dog appears as a co-worker and companion, rather than a pet or livestock.

The closeness of the bond between dog and Sámi reindeer herder has been described by Johan Turi (1979 [1910]). The following paragraphs are my own translation and paraphrasing of the section "About dogs" in his "Stories of the Sámi people" (Turi 1979: 132–134).[3] The legend provides a mythical explanation of the relationship and the important position the dog keeps in Sámi families. It also emphasizes the collaborative aspect of the reindeer-herding livelihood that is not a one-man effort but rather relies on concerted activity between humans and other agents, animated and non-animated.

Turi tells that "[E]ven the dog was once a forest animal. It thought it was getting too much of a hassle to find food in the forest, and it started to get very hungry when the wolf had not been able to bring down a single reindeer." Food was available when the wolf had managed to kill, but some of the other animals were faster and stronger to grab the food and scare off the others.

In that situation, Turi continues, "the dog started to think, 'I will go to work as a herding helper [*renki*] for the Sámi.'" The dog remembered how he had encountered a Sámi herding community (*siida*) and how he had accidentally helped the herder bringing his herd together. Back then, the herder had been shouting and barking like a dog to round up his herd. Upon hearing the

The legend of the dog 255

Figure 13.1 Herding dogs in their daily activities in the seventeenth century
Source: Leem 1956 [1767]: 589–592, tables 45–48).

man engaging with his reindeer in such way, the dog ran towards him barking as well and the fleeing animals formed a herd. The herder offered soup, hoping to hire the dog as a helper. The dog liked the food, but was eyeing scraps and bones, and fled the scene, thinking that the herder would kill it if it started eating those. Returning to the forest the dog started to follow the tracks of a wolf that had killed a hare, but found no more than a foreleg. Following the wolf further, the dog found the leftovers of a fox, and rejoiced over the killing of a competitor, only to find one of his companions, another dog, killed and eaten further down the trail. Now he started to be afraid, "maybe it will kill me, too!" Upon hearing the wolves, the dog started running towards the Sámi dwelling.

"Arriving there it offered itself to the Sámi, 'Take me as a herding helper. I do not want to remain a forest animal any longer.'" The Sámi herder and the dog agreed on payment and treatment, namely soup and something to chew on for the dog, and no scolding when it was unable to do more work. The dog was then asked to find more dogs as helpers. Among those, one had a good sense for dangers, such as approaching wolves. Still today, these kind of dogs can be found, Turi states, "but today no one is able to understand the dog's language, while there are of course some dogs who can understand people. In the old days, all animals, trees, and stones and everything that can be found on the earth spoke to each other, and that is how it is going to be on the judgement day."

As an additional request, the dog asked to be killed by hanging when it gets old, so that it does not have to suffer long. The person who attends to this final request and who had been patient with an overworked dog will have dog luck (*koiraonni*).[4] "Those who have not respected the terms of the contract, will have bad dog luck [*heikko koiraonni*]."

"On judgement day, the dog will be the first soul bearer – and after it all the other natural beings that have been under human command – before those who have asked too much from the animals and who did not even appreciate the animals' work. And the poor animal who did not have a mouth to say that it could not continue to pull the load!" Turi describes how bad-natured people do not stop when they hear heart-breaking sounds from the animals suffering under heavy loads. "One should truly remind oneself that one should not be too harsh to those who work under our command, be they people or natural beings."

Figure 13.2 Turi's drawing of herders and their dogs
Source: Turi 1979[1910]:132; courtesy of Samuli Aikio.

In Turi's account, the dog entered a contract with the reindeer herder, and together they specified the terms and conditions within which the dog would work for the herder and how the herder would take care of it. In my own fieldwork among Finnish Sámi reindeer herders, I have witnessed that this contract is taken seriously until today. In fact, none of my informants has treated a dog badly in my presence. On the contrary, they normally gave dogs a position that is unusual in a Western context – few orders were given to dogs, and this in turn granted them some negotiating power. For example, many of the dog's own decisions were quickly accepted as long as the terms of the contract were not broken, for instance when the dog started attacking the reindeer that it was supposed to protect.

Along these lines, Itkonen (1984 [1948]) describes the process of training a dog for herding purposes. In his book, *Suomen Lappalaiset* ("Finnish Laplanders")[5] one chapter is devoted to "the dog". Here, Itkonen specifies how the dog, according to the Sámi herders, must learn on its own accord and with its own speed, without too much pampering when it is a puppy – in similar ways to how children are taught. This is supported by Myrdene Anderson (1986:9) who claims that "[f]rom earliest puphood, Saami encourage almost any distinctive behavior; much the same pattern obtains with human offspring". It is commonly assumed that if the teaching is too forceful, and the dog is scolded for its activity, it will become stubborn and challenging, and acquire a "wood head", or *muorri oaivi* in Northern Sámi (Itkonen 1984:175). After such a point, the dog will start to be afraid of people, bark at them and no longer take any orders. Hence, the dog is ruined by the attempt to teach it.

Itkonen then describes a teaching method that seems to be more successful, especially with young dogs. In particular, the young untrained dog is sent to round up the herd during a period when less snow is covering the ground, making running easier. It will be allowed to commit mistakes. In fact, it is assumed that it will run through the herd and disperse it, and not be able to gather them afterwards. Anderson (1986:9) describes this in general terms: "Dogs, like children, learn by doing, not by training." Itkonen also reports that when the herder sees the dog getting tired, he will send an experienced dog to quickly gather the herd, knowing that the younger dogs will be watching this and learn from it. "It is better that the dog learns the work by itself, since there is usually only one dog responsible to keep the herd together" (Itkonen 1984:174), with the herd here being 300–600 reindeer. A very good dog can keep up to 1,000 reindeer together during the season when snow is high, albeit not for many days. "When herding, the dog does work ten times more than a person" (Itkonen 1984:177). Hence, a good dog would never be sold, Itkonen points out in a footnote (1984:174), as it is considered to be more useful than a man.

In the same chapter, Itkonen (1984:177) tells stories of dog luck (*beanalihku*, or *koiraonni*, see Turi above). The Salkko brothers, for instance, were famous for their dogs who were sent out in pairs to herd the reindeer without the presence of the herder. The work of the dog was regularly acknowledged in monetary terms: "Arto Sverloff [a Skolt Sámi reindeer herder] recalled that the first time he worked for the association (mid-1950s) the pay was eight Finnmarks (about $2.50) per day, plus one and one-half Finnmarks for one's dog if the herder had an active reindeer dog accompanying him" (Pelto 1973:37).

The close relationship that Leem depicted in the seventeenth century and that Turi explained in terms of a contract is also described by Itkonen, who states that at night, a reindeer herder would have the dog sleeping at his feet, or even be surrounded by about a dozen of the fur balls, moving and sleeping even on top of him. The dog, Itkonen (1984:179) continues, is fed well with blood soup, and during times of hard work eats the same food as the herder – as part of the contract described earlier by Turi.

More recently, Oskal (2000:177) has referred to the concept of dog luck and remarks that "Some people have good dog luck and it is said about them that they have dog luck in their armpit (beanalihku gidavuolli) and this is considered a personality trait".

The legend of the dog in Skolt Sámi narrative

In Skolt Sámi narrative the bond between dog and humans goes far beyond collaboration in reindeer herding. *Piěnn^{a}i màinâs*, the "legend of the dog", tells of a dog who was sent by God to become the son of a Sámi couple. Below is a summary of *Piěnn^{a}i màinâs* as reported by Itkonen (1931:170). The legend unfolds as follows:

Once there was a Sámi couple who wanted to have children but had not succeeded. So they asked God to help them to have a son or, at least, a cat. And if that was not possible, even a dog. A dog was born to them. And so the dog grew up as a son. He went to the forest to hunt and would bring back meat for the meal. Once he asked his mother to bring him a woman. His mother went to an old woman who had three daughters. She offered some dry bacon fat and asked for one of her daughters as a housemaid. The old woman accepted and gave [the mother of the dog] her eldest daughter. They went back home and the woman ordered the maid to clean the house. The maid complained that it was dirty and wondered why there was dog excrement around. The mother answered that dogs meant as much to them as human beings and warned that when her son came back from the forest she should address him as she would address a person. When the son came back and knocked at the door, she went to open it and saw that it was only a dog. She prepared the dinner with the meat he brought and gave him the bones. After dinner, they went to sleep and the maid asked what sort of games the dogs played, and he got angry and bit her breast and killed her. The morning after, before he went to the forest, he asked his mother to get him another woman. The mother went and got the middle daughter, but she behaved in the same way as her elder sister and so was killed in the same way. Finally, the mother brought the youngest sister and this time when the dog came back from the forest, she went to the door and announced that a person had come. The 'dog' wagged his tail for he was happy to be treated as a person. She cooked the food and they all ate together. When she went to sleep with him she did not make any remark as her sister had done. After some time, the mother asked her how her husband was, and she replied that when, at night, he took off his dog-fur he shone with beauty. And his mother asked her how could they take away the fur so that he could keep his human shape. They thought that if the mother lit the fire outside, then when they would go to sleep the woman could kick the fur that he left at the foot of the bed, and the mother could burn it. So they did it. But as he smelled the smoke he woke up and asked about his fur. But she said nothing. He went outside and saw his fur burning. So he decided to go away and told them that they would never find him until they had succeeded in three tasks he would give them. By the time she had succeeded in the first two tasks, the daughter-in-law had found him, but he was already married to the daughter of an ogress. So, his woman hid a brass brush in his clothes. When they all went to sleep in the same bed, the one that he looked at would become his wife. The man looked at his woman, and as the daughter of the ogress realized this, she started to cry until she exploded in half and turned into a mole cricket. The husband told her that she and his mother would not have found him if they had not followed his words. In the meantime, his aged parents had a fire burning on the spindle. A mouse asked them whether it could put out the fire. They replied that the mouse should not to do so because their son was coming home. The mouse did not put it out and their son came back home with his wife (Itkonen 1931:170; Mazzullo 1994:118–120).

The above version of the legend, collected by Itkonen in the 1930s, is clearly about the relationship between humans and non-humans as it was understood in the Sámi community. The mother of the dog painstakingly advises all three sisters that, despite appearances, they should treat her son like a human being. She emphasizes this in the first place by recommending to her potential daughters-in-law[6] that they should address him as a human person. Moreover, she does so long before she discovers that, in reality, at night, her 'dog-son' is a handsome man. However, when the mother realizes that under his fur he is a human being, she makes a serious mistake. Her desire for him to keep his appearance also during the day means that she will have to succeed in three more trials before she can finally have him as a human.

Itkonen also mentions this legend in his later publication, *Suomen Lappalaiset* (Itkonen 1984:528), but his summary stops at the point where the dog is finally happy with the youngest sister and the girl reveals to her mother-in-law that her son is in reality a handsome man. However, the corresponding parts of these two versions presented by Itkonen share the same theme, that is, the acknowledgement of a human status for the dog.

Thirty years after its original publication by Itkonen, the same legend was told to anthropologist Pertti Pelto by a Skolt Sámi, Paavo Moshnikoff.

In his book *Individualism in Skolt Lapp Society* he summarizes it in the following way:

> One of the best known themes in Skolt tales is that of the family who had a dog for a son. He brought them meat from the forest, and the relations in the family were amiable. Then he asked his parents to get him a wife, so they applied to a family nearby where there were three sisters. The oldest sister was brought home to be the dog's wife. When the dog returned from the forest with a big piece of meat they sat down to dinner, but the bride fed the dog just the scraps and the bones of the meat. That night when they retired to their bed in the storehouse he bit her nipples off (killed her). The same sequence of events took place with the middle sister, so finally the youngest sister was brought, and she was naturally kind so she fed the dog the choicest piece of meat, and he was satisfied with her.
> (told by Paavo Moshnikoff of house 23) Pelto 1962:144–145

As we can see, Pelto does not report the whole legend but provides only a very short résumé, and we can immediately identify some substantial differences to Itkonen's account. In this condensed version there is no mention of the recommendation made by the dog's mother to the three sisters that they talk about her son as a human being. In Pelto's version, the dog kills them because they do not serve him good food. Moreover the importance of the relationship between humans and non-humans, an essential element of Itkonen's versions of the legend, is absent from Pelto's account. He introduces the legend to support the Skolt Sámi understanding of "gender roles and nurturance", arguing that for the Skolts, the central importance of the woman lies in the management of the household and the many important skills she should command. This makes the Skolts "practical minded" in their evaluation of women, particularly as prospective wives (Pelto 1962:144).

In Itkonen's earlier version, the term used in the original language to address the dog is *òumàž* ("man" or a "person"). The main reason for the dog choosing the youngest of the three sisters, according to this version, is that she succeeded in recognizing in 'it' the attributes of humanity and personhood, contrary to the visual evidence, and not because she gave it meat to eat instead of bones. The importance of this acknowledgement was re-emphasized when his mother and the maid tried to prevent him from switching back to his canine shape. Their failure to accept him as he was led him to punish them for not being satisfied with his ambivalent appearance and to leave them with three more tasks to solve. In the version presented by Pelto, in contrast, the weight of the tale has shifted to the elements of social roles and upbringing. Although many of these traditional tales are no longer told, I was fortunate to meet a man who could still remember it.

In fact, some thirty years after the publication of Pelto's study, in 1992, I happened to interview the man who had told this legend to Pelto himself.

Paavo Moshnikoff was then 75, and I asked him about this tale. He told me a version similar to Itkonen's shorter version, stopping at the point where the girl reveals to the mother-in-law that at night her son is a human being. Moshnikoff himself maintained that the legend was about the essential relationship between humans and animals, and that each other's importance has to be acknowledged. Respect is unavoidable, he claimed in his conversation with me.

I also interviewed the spokesman for the Skolt community at that time, Sergei Fofanoff, and he told me a version similar to that given to me by Moshnikoff, but repeatedly emphasized that people did not believe that the Sámi couple truly had a dog as a son. He maintained that the point of the story was that the relationship between humans and animals had to be understood on fair terms. But during the interview he expressed his worries and sense of discomfort at the kind of picture I might have drawn of his community. After he had described to me how modernized the Skolt community is now and how much there was still to do in order to bring it up to a standard comparable to that of communities elsewhere, the fact that I was interested in the "legend of the dog" sounded to him very anachronistic.

Discussion: the life of a narrative

Back in the 1990s, a sense of discomfort used to prevail amongst many of my interviewees whenever I asked them whether they knew legends about shamanism, stone-idols (*sieidit*) and human–animal relations. The way they perceived such questions was as if researchers were still trying to revive an exotic image of their culture, the very same one that until recently carried a stigma of backwardness. In the Sámi community there used to be a general tendency to understand any interest in traditional legends as anachronistic. This attitude, in turn, fuelled the collection and publication of traditional tales as memorabilia (rather like antique-collecting in the West) by some Sámi writers, scholars and journalists. The local Sámi radio station has been indeed very active in recording and broadcasting narratives and Sámi traditional singing (*juoiggus*) that might have otherwise disappeared. However, the problem with such institutionalized approaches was that they did not succeed, despite some bottom-up attempts, in engaging the younger generation in the "re-invention" of narratives[7] until the beginning of 2000. It has only been in the past decade or so that a new generation of artists has successfully claimed that space. To put it in Ingold and Kurttila's terms, traditional narratives live through an ongoing process of generation and regeneration, but this can only happen "within the contexts of people's practical engagement with significant components of the environment" (Ingold and Kurttila 2000:192). As we have seen from the example of *Pie̮nnªi màinâs*, the tale has different versions and has survived only because there were still people who could tell them and not just because the tale had been recorded.

When I interviewed Paavo Moshnikoff, the story he told me was shorter than Itkonen's version from 1931 (but perhaps more similar to Itkonen's summary in 1948). The version Moshnikoff gave to Pelto in 1962 is yet similar in length to the one I heard from him in 1992; however, it contains some substantial differences regarding its theme. What had happened? Was the same person telling the same story with different emphasis on the central theme?

Among the many considerations that may have influenced the version he was telling is the fact that the interviews took place more than thirty years apart. Moreover in each case, the relationship with the interviewer and the latter's agenda was very different. Thus Moshnikoff may have given Pelto a version that emphasized the aspect of nurture, knowing that he was concerned with the social significance of the legend, whereas in my interview he knew that my interest was to understand the relationship of the Skolt Sámi people with the animals and the landscape. He might have felt like including some aspects that were relevant to my interests as distinct from those of the previous interviewer. Of course, equally influential is the informant's agenda, as we can see from the response to the same questions that I put to the village spokesman, who agreed to the theme of the legend on condition that it was understood to be no more than an allegory.

The point is that narratives change and that such change occurs not only in the transmission from one storyteller to another, nor only, as noted by Clifford and Marcus, in the translation from oral performance into descriptive writing: "Now data also move from text to text, inscription becomes transcription. Both informant and researcher are readers and re-*writers* of a cultural invention" (Clifford and Marcus 1986:116).

In the case of the different versions of the "legend of the dog", comparison was possible only because the legend had been 'inscribed' by Itkonen in 1931, but that does not mean that once written down the legend ceased to be told. As Cruikshank (2000:155) points out, "Oral tradition permits continuous revision of history by actively interpreting events and then incorporating such constructions into the next generation of narrative". During my fieldwork I often heard anecdotes about people and their dogs, and I constantly witnessed their interaction in everyday life. People nowadays share short stories and normally there is a direct or indirect relation between the event and the narrator, who has either witnessed or taken part in the event – i.e. the practical engagement Ingold and Kurttila (2000) emphasize – or who knows the actors and their dogs involved in it. Narratives of this kind are told among friends and are repeated over and over again. Hence, the next generation of narratives regarding the Sámi herding dog (and other animate beings) may not be told in the traditional format of a legend in the future. While we can trace its main assumptions about respectful engagement between humans and animals, the narrative has lost many of its features that may sound "anachronistic" to our ears today.

Conclusions

The importance of the dog in Sámi pastoral societies has been discussed by Johan Turi (1979 [1910]) and others: according to Sámi tradition, the dog has to be understood as a person and an equal member or partner of the community, with specific tasks and responsibilities, especially in reindeer herding. In a legend being told among the Skolt Sámi, the dog's role goes even beyond this recognized social space, when the dog becomes human.

The "legend of the dog" makes no reference to reindeer, but tells of hunting activities, and thus places the human–animal relationship in times before the Sámi commenced with herding. Similar to the story of the contract made between the dog and the herder, the legend specifies an agreement that is between husband and wife. More generally, it requires humans to make the effort to treat the dog in equal terms, to accept it as a family member and show respect for its work and contribution, while ignoring its different appearance.

I have presented different accounts of this legend, which were being told and recorded over the span of 60 years. These versions of the story have been juxtaposed, starting with the ethnographic collection by Itkonen in 1931, continuing with Pelto's version of the story in 1962, and my own interviews on the story of dog in 1992. The description and analysis of these three instances of the story of the dog have highlighted the role of narratives in societies in general, and in the Skolt Sámi in particular, the lives they live and how they maintain themselves.

In particular, I have described how the same story wears different hats depending on the teller and the audience, and hence, fulfils different social roles (Cruikshank 2000). In the first account (Itkonen 1931), the story of the dog is recorded within a purely ethnographic collection of folklorist heritage. In the second account (Pelto 1962), the story is interpreted in a different way, showing social guidance and gender roles in Sámi tradition. In the third account, presented by the author, but in conversation with the same persons who had told the story earlier to Pelto, quite a different interpretation surfaced. Namely the third account focuses on human–animal relations with almost invisible boundaries between the two realms. However, perhaps due to this shared closeness, this story was not being told easily for fear of being misunderstood by contemporary audiences.

In combination with Turi's account of the contract, we can conclude that this request for respectful collaboration is extended to all living beings and spirits. The symbolic marriage between dog and woman marks the effort of connecting the different communities through the "wedding vow" and with all the social implications and responsibilities (Mazzullo 1994). Stépanoff (2012) emphasizes the need to acknowledge "hybrid human–animal communities", especially among herding communities, where communication between humans and animals takes place in the common accomplishment of tasks. In this joint commitment or co-engagement, "[c]ooperation implies, at least, a triadic relational scheme involving two agents looking together toward a common goal and involving themselves in its accomplishment" (Stépanoff 2012:288). Interaction between Evenki herders and their animals has been described by David Anderson (2000) as taking place within a "sentient ecology" framework, thus emphasizing herders' knowledge of their environment and their understanding based on an extended notion of agency. This long-term interaction develops out of itself and is devoid of any formal account or teaching. Following up on Anderson's argument, Ingold (2000:25) adds the notion of "intuition" to this discussion, meaning the "capacities of judgement and skills of discrimination" upon which sentient being rests.

The stories and legends spelled out the rules for appropriate behaviour to one who was brought up in Sámi society (e.g. Jernsletten 2010). In modern terms, these lessons may sound different, and actual practices may have changed, while the relationship between dog and reindeer herders remains unchanged. The deep appreciation of the skills and abilities of the dog are evident in the ironic analogy of the helicopter as a "flying dog" (Beach 2013), complimenting on the device's versatility, but being aware of its shortcomings.

Considering the importance of the dog in reindeer herding, as well as its endurance, skill and reliability, it can be assumed that herding would not have developed in the same way and at the same scale without dogs. Myrdene Anderson has asserted this in the 1980s: "Only the dog makes the management of semi-wild, semi-domesticated reindeer possible" (Anderson 1986:7). What we can observe by looking at these Sámi stories and legends is the framing of the living space in which relationships were defined and instructions for appropriate behaviour were given.

Acknowledgements

I would like to acknowledge the inputs in this chapter from different anthropological fieldwork I conducted from 1990 until now, in several villages of the municipality of Inari, Lapland. In particular the fieldwork in 1990–1992 in Sevettijärvi and in the cooperative of Sallivaara, and then later in 2012–2014 in Sevettijärvi for the project "Oral History of Empires by Elders in the Arctic" – ORHELIA (2011–2015), funded by the Academy of Finland. The writing of this chapter was made possible through the project "Arctic Ark. Human-animal adaptations to the Arctic environment: natural and folk selection practices" (Arc-Ark), financed by a grant from the Academy of Finland, decision number 286074. I would also like to acknowledge Hugh Beach for his comments on the final proofs and Samuli Aikio for his permission to publish a picture from his book.

I am deeply grateful for the stories and accounts that informants have shared with me in conversations and interviews conducted in those villages, and wish to pay my deepest respect to those who have already passed away.

Notes

1 In this chapter, all translations of publications in Finnish and Sámi languages are my own.
2 Dunia Garcia-Ontiveros, www.historytoday.com/dunia-garcia-ontiveros/treasures-london-library-knud-leem-accidental-ethnologist-lapland (Accessed 18 March 2017). Leem was a missionary with the ambition to make Sámi culture understood so that religious teaching would become more effective.
3 For a full translation of Turi's book into English, see for instance Turi 2011.
4 In Northern Sámi, *beanalihku*.
5 At that time, the Finnish Sámi were commonly referred to as *Lappalaiset*, meaning the indigenous people of Finland.
6 The three sisters were asked by the dog's mother to come to work for her as a *biigá*, "servant", which, in Sámi society, could potentially represent a first step for the parents to get to know the future daughter-in-law. The male version is *reaŋga*, meaning the same. This concept is still acknowledged, although it is not as compelling as it perhaps used to be. During my second period of fieldwork, people often referred to me as my host's *reaŋga*.
7 A vivid example of such need of re-invention is the recent success of a young rap performer from Inari, Mikkal Morottaja, also known as 'Amoc', who sings in Inari Sámi.

Bibliography

Anderson, D.G. 2000. *Identity and Ecology in Arctic Siberia: The Number One Reindeer Brigade*. New York: Oxford University Press.
Anderson, M. 1986. "From Predator to Pet: Social Relationships of the Saami Reindeer-Herding Dog." *Central Issues in Anthropology*, 6(2): 3–11.
Beach, H. 2013. "The Devitalization and Revitalization of Sámi Dwellings in Sweden." In *About the Hearth: Perspectives on the Home, Hearth and Household in the Circumpolar North*. Edited by D.G. Anderson, R.P. Wishart, and V. Virginie, 80–102. Oxford: Berghahn.
Bjørklund, I. 2013. "Domestication, Reindeer Husbandry and the Development of Sámi Pastoralism." *Acta Borealia*, 30(2): 174–189.
Clifford, J. and G.E. Marcus. 1986. *Writing Culture: The Poetics and Politics of Ethnography*. Berkeley: University of California Press.
Cruikshank, J. 2000. *The Social Life of Stories. Narrative and Knowledge in the Yukon Territory*. Lincoln: University of Nebraska Press.
Ingold, T. 1974. "On Reindeer and Men." *Man*, 9(4): 523–538.
Ingold, T. 1978. "The Rationalization of Reindeer Management Among Finnish Lapps." *Development and Change*, 9(1): 103–132.
Ingold, T. 2000. *The Perception of the Environment: Essays on Livelihood, Dwelling and Skill*. London: Routledge.
Ingold, T, and T. Kurttila. 2000. "Perceiving the Environment in Finnish Lapland." *Body & Society*, 6(3–4): 183–196.
Itkonen, T.I. 1931. *Koltan- Ja Kuolanlappalaisia Satuja*. Helsinki: Suomalais-ugrilainen seura.
Itkonen, T.I. 1984. *Suomen Lappalaiset* [1948]. Porvoo: WSOY.

Jernsletten, J. 2010. "Resources for Indigenous Theology from a Sami Perspective." *The Ecumenical Review*, 62(4): 379–389.

Kjellström, R. 1991. "Traditional Saami Hunting in Relation to Drum Motifs of Animals and Hunting." In *The Saami Shaman Drum*. Edited by T. Ahlbäck, 111–132. Scripta Instituti Donneriani Aboensis. Turku: University of Turku.

Leem, K. 1956. *Beskrivelse over Finnmarkens Lapper, Deres Tungemaal, Levemaade Og Forrige Afgudsdyrkelse*. Oslo: Halvorsen & Børsum Antikvariat.

Magnus, O. 1998. *Historia de Gentibus Septentrionalibus [Description of the Northern Peoples* [1555]. London: Hakluyt Society.

Mazzullo, N. 1994. "La Natura Nell'immaginario Sámi. Il Rapporto Con La Natura Attraverso La Rilettura Di Alcune Leggende Dei Kolttasámi E Dei Sámi Del Nord." Settentrione Nuova Serie, *Rivista di Studi Italo-Finlandesi*, 1: 111–120.

Mazzullo, N. 2017. "And People asked: 'We Want to Have Lakes to fish!' And Lakes Were given Skolt. Sámi Relocation after WWII in Finland." *Arctic Anthropology*, 54(1): 46–60.

Oskal, N. 2000. "On Nature and Reindeer Luck." *Rangifer*, 20(2–3): 175–180.

Paine, R. 1994. *Herds of the Tundra: A Portrait of Saami Reindeer Pastoralism*. Washington: Smithsonian Institute Press.

Pelto, P.J. 1962. *Individualism in Skolt Lapp Society*. Helsinki: Suomen Muinaismuistoyhdistys.

Pelto, P.J. 1973. *The Snowmobile Revolution: Technology and Social Change in the Arctic*. Menlo Park, CA: Cummings Publishing.

Stépanoff, C. 2012. "Human–Animal 'Joint Commitment' in a Reindeer Herding System." *Journal of Ethnographic Theory*, 2(2): 287–312.

Turi, J. 1979. *Kertomus Saamelaisista. Muittalus Samid Birra* [1910]. Translated by S. Aikio. Porvoo: Werner Söderström.

Turi, J. 2011. *An Account of the Sámi*. Edited by T.A. DuBois. Chicago: Nordic Studies Press.

Vuojala-Magga, T., M. Turunen, T. Ryyppö, and M. Tennberg. 2010. "Resonance Strategies of Sámi Reindeer Herders in Northernmost Finland during Climatically Extreme Years." *Arctic*, 64(2): 227–241.

14 Dogs in Saapmi

From competition to collaboration to cooperation to now

Myrdene Anderson

Triangulating canines, reindeer, and humans in Saapmi

Since their arrival from western Siberia, coalescing as a linguïcultural group in arctic Fennoscandia around 3000 BCE, the Saami of Lapland (a cross-national region now also called Saapmi) have been associated with both dogs and reindeer. The dog had already distinguished itself from the wolf farther east in centers of its domestication, but both canines figure as actors in conjunction with reindeer and other cervids as objects of human attention (cf. Larson et al. 2012; Schleidt & Shalter 2003). First as hunter-gatherers, the Saami hunted reindeer and other game in competition against wolves but in collaboration with dogs. By 1500 CE, the dog more intimately cooperated with Saami in the herding of their now semi-domestic and half-tame reindeer, as diminishing herds came to be managed and husbanded as owned livestock with decreasing interference from wolves (cf. Bjørklund 2013; Vorren 1973). Today the wolf is all-but exterminated in Saami regions, but as a protected species still impacts smaller livestock farther south in Fennoscandia (Tønnessen 2011).

The theater of these four species, first in the Urals, involved the pairs—of canine(s) and reindeer; of human and reindeer; and of human and canine(s)—all in various stages of familiarity with each other, including the relations between the wild wolf and the domesticated dog. By the time of Saami migrations into Fennoscandia, the dog had become co-dependent with humans, antagonistic with the wolf, compatible with reindeer whether lone or in herds, and amenable to instruction by humans. A half-millennium ago, the free-ranging hunted reindeer came under the control of humans who husbanded and harvested rather than hunting them. The human-wolf relation was still competitive as both species were invested in reindeer, while the human–dog relation gradually shifted from collaboration in hunting to cooperation as both parties shared herding and surveillance chores with the seasonally migrating reindeer. Hence, the reindeer moved from common prey of both human and wolf to a human-protected species, mediated by the dog.

Moving forward to today, Saami reindeer pastoralists herd and husband as a minority within a minority, in four nation-states, in ecologically sensitive zones severely affected by climate change. They participate in local economies, with and without their herding dogs, and, via the export of reindeer meat, in global economies as well. Meanwhile, their regional mutt, the Saami reindeer-herding dog, has become a certified commodity just as its talents on the tundra are challenged by motorized vehicles.

From Siberian steppes to Fennoscandian Saapmi

The Saami in arctic Norway, Sweden, and Finland, and in the northwesternmost corner of Russia, consolidated as a linguïculture long after the first dance of humans, wolves, and wild reindeer on the Mammoth steppes of Eurasia (Schleidt & Shalter 2003; Schleidt 2013)—in process for hundreds of thousands of years. Following Schleidt and Shalter, between one million and one hundred thousand years ago, humans and wolves were first to initiate a co-domestication process, sometimes involving co-taming. Domestication takes place in deep phylogenetic time and taming takes place in shallow ontogenetic time, the first primarily biological and the second primarily social; neither process is unilateral. Consequently, domestication entails co-domestication, taming entails co-taming, and neither process implicates the other.

Ray and Lorna Coppinger and others point out a plethora of ways by which proto-humans and proto-dogs would have volunteered in these processes of domestication and/or taming (Coppinger and Coppinger 2001, 2016; Grimm 2015). The canid could be welcomed as a trash-collector, and the human could be welcomed as a source of leftovers and of grooming; both could be partners in hunting and for shared alarm systems. Then, the salty urine of both canids and humans, and the smoke from fire discouraging insect pests, draws the reindeer into the equation.

By ten thousand years ago and the subsiding of the last ice ages, early humans and wolves had plenty of time to observe each other in their social and subsistence habits. Wolfgang Schleidt (1998) suggests that the more pro-social features of so-called "human nature", elevated in "human culture", coincide with those of the gray wolf: sociality, cooperation, empathy, a sense of fairness, food-sharing, monogamy, and associating in packs. Humans' closest primate cousin, chimpanzees, do not evince these qualities, although the affable sexual habits of bonobos have been judged inspiring. The only residue of alloprimate inheritance in human behavior seems to be what is socioculturally deemed negatively: selfishness, aggression, volatility, boisterousness, Machiavellianism.

However, in ecological zones stressed by heat, cold, or drought, plant-based sedentary economies would be more marginal than lifestyles continuing to practice mobility—gathering, hunting, or ratcheting up to pastoralism. The herbivores favored for husbandry and herding in pastoralism ranged in size, usually being smaller than an adult human. Especially when much larger creatures had to be managed, the dog became the most common herding companion.

Among the Pleistocene megafauna, the wild reindeer can be singled out as offering interesting options as partners for humans in that time, now also offering compelling speculations about the prehistory of the northern hemisphere (cf. Ingold 1980, 1986; Paine 1971; Zeuner 1963). The Saami story is just one slice, but a particularly accessible slice, in Europe's northwest corner.

Hunting to herding

From predation toward taming or/and domestication of canids and cervids

In English, domestication and taming tend to be confused, perhaps because of the polysemous character of "wild", which can mean both "undomesticated" and "untame". Compounding this conceptual problem surrounding the notion of "wild", it appears that our stereotypical model of domestication— involving artificial selection under the control of humans over phylogenetic time—needs drastic overhauling. Coppinger and Smith (1983) have contributed to such a rethinking of the relations of domestication, suggesting that this process can better be described as co-domestication. Hence, in viewing the vectors of domestication and taming, one must not assume that these dynamics are unilateral or human-directed.

Domestication and thereby co-domestication take place in deep, evolutionary, phylogenetic time, through many generations of the participating populations being subjected to deliberate as well as incidental selection, including those recognized in conventional models of husbandry practices. In contrast, taming, via co-taming, takes place in shallow, developmental, ontogenetic time, through the experience of habituation of individual creatures of whatever species, during their lifetimes (Anderson 1986; Ingold 1994; Paine 1964).

Generally speaking, domestication emerges from an information sink, literally respecting DNA, while taming distinguishes itself as an energy sink, as are so many other social phenomena (following Rosen [1985, 1991], considering culture as an anticipatory system). Of course, domestication and taming also emerge through contrasting time frames—analogues as to both process and temporal dimension with the cultural and the social. It follows, indeed, that culture, like domestication, is an information generator and information sink, while society, like taming, is an energy dissipator and energy sink. Culture domesticates, society tames. The Saami dog is both domesticated (given some artificial selection) and tame (given the steady association with humans), while the Saami reindeer is only marginally domesticated by this definition, and not tame, although the castrated draft reindeer have a greater familiarity with both humans and dogs.

At the very least, candidates for taming or domestication have qualities exapting them for the process (cf. Gould & Vrba 1982)—some species virtually volunteering for taming or domestication, or even achieving the new relationship by dint of persuasion or *fait accompli*. Recall here how well the canines, cervids, and humans have accommodated each other.

Similarly, in the taming process, which may or may not accompany a domestication process, and which can take place without either building on or leading to domestication, individual animals differentially select themselves for taming. Whether or not we should be tempted to speak of entering into "co-taming" with respect to plants will be left for another occasion, although even with plants, our co-domestication is not in doubt.

Especially in the intimacy of taming another animal, however, the "tamer" is obviously integral to the process, and it is consequently the larger social relationship that is "tame", not the targeted animal (Ingold 1994). Neither taming nor domestication are or can be totally unilateral, deliberate, or controlled. These relationships co-opt, intensify, and self-organize, far from equilibrium, as throughput processes we might call dissipative structures (cf. Salthe 1993, following Prigogine & Stengers 1984[1979]).

Saami reindeer management today

The stereotype of Saami culture crystallizes around pastoralism—the image of the reindeer and the activities of reindeer herding and husbandry. Crucial to this livelihood, and to the hunting culture that preceded it, has been the reindeer-hunting (now -herding) dog; yet, the dog's station in Saami culture is presently under adjustment.

Today, reindeer-managing Saami—a minority occupational group within this ethnic minority in arctic Fennoscandia—function in numerous interlocking systems that increasingly seem up-ended. Into the twentieth century, the grass-roots practices of pastoralism shaped Saami culture as a whole, to the extent that non-pastoralists voiced envy, while since World War II, external forces have come to dominate all sectors of Saami society, including that involving dogs and reindeer. During the recent historic period, the stereotype of Saami culture was based on a partnership between the Saami, their reindeer livestock, and the reindeer-herding dog, all still organized in pragmatic seasonal, mobile, kin-dominated groups inclusive of their pastoral substrates (called *siida*). These seasonal nomads maintained kinship relations among their more numerous fully sedentary Saami and Fennoscandian neighbors.

These groups were never isolated from the rest of the world; in fact, they had to deal with global phenomena before their respective nation-states came into the picture. Early in the historic period, the Saami on Europe's periphery were affected by the fourteenth-century bubonic plague, by the post-Reformation sixteenth-century crash in the codfish trade, and by their expanding involvement in the somewhat overlapping fur trade. Thereafter, particularly in the twentieth century, Saami were increasingly integrated into local monetized economies, through their subsidized livelihoods, by the welfare state, and then by their self-conscious fourth-world status, their tourist industry, and their being simultaneously protected by and exploited by their respective nation-states (Norway, Sweden, Finland, Russia).

Since Chernobyl in 1986, when contaminated herds particularly in southern regions had to be culled, Saami reindeer livestock remains steady in Norway, or even periodically increases, while the number of reindeer-breeding Saami has decreased as a proportion of the total Saami population, never again to approach 10% (cf. Beach 1990). Herding and husbandry have become a commuter livelihood, with operations coordinated out of seasonal houses rather than constantly moving family tents. Saami incorporate new technology, almost effortlessly adapting it to serve Saami ways. Particularly attractive to Saami are technologies affording greater speed, often in straight lines, such as motor vehicles, planes, and sewing machines.

These trends feed into a trajectory that seems, in retrospect, both ubiquitous and overdetermined. In brief, circumpolar peoples, inclusive of Saami—once hunters of the reindeer and other species, and competitors in still earlier times with other predators such as the wolf—were drawn into increasingly cooperative relationships with both their prey, the reindeer, and their co-predators, the wolf. A spinoff has been the appearance of the co-domesticated dog, first a hunting companion, then a working partner with human herders, and now, in the larger society and internationally, a show breed.

Canine from co-predator to collaborator to partner

Saami exert very little more husbandry over the reindeer when domesticated than they did when wild, although in some areas intensive management practices such as milking contributed to incidental taming as well. For the most part, and especially in contemporary times, herding and husbandry are extensive rather than intensive, and the livestock, while domesticated or semi-domesticated, behave as though wild. Only a few bulls will be gelded for use as draft animals and lead animals. While the other reindeer may be in no way accustomed to handling, as herd animals they tolerate non-predators in their midst without alarm (Anderson 1978, 1986; Baskin 1974).

With the reindeer coming increasingly under the protection of the Saami, and with the domesticated canine on the side of Saami and reindeer, any wolf's resources became marginal. Nonetheless, there would be room in the ecosystem for the wolf today were it not for the animosity of Saami toward this former competitor. Even with regulations protecting the wolf as an endangered species, Saami systematically exterminate any wolf wandering into their areas; wolf populations could survive in the urban peripheries to the south and to the east of north Norway, although some Norwegians are also inclined toward extermination (Tønnessen 2011).

Consequently, in recent times the human-canid-cervid relationships have returned to more straightforward paired relationships of human–dog, dog–reindeer, and reindeer–human, the relationships having much less texture than those of five or ten millennia earlier. Then, humans and wolves were in competitive predation on wild reindeer, which population was accumulating differential amounts of genetic, epigenetic, and experiential information. Now, all three species share largely cooperative rather than competitive relations; strictly speaking, there are no longer predators or prey, unless it is the stray wolf. Humans, dogs, and reindeer now are co-domesticates of a single, shared cultural system, linked by a tight, essergetic web of information and energy. While Saami domestic reindeer management confronts many challenges from exogenous sources—such as simultaneous hostility and protection by the dominant national society—the dissipative structure of the human–dog–reindeer complex can provide a buffer, even a unifying cultural symbol.

From partner to pal to pet (or not)

The reindeer-herding dog, like the Saami child, is treated roughly but affectionately, and given little negative feedback. Instead, because of being rewarded for unique, independent, and innovative behavior, both dog and child ripen into maturity at their own pace, picking up skills as needed or inspired (Anderson 2000). These *laissez-faire* practices result in unique personal and practical characteristics for both dogs and humans, and these peculiarities are actively celebrated, regardless of their utility. For example, the vocal art of yoiking (Anderson 2005) builds on the Saami investment in individuality in every aspect of culture. Whether the dog performs best as a guarding or a herding dog is decided by the initiative of the dog, not through training. Some dogs distinguish themselves as worse than useless, but this situation people tolerate or even enjoy, as it confers some considerable degree of social capital; it also reflects the degree of intimacy in the human–dog bond. It has been noted that the basic unit in Saami society boils down to the individual together with his or her herding dog (cf. Anderson 1978).

All along, the reindeer-herding dog stock absorbed any incidental genes coursing through the region, more pronounced after tourism became a prominent part of the economy after the 1960s. Until recently, a few pastoralist women kept a bitch for breeding, to share male puppies with friends and kin. With few exceptions, male dogs were preferred for herding chores, and even the breeding bitches had to be restrained during periods of estrus—not to control breeding, but to avoid havoc on the tundra. Surplus female pups were immediately culled. Other than the few pastoralist women keeping bitches, no one bothered feeding dogs anything other than ad lib scraps, the scraps being either meat or bread. Some women, though, gathered scraps, boiled them and thickened the gruel, and had designated dog bowls.

Again, with few exceptions, as in the case of the reindeer, there was no selective breeding of reindeer-herding dogs. Any visiting canine might contribute his genes free of charge, and the tradition of welcoming anything different led to the herding dog stock being quite diverse, around a general Spitz model of medium build, bushy fur, curled-up tail, erect ears, and

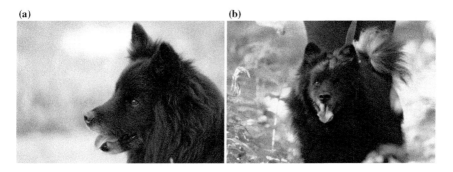

Figure 14.1 Runne-Beana's descendant, Muste-Beana (born 2004 in Finland, photographed in 2012), living with cats in a temperate zone, Indiana, USA

Photograph by Sugata Bhattacharya.

genial demeanor: a regional mutt. In fact, to be working with a dog with the appearance of a hopeful monster, afforded special recognition for the herder. Some dogs live on in narratives (about their appearance or/and behavior, whether positive or negative, but seldom neutral) for several human generations, even without the prompt of a photograph.

Since the late twentieth century, fewer and fewer women have had a priority of maintaining a bitch for breeding purposes, even though the "breed" has become certified, and a commercial item far beyond Saapmi, but not by Saami. In the world of registered breeds, since World War II, one will find at least three competing breeds standing in for the basic Saami reindeer-herding dog, their labels ironically sorted by nation-state: the Finnish Lapphund, the Swedish Lapphund, and a short-haired Lapponian Herder. Such dogs, whether shown in competitions or simply held as household pets, as they are at least throughout Europe and North America, have much going for them—gentle, energetic but compliant, and eager to herd, even children and cats.

I am not the only person outside Saapmi to be guarded by a Saami herding dog—in my case, Muste-Beana, the descendant of Runne-Beana, the dog who adopted me when I first arrived in the field, near Kautokeino, Norway, just before spring migration in 1972 (Anderson 2006, 2016). Whereas at that time, no dogs of any type were held as pets by the nomadic population, farming and fishing families could keep dogs with roles falling in our "pet" category. Some pets were of the traditional herding dog stock by convenience, but most of these dogs had more provisional backgrounds. By the end of the twentieth century, sedentary Saami were finding ways to adopt seemingly random breeds. Today, reindeer-herding families may also have dogs as pets, but these are not herding dogs from the indigenous stock; instead, they will be from a range of official breeds, seldom two alike, reflecting again the Saami passion for individuality and independence. Forty years ago, no one could imagine

Figure 14.2 Another descendant of Runne-Beana, Muste-Junior (Yuni) in Calgary, Alberta, Canada
Photograph by Ada Jaarsma.

that the herding dog could become superfluous, for the dog helped establish the status of his human partner, yet this has transpired.

In Saapmi itself, where a few dogs are still involved in some reindeer-herding operations, more and more families rely on snowmobiles and all-terrain vehicles or even planes for herding. These families may be the ones bringing in dogs of exotic breeds, often small in stature, that are kept indoors as sheltered pets, by women, who were once the breeders of herding dogs, and by children. Yet, these same families may take their pets out to the tundra for seasonal outings—early summer reindeer roundups for calf-marking and autumn roundups for husbandry tasks and slaughtering while the reindeer are sleek from summer grazing—and let the short-legged and short-haired canines try their hands and feet at herding chores. Most of these herding families claim that these dogs, whether certified breeds or mutts, function quite satisfactorily with the reindeer herd.

From center to periphery to center again: The Saami herding dog, the yoik, the drum, and shamanism

One does not often find traditional Saami reindeer-herding dogs in Saapmi nowadays, and those few are apt to be black, and named Muste! This name relates to a root for "black" in some other Finno-Ugric languages, but not in Saami, where "black" is *čahppat*. Other dog colors and patterns have disappeared, along with the special names for them.

Reindeer-husbandry remains the Saami occupation par excellence, conferring prestige on its relatively few practitioners—prestige both from within the ethnic minority and from without. But herding and guarding dogs have become peripheral to the lifestyle, even as the lifestyle has become an industry, its inputs now commercial technologies, its products becoming commodities. Increasingly, the only dogs involved in Saami pastoralism are tokens, imported from other cultures, while the original reindeer-herding dog has assimilated into a new context elsewhere in the world: as a show dog.

Other elements of Saami culture also thrive on the periphery of Saapmi, at least in Europe and North America. The Saami shaman drum has become a commodity item outside of Saapmi. The drum, more than shamanism itself, had disappeared several hundred years ago, prohibited and destroyed by edict of the religion of the colonizer. As to shamanism, the adventuring tourist can even enroll in workshops, elsewhere in the world, to study Saami (and other) shamanic journeying and healing, accompanied by the drum.

Perhaps few outsiders will encounter a Saami herding dog or any purported Saami drum or a shamanism study group, but everyone will regularly hear the traditional Saami chant, the yoik, sometimes but not always rendered by a Saami vocal artist, if not solo, then in improvised rounds.

As a folk embracing mobility, the Saami are truly hospitable and generous. It is ironic that Saapmi as a cultural center should have been so generous as to give away, rather than loan, so much of its cultural property; or, on reflection, was it stolen?

Bibliography

Anderson, M. 1978. Saami Ethnoecology: Resource Management in Norwegian Lapland. Ph.D. dissertation, Department of Anthropology, Yale University.

Anderson, M. 1986. "From Predator to Pet: Social Relationships of the Saami Reindeer-Herding Dog." *Central Issues in Anthropology*, 6(2): 3–11.

Anderson, M. 2000. "Saami Children and Traditional Knowledge." In *Ecological Knowledge in the North: Studies in Ethnobiology* (Studia Ethnobiological 9). Edited by I. Svanberg and H. Tunon, 55–65. Uppsala: Swedish Biodiversity Centre.

Anderson, M. 2005. "The Saami Yoik: Translating Hum, Chant, or/and Song." In *Song and significance: Virtues and Vices of Vocal Translation*. Edited by D.L. Gorlée, 213–233. Amsterdam: Editions Rodopi.

Anderson, M. 2006. "Space, Time, Motion, Habit, and Saami 'Nomadism.'" *Koht ja Paik / Place and location: Studies in Environmental Aesthetics and Semiotics*, 5: 119–129.

Anderson, M. 2016. "Runne-Beana: Dog herds ethnographer." *Ethnobiology Letters*, 7(2): 32–40.

Baskin, L.M. 1974. "Management of Ungulate Herds in Relation to Domestication." In *The Behaviour of Ungulates and its Relation to Management*. Edited by V. Geist and F.R. Walther, 530–541. Proceedings of an International Symposium, University of Calgary, 2–5 November 1971. Morges: International Union for Conservation of Nature and Natural Resources, IUCN Publication New Series 24(2).

Beach, H. 1990. "Coping with the Chernobyl Disaster: A Comparison of Social Effects in Two Reindeer-Herding areas." *Rangifer*, 10(3): 25–34.

Bjørklund, I. 2013. "Domestication, Reindeer Husbandry, and the Development of Sámi Pastoralism." *Acta Borealia*, 30(2): 174–189.

Coppinger, R.P. and L. Coppinger. 2001. *Dog: A Startling New Understanding of Canine Origin, Behavior, and Evolution*. New York: Scribner.

Coppinger, R.P. and L. Coppinger. 2016. *What is a Dog*. Chicago: University of Chicago Press.

Coppinger, R.P. and C.K. Smith. 1983. "The Domestication of Evolution." *Environmental Conservation*, 10(4): 283–292.

Gould, S.J. and E.S. Vrba. 1982. "Exaptation—A missing term in the science of form." *Paleobiology*, 8(1): 4–15.

Grimm, D. 2015. *Citizen Canine: Our Evolving Relationship with Cats and Dogs*. New York: Public Affairs.

Ingold, T. 1980. *Hunters, Pastoralists, and Ranchers; Reindeer Economies and Their Transformations*. Cambridge: Cambridge University Press.

Ingold, T. 1986. "Reindeer Economies: And the Origins of Pastoralism." *Anthropology Today*, 2(4): 5–10.

Ingold, I. 1994. "From Trust to Domination: An Alternative History of Human–Animal Relations." In *Animals and Human Society: Changing Perspectives*. Edited by A. Manning and J. Serpell, 1–22. London: Routledge.

Larson, G., E. Karlsson, A. Perri, M.T. Webster, S.Y.W. Ho, J. Peters, P.W. Stahl, P.J. Piper, F. Lingaas, M. Fredholm, K.E. Comstock, J.F. Modiano, C. Schelling, A.I. Agoulnik, P.A. Leegwater, K. Dobney, J.-D. Vigne, C. Vilà, L. Andersson, and K. Lindblad-Toh. 2012. "Rethinking Dog Domestication by Integrating Genetics, Archeology, and Biogeography." *Proceedings of the National Academy of Sciences USA*, 109(23): 8878–8883.

Paine, R. 1964. "Herding and Husbandry: Two Basic Concepts in the Study of Reindeer Management." *Folk*, 6: 83–88.

Paine, R. 1971. "Animals as Capital: Comparisons among Northern Nomadic Herders and Hunters." *Anthropological Quarterly*, 44: 157–172.

Prigogine, I. and I. Stengers. 1984. *Order Out of Chaos*. New York: Bantam, New York.

Rosen, R. 1985. *Anticipatory systems: Philosophical, Mathematical, and Methodological Foundations*. Oxford: Pergamon.

Rosen, R. 1991. *Life Itself: A Comprehensive Inquiry Into the Nature, Origin, and Fabrication of Life*. New York: Columbia University Press.

Salthe, S.N. 1993. *Development and Evolution: Complexity and Change in Biology*. Cambridge, MA: MIT Press.

Schleidt, W.M. 1998. "Is Humaneness Canine?" *Human Ethology Bulletin*, 13(4): 1–4.

Schleidt, W.M. 2013. "Communication: The Quest for Understanding Behavioural Complexity." *Nova Acta Leopoldina NF III*, 380: 61–75.

Schleidt, W.M. and D. Shalter. 2003. "Co-Evolution of Humans and Canids: An Alternative View of Dog Domestication: Homo Homini Lupus?" *Evolution and Cognition*, 9(1): 57–72.

Tønnessen, M. 2011. Umwelt transition and Uexküllian phenomenology: An ecosemiotic analysis of Norwegian wolf management. PhD dissertation, University of Tartu, Estonia.

Vorren, Ø. 1973. "Some trends of the transition from hunting to nomadic economy in Finnmark." In *Circumpolar Problems: Habitat, Economy, and Social Relations in the Arctic; A Symposium for Anthropological Research in the North, September 1969.* Edited by G. Berg, 185–194. Oxford and New York: Pergamon Press.

Zeuner, F.E. 1963. *A History of Domesticated Animals.* London: Hutchinson.

Zeuner, M.A. 2015. "Core questions in Domestication Research", *Proceedings of the National Academy of Sciences USA*, 112(11): 3191–3198.

15 Conclusion
Dogs in the North

Jan Peter Laurens Loovers, Robert J. Losey, and Robert P. Wishart

Introduction

Dogs are now omnipresent across the globe and in some settings are subjects of great affection and importance. Human–dog relations across the North, however, vary in remarkable ways, often being far more complex than the owner-pet connections that are so familiar to us today. The contributors in this volume illustrate how dogs have become part of and are interwoven into northern lives in diverse ways. These stories of dogs and their human companions stretch back through the millennia into the elusive past. While the chapters gathered here offer many examples of such variability, there are also striking similarities and commonalities that offer new insights for the ever-growing human–animal studies literature and many disciplines' changing understandings of the history of domestication.

Challenges of the animal turn

Academic attentions are ever turning, or arguably returning, to (new) themes. Harriet Ritvo (2007) could be credited with identifying and coining one such redirection, namely the *animal turn*. Being quick to note that the scientific study of animals has a long tradition stretching back to Aristotle, she argues that the focus on animals in the humanities and social sciences has gained much prominence in the last several decades (ibid: 118–119), flowing out of the broader posthumanist movement (see Wolfe 2010, 2011). Subsequently, this has led to a turn among some in the social sciences from human-centred approaches to animal-centred approaches. A decade later, the field of animal studies has become widely incorporated into historical and contemporary academic subject areas ranging from law, literature, and social sciences, to medieval studies and archaeology. Cary Wolfe, however, is critical towards the posthumanist emphasis in much of these studies:

> Once we understand that 'the human' and 'the animal' are relics of a philosophical humanism that flattens the actual complexity and multi-dimensionality of what are, in fact, many different ways of being in the

world that are shared in myriad particular ways across species lines, then the question of the animal – and of the animality of the human – cannot help but open onto fundamental issues that are best thought not as problems of distinct and discreet ontological substances, but rather in terms of processes, dynamics and relations – what Donna Haraway (2007) winningly calls 'contact zones' between human and non-human life forms and the environments, technologies, prostheses, and practices in which they are embedded as beings both acting and acted upon.

Wolfe 2011: 3

Taking Wolfe's critique seriously in many ways involves making decisions about which facets of the story one wants to illuminate or dismiss. Or, put another way, which lines of relations (cf. Deleuze and Guattari 2003; Ingold 2007) one wants to follow. Lines intersecting with dogs and people are emphasized here, but other things and beings are also always intertwined across the North – sleds, fish, reindeer, landscapes, and so on. Giving emphases to such relationships helps to undermine long dominant and often inaccurate narratives, but also allow engagement with other challenges.

One of these challenges is a very basic one: is it in fact possible to give voice to animals? Is it correct to speak of multi-species, or inter-species, ethnographies when it is human fingers that move across the keyboard and put down these chapters? In some ways, this ethnographic dilemma has parallels in archaeology, where generations of scholars have questioned how to speak about (most often human) relationships in the past, where direct communication with those involved is no longer possible. Both ethnography and archaeology have always involved speaking for others, with all of the obvious problems this entails. Perhaps in the animal turn we are not really giving voice to animals but rather no longer speaking as if they are irrelevant to 'our' stories, experiences, and histories. We return to the conundrum of giving voice to animals at the end of this conclusion, but first move to the story of domestication and how dogs came into being.

Domestication

Animals, as Ritvo points out, have been the primary loci of attention for the natural sciences and philosophy for a far longer period. Foundational and massively influential over the last two centuries is Charles Darwin's *The Origin of Species* (2009 [1859]), which identifies humans as the evolutionary descendants of other animals. Paradoxically, while forcefully arguing for human and animal lives both as the products of evolution, Darwin's *The Variation of Animals and Plants under Domestication* (2010 [1868]) and *The Descent of Man* (1998 [1874]) retained and reinforced anthropocentric understandings of humans as the pinnacle (and arguable mutant) of the animal kingdom. Whereas humans first had received domination over animals by God's decree, now humans had evolved the capacity to domesticate lesser animals. Darwin relied heavily on the notes of explorers and settlers to make his claims, and furthermore drew heavily on the work of his cousin Francis Galton. Pearson, who has written an extraordinary biography of Galton, includes a letter of Charles Darwin to his cousin with the request: 'I continue much interested about all domestic animals of all savage nations, though I shall not take up cattle in detail. ... Anything about savages taking any the least pains in breeding or crossing their domestic animals is of particular interest to me' (Pearson 1924: 71). These interests of Darwin manifest in his work on natural selection and in establishing theories on both animal and human breeding. Galton, the eugenics theorist, was more than keen to follow up on such beliefs (ibid: 74).

Near the end of the nineteenth century, Galton included the chapter *Domestication of Animals* in a controversial book on eugenics (1883). The chapter was almost a replica of a much earlier version, *The First Steps Towards the Domestication of Animals* (1863), written twenty years earlier. Galton starts the chapter with an evolutionary understanding of domestication and humanity. He was not so much interested in theriophilic questions of animal suffering and human morality towards animals, but more about how the rise of civilization could be understood through the domestication of animals. Galton (1863: 4) complains that much of the literature by Western travellers across the globe does not specifically focus on the 'rearing of animals' by Indigenous peoples. To fill in this gap, he corresponded with a number of 'scientific explorers' and fur traders.[1] Building upon these brief accounts from several continents, Galton identified the conditions of animals and their surroundings that were most suitable for domestication:

> 1, they should be abound in the wild state; 2, the natives should be hunters; 3, the animals should be hardy; 4, they should have an inborn liking for man; 5, they should be comfort-loving; 6, they should be found to be useful to the savages; 7, they should breed freely; 8, they should be gregarious.
>
> Galton 1863: 15

He ponders why modern man has only succeeded in improving the domesticated races but not added new ones, and concluded:

> a vast number of half unconscious attempts have been made throughout the course of ages, and that ultimately, by slow degrees, after many relapses, and continued selection, our several domestic breeds became firmly established.
>
> Galton 1863: 17

This conclusion was in stark contrast with domestication theories that arose at the end of the nineteenth century. As Rebecca Cassidy (2007: 2) points out, most academics at the time argued that 'the domestication of plants and animals' was considered to be 'a human achievement based on breakthroughs in knowledge'. In other words, it was human uniqueness and the evolution of higher intelligence that enabled the successful domination over others.

V. Gordon Childe has been particularly influential in formulating another early and popular evolutionary, or anthropogenic, approach towards domestication. Childe follows a similar path to Lewis Henry Morgan's work on human stages of evolution. He argued that civilization of humankind unfolded with the domestication of animals and plants. The dawn of civilization, thus, started with the human mastery over animals and plants, which was tied to climate changes and the subsequent crises that humans faced. There was a shift from 'food-gatherers' or Morgan's savages, roaming along ever in search for food – to 'food-producers', or Morgan's high-barbarians and the civilized, who developed more sedimentary lives. Indeed for Childe this was the 'great revolution' where men would become 'masters of their own food supply through possession of domesticated animals and cultivation of cereals' (1929: 42). Childe envisioned earlier cases of domestication (such as the dog) as rudimentary, while the cultivation of plants and the control over animals that sprouted in the Middle East was much more sophisticated and entailing the next evolutionary intellectual step up on the civilized ladder.[2] This was of course aligned with the shift from hunting and gathering to pastoralism and agriculture, and the technological improvements involving manipulation of new minerals such as iron, copper, and bronze. Or paraphrasing his words, it was both the next phase of human independence from the environment as well as an expanded capacity to exploit that environment (1958: 15). This revolutionary achievement was made possible through control and domination. Notice that the discourse differed greatly from that of Galton, where at least the characteristics of animals were in part critical to domestication. For Childe, domestication was a threshold event and unidirectional process where humans were the principal active forces.

Juliet Clutton-Brock in some ways took up Darwin's and Galton's arguments, and her perspectives in many ways typify how domestication is now widely understood and explained. Clutton-Brock has argued specifically that domestication entails human control and conversion of animals into property (2012). Further, her definition of the domestic animal, as 'one that has been bred in captivity for purposes of economic profit to a human community that maintains total control over its breeding, organization of territory, and food supply' (1999: 32), is often cited in recent work on domestication and neatly illustrates anthropogenic approaches. Galton, so she claims (2012: 2), eloquently shows how nature hovered over nurture. It is human nature to nurture (to care for, dominate, and control) while it is in the nature of domesticated animals to be subordinate or nurtured. The question of nature and nurture in domestication is characterized by Clutton-Brock as consisting of two processes: biological and cultural. The biological process of domestication is 'an evolution that mimics the sequence of events in the differentiation of island races of wild animals from their mainland ancestors' in which there are genetic changes of the resulting generations due to selective breeding, namely Darwin's methodological or 'artifical' selection (2012: 3–5). In other words, the argument is that through breeding a new species is produced which differs from its ancestors and which would not have appeared through natural selection alone. Following this model, dogs have become genetically, morphologically, and behaviourally different from wolves through human-directed isolation from other wolves and interbreeding.

Second for Clutton-Brock is the cultural process of domestication, which in essence involved the incorporation of animals into human cultures. Clutton-Brock describes culture as 'a way of life imposed over successive generations on a society of humans or animals by its elders. Where the society includes both humans and animals then the humans act as the elders' (1999: 32). Taking an animal out of the 'wild' and domesticating it implies that the animal's culture of being wild is replaced by that of being domestic. The animal subsequently needs to acquire a new set of social relations which then become its culture. The domestic animal thus is both a cultural artefact and has culture. Clutton-Brock (ibid: 30–31) is at the same time somewhat sceptical towards a clear distinction between 'wild' and 'domestic' and reasons that a degree or scale of familiarity and fear divides the two. In her words, 'the lack of fear is the essence of tameness, but the extent of this fearlessness depends on the complex characteristics of the species as well as the individual temperament of the animal' (Clutton-Brock 2012: 7).

In sum, Clutton-Brock's perspective is that while all organisms are subject to 'natural selection [occuring] in response to environmental, climatic, and other conditions combined with reproductive isolation', domestic animals and plants also change through artificial selection by humans (ibid: 2). Having said this, so Clutton-Brock argues, all organisms and social-cultural structures are bound to biological processes of evolution. The 'primitive' humans, clothed with behavioural structures, had become social hunters that would tame and control animals through evolutionary leaps. 'Each of these surges was a progression towards increasing mastery over the environment and pressures that control the evolutionary success or failure in all other forms of life' while still being 'tied to physiological adaptations formed in our early hominid ancestors as a response to tropical climates, and we are still tied to behavioural adaptations that evolved at a larger stage in hunters of large prey' (1999: 3).

Most scholars involved in the animal turn have rejected such anthropogenic approaches, in part because they characterize domestication as a unidirectional process of increasing dominance, often situated in the far distant past, and structured largely around human decision-making and intent – it is something that was done to passive animals by humans and is largely conjectural. These broad accounts from Darwin, Galton, and Clutton-Brock are also world-making myths, attempts to describe and explain on-going human–animal practices and relationships, genotype and phenotype changes, and how all of this changed over thousands of years. Such macro-scale accounts gloss over and hide untold numbers of interesting and subtle processes of domestication, particularly the lived experiences of being with animals in the North highlighted in this volume.

Co-habitation and co-existence

The idea of human control and domination is widely contested by a more recent movement within human–animal studies and related disciplines, including anthropology. This movement emphasizes the mutuality, or symbiosis, between humans and animals in which they are 'co-dependent' or form 'partnerships'. For example, Margo DeMello describes dogs as 'man's first nonhuman partner' (DeMello 2012: 194). Such notions, though, emerged in academia more than half a century ago. Frederick Zeuner, an archaeologist and colleague of Childe's, pioneered the notion of symbiosis in relation to domestication (Russell 2002, 2011). In *A History of Domesticated Animals*, Zeuner (1963: 36–55) argues that scavenging practices of particular animals in the vicinity of people can be considered as the emergence of domestication. For example, he argues that in 'prehistory' there were scavenging wolves who came to live on the periphery of human settlements. A co-operation between humans and these canines in hunting other animals eventually led to domestic dogs. Zeuner goes on to say that the 'comradeship between man and wolf led to a driving of certain nomadic animals' (ibid: 61). Coppinger and Coppinger (2001) termed this process 'self-domestication', arguing that dogs emerged not through human domination or control, but rather by a select subset of wolves adapting to a new niche – the human habitation, and the remains of food left around them. This is quite a different narrative from Childe's chronicle of control and domination in which the human 'captured' the wild animal and mastered them.

Zeuner is quick to note that this unequal partnership, in which one species benefits or is parasitic on the other, is still symbiotic. As Nerissa Russell (2011: 211) points out, however, while Zeuner denies human intentionality in the origin processes of domestication, he nonetheless positions humans as dominant. Symbiosis, then, still remains something of a human enterprise where the 'ultimate dominance of the human partner is, of course, the result of [his/her] superior intelligence [over the animal]' (Zeuner 1963: 111). This struggle in archaeology (and elsewhere) to understand animals as something other than the objects of human possession and intent persists, despite these earlier arguments that domestication involves significant animal initiative and action.

Other theoretical explorations have also taken a synergetic approach, but have been more critical towards a clear human–animal division. Kohn (2007), for example, elaborates on the entanglements between dogs and humans. He argues that through the 'mutual attempts to live together and make sense of each other, dogs and people increasingly come to partake in a shared constellation of attributes and dispositions – a sort of shared trans-species habitus' (ibid: 7). Rather than focusing on human–dog relations as domestication, whatever that might be, or human dominance, Kohn (2007: 6) argues for attention to 'a larger series of processes and relations that exceed the human', and the ways in which different forms of life sustain each other.

Donna Haraway has been one of the most outspoken and influential anthropological scholars within the literature on dogs. She describes domestication enigmatically as 'an emergent process of co-habiting, involving agencies of many sorts and stories that do not lend themselves to yet one more version of the Fall or to an assured outcome for anybody' (2003: 30). Both in *The Companion Species Manifesto* (2003) and *When Species Meet* (2007), Haraway elaborates on the entanglements between humans and canines. Companion species, to Haraway, concern a 'becoming with'. Building on a variety of studies and examples, Haraway (2007: 26) contemplates 'the flow of entangled bodies' that enact each other. Companionship is all about historical situated relations in the 'worlding' between humans, animals, technologies, landscapes. Much like Kohn, dogs are not so much man-made, but rather humans and dogs (and a myriad other things and being) act to create one-another.

In his article *From Trust to Domination*, Ingold reformulates the anthropogenic approach and critically asserts the evolutionary approach (1994). The earlier mentioned studies of Darwin, Galton, Childe, and Clutton-Brock had a strong evolutionary flavour in which hunter-gatherers were seen in most cases as more 'natural', 'wild', 'uncivilized', formulations that have remained persistent. Ingold commences his article with Darwin's disgust of encountering Tierra del Fuego inhabitants who are nothing short of being savages. Like their Palaeolithic ancestors and contemporary hunter-gatherers, Darwin found these inhabitants exemplary as those who had not yet made the revolutionary leap and thus continued to roam in the wild acting out their uncivilized behavioural structures of natural desires to reproduce and scavenge for food. Or, in Childe's words, they had remained food-gatherers rather than food-producers. Ingold takes a stance against such a demeaning perspective of Indigenous peoples. One of his main critiques, and at the core of his monumental *The Perception of the Environment* (2000), is that anthropogenetic (that is again, human control and domination over animals) approaches make a problematic distinction between nature and culture that places humans outside the environment. For example, the earlier scholars illuminated notions of 'human nature' (Galton), 'intellectual revolution' (Childe), and 'behavioural adaptations' (Clutton-Brock) to reinforce a clear separation between nature and culture, and respectively animal and human. Recount how Childe argued that domestication implied a further human separation from the external environment. This is strongly and fruitfully challenged by Ingold in all of his recent works. Ingold outlines that the relationship of animals and hunting-gathering Indigenous peoples, including those of the North, is based upon trust and sharing whilst the relationships between animals and pastoralists is based on domination. It is crucial for Ingold to make this distinction and by doing so we can see how he moves away from, and yet paradoxically still incorporates other anthropogenic and evolutionary approaches. For Indigenous peoples who are hunting and do not possess domesticated animals, Ingold shows that the hunted animals give themselves to the hunter and that the hunter seeks revelation rather than control. Such is said not to be the case for the pastoralists, which Ingold describes as keeping animals as non-human slaves. Thus it is in the social relationships between animals and humans that the mastery over animals needs to be situated. This mastery, to restate, does not entail for Ingold a human position above animals or outside the environment, but rather a specific set of relations based on the control and domination of animal lives by humans. Kristin Armstrong Oma (2010) considers Ingold's rigid distinction between trust and domination over-simplified, and illustrates how pastoralists establish relationships of trust with their domesticate animals. She argues instead that humans and domesticated animals make a 'social contract', and that such a contract 'defines the terms of engagement and the duties, responsibilities and rights of the parts involved' (ibid: 178). Unlike the anthropogenic approaches, Armstrong Oma speaks of mutual becomings where human–animal relations are based on reciprocity and influence one another. While her critique of Ingold is fruitful, Armstrong Oma twists the argument around. Trust becomes an economic condition for a productive, intimate relationship with domesticated animals while hunting is coloured with brutality and disengagement. Both Ingold and Oma Armstrong provide polarizing accounts, lumping human–animal relations and practices into generalized and stark categories.

David Anderson (2014) reconsiders the notions of wild and domesticate, while at the same time drawing on these earlier debates. He commences with making a similar distinction as Ingold between the Western society and the Indigenous society; or between cultures of control and cultures of reciprocity. 'Culture of control' relies heavily on ideas similar to those seen in anthropogenic approaches as well as Ingold's discussion of domination. The 'culture of reciprocity', on the other hand, is much more aligned with the approaches of symbiosis and co-existence. D. Anderson, however, gives a small but important twist and emphasizes the importance of ethnographic fieldwork to illustrate how aspects of 'culture of control' and 'culture of reciprocity' are brought together within single communities. His example comes from working with Evenki reindeer herders in Siberia. He focuses on 'architectures of domestication' (see also Anderson et al. 2017) to make his case. Architectures of domestication such as fences or corrals have often been described as places of control and domination. D. Anderson shows that such places do not necessarily imply dominant relationships and can be considered a 'physical setting' where 'people and animals [come] into co-existence creating a mutual interest in a common life together' (2014: 20). In this sense, Anderson speaks of 'architectures of relations' where intimacy, proximity, and distance are made possible by channelling movement. This does not mean that there are no elements that could be designated as entailing control or domination or trust. Anderson et al. (2017) question in the specific context of northern lives whether it is even possible to maintain stark contrasts by characterizing domestication as either domination or mutual.

Intimacy, ambiguity, introgression

The emotions involved in being with other animals are complex, fluid, and often ambiguous, but at the same time are important and often unappreciated elements of domestication. Relations of intimacy with dogs in the North are perhaps easiest to make sense of, but they are by no means consistent, even over the lifetime of an individual animal. Intimate relations between people and dogs appear to have a history spanning thousands of years. Darcy Morey (2010), Losey et al. (2013), Perri (2016), and several contributors to this volume have described archaeological examples of dog burials from many regions. These authors argue that the burials indicate close emotional bonds between these canids and humans, dogs achieving other-than-human personhood, or recognition of these animals' critical roles in successful hunting in some settings. Morey (2010) in particular notes that over the last 10,000 years, dogs appear to have been buried far more often than any other animals. It would appear then that a deep appreciation and even reverence for dogs is not merely a facet of modern pet-keeping but rather emerged long ago.

Such intimate ways of being with dogs, however comforting, cannot hide the fact that human–dog co-habitation and domestication involves culling, eating, and other harsh treatment of dogs, as well as enormous on-going efforts among both people and dogs to maintain their interwoven worlds. Dogs of course resist and have their own agendas, which only sometimes align with those of their human counterparts, and this sometimes manifests in violence. Having an effective human–dog world, particularly where our two species work together, requires socialization, 'taming', or 'crafting' (Loovers 2015) of each generation of both parties, and of course also the fashioning and repairing of the other material things involved in these relationships. Perhaps co-taming and co-crafting are more accurate, as with other domestication processes, these too are multidirectional. Dogs are also understood as impure and unclean in some areas of the North (Willerslev 2007), in part due to their smell and indiscriminate eating and sexual practices. In many different ways, ambiguity rather than continuity characterizes the ways in which human–dog relations play out in the North.

Domestic worlds have arguably been disastrous for those canids with far less intimate relations with people, particularly when viewed over the long term. Coppinger and Coppinger (2016) estimate that there are now at least 850 million dogs on earth. In terms of population size, dogs are clearly remarkably successful. Their closest living relatives, grey wolves, now number around only 400,000 individuals. In other words, dogs now outnumber grey wolves by a ration of ~2500 to one. Wolves clearly have had difficulty competing in an increasingly human world, where they constitute a continually shrinking portion of the *Canis* genus.

Perhaps most troubling for our understanding of domestication, and seemingly most problematic for wolves, is that the breeding is directly controlled by humans in no more that about one-fourth of the massive global dog population (Lord et al. 2013). One might assume then that dog–wolf interbreeding quickly results in total genetic swamping of the vastly smaller wolf population. The reality is that while wolf–dog interbreeding is widely claimed to occur in the North and elsewhere, dogs and wolves are now very different animals, even at the level of basic biology, making interbreeding far less likely than expected. Dogs are famously promiscuous, and females can and do produce single litters with multiple male partners. Perhaps most importantly, dogs have evolved the ability to reproduce at virtually any time of the year, while northern wolves (and other non-domestic canids) can do so for only one short period yearly, often no more than six weeks. The period when dog introgression into the wolf population is possible is thus relatively short. Wolf interbreeding into dog populations is also similarly limited, as male wolves are only capable of fertilizing female dogs for the same short period of each year, while their male dog counterparts could potentially do so at nearly any time. This is not to say that some interbreeding has and does not occur, but rather that at the level of reproduction, dog and wolf intimacy is greatly constrained because the worlds of these two canids are now quite different.

Shared bodies and emotions

For archaeologists, of course, dog skeletons are of the essence. Losey et al. (this volume) point to signatures that are embodied, or 'inscribed' as we would call it, in the dog bones. These 'osteological signatures' provide insights into the lives of the respective dogs in whether they were hauling freight, being hit or maltreated, or other things. But not only this, the authors claim that the 'chemistry of the region's bedrock is in a sense "written" in them while they form'. The land, it could be concluded enigmatically, is written in the bodies of humans and dogs (and other beings for that matter). One facet that is 'written' in the bodies is that of the dog's diet as Losey et al. and Viranta and Mannermaa show. Losey et al. point out that the osteological signatures of the dogs provide insights into the different ecological settings where dogs lived. Some dogs were highly dependent on a fish diet while other dogs would eat more meat. Viranta and Mannermaa exemplify that human and animals shared the same diet. In this sense, the osteological signatures between humans and dogs would not be that different. More recent ethnographic examples further the idea that humans and dogs eat similarly. Hastrup suggests that there is competition between humans and dogs for the same resources and she is echoed by McCormack. M. Anderson, however, exemplifies that dogs receive scraps from humans. Wishart shows that the dogs and humans share the same provisions of the land, meaning fish and meat. Strecker's contribution is the most elaborative and she shows how salmon is an essential staple for the dogs and the people, but also how fishing laws and rights have altered this. We will turn to the processes of colonialism below, but now it is suffice to say that part of 'settler colonialism' has been the control of dogs' feeding habits and subsequently altering the signature. Or, in other words, the bodily lives of the dogs and humans are 'rewritten' through such practices. Oehler, in his chapter, speaks about the 'embodied perspectives of the landscape'. For Oehler such embodiment of the landscape means a heightened alteration of perception and bodily accustomation as the dog with the illustrious name White Sheik shows. Indeed, he goes on to speak about 'perspectival sharing' through shared bodies. Hunting with dogs, one becomes attuned to the gaze of the other. The dog, thus, guides the human hunting-partner to become attentive to particular sensitivities and vice versa. Such sensitivities and the sharing of bodies are not only between humans and dogs as Davydov and Klokov, Strecker, Mazzullo, and M. Anderson underscore (see also D. Anderson et al. 2017). All of them bring reindeer into the narrative. These shared triangulations are not always without tension and ambivalence (to turn back to Hill's chapter). Strecker, for example, speaks about the bad match between reindeer and dogs while M. Anderson has been discussing the human-reindeer-dog triangulation over thirty years.

In the stories of northern dogs and their humans one cannot help but notice elements of attunement, sensitivity, and 'perspectival sharing'. Here emotions and mood come into play as touched upon by the Indigenous teachers in Oehler's and Loovers' chapters. In recent years, there has been an increasing theoretical move to include affects and attunement in the discussion of inter-species relations. Flowing out of Spinoza, and subsequently Deleuze (and Guattari), these discussions elaborate on bodily affects. Seigworth and Gregg describe affect as 'a gradient of bodily capacity – a supple incrementalism of ever-modulating force-relations – that rises and falls not only along various rhythms and modalities of encounter but also through the troughs and sieves of sensation and sensibility' (2010: 2). The authors are quick to note, paraphrasing Spinoza, that there is not a Cartesian duality between mind and body but that 'body and cognition' are very much entangled. Here we could recount Mazzullo's discussion of the sensibilities of dogs. Such an unfolding field of relations entails confluences and divergences in which beings (dogs and humans – but also other beings and things – in this particular volume) come into existence and grow or wither and decay and perhaps grow again etc. Within these flows of growing and decaying, attunement and emotion play a role in the in-between entangling. Jason Throop in a recent article argues that '[t]o be attuned to relationships that constitute the world is thus to always already be situated and responsive to the various possibilities and limits arising within that world' (2017: 202). In other words, one is *corresponding* to one another (cf. Ingold 2010; see also Loovers 2015: 113). In one way or another, all contributors address such correspondence between humans and dogs while framing it differently. We learn that Losey et al. speak of mutualism and the emotional bond between dogs and humans. We have already noted Oehler's shared bodies and the attunement of moods between hunter and dog. Davydov and Klokov talk about joint activities and co-existence. Strecker, in her turn, writes about how socio-economic colonial practices affect and even change the dogs. Hill, as we have seen above, discusses the entanglement between humans and dogs and considers them as co-dependent and co-inhabitants of particular places. McCormack addresses the joint societies and collective action that shape human and dog relations. In similar vein, Wishart teases out Haraway's companion species and picks up on inter-species partnerships. Lévesque, likewise, speaks of dogs as human companions but adds notions of kinship into the equation. Loovers illustrates the effort that goes into working together between humans and dogs to make relations possible. Hastrup, too, engages with Haraway's work on companionship but argues that these are not fixed but rather open-ended assemblages. Again, we read about companions in the chapter by Viranta and Mannermaa. This resonates with Mazzullo's account of dogs as companions but here he adds that dogs are co-workers. Finally, we get to M. Anderson who concludes with the notion of co-domestication as we have already discussed in some detail.

Conclusion: refrain and (dis)concert

To conclude, the confluence between humans and dogs is not always smooth. Donna Haraway shows that in contemporary US-dog relations, there is an aspect of *biocapital* (a word play on Marx's *Capital*) in which animals become commodities and are also the consumers of commodities. Haraway (2007: 55) expands on working dogs as biotechnologies that are produced and reproduced within the capitalist market. Haraway, however, is quick to note that working dogs should not be viewed as slaves or wage-labourers. She concludes that '[p]eople and dogs emerge as mutually adapted partners in the naturecultures of lively capital' (ibid: 62). She states that '[t]he working dogs [she refers to herding dogs] are the means and offspring of colonial conquest, the international meat and fibre animal trade, US western ranch economies and ecologies, Native American resistance to the US Army, and sports and entertainment culture' while 'non-working dogs are the offspring of class, race, and gender formations that are rooted in the conformation show world and affectional pet culture' (ibid: 105). Leaving aside the larger part of her argument, we want to finish this volume with the 'dark anthropology' that McCormack addresses. The notion of 'co-' in the above summary of all the contributors is not a monologue story but rather emerges in many different forms; forms that sometimes take the shape of violence. Hastrup's notion of refrain coupled with Losey et al.'s mention of concert, albeit *en passant*, reminds us of the difficulty of telling individual stories that are in essence metonymic. Kathleen Stewart argues: '[w]hat is, is a refrain. A scoring over a world's repetitions ... Refrains are a *worlding* ... Events, relations, and impacts accumulate *as the capacities to affect and be affected*' (2010: 339, emphasis added). Refrains, however, are not always harmonious or indeed pleasant to 'hear' for certain people and colonialism often presents us with a cacophony of actions, policies, and assumptions which become clear in their intent when examined along the various colonial frontiers presented here. Indeed, several of our contributions have shown that there can be *dis*concert between humans and dogs, or more accurately between particular relations of dogs and humans that are deemed not to be part of the refrain or concert that the nation has in mind. Indigenous people and dogs in the North certainly have been affected by colonial practices, while in certain cases have successfully confronted such events. Hastrup speaks of dogs as *territorial engineers* who make territory; that is, they make sensual worlds. Colonial agents demolished such engineering by putting in place health and safety measures that bound dogs to a narrow spot or killed them if loose. Lévesque's account spells out how Canadian officials counter-acted on the lives of Inuit with their dogs through killing or healing, depending on what harmony they wanted to establish. Dogs, perhaps paradoxically or ironically, have been mediators of colonialism, as Hill alludes to. Wishart speaks of dogs as actors in colonial transformations with his chapter on police forces in Canada. McCormack, too, shows how dogs enabled the 'settler colonialism' to take shape and how they brought along with them agents of disease, control, and increasing dependency. In Siberia, as Strecker points out, dogs played a similar role in the movements of Imperial and Soviet settling policies. Finally, M. Anderson critically asserts the renewed breeding of the Saami herding dog as a possible act of theft, in which the knowledge and lives of Saami dogs are silenced and reshaped into commodities. Colonialism worked through the simultaneous attempt to reform relationships while imposing authority over those relations; dogs in the North became caught up in these actions. It is a fact in this work, that the very dogs which made the imposition of colonial agencies possible in the North could be the siblings of those working in concert with the people who were being affected by this new version of control. Does one become a bad dog in their complicity while the other is understood to be more noble? No, they are both part of the complex unfolding of repeated events in the North.

Notes

1 Charles Darwin seems to have replicated these sources in his theoretical treatise on domestication.
2 Note that most of the ideas on domestication derived from archaeologists working in the Middle East (D. Anderson et al. 2017). Contributions from Losey et al., Hill, Viranta and Mannermaa, McCormack, and M. Anderson which focus on the circumpolar North provide quite a different perspective. As with the other contributions in this book, they show that notions of domination and control are too simplistic and that Indigenous people and dogs have had an intricate and complex relationship of crafting lives together.

Bibliography

Anderson, D.G. 2014. "Cultures of Reciprocity and Cultures of Control in the Circumpolar North." *Journal of Northern Studies*, 9 (2): 11–27.

Anderson, D.G., J.P.L. Loovers, S.A. Schroer, and R.P. Wishart. 2017. "Architectures of Domestication: On Emplacing Human–Animal Relations in the North." *Journal of the Royal Anthropological Institute*, 23 (2): 398–416.

Armstrong Oma, K. 2010. "Between Trust and Domination: Social Contracts Between Humans and Animals." *World Archaeology*, 42 (2): 175–187.

Cassidy, R. 2007. "Introduction: Domestication Reconsidered." In *Where The Wild Things are Now: Domestication Reconsidered*. Edited by R. Cassidy and M. Mullin, 1–25. Oxford and New York: Berg.

Childe, V.G. 1929. *The Most Ancient East: The Oriental Prelude to European Prehistory*. New York: Alfred A. Knopf.

Childe, V.G. 1958. *The Dawn of European Civilization*. New York: Alfred A. Knopf.

Clutton-Brock, J. 1999. *A Natural History of Domesticated Mammals (2nd edition)*. Cambridge: Cambridge University Press.

Clutton-Brock, J. 2012. "Introduction." In *Animal Turn: Animals as Domesticates*. Edited by J. Clutton-Brock, 1–9. East Lansing: Michigan State University Press.

Coppinger, R. and L. Coppinger. 2001. *Dogs: A Startling New Understanding of Canine Origin, Behavior, and Evolution*. New York: Scribner.

Coppinger, R. and L. Coppinger. 2016. *What is a Dog?* Chicago: University of Chicago Press.

Darwin, C. 1998 [1874]. *The Descent of Man*. Amherst: Prometheus Books.

Darwin, C. 2009 [1859]. *The Origin of Species and The Voyage of the Beagle*. London: Vintage Books.

Darwin, C. 2010 [1868]. *The Variation of Animals and Plants under Domestication, Volume 1*. Cambridge: Cambridge University Press.

Deleuze, G. and F. Guattari. 2003. *A Thousand Plateaus: Capitalism and Schizophrenia*. London: Continuum.

DeMello, M. 2012. *Animals and Society: An Introduction to Human–Animal Studies*. New York: Columbia University Press.

Galton, F. 1863. *The First Steps Towards the Domestication of Animals*. London: Spottiswoode & Co.

Galton, F. 1883. *Inquiries into Human Faculty and its Development*. London: J.M. Dent & Company.

Haraway, Donna. 2003. *The Companion Species Manifesto: Dogs, People, and Significant Otherness*. Chicago: Prickly Paradigm Press.

Haraway, D. 2007. *When Species Meet*. Posthumanities, Volume 3. Minneapolis: University of Minnesota Press.

Ingold, T. 1994. "From Trust to Domination: An Alternative History of Human–Animal Relations." In *Animals and Human Society: Changing Perspectives*. Edited by A. Manning and J. Serpell, 1–22. London and New York: Routledge.

Ingold, T. 2000. *The Perception of the Environment: Essays in Livelihood, Dwelling and Skill*. London and New York: Routledge.

Ingold, T. 2007. *Lines: A Brief History*. London and New York: Routledge.

Ingold, T. 2010. "Drawing Together: Materials, Gestures, Lines." In *Experiments in Holism: Theory and Practice in Contemporary Anthropology*. Edited by T. Otto and N. Bubandt, 299–313. Chichester: Wiley-Blackwell Publishing Ltd.

Kohn, E. 2007. "How Dogs Dream: Amazonian Natures and Politics of Transspecies Engagements." *American Ethnologist*, 34 (1): 3–24.

Loovers, J.P.L. 2015. "'Walking Threads, Threading Walk': Weaving and Entangling Deleuze and Ingold with Threads." *The Unfamiliar*, 5 (1&2): 107–117.

Lord, K., M. Feinstein, B. Smith, and R. Coppinger. 2013. "Variation in Reproductive Traits of the Members of the Genus Canis with Special Attention to the Domestic Dog (Canis familiaris)." *Behavioural Processes*, 92: 131–142.

Losey, R.J., S. Garvie-Lok, J.A. Leonard, M.A. Katzenberg, M. Germonpré, T. Nomokonova, M.V. Sablin, O.I. Goriunova, N.E. Berdnikova, and N.A. Savel'ev. 2013. "Burying Dogs in Ancient Cis-Baikal, Siberia: Temporal Trends and Relationships with Human Diet and Subsistence Practices." *PLoS One*: e63740.

Morey, D.F. 2010. *Dogs: Domestication and the Development of a Social Bond*. Cambridge: Cambridge University Press.

Pearson, K. 1924. *The Life, Letters, and Labours of Francis Galton. Volume II*. London: Cambridge.

Perri, A.R. 2016. "Hunting dogs as environmental adaptations in Jōmon Japan." *Antiquity*, 90 (353): 1166–1180

Ritvo, H. 2007. "On the Animal Turn." *Daedalus*, 136 (4): 118–122.

Russell, N. 2002. "The Wild Side of Animal Domestication." *Society & Animals*, 10 (3): 285–302.

Russell, N. 2011. *Social Zooarchaeology: Humans and Animals in Prehistory*. Cambridge: Cambridge University Press.

Seigworth, G.J. and M. Gregg. 2010. "An Inventory of Simmers." In *The Affect Theory*. Edited by M. Gregg and G.J. Seigworth, 1–25. Durham and London: Duke University Press.

Stewart, Kathleen. 2010. "Afterword: World Refrains." In *The Affect Theory Reader*. Edited by M. Gregg and G.J. Seigworth, 339–353. Durham and London: Duke University Press.

Throop, C.J. 2017. "Despairing Moods: Worldly Attunements and Permeable Personhood in Yap." *Ethos*, 45: 199–215.

Willerslev, R. 2007. *Soul Hunters: Hunting, Animism, and Personhood among the Siberian Yukaghirs*. Berkeley: University of California Press.

Wolfe, C. 2010. *What is Posthumanism?* Minneapolis: University of Minnesota Press.

Wolfe, C. 2011. "Moving Forward, Kicking Back: The Animal Turn." *Postmedieval: A Journal of Medieval Cultural Studies*, 2: 1–12.

Zeuner, Frederick E. 1963. *A History of Domesticated Animals*. London: Hutchinson & Co LTD.

Index

Note: Page references in **bold** refer to tables; page references in *italics*, to figures.

Agriculture Abuse Act 180
Alaska 76, 79, 87, 92–9, 164; coastal 4, 87–8, 89, 91–2, 97; literature 96; northern 93–4, 96, 98; Northwest 87–9, 92–3, 95, 97; Siberia 107; southern 87; Southwest 94
Alaskan Malemute 105, 115
Alberta 105
Algonquian 113, 120, 124, 129, 139; language family **124**
Almeö *234*, 235, **244**
Anderson, D. 264, 285
animal turn 28, 153–4, 278–9, 282
apocalypse 191–2
assemblage: archaeological 92; of beings 4, 6; faunal 91; of human, animal and material agents 213–14, 219, 230, 289; of perspectives 29, 33, 41; of technologies 216
attacks by dogs 175–6, 180, 218
Avanersuaq 212–13, 215, 217–18, 222, 227–8, 230

Beringia sled dog race 64–5, 75
Bible 193–4, 208
Birnirk 92, 95, 99
bone functional adaptation 13, 15
bones: of dogs 9, 16, 18, 87, 89, 91, 94–5, 125, 233, 236–41, 287
breeding dogs 4, 13, 45–8, 53, 65, 78–9, 118, 161, 196, 200–4, 208, 226, 271, 273, 280–1, 287, 290; interbreeding 3, 109, 113, 195, 282, 287; selective 132, 282; stock 160
burials, of dogs 6, 15, 87, 89, 118, 286; Baikal 12; Eskimo 98; in Fennoscandia 233, 235, 238–40; Ipiutak 88–9, 91–2; Skateholm 236; Siberian 11, 120
Buriat: settlers 28; dogs 47
Buriatia 19, 28
British Columbia: northern 163, 174

canine hepatitis 178, 183
Caribou 19, 93, 95, 123, 129, 174, 191, 200, 204
castration of dogs 36–7, 65
Chipewyan: Athapaskan language family **124**; ideas of food 125; knowledge 121–3; people 111, 115–16, 119, 121–3, 125–8, 132–3, 135–7, 197; sleighs 112; symbolic system 125–6
Christianity 135, 194–5
Chukchi: people 47–8, 66; Sea 87–8, 92; sled dog 54
Chukotka 48–9, 50, 64, 89, 91; coasts of 88–9, 91–3, 97
co-domestication 1, 7, 51, 268, 269–70, 289
co-existence 45–6, 50, 56–7, 283, 285, 289
co-habitation 11, 283, 286; vs codependency 98
co-taming 268–70, 286
codependency: between human and dogs 87; vs cohabitation 98; *see also* dependency; interdependency
Common Indian Dog 195
companion species 6, 139, 213–14, 217, 224, 228, 230, 284, 289
companion, dog as 1, 9; hunting companion 5; in Northern Canada 6; in Northwest Greenland 6
collaborator, dog as 271

colonialism 5, 6, 172, 174, 184–5, 288, 290
cooperation 1, 268; dog and human 98, 152, 160, 267; dog and reindeer 48; in HDR-communities 53, 56–7; human–animal 166; interspecies 7, 152; of dogs 155
Coppinger, R. and Coppinger, L. 268, 283, 286
Cossacks 67, 69
coworker, dog as 254
crafts of domestication 13
Cree: Algonquian language family, y dialect 124; elder Louis Bird 119; people 121, 123, 125, 130, 133–5, 137, 174; Plains 113; social universe 125; term for dog 111, 113; traditions 136; values 124; Woodland 113
cremation of dogs 13, 237–8, 240
Cumberland Sound 183, 185–6

Dawson City 165, 196
Dene: Athapascans 5, 113, 120, **124**, 129; Dene Tha 192; mythology 127; people 121–2, 124, 126, 128, 132, 135, 137, 193, 203; traditions 126, 136, 139
dependency: of dogs on humans 128; of humans on dogs 227, 290; *see also* codependency; interdependency
diet: of ancient dogs 19, 109, 237; based on fish 19, 152; of Danish dogs 237; of dogs 4, 9–10, 287; dogs and domestication 17–18; of dogs in Kamchatka 64–6, 77; of dogs in Oka 31; of sled dogs 152; *see also* salmon
dog teams 5, 16, 61, 64, 69–72; amongst Gwich'in 196–7, 200–3, 205, 208; Inuit 181, 183–4; in the Mackenzie Basin 106, 112, 137; in Northwest Alaska 93–4, 99; in Northwest Greenland 223, 226–7; in race competitions 73–4, 77–8, 80; in the Western Canadian Subarctic 159–62, 167
Dolgan: people 51–2; reindeer herders 49, 51
domestic: animals 49–50, 55–6, 67, 106, 110, 233, 237, 243, 280–2; breeds 280; culture 282; dog 91, 94, 108–10, 113, 126, 138, 233, 236, 244, 283; evolution of domestic animals 8; mode of production 131; reindeer 53; relationship 152; semi- 267; skeleton of domestic animals 9; socio-spiritual world 66; stock 36; way of life 109; -wild dichotomy 152, 282; worlds 286
domestication 1–3, 8, 9, 13, 48, 50, 155, 252, 268, 278–80, 283–4, 286–7; anthropogenic approach towards 281–2; archaeological research on 20; architecture of 47, 52, 285; crafts of 13; of the dog 8–10, 17–20, 106, 108–10, 124, 267; horse 10; multi-species aspects of 20; mutual 7; mutualistic aspects of 9; process of 8, 52, 54, 106, 124, 268, 281–3, 286; reindeer 11; 'sustained canid domestication' 109; and taming 269–70
Dorset 215–16
Deering 89, 91, 94
Denmark 212, 233–4, 236–9; Mesolithic cemeteries of 235; northern 237; western 238, **244**
distemper 119, 134, 178, 223

emotions 286–8; mobile 230
enskillment 13
Ekven 91, 95
Esquimaux dog 113, 115, 118; *see also* Husky
Evenki: dogs 47; herders 51–2, 264, 285; people 47, 50, 55

Fennoscandia 6–7, 233, 242; archaeological dog finds **244**; arctic 267, 270; human occupation of 234; northern parts of 237, 251; prehistory of 235; settlement sites 238; southern 241
Finland 233–41, 243–4, 251, 253, 268, 271, **273**
Finnish Spitz 242–3, 245
fish 65, *75*, 200
fishing 62
food shortage 216
Fort Chipewyan 105, 116, 131, 133–5, 157, 163
Fort McPherson 156, 165–6, 193–6, 199–200, 202, 207
fuel 57, 73, 77, 162, 199–200, 208
fur of dogs 1, 62, 95, 118, 237, 259
fur trade 105, 118, 131–3, 135, 162, 193, 196, 270; and dogs 5, 106–7, 112, 120, 137, 155, 166; pre- 112, 129–30; transport 113, 137, 195

genetics 87, 108, 111
Great Slave Lake 131, 143n36, 162–3

Greenland 6, 92, 94, 99, 110, 212–13, 218, 224–5; North 224; Northwest 6, 212, 215–16; South 220, 222; West 223
Gwich'in: dog teams 196; guides 156, 165; people 6, 191, 194–5, 197–205, 208; prophecies 208; Teetl'it 191, 193–4, 198, 200; Vuntut 202–3, 207

habitual activity 13
Haraway, D. 139, 174, 213, 279, 284, 289
Hare Indian Dog 111, 113–14, 115–17, 118, 129, 195
harnesses: for dogs 13, 15–16, 20, *63*, 92, 105, 112, 127, 182, 215, 218; and dog training 204–5; prehistoric 242
harnessing complements 89
HDR *see* Human–dog–reindeer communities
health of dogs 8, 64, 159–60, 222; dental 19; menace to 184, 186
horses: amongst *Canadien* workers 137; domestication 10; amongst Evenkis 50; herding 17; in human graves 240; in Kamchatcka 63; Mountie patrol 158; in Oka district 28–9, 33–5, 37, 41; amongst Plains Cree 113; in Yakutia 47; amongst Yakuts 66; Vikings 239
Hudson Bay Company 111, 131, 133, 156, 163, 174, 193, 197; and dogs 113, 115–16, 119, 160
human–dog–reindeer communities 45, 51, 53, 55–7
hunting by dogs: 33
hunting with dogs 1, 4–6, 283, 285–6, 288–9; in Alaska 93; in Fennoscandia 233, 237, 241, 243, 245; amongst Gwich'in 195; in the Mackenzie Basin 129–30; in northern Quebec 175; in Northwest Greenland 213–15, 223, 227–8, 230; in the Oka district 28–34, 41; in Sápmi (Saapmi) 254, 267–8; in Siberia 13, 16–17, 48, 56
Husky 118
hybridization of dogs: with other dogs 111, 118, 132; with wolves 115

identity: ethnic 72–3, 79; native 73–4; social 241
Ingold, T. 29, 41, 120, 138, 261–2, 264, 284–5
interdependency: between dogs and humans 30
intimacy 270, 272, 285–7

introgression of dogs: 242, 286; with wolves 287
Inughuit 6, 212, 216, 225, 228–9
Inuit: Alaskan 198; Canadian 94, 96; Cumberland Sound 183, 185; dogs 5, 107, 158, 172, 175, 184; Iqaluit 183; Nunavik 172, 174; Nunavuk 174, 184; people 6, 16, 107, 158, 172, 174–86, 215, 290; Qikiqtaaluk 172, 188n27; Thule 215–16
Ipiutak 87–92, 95, 98–9; period 89
Iqaluit 174, 180–3, 185
Itelmen: culture 68; hunters 71; people 66–9, 71

Kamchadal 70
Kamchatskaya Ezdovaya 63–5; *see also* Kamchatka sled dog
Kamchatka 4, 10–11, 61–5, 67–72, 75–9; Central 70, 78; coast 87; Northern 62–3, 71–5, 77–80; Southern 78; Soviet economy in 71; winter tourists in 77
Kamchatka sled dog 61–2, 64
Kohn, E. 106–7, 139, 213, 225, 227–8, 283–4
Koryak: hunters 71; people 66, 69, 72
Kangiqsujuaq 174–5, 179–80, 85
kinship 124–5, 127, 175, 270, 289
Klondike Gold Rush 160, 196–7
Kola Peninsula 234, 251
Kuujjuarapik 174–6, 178–9, 185

Labrador 160, 174; dog 196–7
landscape: 13, 19, 80, 120, 214, 217, 279, 284; appropriation 45–6, 50, 53, 57; as an assemblage 229–30; embodied perspectives of 28–9, 40, 288; High Arctic 212; of hunters 6; hunting 32, 34, 41; legal 152; northern 45; political 4; post-glacial 235; relationship with 262
Laika: East Siberian 35, 48, 50–1, 54; Russian 242
Lake Athabasca 105, 116, 127, 131, 133–5
Lake Baikal 10–12, 19
Lapland 234–5, 240, *244*, 267; Finnish 251, 253
loose dogs 30, 93, 105, 112, 200, 225; Dog Ordinance 180–1, 183; Inuit 175, 180; killing of 176–8, 181, 186, 290; in polar-bear-hunt 227–8
Losey, R. 3, 19, 87, 94, 99, 120, 286–9
Lundehund 243

Mackenzie River 115–16, 119, 129–31, 134–5
movement: coordination of reindeer herd 56; of dogs in hunting 40, 50, 54; limit 52; of predators 56;
multi-species ethnohistory 137
multi-species ethnography 28, 106–7, 139
Muskrat period 197

naming dogs 96–7, 99, 113, 119, 125, 128, 160, 166, 175, 226, 243, 274–5
Nenets: herders 49–52, 54; reindeer herding dogs 54; Yamal 49
non-domestic: canids 287; dog 244; reindeer 254
non-human persons 46, 106, 120, 122
North West Company 131, 133–5, 162
NWMP *see* North West Mounted Police
North West Mounted Police 152, 156, 157–8, 60–4, 197
Northwest Territories 173, 175, 180
North American Dog 113, 118
Norway 125, 233, 239, 241, 243–4, 268, 273; Northern 234–5, 271; Southern 237; Stone Age 241
Nunavik 172–4, 180, 184–5
Nunavut 94, 174

Ob' River 19
Ojibwa: 123, 134
Oka 28–30, 34–6, 235
Oka-Soiot *see* Soiot
Old Bering Sea 89, 91, 92, 95
ontological turn 28 *see also* de Castro V.
ontology: Athapascan 5, 120; Chipewyan 120–1
oral tradition: 135, 262; in children education 129; Dene 136, 139; in Subarctic ethnography 106; Sámi 7, 253; about wolves 123 *see also* tradition concerning dogs
Östra Vemmerlöf 227, *234*
other-than-human personhood 10, 13, 286 *see also* non-human persons

packs carried by dogs 15–16, 93, 105, 111–13, 130, 141, 195, 201, 204
Peel River 166, 191, 193
pets: dogs as 6, 65, 105, 108, 113, 125, 130, 201, 204, 233, 252, 254, 272–4, 278, 286, 289
personhood: and autonomy 50; of dog 99, 260
perspectival sharing 4, 28–9, 41, 288

polar bear 219, 227
policy: anti-sled dog 79; of Canadian government 152, 156, 174–5, 185–6; of control 167; sedentarization 54
posthumanism 213
Primor'e 18–19
provisioning of dogs 4–5, 10, 17, 88, 93, 162; in exchange for traction 99; with freshwater fish 19; *see also* diet; salmon

Qaanaaq 212, 214, 218, 227
Qikiqtaaluk 172–4
Qikiktani Truth Commission 184
Quebec 118, 137, 172–3, 175–7, 185; department of Agriculture 178; governments 172, 175, 180; Northern 174, 179

rabies 119, 178–9, 223–4
RCMP *see* Royal Canadian Mounted Police
reindeer: 45, 279, 288; based economy 242; and dogs 48–57, 254–5, 257, 263–4, 267, 270–1, 288; domestication 11, 13; fur 62; GPS collars 252; hunted 267; in Kamchatcka 67; in Oka 27–9, 41; meat 268; remains 19; Sámi 7; in Siberia 4, 46, 285; stray 253; transport 48–9, 61–3, 69, 79, 251
reindeer herding: dogs 36, 46, 49, 51, 53–4, 62, 65, 268, 289; and dogs 13, 15, 28, 47–8, 56–7, 251, 253–5, 258, 263–4, 267; Saami reindeer-herding dog 268, 270, 272–5, 290; Sámi reindeer-herding dogs 241–2, 262; *see also* training of dogs
RNWMP *see* Royal North West Mounted Police
Royal Canadian Mounted Police 107, 152, 156–61, 163–6, 174–5, 183, 185–6, 197–8
Royal North West Mounted Police 152, 196
Russian Far East 61, 68, 72

sacrifice: of animals 12, 238; of dogs 49–50, 66, 96, 113, 125, 136, 237, 240; of reindeer 49
sable: hunt for 28, 31–3, 36–40
Saian 28
salmon: 68–9, 73–4, 79, 164; for dogs 4, 62, 64–6, 70–2, 163, 287; fishing regulations 74; poaching 73–4, 77, 80

Sámi: culture 253; dwelling 256; family 253–4; Finnish 257; herding dog 262; hunters 254; Norwegian 254; offering sites 240; oral tradition 7, 253, 263; people 7, 234, 241–2, **244**, 251–4, 256, 261; reindeer herders 252, 254, 256–7; reindeer herding 251–2; shaman 254; Skolt 251, 253, 258–63; society 264; stories 264

Saami: culture 270, 275; herding dog 268–9, 273–5, 290; people 7, 257, 267–9, 271–3, 275; reindeer 269; reindeer management 270–2, 275; society 270, 272

Saami herding dog 241–2, 268, 270, 272–5, 290

Sápmi/Saapmi 234, 251, 267–8, 273–5

sedentarization 54, 218

self-domestication 17, 283

Siberia 1, 3–4, 8–10, 13, 45–6, 50, 53, 55, 87, 94, 107, 122, 215, 285; canid burials 11–12, 89, 120; colonization of 68; dog diet 17–18; dog harnesses 15; eastern 110–11; food sharing 51; means of transport 48, 57, 290; sacrifice of dogs 49; South Central 28; western 10, 18, 267

Siberian Husky 35, 65, 105, 115

Ski-Doo 131, 204–5; see also snowmobile

skills 6, 199, 222, 260; of dogs 47, 92, 161, 215, 253; of hunting dogs 29, 32–6, 41, 54, 242; of hunter 127, 226, 228; learning 129, 272; of perception 139; of reindeer-herding dogs 51, 54, 264; sensorial 41; of sledge dogs 54, 201; traditional 252; transmission of 53; in working with dogs 167

slaughter of dogs 5, 119, 158, 172, 174

sleds 279; in Alaska 93; in Fennoscandia 239, 241–2; amongst Gwich'in 195–6, 201; in Kamchatka 61–3, 66–8, 70, 72–3, 75, 77–8; in the Mackenzie Basin 105, 107–8, 111–3, 116, 118, 132, 137; in Northwest Greenland 215; in Siberia 13, 17, 20; in the Western Canadian Subarctic 156, 158, 165

sled dog racing 6, 16, 65, 68, 76, 78, 80, 108, 201, 206

sledding: dog 15, 16, 108; dog vs reindeer sledding 79

snowmobile: 67, 77, 155, 159, 199, 252; vs dog 4, 57, 62, 72, 75, 105, 179–80, 183, 186, 191, 201, 253, 274; revolution 57; see also Ski-doo

social contracts 285

socialization: animals' 47; by children: 47; human–dog 286; process 53

Soiot: dogs 29–30; households 28, 31; people 4, 28–30, 37, 41

sound: cognition 56; of dogs 214, 256; territories made by 214–15; of the whip 219

spondylosis deformans 16

stable isotope analysis 18

starvation 119, 127, 130, 134–5, 223–4; see also food shortage

stray dogs 177, 180–1, 185–6, 218–19

subsistence 6, 30, 74, 34, 92, 132, 235; economy 73, 237; environment 74; fishing 74, 80; habits 268; practices 88, 99, 155, 237; resources 98

Sweden 233–40, 242, **244**, 268, 271

symbiosis 9, 283, 285

Taimyr 48–9, 51–2, 54, 56–7

taming 251, 268–9, 270, 286; incidental 271

terminology 124

Thule 4, 87–9, 92–5, 98–9, 212, 215–18, 222–5, 227–8

Tofa: dogs 30–2, 37; hunters 31; people 28, 34; tradition 31, 37

tradition concerning dogs: Chukchi 50; human–dog–reindeer communities 53; Kamchatkan 78; in the Mackenzie Basin 7, 105, 107, 120, 126, 129, 136–7, 139; Mongolian 37; Sámi 7, 251, 253, 263; Siberian 4; Tofa 31, 37

training of dogs: in Fennoscandia 272; amongst Gwich'in 204–6; for hunting 31–2; in the Mackenzie Basin 129, 137; in Northwest Greenland 226; for reindeer-herding 51, 257; in Siberia 52, 53; for sled racing 62, 78; in the Western Canadian Subarctic 161

transportation, dogs for 1, 4–5; in Fennoscandia 240, 242; amongst Gwich'in 6; in Kamchatka 62, 68–75, 77, 79; in Kuujjuarapik 178; in the Mackenzie Basin 5, 105, 108, 112–13, 129–30, 137; in Northwest Alaska 88, 92–3, 99; in Northwest Greenland 215–16, 226; in Siberia 13, 47–8, 49, 50, 56–7; in the Western Canadian Subarctic 155, 158–9, 162, 167

trapline 197

trapping 93, 130–4, 137, 191, 197, 199–200; economy 156
trauma in dogs: 32; lesions in bones attributed to 94; related deformations 16
Tustuk River 33, 35

vaccination of dogs: 185
Viking **236**, 238–9, 242, **244**

whaling: 98, 195–7; and dogs 98
whips 20; dog whips 93–4
wild: animal 125, 281, 283; dogs 118, 177, 220; and domestic 53, 138, 233; game species 236; hunter-gatherers 284; men 217; mountain reindeer 234–5; polysemous character of 269; reindeer 251, 254, 264, 268–9, 271–2; semi- 220, 264; state 280; taking an animal out of the 282; vs domestic 9, 53, 56, 152, 282, 285; wolf 267

wolves: 19, 28, 107, 118–19, 124, 127, 134, 220, 252, 256, 287; agency of 106; ancestral 110; breeding dogs with 202; competition against 267; and dogs 113, 118, 120, 287; dogs killed by 30, 112; dogs mixed with 242; domestication of dogs from 10, 17–18, 108–9; fear of 122; grey 286; human concept of 125; hunting 123; and people 1–2, 110, 123, 139, 268, 272, 283; and reincarnation 121; terms for **124**; vs dogs 19, 62, 115, 128, 282

Yakutia 10, 47, 52, 64
Yamal 49–51, 53
Yukon 161, 164, 193

Zabaikal 47, 56
Zhokhov Island 10, 87, 242